Dear Pastor,

Ministry Advice From Seasoned Pastors

John R. Cionca, Editor

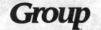

Group
Loveland, Colorado
www.group.com

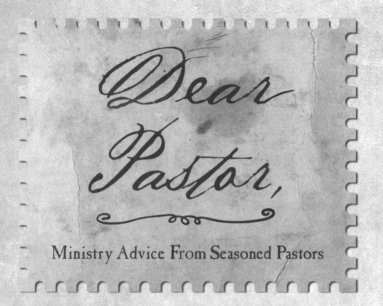

Dear Pastor,
Ministry Advice From Seasoned Pastors

Visit our Web site: **www.group.com**

Credits
Compiling Editor: John R. Cionca, Ph.D.
Acquisitions Editor: Alan Nelson
Chief Creative Officer: Joani Schultz
Editor: Amber Van Schooneveld
Art Director: Jean Bruns
Book Designer: Pamela Poll, www.pamelapoll.com
Cover Designer: Jay Smith/Juicebox Designs, www.juiceboxdesigns.com
Print Production Artist: Pat Reinheimer
Production Manager: DeAnne Lear

Library of Congress Cataloging-in-Publication Data

Dear pastor : ministry advice from seasoned pastors / John R. Cionca, editor.
p. cm.
Includes index.
ISBN-13: 978-0-7644-3436-5 (pbk. : alk. paper)
1. Pastoral theology. 2. Clergy--Correspondence. I. Cionca, John R., 1946-
BV4011.3.D43 2006
253--dc22

2006024674

10 9 8 7 6 5 4 3 2 1   16 15 14 13 12 11 10 09 08 07
Printed in the United States of America.

Dedication

To

JEAN CUTSHALL

And in Memory of

ROBERT CUTSHALL

Servants of the Church
Providers of Christian Resources
Friends to Pastors

Table of Contents

The Family

The Congregation

The Community

Colleagues and Support

Change and Conflict

Preaching

Self-Care

The Journey

Contributors

Larry Adams
Golden Hills Community Church
Antioch-Brentwood, California

Benjamin Alicea-Lugo
St. Paul's Evangelical Reformed Church
Perth Amboy, New Jersey

Gene Appel
Willow Creek Community Church
South Barrington, Illinois

Roger Ball
First Baptist Church
Tempe, Arizona

Randy Berg
Calvary Christian Church
Hastings, Minnesota

Greg Bourgond
Heart of a Warrior and Bethel Seminary
St. Paul, Minnesota

Jill Briscoe
Elmbrook Church
Brookfield, Wisconsin

Douglas J. Brouwer
First Presbyterian Church
Ann Arbor, Michigan

Alicia D. Byrd
St. Stephen's AME Church
Owings Mills, Maryland

Richard P. Camp Jr.
Chaplain, United States Military Academy, 1973-1996
Director, A Christian Ministry in the National Parks
Freeport, Maine

Dear Pastor,

Timothy Chan
Gaithersburg Chinese Alliance Church
Gaithersburg, Maryland

John R. Cionca
Ministry Transitions, Inc. and Bethel Seminary
St. Paul, Minnesota

David C. Cooper
Mount Paran Church of God
Atlanta, Georgia

John Crosby
Christ Presbyterian Church
Edina, Minnesota

Darryl DelHousaye
Scottsdale Bible Church and President of Phoenix Seminary
Scottsdale, Arizona

Richard L. Dresselhaus
Assemblies of God
San Diego, California

David C. Fisher
Plymouth Church of the Pilgrims
Brooklyn, New York

Michael W. Foss
Prince of Peace Lutheran Church
Burnsville, Minnesota

Randy Frazee
Willow Creek Community Church
South Barrington, Illinois

Vernon Grounds
Denver Seminary
Littleton, Colorado

Jan D. Hettinga
Northshore Baptist Church
Bothell, Washington

Bill Hull
Author and Teacher
Long Beach, California

Contributors

Joel C. Hunter
Northland, A Church Distributed
Longwood, Florida

Joey Johnson
The House of the Lord
Akron, Ohio

Steve Johnson
President, Vision USA
Kissimmee, Florida

Knute Larson
The Chapel
Akron, Ohio

LeRoy Lawson
CMF International
Payson, Arizona

H.B. London Jr.
Vice President, Ministry Outreach/Pastoral Ministries
Focus on the Family, Colorado Springs, Colorado

Gordon MacDonald
World Relief Chairman
Belmont, New Hampshire

Les Magee
Teacher
Boulder, Colorado

Alan Nelson
Executive Editor of Rev! Magazine
Fort Collins, Colorado

Earl F. Palmer
University Presbyterian Church
Seattle, Washington

Dwight Perry
Great Lakes Baptist Conference
Rothschild, Wisconsin

Fred W. Prinzing
Dean and Professor Emeritus, Bethel Seminary
Everett, Washington

Dear Pastor,

Haddon Robinson
Gordon-Conwell Theological Seminary
Hamilton, Massachusetts

Bob Russell
Southeast Christian Church
Louisville, Kentucky

Pete Scazzero
New Life Fellowship
Elmhurst Queens, New York

Wayne K. Schmidt
Kentwood Community Church
Grand Rapids, Michigan

Jerry Sheveland
President, Baptist General Conference
Arlington Heights, Illinois

Joseph Stowell
Harvest Bible Chapel
Rolling Meadows, Illinois

Doug Talley
Church of God Ministries
Lakeland, Florida

Carol A. Travilla
Pathfinders
Tempe, Arizona

John Vawter
You're Not Alone, Inc.
Scottsdale, Arizona

Tony Vis
Meredith Drive Reformed Church
Des Moines, Iowa

Dan Yeary
North Phoenix Baptist Church
Phoenix, Arizona

Penny J. Zettler
Teacher
St. Paul, Minnesota

Acknowledgments

This resource would not have been possible without the vision, encouragement, and support of many ministry colleagues.

First, appreciation is due to the team of writers who provided wise counsel. These seasoned pastors are all in demand because of their personal ministry effectiveness, publications, and conference speaking. Nevertheless, with plates overflowing, they still wanted to participate in a resource designed to help younger colleagues in their pastoral journeys.

Second, I express my gratitude to a core of supporters who financed the project. Their generosity made possible writing stipends and editorial expenses. Each has a heart for pastors, understanding the growing complexity of the clergy role. And each has a love for the church, recognizing the expanding possibilities before her.

Third, appreciation is given to Gloria Metz, Rebecca Reeves, Sara Norton, and Amber Van Schooneveld for the seemingly unending task of transforming editorial revisions into the final product that is before you.

Finally, ultimate love is expressed to the Lord of the church, who has breathed his life, passion, and gifts into this team of servants, that in return they can offer him the highest praise!

Preface

We all know the verses: *"He appointed twelve...that they might be **with** him and that he might send them out to preach"* (Mark 3:14). *"When they saw the courage of Peter and John and realized that they were unschooled, ordinary men, they were astonished and they took note that these men had been **with** Jesus"* (Acts 4:13).

And we understand the concepts—the Christian faith is more caught than taught, and ministry effectiveness is best learned contextually from role models. But for many of us, the race and pace of pastoral work keeps us isolated within our own ministries. We lose sight of our mentors. *Doing* crowds out *being*. And the last thing we take time for is personal reflection. Preach your best sermon, and another one is due in seven days. In fact, the better the message was last week, the higher you raise the bar for next week. Do a good job of counseling, and more church members await your advice. Teach well, and more people need instruction. Warmly welcome visitors, and more will arrive desiring personal care. Implement a significant change, and another challenge is before you. The bottom line for clergy is that the loop never closes.

But we don't have to be victims of this cycle. We can take time, even daily, to reflect on our service, to reassess priorities, and to focus on the significance of our calling.

So I invite you to spend some quality time *with* a team of pastoral mentors. These seasoned ministry colleagues offer insights into our inner lives, our relationships, and our Christian service.

These letters have been collected over the past decade. And since transitions are a common reality of pastoral life, a number of the authors have made significant contextual changes since their letters were originally penned. A few have relocated to new congregations. Three have become denominational executives. Two have moved into teaching. Several have retired from church work yet remain active in writing, teaching, interim work, and missions. Surprisingly, two senior ministers, Gene Appel (from Central Christian Church in Las Vegas) and Randy Frazee (from Pantego Bible Church in Arlington, Texas), have transitioned into the same new congregation—Willow Creek Community Church (South Barrington, Illinois).

No doubt, some of you will pick up this volume and read it cover to cover. Perhaps others will go first to a specific topic or particular author. But the collective counsel is best digested in small bites. I suggest you read each letter several times—jotting down your thoughts and reflections.

Better yet, invite two or three ministry colleagues to also read the letters, and meet every two weeks to share your reflections with one another. The ongoing accountability, encouragement, and prayer can draw you closer together as pastors and friends.

May God continue to receive great honor through your faithful kingdom service.

God's best!

John R. Cionca

Focus

If I Could Begin Again

Dan Yeary

North Phoenix Baptist Church, Phoenix, Arizona

Dear Chris,

If I could turn back the calendar and begin my ministry again, I would give even more attention to seven important ministry emphases. I have benefited from these practices throughout my pastoral tenure, but I have also struggled to maintain them as priorities amid the daily press of service.

What would I tell a young pastor? The same thing that I remind myself, and the same thing I would pass on to a tenured pastor.

First and foremost, never forget that there is no substitute for a personal, intimate, private relationship with Christ on a daily basis. Never allow yourself to neglect the opportunity of personal communion with Christ. Without that connection, life and ministry will misfire. The greatest temptation you will face when busy in ministry will be to neglect the need to feed your own spirit. Very few people, even your most devoted church members, will fully understand, appreciate, and protect your need for study and prayer. Establish it as your highest priority, and let *nothing* interfere.

Second, remember that your first ministry is to your family. You may not be the only pastor they have, but you are their only spouse and parent. Your children will love neither the Lord nor the church if they have to compete with either for your affections. God gave you a family as a sacred trust. Treat them accordingly. No meeting of any committee or theological organization should take precedence over the priority needs of your family. In your entire life, have you ever known a minister who, on his deathbed, wished he had spent more time in committee meetings? Since there are no committee meetings in heaven (I hope), I suggest the priority meetings of your life be at your own address with your own family—and with great frequency.

Next, I would *Sabbath more and Sunday less*. It is a tragic mistake to assume that Sunday is a day of rest for any minister. Yet most folks will make that assumption. You must not. Don't break the Sabbath—establish a day. Preserve it doggedly. Demand it with the tenacity of a pit bull. A Sabbath will replenish your resources and restore your soul. When you are constantly drained on every possible level, your own spiritual refreshment is vital to the effectiveness of your ministry. To be a Sabbath breaker is not just breaking a commandment, it is also breaking your commitment.

If you haven't already done so, Chris, discover, select, and maintain an accountability group. Lone Ranger ministers will inevitably be ambushed. A minister cannot maintain the best of spirituality and moral integrity without a special trust group. Find an accountability team to whom you can trust your life. Ask them to hold you accountable on a consistent basis. You could do the same for them, and it will be a blessing of untold proportions. This will be a difficult task to establish. Accountability is instinctively resisted and feared. The benefits, however, are beyond value.

Fifth, respect your body as the temple of the Holy Spirit. Condition it and bring it into submission. Find something on which you can expend enormous physical energy outside of your basic responsibilities. Find something inanimate to hit that will not be injured or hit back. Golf, tennis, racquetball, cycling, and running are all marvelous expenditures of healthy energy that replenish the body. This, too, is more important than the next board meeting or the last one. Fatigue makes cowards of us all. An exercise regimen has enormous benefits.

And, dear friend, never speak a word of condemnation or criticism regarding one of your ministry brothers or sisters—even through innuendo. Remember, God has to compromise to use any of us (the degree to which will only be known when we get to heaven). Celebrate, pray for, and encourage your colleagues in the cloth. We have too many enemies on the outside, so let's not take potshots on the inside. You can learn from anyone, even a bad example. Since lighthouses are not set up to compete with one another, there is no sensible reason for competitive lighthouse keepers. Our ultimate test of leadership is not how many building campaigns we've led or the size of our budgets, but whether or not we have helped men and women become like Jesus. So become a minister to your fellow ministers in this great enterprise.

And last, always remember that you are an authentic, unique creation of God. He has gifted you according to his desires, and you are never required to follow anyone's footsteps or compete with anyone in ministry. Even when some dear soul in your fellowship is convinced that you are the successor to Billy Graham...don't believe it. God will create that person in his own good time. Don't take yourself so seriously. Send your ego on a trip, and don't accompany it. Learn to laugh at yourself, life, and all circumstances. It is part of the command of Scripture that we rejoice in all things. Down-to-earth, authentic, humble spirits are blessed and used by God to the maximum.

Your brother,

Dan

So do not throw away your confidence; it will be richly rewarded. You need to persevere so that when you have done the will of God, you will receive what he has promised.

Hebrews 10:35-36

Never Open Your Mail on Sundays

Penny J. Zettler
Faculty Associate, Bethel Seminary, St. Paul, Minnesota

Dear Rebecca,

Never open your mail on a Sunday! I assure you, this is one of the best pieces of advice I offer colleagues new to the ministry. It's not a warning about exploding letter bombs. It's about a threat that is potentially deadly to the spirit and to worship: distraction. On the Lord's Day, we must maintain a single focus.

Therefore, on Sunday mornings I don't check e-mail, pick up voice mail, or attend to anything in my office inbox. If I'm tempted, I remind myself of my own advice: *Leave it alone. Another time. Later!* A poison pen letter or mail that contains a lovely compliment is best digested at another time.

I settled on this guideline one Sunday when an innocent white envelope was placed in my office inbox. I didn't recognize the handwriting and tore into the letter with enthusiasm and curiosity. There were four pages of lined notebook paper filled with advice, detailing—at what I felt was an excessive length—how mistaken I had been in my last sermon on interpreting the ministry of angels. I thought the sermon had been especially helpful. The letter seemed mean-spirited and small-minded. I was thrown off guard, frustrated, and brokenhearted.

That's not where I am called to be on Sunday mornings.

As a pastor, my task on Sunday mornings is to stay focused on the work I am called to do. Whatever my ministry responsibilities, I do not need to be distracted during these key hours. If I lead the worship, I need to be ready to worship with my whole heart. If I preach, my attention needs to be centered on that crucial task. If I teach the junior high youth or organize the nursery, *that's* were I need to center my whole self.

On Sunday mornings, I seek personal engagement with the family of God that gathers for words of hope. This is my chance to look into people's eyes as I ask, "How's it going?" I want to do more than hear a pat answer—I want to look for health, sadness, joy, and need. I also want to connect with the congregation through touch as I hug, give a handshake, or encourage with an arm around the shoulder. If I am deeply available, I can hear their whispers and can whisper back to them God's words of love and grace.

As I number them, I'm amazed at the ways I've been drawn away from this primary task. Focused, relational ministry isn't easy. Invitations to distraction are always present. I remember an encounter with an aggressive leader of a local group who needed to rent the church and needed an answer *now*! Wasn't I the pastor? Didn't I know the church calendar? This was important—to him. To me, it felt like an encounter with a bulldozer. People who will steamroll you and your focus are not just present in *my* congregation, friend. Stay focused. If not, your passion on the Sabbath will be flattened.

Or consider these situations: We have an unusually lovely sanctuary, so it's not uncommon to meet a young couple who has come full of smiles and hope on Sunday morning to arrange their wedding. They want to meet me, to know how much it costs for a wedding, to inquire about availability, to meet the wedding consultant, and so on. There are also people who come to our services to introduce their ministry to us with no prearranged appointment. They want to present themselves, explain their gifts, and discuss opportunities for the future. Could this be an opportunity from God?

For us, the answer is that we just don't do that kind of business on Sundays. We focus. We come to be molded and changed by our corporate encounter with God. This is our top priority. So we sweep aside distractions, step around energy drains, and avoid the black holes of doing business by saying, "Please call the office on Monday; we'd love to help."

In many ways, I am the one who decides what Sunday mornings will hold for me and for my congregation. If I believe God wants us to be as free of distraction as we can be, I need to make choices that lead to that point of focus. This I know: God wants us completely there with him in worship—wholly attentive, loving one another as we grow together.

On a recent Sunday morning, a plain white envelope, plump with potential, with my name written on it in unknown script, rested invitingly in my box. I picked it up, shook it a little, and then thought better of the temptation. I put the unopened envelope back in the box for Monday and entered the sanctuary to say "I love you" to God.

Becky, don't open your mail on Sundays—you have better things to do!

Joyfully,

Penny

Focus

If you keep your feet from breaking the Sabbath and from doing as you please on my holy day, if you call the Sabbath a delight and the Lord's holy day honorable, and if you honor it by not going your own way and not doing as you please or speaking idle words, then you will find your joy in the Lord.

Isaiah 58:13b-14a

Engraved on His Palms

John Crosby
Christ Presbyterian Church, Edina, Minnesota

Dear Harry,

Recently a 50-year-old pastor told me, "When I started in ministry, I was called aside by an older pastor. He showed me his Bible with my name and several others written in the flyleaf. He mentioned his commitment to pray daily for my life and ministry. I was so taken by his initiative that when I turned 40, I likewise picked out 10 young pastors and did the same. But now a decade later, there are only four names left in my Bible: The other pastors have resigned or been forced out of ministry by financial pressures, bad health, sexual misconduct, or failing marriages. When I shared this situation with my mentor, he showed me his Bible. Mine was the only name left." Yes, Harry, ministry is filled with casualties, spectacular and quiet.

Pastoral ministry has always been hard. Perhaps today it's even harder: unending phone calls, jam-packed schedules, and either too many empty parking spots or too few. Add to this our own sinfulness, frailties, and shortcomings as leaders. Sometimes, as pastors, we fall by the wayside because we lose the battles common to us all—the world, the flesh, or the devil. Brothers and sisters are spiritually neutralized by sensuality, money, failing family relationships, or any of the myriad pitfalls of the day.

But just as often, so many pastors gradually lose the sense of calling, which is far more subtle and difficult to detect. Slowly, the compelling urgency that brought them to ministry seeps away in the face of phone calls, appointments, arguments, and the struggle for balance in the busyness of modern life. As the wag admonishes, "It doesn't matter if you burn out, rust out, or drop out; you're still out."

But I don't want *out*! I want to finish strong. I want to be a healthier person at retirement than when I first became a pastor. I'm saddened when I hear of yet another talented pastor who has become a casualty of the stress of ministry. And I admit that *but by the grace of God go I.* With all that's within me, Harry, I want to stay passionate about my calling.

And in times of stress, it's *imperative* to remember why we got involved in ministry in the first place. Nothing strengthens the servant of God better than a good reminder of the deep love of God and of his gracious calling. Let me share such a reminder with you.

In 1984, I led a group of high school students to Haiti on a mission. On the preparatory trip, as we flew in, the plane dusted the beach where we were to land, drawing in hundreds of children, all barefoot and many naked. The Haitian missionaries who ran the local clinic were our hosts and ended the tour with a visit to the cinder-block clinic. Native nurses showed us the facility with pride, though it was crude even by third-world standards. Lining the halls and reception area were families with their children, waiting patiently for hours.

In the last room, there was a little boy about the size of my 4-year-old daughter. His arms and legs were covered with newspaper: The disease that had ravaged his body left him with sores that he picked constantly, and the clinic couldn't afford to change bandages hourly to prevent infection.

"His name is Jean," said one of the nurses, "and we almost lost him. Sometimes they just bring the little ones out of the hills too late to be saved." She asked me to lift up the boy so they could change the sheets. He felt tiny and frail. He slumped into my chest, where he felt like a little furnace, soaking us both with sweat. After what seemed an eternity, I put him down, ruffled his head, and left the clinic.

Out in the Jeep, I wiped my hands off on my thighs, looked down and saw that the ink from his newspapers had smeared all over my hands (and now my pants as well). Hard as I rubbed and cleaned for the next day, the ink had stained too deeply to be removed: a powerful reminder of my little friend, Jean. And then I was reminded of Isaiah's words, "See, I have engraved you on the palms of my hands; your walls are ever before me" (Isaiah 49:16).

When I came to Christ, it was with the sure conviction that I would be held safely in the hand of God—his love for me sealed on the palms of Christ. When I felt called into ministry, it was with the sure conviction that the pain and brokenness of others had stained my hands, compelling me to reach out with God's love to others.

So, Harry, when you're tempted to forget why God has brought you into ministry, look down at your hands. Remember what you are holding, and pray that the ink of the pain of others never rubs off of your heart or your hands.

Your brother in Christ,

John

Can a mother forget the baby at her breast and have no compassion on the child she has borne? Though she may forget, I will not forget you! See, I have engraved you on the palms of my hands.

Isaiah 49:15-16

The Money Trap

Joseph Stowell
Harvest Bible Chapel, Rolling Meadows, Illinois

Dear Ralph,

Years ago, a friend said to me, "Joe, if you want to be effective for Christ, master the three W's: *Work:* Don't be lazy. When you work, work hard. *Women:* Be a one-woman man, and make sure you live so that all the women in the flock feel safe with you. *Wealth:* Never serve the Lord for money. Don't be seduced by getting more or be discouraged by not having enough. And never compare your salary to what others are getting."

All of these issues are important, dear friend, but I want to talk to you about the money trap.

Money has phenomenal power to manipulate our attitudes and actions. And although it's true that no one can live *without* it, no shepherd can afford to live *for* it. As soon as we begin to do what we do for financial gain, we endanger everything in our work for the Lord.

God taught me a major money lesson early in my ministry life. While in my first pastorate, a small church plant in Ohio, I was asked to speak at a youth banquet in neighboring Indiana. At the time we were living on a subsistence-level income, and given this financial pressure, part of the intrigue of the invitation was the ever-alluring honorarium.

I drove to the banquet, gave my talk, said my prayer, and when it was all done, I waited for the coordinator of the evening to hand me the envelope. He didn't seem to be real quick on the draw, so I stayed and helped them take down the chairs. Still nothing was forthcoming. I gave them a hand as they rearranged the tables, chatting and lingering as long as I could. Finally, after nearly everyone was gone, I got in my car and drove home.

As I crawled into bed in the wee hours of the morning, I fell asleep wondering why I had not gotten paid—not even a check for expenses! I was so consumed with this disappointment that I gave little thought to the fact that I had ministered for the Lord, helped his church, and perhaps even been used for a supernatural transaction in someone's life.

Through the days ahead, I felt my heart sour. I grumbled that they had taken advantage of me. I brooded over the thought that they would have treated an important speaker better. But after several days of this less-than-admirable response, the Spirit began to work on me. Why had I gone there: for money or for ministry? Was it for cash or for Christ that I had given my time that night? And hadn't I already learned that God would supply my needs in his way and his time? When it came to provision, was it the responsibility of people around me, or was my prosperity managed through God's hand? I felt a growing sense of shame at my crude, cash-oriented focus on ministry.

It was at this point that I confessed my sinful attitude and made a commitment: From that time on, I would never again serve for financial gain. It was a defining and liberating moment that has changed the course of my life in ministry ever since. Interestingly, the next day, a check for expenses and an honorarium came in the mail. I'm convinced that God delayed that supply until I had gotten a grip on this foundational principle of ministry.

However, the money-trap story isn't over. While I had the honorarium part of it figured out, the salary issue soon began to haunt my heart. In the early days of that church-planting experience, Martie and

I found that the sacrificial generosity of the flock stimulated a sense of gratitude in our hearts toward them. As the church began to grow and flourish, however, that attitude began to change. Not only was the work of the ministry more demanding, our family was also growing. We needed a bigger house, and, from our perspective, the increases in salary were not commensurate with the church's growth.

It's interesting that the same congregation that brought us joy in their supply in earlier days had now become a source of frustration. It tarnished our view of the ministry and the people to whom we ministered, and it created jealousy in our hearts when we heard how other pastors were treated.

Fortunately, I eventually realized this wasn't my church's problem. The problem was mine. My focus was all wrong…again. Instead of focusing on the Lord as the primary source of provision for my needs, I had wrongly viewed the congregation as my provider. It's no wonder I ended up struggling with my feelings toward some of them. What a damaging distortion of a shepherd's perspective, especially given the fact that God had worked overtime to prove he could and would provide for all our needs.

I repented…again.

Here's the lesson: Don't ever let your guard down when it comes to the seductive power of money. Just when you think you've mastered the monster, it's there again in your face, wanting to be in your heart. Instead, keep your heart focused on the Lord, our true provider.

Sincerely,

Joe

People who want to get rich fall into temptation and a trap and into many foolish and harmful desires that plunge men into ruin and destruction…But you, man of God, flee from all this, and pursue righteousness, godliness, faith, love, endurance and gentleness.

1 Timothy 6:9, 11

Get a Life!

Gordon MacDonald
World Relief Chairman, Belmont, New Hampshire

Dear Tim,

Few paragraphs of Scripture have impacted me as much as those describing the attitude of John the Baptist when he learned that the crowds that once came to him were now going to Jesus. In short, he was losing his job.

I've seen many lose jobs, and the sight isn't pretty. People usually get defensive, angry, and vindictive. This is the problem: The person and his or her job became indistinguishable.

Not so with John the Baptist. John's thinking (as recorded in John 3:27-30) goes like this: A person in ministry only possesses what is given to him from heaven. From the beginning, he must be quite aware that he is not (and never will be) the anointed one (the Christ). Ultimately, his task is to direct people to Christ so that they forget about the person and remember only the Savior.

Sounds good, right? But watch out! Once you enter the ministry, the entire system will conspire in clever ways to make you forget everything John said. You will be overwhelmingly tempted to step from the best man's position to that of the groom and accept (if not invite) adulation that simply doesn't belong to you. As your work and skills grow and your ability to lead broadens, you will face the seduction of assuming that people need *you* more than they need *him.*

Keep in mind that some day the job you've been called to do will come to an end. For your own well-being, Tim, you need to cultivate a healthy John-like perspective. If you fail to make this distinction, you may become like those who end life in bitterness and disillusionment. They resent the next generation, which takes their place. They cannot rejoice in the success of others or in the growth of the kingdom that is happening without them. They don't know what to do with their time or how to live life as a normal, unknown person. They discover that their marriages, their friendships, and their relationships in the community are all in trouble because they were defined by a ministry that is now in the past. Their minds become dull because the only intellectual exercise they knew was preparing sermons. Their leadership skills go flat because they never learned to exercise them anywhere but the church. Their own sense of self-esteem plummets because it is predicated on the applause of people, which they don't hear anymore.

Now for the good news. I've known some who didn't fall into this trap. When I've talked to them about these things, this is what I've learned. First, they cultivated a marriage that was not ministry-driven. Sadly, ministers can love their spouses for the things they do for the ministry. And many a spouse has loved the person in the pulpit, the person the congregation admires, rather than the real person apart from the public ministry. The people I admire, Tim, made sure their marriages were healthy with or without public activities.

Second, they made sure there were friends out there whose affection would last beyond the days of ministry. You won't believe this until you've experienced it, but I need to warn you: Ninety percent of those who love you as a pastor will transfer that love to the next guy rather quickly. And that's OK. In fact that's how it should be. You don't need a crowd, but do cultivate a few close friends over time.

Third, they maintained a personal center of living that wasn't defined by ministry. It included intellectual pursuits, leisure activities, and interests that weren't antithetical to their ministries but not driven by them either. Some of my favorite people have entered the larger community as coaches, volunteer firefighters, charity workers, and school volunteers. One pastoral couple I admire took up ballroom dancing and developed relationships with a host of people they would never have met in the church parking lot.

Let me wrap up with a story. When I was a teenager, we would occasionally drive up to a ghost town in the Rocky Mountains. Its only inhabitant was an old woman who was mentally unbalanced. Among her peculiar behaviors, she would threaten unwanted visitors with a shotgun. One day it became necessary for state authorities to take her away to the state hospital. When they tried to bathe her, they couldn't remove her hat because she had worn it for so many years that her hair had grown up into the fibers of the fabric. Thus, it became necessary to cut off her hair to remove her hat.

I think you know where I'm going. Don't let your pastoral role so enmesh itself in your person that when your tenure of leadership ends, your personal life ends also. Know what can be laid aside with grace and what can go on...because it's the real you. Learn from John the Baptist. He was an expert on such a matter.

Warmly,

Gordon

To this John replied, "A man can receive only what is given him from heaven. You yourselves can testify that I said, 'I am not the Christ but am sent ahead of him'... He must become greater; I must become less."

John 3:27-28, 30

Personal Reflections on

Focus

Inner Life

Godly Passion or Adrenaline Rush?

Wayne K. Schmidt
Kentwood Community Church, Grand Rapids, Michigan

Dear Josh,

I'd been warned about cheap substitutes. Using someone else's sermon in place of an original creation of one's own is a well-known and tempting substitute. However, one cheap substitute that no one ever told me about is the substitute of adrenaline. It masquerades as passion from God, but it can imperil our lives and ministries.

I entered ministry full of zeal. My heart skipped a beat when I read about the Apostle Paul's ambition to preach the gospel where Christ was not known. I could sense his passion and longed to replicate it in my life. Yes, I knew that Scripture banned selfish ambition, and I constantly monitored what *created* my ambition—vision from God vs. selfish desire—but I failed to keep an eye on what *fueled* my ambition.

Now, there is nothing wrong with a little adrenaline. The God-given glands provide extraordinary energy when we face emergencies. But I developed an adrenaline addiction. I began to perceive every worship service, planning meeting, and discipleship time as necessitating that adrenaline rush. And like many addicts, I was in denial about its impact on myself and those around me. I missed the warning signs.

Over the years I've created a list of questions to highlight the differences between adrenaline and passion from God. I review it every so often to keep my glands in check. Here's a sampling of the questions on my list:

Am I able to enter into and enjoy quiet times with God? Adrenaline stifles reflection. When living off adrenaline, the tachometer of the soul indicates my internal engine is revving. There is a fundamental incompatibility between a reflective soul and a revving internal engine. I can't be still and know that he is God because *doing* overwhelms *dwelling* in God's presence. I rush through my religious routine so I can check spiritual disciplines off my to-do list.

On the other hand, godly passion springs from reflection in God's presence. His gentle whisper helps me understand who I am as his child and what he desires to accomplish through me that day. His leadings become clear, and I long to spend my time living them out.

Are my relationships becoming superficial? Adrenaline creates intensity—self-generated energy that either results in high productivity or, sometimes, just frantic activity. I begin to hydroplane through life and develop superficial relationships with God, family, and friends. They get my emotional leftovers as I exhaust myself. In contrast, Spirit-generated passion makes room for intimacy with God and others. The Spirit, who gives me a power surge when needed, also slows me down to deeply interact with others.

How am I managing my time? Adrenaline subjects me to the tyranny of the urgent. There is a compulsive desire to make every minute matter. This urgency undermines any sense of priority and falsely signals that anything waiting to be done must be done now. I begin to hurry everywhere and hurry everything.

Passion from God, however, keeps me in tune with the rhythms of life. The wisdom of Ecclesiastes assures us there is a time for everything. I can wait upon God for the seasons of opportunity he will provide.

Am I burning out? Adrenaline is great for sprinters, but for marathoners it creates an overly aggressive early pace that leaves them with no reserve for the crucial stretch to the finish line. The stress that adrenaline generates prematurely ages me physically, emotionally, and spiritually. God designed me to experience it in periodic spurts, and a constant flow wears me out. On the other hand, passion from God fosters perseverance, which develops my character and deepens my ministry as the days go by.

Listen, Josh: For too many years, I lived my life as an adrenaline addict—with routine devotional times, superficial relationships, and perpetual busyness. I was vulnerable to burnout, family breakup, and carelessness. By my mid-30s, I was thinking more about retirement than a fruitful ministry for decades to come. Now in my mid-40s, I am learning how to enjoy the varied paces of life. I love those occasions when God says "full speed ahead," but I also cherish those times of more quiet reflection.

Here are some ways I'm learning to ensure my passion comes from God.

• Godly passion blossoms when I remember the Sabbath no-load principle. When I have one full day off each week as a release from the routine, I live more fully the other six days.

• As soon as I feel an adrenaline surge, I quiet my heart. I ask God to calm this area of personal weakness. While the external difference may be indiscernible, my soul is at peace rather than having to power up.

• I begin my day on my knees. This posture of submission to God before the day's activities begin reminds me he'll provide my daily energy needs.

• I take rest periods throughout the day. I stop to close my eyes for a moment of gratitude, listen to a worship song, or take a deep breath and review a Scripture verse. These rest stops check my flow of adrenaline and open the channels for his passion to flow.

• In my biweekly meetings with an accountability partner, I share the level of peacefulness in my private world.

So, Josh, don't believe the lie that a continual adrenaline rush means you're on the cutting edge of ministry. In reality, it takes the edge off your ministry and off your life. Instead, live in the power of the passion that God gives—it is the fuel of eternally significant ambitions. You'll love it as I do.

In Christ,

Wayne

For this reason I remind you to fan into flame the gift of God, which is in you through the laying on of my hands. For God did not give us a spirit of timidity, but a spirit of power, of love and of self-discipline.

2 TIMOTHY 1:6-7

Heart Surgery

Greg Bourgond

Heart of a Warrior and Bethel Seminary, St. Paul, Minnesota

Dear Ray,

Early on I was committed to discipling others in the faith. I wanted them to enjoy the full benefits of being a member of God's family. I did my best to help them understand what it meant to be a fully devoted follower of Christ. Some got it; others did not.

So I redoubled my efforts. I taught them the basics about the empowerment of the Holy Spirit, the importance of prayer, the authority of Scripture, spiritual disciplines, the community of faith, the stewardship of our giftedness, and so on. Some experienced the abundant life that Christ promised; others did not.

Then one day I was reading the Bible, and I came across a passage that changed my life and my ministry from that point forward—"Above all else, guard your heart, for it is the wellspring of life" (Proverbs 4:23). For all those years, I had focused on the wrong battlefield. I had been pushing for a change in outward practices without realizing how much these actions flow from a healthy Christian heart.

What passes as discipleship in many circles today is no more than behavior modification. If we can get people to do the right things, they will become the right people. Boy, was I wrong. The battlefield for transformational change is the heart, not behavior.

Well-meaning efforts to control our behavior seldom last. Removed from self-imposed restraints, our tendency is to lapse back into actions that we despise. In desperation, we make sincere commitments to read our Bibles *more*...to pray *more*...to witness *more*...to go to church *more*...only to find out that *more is producing less* in our lives. We're on the wrong battlefield.

When Samuel visited the house of Jesse to anoint the next king of Israel, the eldest son, Eliab, was paraded before him. He had all the appearance of a king—regal stature, bearing, and presence. But God stopped Samuel in his tracks. He reminded him, "Do not consider his appearance or his height, for I have rejected him. The Lord does not look at the things man looks at. Man looks at the outward appearance, but the Lord looks at the heart" (1 Samuel 16:7).

The enemy wants us to think the battleground is our behavior, while he knows it has always been the heart. And he desires to use us as a means to an end. His objective is to corrupt us so our behavior brings discredit upon the Father and keeps others from coming to a saving knowledge of Christ. After all, if our behavior is no different from the world's, why would anyone be interested in salvation offered through Christ? Winning the battle for the heart is essential to freedom from bondage, Christian maturity, and Christ-like leadership.

When I studied the Scriptures on the heart, I was astounded by the richness of meaning. The heart, you see, is comprised of our beliefs, values, attitudes, and motives. Outward behavior can act as an influence on the heart. And behavior can solidify what is stored in the heart, like an internal feedback loop. But what originates in the heart is actually what motivates external actions.

I should have realized this earlier. After all, didn't Jesus teach that "from within, out of men's hearts, come evil thoughts, sexual immorality, theft, murder, adultery, greed, malice, deceit, lewdness, envy, slander, arrogance and folly. All these evils come from inside and make a man 'unclean' " (Mark 7:21-23). If our beliefs, values, attitudes, and motives are not carved by God's scalpel, the Bible, they will likely be shaped by other influences including friends, circumstances, the world, and the adversary himself.

Christian transformation happens as the mind of Christ permeates our inner selves. As his Word forms our beliefs, we begin to value what he values. As we follow the leading of the Spirit, he renews our attitudes and motives. And from this growing Christ-like character, outwardly flows behavior that glorifies God. To change behavior, we must have a change of *heart.*

Not too long ago, I was asked to address prominent pastors in a particular denomination. I asked them what the primary function of their role as pastors was. They responded with declarations of their life purpose or their visions for their churches. I countered that I believed their primary function was heart surgery. We are called to facilitate heart transformation in the lives of Christ followers. With the empowerment of the Holy Spirit, the authority of God the Father, and the strength of Jesus Christ, we are to move others toward victory by focusing on the source of our behavior, the heart.

So, brother, you are really a surgeon commissioned by God to perform heart surgery with his help. The world doesn't really care what we have to say until they observe how we live. And the way we live won't be transformed without this surgery. We are called to live in bold relief against the backdrop of our culture, always prepared to give a defense for the hope that is in us.

In his strength and to his honor,

Greg

For the grace of God that brings salvation has appeared to all men. It teaches us to say "No" to ungodliness and worldly passions, and to live self-controlled, upright and godly lives in this present age, while we wait for the blessed hope—the glorious appearing of our great God and Savior, Jesus Christ, who gave himself for us to redeem us from all wickedness and to purify for himself a people that are his very own, eager to do what is good.

Titus 2:11-14

Tend Your Inner Life

Michael W. Foss
Prince of Peace Lutheran Church, Burnsville, Minnesota

Dear Bill,

I am so glad for the opportunity to encourage you in this great adventure—the ministry of the gospel of Jesus Christ. It is God's calling for each of us, and our Creator has already given you what you'll need to accomplish and grow your ministry: your inner spiritual life. In the power of God's Holy Spirit, I urge you tend your inner life; it's God's vehicle for your call.

I remember how eagerly I entered the ministry of Jesus Christ. I was enthusiastic in preparing sermons, attending meetings, and working with others. In three years, I had made a good beginning. But what no one told me was that my profession could actually become an impediment to my practice of the faith. There grew within me a gnawing longing, which I could not understand. Something was missing. One day, in conversation with my wife, she asked if my *public* prayer and Scripture life had replaced my *personal* one. And I knew immediately that she was right. I knew I needed to get back to the basics and return to my first love.

Prayer has always been a way of life for me, but now that I was praying so frequently in public, I found my personal prayers sounded like the ones I would give at a Rotary meeting. They became polished and eloquent. But I longed for the intimate, unrehearsed times of conversation with my Savior that had been the staple of my inner life. So I began taking time again to simply talk to the Savior. The simplicity and honesty of these times truly are refreshing and freeing. And the warmth of these moments with God in prayer began to relight my passion for Christ.

I am not the kind of person who can pray at one time of the day, every day, for very long. I tried it…it was helpful for a season. Now, I simply *talk* with God all the time—as I come and go or as I have moments to myself.

However, I have discovered that I need to slow down, even stop, in order to *listen* to God. Now I look for those moments—no, I *forge* such moments out of my days. My passion for ministry has taken on an inner confidence because of my intimacy with my faithful Friend. I can always go to him, and I always receive strength, comfort, and joy. I urge you to remember the place of prayer in your daily life. Stay connected to the One who will see you through all the seasons of your ministry.

A second great joy of our calling is the opening of God's Word to others. Few things can match the sheer pleasure of watching someone's spirit light up at the discovery of spiritual truth through the Bible. However, as my ministry grew during those first three years, I found that I read God's Word increasingly with an eye for others. My approach to the Bible was increasingly not *What is God saying to me?* but *What is God saying to our congregation through me?*

Both are good questions. Both have their place in our lives. What I discovered was the lesson of Hosea the prophet. Hosea's ministry began first with a word of God *to* the prophet, and then that word became a word to the people *through* the prophet. My soul was hungering for God's Word to once again come alive in my own life.

I remembered my grandfather sitting in his chair, beneath the floor lamp, reading the Bible. I remembered my own times of discovery in God's Word—how a passage of Scripture, which I had read dozens of times, would suddenly emerge into an entirely new light by the illumination of the Holy Spirit.

So, I began to intentionally read the Bible again—not in preparation for a sermon, but just for the joy of meeting God. And through these times, I've discovered that I have even more to pass on than ever before! Out of the personal reading of God's Word came an inner integrity of witness that had gotten lost in the *doing* of my ministry. So I urge you, Bill, take time with God to allow his Word to refresh your soul, enliven your heart, and strengthen your ministry.

Take seriously the need to tend your inner life. I discovered that our outer life of ministry can absorb the inner life of the soul. Be careful of this seduction! The most important work of ministry that you and I can do is keep praying and reading the Scriptures *for ourselves!* As God feeds us, we will be equipped to feed the saints.

I thank God for you and your calling. We are partners in the greatest adventure possible to human beings—the life and ministry of the faith.

Your fellow servant in Christ Jesus,

Michael

But we have this treasure in jars of clay to show that this all-surpassing power is from God and not from us.

2 Corinthians 4:7

Personal Reflections on

Inner Life

Significance

Success?

Larry Adams
Golden Hills Community Church, Antioch-Brentwood, California

Dear Paul,

Last week I worked through the stacks of mail that had accumulated during my family vacation. Sitting at the bottom of the pile, two pieces caught my eye. They couldn't have been more opposite from one another. One was large, professionally printed, and multicolored. The other was small, hand-labeled, and plain. One was a must-see experience; the other a heartfelt thanks. The one told me about some of America's most dynamic and successful pastors. The other told my wife and me about our example of faithfulness that had given another person hope.

The brochure offered success…the letter exampled it.

My wife Karla and I have been in pastoral ministry for over 20 years. We've served in associate positions in churches of less than 100 and, for the last 16 years, in the senior pastorate. We have seen our church plant grow from infancy to more than 2,500. I share that brief history for one reason—to let you know that at every level the pressures to succeed have been real and relentless.

But for too many years, I labored under a faulty definition of success. As a youth pastor, I thought success was measured by how many kids swelled our youth group or how many hands were raised at meetings. As a church planter, success seemed to be defined by growth and how fast one could get off of denominational support. Yet as our church grew beyond 500, then 800, and then 1,000, I noticed the pressures to succeed never went away.

Today's cutting-edge leaders are usually described with phrases like *change agent, paradigm shifter,* and *difference maker.* They are introduced as dynamic strategists, innovators, revolutionaries, and entrepreneurs. We hear that successful pastors take bold risks and are articulate, charismatic, and visionary. They know what they want, they have their fingers on the pulse of the culture, and they continually make accurate assessments regarding what will attract people in droves and keep them happy. It seems like we must have the entrepreneurial skill of a Bill Gates and the servant hands of a Mother Teresa. Who can measure up?

Contrary to the subliminal tug within us, however, our lives do not need to clone those successful conference speakers. Yes, many are effective leaders, but success doesn't require that *your* church become like *their* churches. Success is not being featured as a keynote speaker in an upcoming national seminar. It's not in pastoring a megachurch or publishing a bestseller. Success is becoming what God wants each of us to be as a person and in fulfilling the ministry he wants us to have as pastors. God wants us to be living, breathing, touchable jars of clay filled with the treasure of Jesus.

Often, in the face of another important ministry decision, I find myself prayerfully reminding the Lord that I don't seem to have what those other guys have. The Lord graciously reminds me that I'm thinking too much about succeeding and not enough about seeking. Then a deep peace from God assures me that he is not asking me to be like those guys…he is asking me to be like him.

Now this doesn't mean that cultural issues and ministry strategies aren't important to me. At every level of church growth and development, I have sought God's wisdom, devised program strategies, solidified core values, and assessed outcomes. There is never a place in ministry for sloppy theology, laziness, or passing the buck. We need to pray hard, study hard, and work hard. We need to keep in touch with our community and our world. But effective ministry is more than vision, culture, and strategies. Take heed, Paul. Remember that ministry is also a mystery and, above all, a spiritual work. Therefore, we need to seek God's mind and heart and obediently follow what he reveals for our particular situations.

I have also been greatly encouraged to realize that when God calls us to serve him, he defines success not in terms of strategies and outcomes, but in terms of Christ-like character. He didn't say we had to be CEOs, change agents, or paradigm shifters to be successful in ministry. He said we simply need to walk in a way worthy of him. Neither did he use a long list of marketing terms to define entrepreneurial potential. He describes the secret to success with words such as *humility, gentleness, patience, perseverance, holiness, faithfulness,* and *truth.* The more others see Christ reflected in our lives and in turn desire to draw nearer to him, the closer we come to living a life and having a ministry that God would call a success.

Yes, it's an awesome privilege to bear the name of Jesus and to lay our lives down in service to him. With this privilege comes the divine calling to walk worthy, to become a vessel fit for his use, to know him, and to make him known.

Two pieces of mail—one offered success, the other defined it. One version of success may lead to having our names inscribed on the pages of a glossy brochure. The other will mean that God was pleased to use us to inscribe Jesus' name on another human heart.

Hey, Paul, have you checked your mail lately? Perhaps God's acknowledgment of success is closer than you think. It may even be waiting for you buried beneath the mountain on your desk.

Your brother,

Larry

As a prisoner for the Lord, then, I urge you to live a life worthy of the calling you have received. Be completely humble and gentle; be patient, bearing with one another in love. Make every effort to keep the unity of the Spirit through the bond of peace.

EPHESIANS 4:1-3

Yearning for Significance

Earl F. Palmer
University Presbyterian Church, Seattle, Washington

Dear Pete,

From the time I was a boy, I wanted to do something significant. I wanted to make a difference in the world, to leave a mark of my own. I remember the time a high school buddy and I found a small lake on the lower slopes of Mount Shasta. When we looked closely at the U.S. Geological Survey map, we noticed that the lake was unnamed. We made a pile of rocks at the site, and from that moment on, we called it Lake Palzag to honor both our names: Earl Palmer and Harry Zagorites.

For some reason, the name didn't endure (maybe it was too hard to spell). But my desire to be significant and leave a mark stayed with me. Now I am a man, a husband, a father, and a pastor—and I still want to make a difference.

I have been wondering about this unique human motivation to leave a mark. What do you think, Pete? Is it good or bad? Personally, I've come to the conclusion that it can be both. But I think the good may outweigh the bad.

The bad desire for significance is called pride—a disease that preoccupies me with my own importance. The result is a long list of desperate attempts to ensure recognition, inevitably leading to bitterness and despair (because most people just don't care about my personal ambitions). Pride becomes an unforgiving and humorless master of the soul. It spoils hard work because it's too serious, too self-referential, and too idolatrous. And pride's feeble attempt to ensure our own significance is ultimately in vain: We are not the lake on the map, we are only the finders of the lake. (And if the truth were known, the mapmaker found it before we did.)

Despite this bad yearning for significance, there is also a good yearning. From the beginning of man, God designed and encouraged within us the drive to leave a mark when he allowed us to name the animals. He is the creator of them all, but he calls the grand animal of Africa *hippopotamus* because man thought up that name. Wow! We should never ignore this mystery: God himself cares about our significance, the mark we leave.

What then is the greatest significance we can experience in our own life journey? I think the answer is simple and profound: It is in helping others discover the mystery of their significance in God's eyes. The words and deeds that show the love of Jesus Christ to another person are the most significant acts of my life. Remember the servants in Luke 19 who invested their master's talents? The Owner of the estate has given *me* treasures of the estate to invest in others. And something much better than egotistical pride is the result: It is the accolade of the Lord at the end of the day: *Well done, good and faithful servant.*

And in this divine praise, we discover the cure for pride, that negative quest for significance. People become desperate for recognition because they feel lonely and unnoticed; they feel a lack of inner significance. The best cure for pride is an unequivocal and total endorsement by someone who really matters—God. When we realize God freely deems us significant, we won't chase after significance in pride.

What makes this mystery so delightful is that God considers it a joy. He wants us to exercise this impulse to leave a mark. Could it be that he loves our simple lake-naming? Does he say something like, "Well done! You showed them my lake. By the way, the name sounds funny, but I like it. It has a kind of ring to it—Lake Palzag! Yes, that *is* a funny name." And then there is laughter in heaven for the end of insignificance.

Warmly,

Earl

His master replied, "Well done, good and faithful servant!
You have been faithful with a few things; I will
put you in charge of many things. Come and
share your master's happiness!"

Matthew 25:21

Age, Achievements, and Acceptance

Joel C. Hunter
Northland, A Church Distributed, Longwood, Florida

Dear Roberto,

As I approach another birthday, it seems appropriate to consider the relationship age has with perceived ministry accomplishments. We often see ourselves in competition with peers and with our biological clocks.

If we're doing better than we estimate most of our age group is doing, we feel affirmed and relieved. If you have a family background that demanded more discipline and expected more excellence than most, the early returns when comparing your achievements with peers may rate you high above average. This manner of comparison can be a morale booster much of your life—if you do well in conventional terms. It only starts to fail when you get into your 40s and there are people much younger who are out-achieving you. Then the fallacy of this approach becomes apparent.

We need to watch out for several pitfalls of the tendency to compare ourselves with our peers. First, many adults tend to settle for mere survival in their early years. But survival should never be our goal, not even in the direst conflicts (let alone everyday life). Ironically, aiming only at survival ensures failure. We were made to make a positive difference that no one else can make. We are all as singular as Adam in the garden. Yet, I see ministers my age still just trying to survive. They have carried that mind-set since they began pastoring. Comparing ourselves with those who are merely trying to survive isn't the correct standard to use!

Another pitfall of comparison is that we begin to believe that God's timing is connected to our calendar. Success is cumulative, but it is not consecutive. One success does not always lead to another. It can be easy for ministers to become frustrated that they aren't "more successful by now." We think accomplishments are a sign of some sort of spiritual seniority. But this is a lie. Watch out *at any age* for an imagined "accomplishment" in which you're not carrying a basin and towel.

The last pitfall I'll mention is this: Unlike any little league sport, the competition is never your peers. The competition has always been the same, whether in serpent form or slithering whisper. It is his lies that you need to leave in the dust, his lies that make you strive for success over servanthood. Your *allies* are other Christian leaders and churches. The *competition* is whatever stands between them and Jesus.

I celebrate this birthday relieved that I haven't messed up royally in my years in ministry. Given my nature and my past, this is literally a miracle of God's grace.

I'm glad I don't have to be afraid of growing older; in fact, I'm looking forward to it. I wouldn't go back to any age for anything. I've got a wonderful wife, great sons, a terrific daughter-in-law, and a grandson who appears to me to be as close to perfect as is humanly possible. I've earned my gray hair and wrinkles, and in spite of looking more like a Shar-Pei dog, I still have years of doing good yet to come.

The glory of aging, especially in professions where the mind is capital, is credibility. And credibility really comes from two sources: faithfulness and wisdom.

Faithfulness is doing the same helpful things week after week, year after year. When our forefathers in the Bible wanted to remind each other of God's credibility, they would repeat how faithful he was in acts of grace over hundreds of years. Young people, without much of a record of faithfulness, may try to substitute promises. Don't do that; there is no substitute, so just keep helping consistently.

The other source of credibility is wisdom. The older you get, the more you can tell the difference between knowledge that is good for the moment and wisdom that is good forever. Keep pursuing wisdom, friend, and your credibility will grow.

Personal reward, peace, and acceptance are found not so much by achievements touted by others, but through faithful service in each stage of ministry. May our Lord continue to bless you over all the seasons of your Christian leadership.

Yours because I'm his,

Joel

Be faithful, even to the point of death,
and I will give you the crown of life.
Revelation 2:10b

Quit Squinting

LeRoy Lawson
CMF International, Payson, Arizona

Dear Josiah,

If my close friends knew what I was doing now, they'd be scoffing. "You're doing what? You're giving advice to a young minister?" They would tell you to get your career counseling from someone else. They've been shaking their heads over my decisions for years. Why, they ask, would anybody in his right mind transport his young family from a solid pastorate in Oregon to teach at an obscure Christian college in Tennessee? Or walk away from a college vice presidency to pastor an urban church? Or later leave that growing Indianapolis church for one just half its size in the Arizona desert?

Why would one assume the presidency of a Christian college in California while remaining as pastor of the Arizona congregation and still be at both jobs eight years later? Many of my friends also disapprove of my motorcycle, shake their heads at my bungee jumping, and question other activities. "Surely," they would scold, "you don't want any young ministers to become like you!"

They're right. You shouldn't imitate me. Or any other minister, for that matter. God called you to be yourself—your best self—and nobody else.

My only advice for you is this: Practice the *Isaiah Principle*. You'll find it in Isaiah 6:1-8, where this shaken future prophet confronts his God, to his initial dismay. He has soiled his soul and cannot clean it up. He is trespassing where only holiness belongs. He has no right to be in the Temple—neither he nor any of his kind.

Then comes the purifying touch of burning coals. Thanks to this grace, Isaiah now can dare to hear and even serve God. "Here am I," he says. "Send me." And Isaiah's words, slightly altered into the Isaiah Principle, have guided me for four decades: *Here am I; use me.*

Like Isaiah, my ministry commenced with this dual vision of God's holiness and of my nearly paralyzing unholiness. The result of this double vision is the tic I've developed. I tend, when looking toward God, to squint. Isaiah worried about his unclean lips; I fret over my unseeing eyes. We can't dwell in the midst of a people of little faith without sinfulness and cowardice infecting us, too. Even when convinced of our calling, we still squint. To look boldly toward our Savior or those mountains he challenges us to move is beyond us. *Conservatism, laziness, fear*—what word accounts for your timidity when God lays his challenges before you? Why do you narrow your field of vision to the merely manageable?

After a lifetime of ministry, I have few regrets. One that nags, though, is this: I can't help wondering what adventures God would have empowered me to undertake, if only I had trusted him more boldly. T.S. Eliot's J. Alfred Prufrock lamented, "I have seen the moment of my greatness flicker...And in short, I was afraid." I quote him with more empathy than I like to admit.

Here's just one example of my shortsightedness. When I was on the campus of Pacific Christian College to be interviewed for the presidency, one of the vice presidents and I were surveying the campus from the second story of the main building. The view was less than inspiring. The diminutive college of 500 students was squeezed onto 11 densely packed acres, bound by California State University at Fullerton on the north and businesses and apartment buildings on the other three sides. "Well," my disappointment sighed, "there sure isn't any room for expansion, is there?"

"There's plenty of room," the vice president retorted.

"Where?" I asked.

He pointed skyward as he answered, "Up. This area is zoned for 10 stories." He was right, and today I'm writing from the seventh floor at Hope International University. This is the blessing of looking up rather than squinting.

If I had these 40 years of ministry to do over again, I'd open my eyes wider. Instead of routinely asking of every new proposal, "How can we possibly do it? How will we fund it?" I'd be quicker to ask, "Why not?" Doesn't James 4:2 say, "You do not have, because you do not ask God"?

And doesn't Jesus insist, "Everything is possible for him who believes" (Mark 9:23)? And what about Matthew 7:7-8, "Ask and it will be given to you; seek and you will find; knock and the door will be opened to you"?

Even as I cite these references, though, something in this minister emeritus starts to explain what is really meant by them, how we have to consider the context, the extenuating circumstances, the difference between Jesus' day and ours—in other words, I still haven't cured this tic, this self-defeating propensity for blinking away the possibilities.

Peter had it right. When his gaze was fixed on Jesus, he could walk on water (Matthew 14:25-33). When he diverted his eyes to the wind, he sank. Diverting your eyes—that's just a less obvious form of squinting, isn't it?

This, then, is my advice: Apply the Isaiah Principle. First, deliver yourself to the Lord to be cleaned up. Second, offer yourself to be used in any way he desires. Finally, always fix your gaze steadily on him and the opportunities he lays before you.

And don't squint!

Yours in Christ,

LeRoy

> *Now to him who is able to do immeasurably more than all we ask or imagine, according to his power that is at work within us, to him be glory in the church and in Christ Jesus throughout all generations, forever and ever! Amen.*
>
> EPHESIANS 3:20-21

Don't Touch the Glory

Steve Johnson
President, Vision USA, Kissimmee, Florida

Dear John,

Recently I've been reminded of how wonderful it is to have God's call on my life. In the church I serve, there are several young men who have expressed an interest in becoming pastors. Their enthusiasm and adventurous spirit to go forth in the power of the gospel to change the world takes me back over 20 years to when I first felt called to serve God in this way.

Many who start the race of pastoral ministry don't finish the way they expect. They get sidetracked by the many hazards that prevent us from completing the task to which we've been called. I'd like to caution you about one particular hazard that could have destroyed my effectiveness in pastoral ministry.

To give you a little background, I became a Christian when I was 16. My older brother Paul was very instrumental in the process of my conversion. We both became church planters in our early 20s while we were working our way through college and seminary. We had a wonderful plan to see new churches started all over the country that would be effective in bringing the gospel to our generation. These were days of great vision and believing that God could do the impossible.

However, my desire to serve God often was shadowed by a dark side within me. I was very concerned about being successful. I wasn't completely sure what success meant, but I knew that's what I wanted in my life. For me, my brother Paul set the benchmark of what it meant to be successful. And it always seemed to be escalating. My pursuit of this elusive sense of accomplishment led me into many struggles with pride. I have since found out that pride might be the number one struggle that most church planters face. We are torn between the honorable pursuit of serving God and the ugly quest to be seen as successful.

I recently heard some advice given to an up-and-coming pastor from a pastor near retirement age. He said, "Don't touch the glory." How true. All of the glory needs to go to God, yet all too often we want people to know about our successes.

I can remember times it became difficult to celebrate the seasons of blessings that others were enjoying. I tried to act like I was happy for them, but I have to confess that I wondered how it made me look. God was doing great things in the ministry he had given me, but I wanted more. I was in the midst of a battle. I really wanted to be like Christ, yet I fought with this terrible need for self-promotion.

In the early days of our church-planting movement, we hired a very sharp young man named Tom. Tom and his wife had just graduated from seminary and had a passion to see the gospel shared in our home state of Wisconsin. Tom came to pastor our third church plant. My brother Paul and I had made a pact that we wanted each new church plant to do better than the previous. The problem was that now we were using someone else. The question arose in my soul: Do I really want to bless Tom with success?

Tom became a great church planter. God blessed his ministry in Whitewater, Wisconsin. My church in Oshkosh, Wisconsin started six months earlier; thus we were always six months ahead of the Whitewater congregation. Our attendance, offering, and move to our first building were almost exactly six months ahead of the church he had started.

There was an unspoken competitiveness that existed in my heart toward Tom. He later shared that he felt the same way toward me. Although this battle raged inside both of our hearts, we didn't confront and confess this attitude as sin until several years later. It was a day of humbling my heart and asking God and Tom for forgiveness. From that point on, I became a cheerleader for Tom.

Some time later I was given an opportunity to serve on a search committee as mission director for our state. Not only did I recommend Tom, but I tried my best to see that his job description and salary were adequate.

I can't say that I no longer struggle with pride. I think we all do. However, I'm now more aware that pride is an incredibly dangerous problem that depletes the leader rather than building him or her up. As ministers of God, we must purge this attitude from our lives or we will be destroyed by it.

We have been called to serve God. We are not going to be evaluated by him in comparison to others. Rather, he will hold us accountable for what he has entrusted to each of us. We can truly celebrate victories in other people's lives and ministries and also enjoy the seasons of blessing that God gives us. After all, it's all for God's glory, not ours.

Let me give you a postscript to this story, John. Not too long ago, Tom and I were attending the same conference, so we decided to room together. One evening Tom got down on the floor and did 50 push-ups. Likewise, I took my turn. When I finished, Tom asked me how many I had done. I told him I only had the strength to do 49.

Your co-laborer,

Steve

When pride comes, then comes disgrace,
but with humility comes wisdom.

Proverbs 11:2

Personal Reflections on

Significance

The Family

Capturing Time

Randy Berg
Calvary Christian Church, Hastings, Minnesota

Dear Manuel,

Admit it, as pastors we keep strange hours. Some days we start with an early 6:00 a.m. breakfast study, have meetings throughout the day, and conclude with an evening activity. Not every day is maxed out, but hard work seems synonymous with effective ministry.

While this situation is inherent to the pastorate, I don't think it has to keep us from our families. Even though some days require being out early or away from home at night, I have learned several ways to maximize time with my family.

As a pastor, I need to remember that my schedule is largely determined by me. Other people may have expectations for my time, but ultimately I decide what is going to be placed on my schedule. Obviously, some events are steadfast and immovable, but appointments, administrative work, and study time can be adapted to my schedule. There is no question that I am available for hospital emergencies, family crises, and babies that are born at inconsiderate hours. In one sense, I'm on call 24 hours a day, but I don't have to jump at everything. In reality, I have flexibility in my daily work as a pastor. When I make it a habit to take an early look at events and opportunities before me, I can make sure that priority activities with my family are included in my schedule.

Let me pass on to you some of the things that I've done to capture time with my family.

When our children were in elementary school, my schedule allowed me to be the only male parent accompanying the class on field trips. I went to museums and concerts with my children and their friends, and I got to know teachers and other parents on these escapes from the office. It usually took either a morning or afternoon until 3:00, so I shifted my schedule accordingly.

I have also made it a point, if at all possible, to be around after school when my kids are home. I might just stop by for a few minutes to see how things are going and then return to work. Sometimes I pick them up from school, and they con me out of a pop or a burger. Once we pulled the middle seat out of our minivan and ate French fries around a low table in our "limousine." Captured moments such as this are priceless.

When my children participate in after-school sports, my schedule allows me to stop by practice and watch for a while. When I'm at games, I don't bring a book to read: I'm there to watch them play and show that I'm proud of them.

This week, our church has town meetings Monday through Thursday night. Does this mean I'll be running from morning until night, breezing in only for a quick dinner? No. I'll go out for a cup of coffee with my wife this afternoon and later be available to help my son work on his car or play basketball or whatever else may be going on.

The ministry of presence among my own family is of critical value. My job allows me to control my schedule. I can choose to be a driven pastor, squeezing every minute to build a church. Or I can choose to be a balanced pastor, not sacrificing my own family for the church family.

Some pastors' kids watch the church steal their parents. But this doesn't have to be the situation. If we allow it and don't educate our congregations, we ourselves are at fault. I want my kids to grow up thinking it was really great having dad be a pastor. Let's make sure we talk about the benefits with our families. They're quick to pick up on the challenges of the ministry. Let's help them also see the blessings.

Lewis Bird, a professor in marriage and family, reminded our class one day about the importance of giving time to our children. He said, "Remember, your children will rise up and call you something. For me, I want that something to be positive rather than negative, and I think my chances are better if I capture time with them and share my life with them now while I have the opportunity."

I only have a window of a few prime years with my children, as do you, Manuel. After that, they'll get busy and have other interests. I consider it a crime if I'm working all the time when these windows of opportunity are open. I can't afford to be a workaholic while my kids are living at home. When they are gone, I can increase my load, but not now.

As you grow in your professional ministry skills, dear friend, likewise become more effective in capturing time for your family.

Praying for balance in your life,

Randy

Be very careful, then, how you live—
not as unwise but as wise.

Ephesians 5:15

Listen to Your Spouse

Doug Talley
Church of God Ministries, Lakeland, Florida

Dear Scott,

As you begin your ministry, I'd like to pass on some helpful advice I received when I first began pastoring—listen to your spouse. Listening to my wife has not only increased my understanding of people and situations, but it has also saved me from some serious blunders. Let me explain what I mean.

First, my wife has a great sense of intuition when it comes to people's motives, especially women's motives. When I was in seminary, I heard stories about women who were attracted to pastors, but I never thought much about it. Cindy, however, is very much aware of the possibility that other women might find me attractive. (I suspect this has a lot more to do with the role I fill than with my personality or looks.) I don't fully understand it, but she's able to intercept subtle communications from other women and quickly detect when motives are questionable or simply impure.

Cindy seems to have built-in radar, which sets off a warning signal when someone begins to demonstrate an inappropriate interest in me. I'm totally oblivious to these warning signals—or I don't want to admit their existence to myself because such attention can be flattering. After her intuition proved to be accurate on several occasions, I was convinced she knew what she was talking about. I asked her to please let me know when her radar goes off and to help protect me from any possible situations and persons that could compromise my integrity. She has eagerly complied, and I've been able to take evasive action to protect myself from potentially dangerous situations.

Second, my spouse seems to have a sixth sense about persons who will serve well in various ministry positions, as well as persons who will not. This especially applies to leadership roles in the church. During the early years of my ministry when she would express a reservation about someone serving in a particular position, I just thought she was trying to tell me what to do. Even though she would give me specific examples based on her interaction with that person or observations from that person's interactions with others, I chose to exercise my executive privilege. After all, I was the senior pastor!

About this same time, I heard a conference speaker say that pastors need to listen to their spouses regarding whom to recruit for ministry positions. His statement caused me to have flashbacks. I began seeing faces of people I had invited to a ministry who didn't fit the role for which I had recruited them. Sometimes the person's spiritual gifts and abilities didn't match the ministry role. Other times there was a personality mismatch or weakness that restricted their individual effectiveness or even caused problems. As I pictured those people, I could hear my wife expressing her reservations. Even though my male ego tried to resist admitting she was right, I knew if I was going to be an effective leader who surrounded himself with the right people, I needed to tap into her wisdom.

Since then, there have been a few times I have not heeded Cindy's advice. I knew I was taking a bit of a risk. However, I thought I could either manage the person and any situations that developed or that the person had hidden leadership ability that my wife simply wasn't seeing. Despite my optimism, her insight continues to be extremely accurate.

Third, my spouse has helped me work through my feelings when people choose to leave the church. People change churches all too often in today's world, and it always hurts me when they do. While people will say it's not personal when they leave, I often feel otherwise. Cindy has helped me sort through my feelings. Sometimes it is personal. The individual involved just doesn't like me. Most of the time, however, there are other reasons. By talking me through these situations, my wife has helped me work through my disappointment and feelings of inadequacy so I can move forward in ministry.

Fourth, my spouse has helped me evaluate various ministry opportunities we've been offered. My first invitation to serve came when we were in seminary and I was looking for ministry experience. I didn't think the church position was the best fit, but I felt like my choices were limited. Against my better judgment, I was about to accept it. My wife was able to convince me that a bad ministry fit does not yield a good experience. As I reconsidered the opportunity, it dawned on me that she understood my gifts, abilities, and temperament better than I did. I declined the position.

Now, more than 20 years later, I realize Cindy saved me from making a bad decision. Declining that ministry opportunity soon led to my first, and thus far, only pastorate, which has lasted over 19 years. During this time, there have been several enticing ministry opportunities presented to me. She has helped me sort through each one and seek the mind of God.

Scott, God has given you a wonderful wife who complements you well. Remember that together you are in the Lord's service. And since spouses don't have the same experiences, spiritual gifts, and abilities, they bring a balancing insight and perspective to each of our ministries. So let's keep listening to our spouses. And I believe we'll exalt them for their tremendous contribution to our kingdom partnership.

Sincerely,

Doug

A man's greatest treasure is his wife—
she is a gift from the Lord.

Her words are sensible, and her advice is thoughtful.
Proverbs 18:22; 31:26
(Contemporary English Version)

Avoiding the "Either/Or"

Bob Russell
Southeast Christian Church, Louisville, Kentucky

Dear Brian,

Aristotle taught that the best path lies in the mean. The secret of so much of life is avoiding the extremes. We tend to excel at and focus on *either* this *or* that, but we have a hard time balancing two extremes. If you want to have a long and prosperous ministry, you would be wise to remember to keep a proper balance in three important areas of ministry.

First, *avoid the "either/or" regarding tolerance and truth.* One dimension of an effective ministry is the ability to stand for God's Word while at the same time expressing God's love. In Ephesians 4:15 Paul reminds us to speak "the truth in love." This balance is not easy to maintain. A few years ago, a wealthy business owner in our town pledged a half million dollars to our building program. Then he asked me to perform his wedding—his third. The circumstances of his divorce didn't measure up to the church's guidelines for divorce and remarriage, so I had to tell him I couldn't oversee his wedding, even though it was really tempting to find a way to fudge on our policy just this once. There will always be influential and likeable people you want to accommodate or even grieving people to whom you want to give hope. But don't give in. Always hold fast to the Word of God.

But don't forget to speak the truth *in love.* A colleague of mine preached his first sermon at his home church while he was still a student in Bible college. Throughout the message he scolded his church for all they'd been doing wrong the last 20 years. When he was finished, his pastor said, "Well, you did fine, son. But remember, you can't preach the love of God with a clenched fist."

Second, *avoid the "either/or" regarding ambition and contentment.* A spiritual gift is like a garden tool—it only works if you exert enough effort. I've seen more people fail in ministry because of a lack of discipline than a lack of talent or training. One of the turning points of my ministry came during my first preaching position just after I graduated from Bible college. I was the first full-time minister this church had ever employed, and there was no place to study at the church. My wife left for work at 7:15 a.m., and I was home alone. I had some choices: I could read the paper, watch television, drive down to the donut shop, or try to get up a golf game. But I decided that I would dedicate those hours each morning to studying for my Sunday sermon. That discipline has stayed with me to this day.

Make the most of the gifts that God has given you. Work hard. Proverbs 10:4 says, "Lazy hands make a man poor, but diligent hands bring wealth." The servant God will use to the fullest is not the most gifted, but the most diligent.

Also, remember, friend, to balance ambition with contentment. A lot of overly hardworking pastors are discontented, restless, and always on the lookout for what they consider an ideal church. Ambition is a wonderful motivator, but it must in balance. Develop a sense of satisfaction from simply doing your best. God evaluates his servants not by statistics but by faithfulness.

Third, *avoid the "either/or" regarding your calling and your family.* I'm sure you see your ministry as a calling. And this is a great privilege. However, you can get so caught up in ministry that you neglect your family.

I made the mistake early in my ministry of leaving the house every available evening to go out calling on potential members. My wife was so supportive that she never complained. But she was lonely at times, and that was unfair. Thankfully, by the time my children came along, I had learned the importance of being home to eat with them, to put them to bed, and to develop a close relationship with them. One year, my sons were both playing on different basketball teams, and they had games four nights a week. I put the games on my calendar and only missed one or two the entire season. It was amazing to see how God blessed our church during that year. I learned that the church doesn't have to revolve around me.

I've often heard that the best thing a father can do for his children is to love their mother. Similarly, the best thing you can do for your ministry is to love your family. I'd challenge you to be lovingly faithful to your mate and deeply attentive to your children—this is your first calling.

The answer to life's challenges is often in the mean, so keep your balance, Brian. Speak the truth, but do it in love. Work hard, but be content. And be true to your calling, but remember your family. Then God will honor your ministry, bless your family, and bring fruit to your labor.

Your friend in Christ,

Bob

See that what you have heard from the beginning remains in you. If it does, you also will remain in the Son and in the Father. And this is what he promised us—even eternal life.

1 John 2:24-25

Personal Reflections on

The Family

The Congregation

Community

Knute Larson

The Chapel, Akron, Ohio

Dear Nathan,

He was so timid yet so talkative. He was awkward, socially and emotionally, likely related to an accident when he was younger. He would wander the halls at our church, sometimes sit in on a class, and even volunteered a bit. No doubt he was looking for family.

One day he attended one of our Sunday classes. After the lesson, as the class was beginning to dismiss, one of the men asked, "Eric, would you like to join our group?"

Two days later, Eric related to me the following: "No one ever asked me to join a group. All my life I've been in and out of different things, even trying churches, yet no one ever asked me to become a part of their group."

Eric's amazement illustrates the hunger for community that is all around us. His surprise makes me realize that we can always do a better job of extending Christ's invitation to become a part of his body. When Jesus asked us to join his group, he also asked us to extend to others the same love, forgiveness, acceptance, and fellowship he offered us. He desires that many more know his fellowship found in Christian community.

Nate, you and I both know what true friendship is like. Sometimes we've just sat with a buddy, no words exchanged, comfortable together even in our silence. On other occasions we've needed to vent—share deep frustrations or even our sin struggles—and still feel respected and loved by our friend.

But so many people miss this kind of community. They don't know the love of a friend or the joy of fellowship. More troubling still is that they may never understand much of Christ's love if they don't see it embodied in us, the church.

Let me explain. The only way many people experience church is in the worship service. Worship is essential and good, for it is what we were created to do. However, we were also created for community, and the typical worship service is not designed for relationship building.

Community is where people can know each other, where they can be honest, and where they can ask questions. Community is where people can pour out their hearts and where they listen with a sympathetic ear. Community is where folks are allowed to straddle a fence on little issues that aren't clear in the Scriptures, where they can say, "I don't know," and where they can even differ respectfully with a brother or sister. Community is where friends overlook offenses or follow Matthew 18 when confrontation is necessary. Community is an atmosphere of cooperation that majors on the gospel and its love and concern for the world. Community is discipleship, fellowship, and accountability carried out in love.

Nathan, long ago I noticed if I preach about love but don't show it myself, I am just a loud, clanging cymbal. Likewise, if I merely talk about loving relationships and encourage people to build them but do not establish a system within the congregation to accomplish this, our people will not have the fellowship they need. Sure, some folks will take the required initiative to build relationships with others. But as you are aware, too many people simply fall through the cracks when we leave this to chance.

Therefore, I urge you, friend, to build into your church many small groups and midsize communities. At our church, we have classes that meet on Sundays. These same groups then also gather during the week as extended families for discipleship, social events, and outreach. They notice when someone is missing, and they care for those who are sick. They have become the vehicles in our church for carrying out all of the "one anothers" in Scripture.

As leaders in our churches, the most important thing we can do to enhance community is to cultivate an overall atmosphere that communicates we are family. That atmosphere begins with our own modeling. For example, sometimes I refer to my own small group from the pulpit, just to remind people that pastors also need fellowship and accountability.

The example of our executive leadership is also important. Therefore, I make sure our leaders are in community—all of us need that smaller group where we contribute our gifts and love or where we meet people out of work, in pain, or perhaps fighting cancer.

The bottom line, Nate, is that people will recognize authentic community by the way we greet others in the hall, talk from a heart of love, send notes, or work together as a team. Our daily demeanor will reveal whether we're just interested in numbers and looking good or if we really value people. My prayer for each of us is that we guide our churches in extending Christ's community to one another.

In the good yoke,

Knute

Let us not give up meeting together, as some are in the habit of doing, but let us encourage one another— and all the more as you see the Day approaching.

Hebrews 10:25

The Gift of Diversity

Benjamin Alicea-Lugo
St. Paul's Evangelical Reformed Church, Perth Amboy, New Jersey

Dear Timoteo,

During my ministry I have learned that Jesus calls us to serve people who are like us, who are almost like us, and many who are not like us at all. I've come to realize that it's important to accept differences among people and to love each one appropriately. These differences are usually defined by appearance, geographical origin, or a person's station in life. As a young man, I recognized diversity but did not necessarily value diversity. I now understand that seeing human diversity as a gift from God is an important step toward effective ministry.

I have heard many sermons that say God doesn't care whether you are white or black or brown or red, or what language you speak, or in what part of town you live. These sermons assume that our particularities should be ignored and that they should not get in the way of our unity in Christ. The result of this kind of preaching is that we homogenize our differences. We claim to be above discrimination, and we settle for a Christianity that distrusts diversity and promotes sameness under the banner of Christian love.

As I reflect on this understanding of diversity, I realize that I was invited to become a Christian by leaving my own particularity at the altar, as if my uniqueness was sinful or disruptive to my newfound faith. But please notice, Timoteo, that the Gospels paint a different composite picture of the body of Christ—a much richer picture.

Jesus loved John the Baptist although he seemed strange to many.

He called disciples from the working class and from the professionals. The woman at the well was from Samaria, a despised neighboring region. Matthew was a hated tax collector. Mary Magdalene, an unlikely believer, became the first to proclaim Christ had risen. All were accepted with their particularities and unique differences.

The early church gave evidence of the affirmation of diversity in ministry and church growth. The book of Acts shows us an emerging Christian church breaking free from parochial views. It shows a church moving beyond the geographical limits of Jerusalem, seeking to engage communities outside the synagogue and in the marketplace of major cities. It is a church creating and celebrating the gift of a pluralistic body of Christ.

The Holy Spirit descended at a time when there were many nations represented in Jerusalem and invited the crowd to hear the gospel in their own tongue. On the birthday of the Christian church, its diversity was assured. The gospel was proclaimed to the insider and outsider, the local and distant, the religious and secular, the elite and common, and the Jew and Gentile.

The history of the New Testament church supports the idea that ethnicity matters. Geography matters. One's profession or occupation matters. It matters because it gives context to our identity and helps define our place in the world. The particularity of our human existence is one of the gifts God provides. It is part of the beautiful tapestry he is creating among us. He *redeems* our particularity; he doesn't replace it. Through this gift God enables us to truly love one another. We are a community that has differences in color, language, race, and class. To see ourselves differently is to practice ministry with a serious blind spot. It is a form of human denial and fails to honor one of the outcomes of the cross.

In the Scriptures, the particularity of a group helped determine the nature of ministry to that group, and it should today as well. Ministry to the poor and under-employed is significantly different from ministry to the educated and upwardly mobile. Ministry to groups that enjoy power and privilege is different from ministry to groups that are on the margins of society. And ministry to people of color is different from ministry to people in an Anglo culture. This is true not only because God made us different but also because our faith is fleshed out in different contexts inside and outside of the church.

The Christian faith is the answer to all the world's questions if we keep in mind that we all have different questions, shaped by our particularity. God is the answer to the many questions shaped by our diverse human reality. If we assume we are all the same, we miss the opportunity to see the gospel applied to our unique situation and to the full range of the human experience.

Finally, Timoteo, the most compelling picture of diversity found in Scripture is the image of all humanity standing before God's throne in the book of Revelation. People of every land and ethnicity will participate in this incredible gathering. I get a tingle down my back just thinking about it. God will acknowledge us for who we are, where we came from, and the place where we found Jesus. Our common denominator is our union with Christ. And the greater our diversity, the more it elevates his greatness in drawing all kinds of people to himself.

What a glorious day it will be, and what a glorious day it can be today when we appreciate the beauty of our differences and celebrate our particularities. Appreciate the characteristics of the people you serve, and you will serve them more effectively.

En el servicio del maestro,

Benjamin

After this I looked and there before me was a great multitude that no one could count, from every nation, tribe, people and language, standing before the throne and in front of the Lamb. They were wearing white robes and were holding palm branches in their hands. And they cried out in a loud voice: "Salvation belongs to our God, who sits on the throne, and to the Lamb."

Revelation 7:9-10

Protecting Our People From Ourselves

Jan D. Hettinga
Northshore Baptist Church, Bothell, Washington

Dear Doug,

For three years Jim worked his way into a full-time staff position. Along the way, he headed up several different ministries, finally settling in as the pastor of small groups. When the church hit 1,000 in average attendance, plans were laid to start another church. Jim was selected as the lead pastor.

The same plan was used that had worked so well for the young mother church. A strong core group was established, and soon Jim and his wife found themselves leading a church of their own. That's when a troubling pattern began to appear. Whenever a strong, gifted leader would become part of the body and begin to exercise his gifts, Jim would find some way to alienate him. As the months went by, only people who were no threat to Jim were recruited. At the end of three years, the embryonic church collapsed. Jim had pushed away the very people he needed most. Somehow, he forgot an important practice—to protect his congregation from himself.

Churches self-destruct and pastors quit for a variety of reasons, but here are some common themes associated with the demise: pride and egotism, selfish ambition, obsession with power and control, competitiveness, rivalry, malicious attempts to destroy those considered "the opposition," arrogant insistence on "my way or the highway," and stubborn self-righteousness. Unfortunately, these are the sins that plague both pew and pulpit. The command to love above all is neglected, and the image of Christ is destroyed and defaced in his church.

So how can we avoid this potential pitfall, Doug? How can we assume command, yet protect our people from abusive leadership? It may just be that, like the Apostle Peter, our ministry effectiveness can only begin after we see our natural abilities fail.

You'll remember that Peter was bold and confrontational by nature. He alone joined his Lord for a walk on the Sea of Galilee. In the garden of Gethsemane, he defied the Temple guards, sword in hand, to defend Jesus. This was typical. Peter was assertive, aggressive, and strong-willed.

When Jesus predicted that Peter would deny him three times, Peter was offended. Yet at the fire outside the door of the high priest's courtyard, when a servant girl asked, "You are not one of his disciples, are you?" Peter mumbled in abject cowardice, "I am not" (John 18:17). Within minutes, he denied his Lord twice more...ultimate humiliation! His worse personal nightmare became reality. He had failed at the very place of his strength.

Peter never forgot this first rite of passage into kingdom leadership. The raw material of personality and self-confidence was broken down so the power of God's Spirit could produce a transformed leader. Only now was he ready to be the mouthpiece of God on the fabulous Day of Pentecost. In the face of a hostile culture, he proclaimed the first sermon of the church era. The Spirit's use of his brokenness was a thing of rare beauty and effectiveness.

Here was a strong, courageous leader with the ego-proofing of God-centeredness being increasingly developed. He was still capable of assertive confrontation (see his rebuke of Ananias and Sapphira in Acts 5), but it wasn't a competitive, self-oriented drive that motivated him. He was at God's disposal, doing God's business, in God's power. The issues of self-worth, self-image, self-in-control, and self-centeredness were being replaced with the reign of the Spirit in the throne room of his inner being.

A test of Peter's ego is reported in Galatians 2. It is a situation of confrontation between peers—apostle in the face of apostle. Paul was on the "dishing out" end, and Peter was on the receiving end—and Paul was right! Peter accepted the rebuke and humbly corrected his course. He had come a long way in his spiritual formation!

After 30 years in pastoral ministry, I have come to the conclusion that the first duty of those of us in Christian leadership is to protect our people from ourselves...specifically from what remains of our old self-in-control nature. Oh, I am not minimizing the danger of the world and the devil. I am simply observing from the vantage point of long experience that we are often our own worst enemies. All too often, stuck in our unresolved ego issues, we rend and tear the sheep entrusted to our care and, in turn, are bitten and devoured ourselves.

The safest, healthiest, most effective ministry leaders are those who tap into greater grace through lifestyle repentance and voluntary humility. Peter learned this bedrock principle in the school of hard knocks—and he learned it well. God resists the proud! God strips the mantle of his favor from those who refuse to allow him to break up their dangerous inner egoism.

The great news, Doug, is that God freely gives his grace to the humble. Christian leaders thrive on grace. It is the spiritual empowerment that flows from the process of submission to Christ. Grace-based, God-exalted leadership is trustworthy. It follows in the footprints of the safest and most substantial of all leaders—the slain Lamb of God, who is worthy to receive honor, power, and glory!

Your fellow servant,

Jan

Young men, in the same way be submissive to those who are older. All of you, clothe yourselves with humility toward one another, because, "God opposes the proud but gives grace to the humble." Humble yourselves, therefore, under God's mighty hand that he may lift you up in due time.

1 Peter 5:5-6

You've Got to Laugh a Little

Alicia D. Byrd
St. Stephen's AME Church, Owings Mills, Maryland

Dear Allen,

I've always taken life seriously. When I gave my heart to Jesus at age 10, I sought to live a life pleasing to God. My Christian mentors helped me understand that you can't play with Christianity. However, they didn't teach me that Christians can and should also laugh.

We talk so much about the joy of the Lord being our strength. Joy helps us transcend emotional distress and worries. We don't understand how God's joy works, but it releases us from all that binds us spiritually, emotionally, and mentally. It's good to experience God's joy. And it's good to appreciate laughter and learn how to incorporate it into our ministries.

I learned this early in my church service.

It was just the third week of my first pastorate, and I had been preaching timeliness to the congregation. Ironically enough, on one Sunday morning, a couple of last minute phone calls tied me up at home. So I made the unwise decision to speed on my way to church. Making up time, I was only five minutes late and almost to the church when I was caught in a speed trap.

I tried to explain to the officer that I was the new pastor of the little church down the road and was trying to get to church on time, but his only response was, "That is no excuse." While he ran my license and tags, I could see members drive by on their way to church. I groaned in my spirit—embarrassed and worried. With a ticket in hand and prayer for God's help, I continued my drive to the church. When I turned into the lot, the Lord gave me a new opening for that day's sermon: A Second Chance.

I started, "At some time in our lives, we all need a second chance. Even pastors who violate the speed limit on the way to church need a second chance." This initiated smiles and laughs from both pastor and congregation, and it helped me learn the importance of being able to laugh at myself.

Over the course of my ministry, God has provided other opportunities for me to laugh with others. Sometimes we've laughed over my pulpit mannerisms. I'm sure you realize that children especially like to model what you say and do in the midst of worship. When the Holy Spirit gets hold of me, I sometimes spin around, and kids love to mimic this. Rather than take offense, I laugh with them and consider it an open door for me to teach about ways the Holy Spirit can move through us.

Another interesting event happened last January when a 7-year-old boy told me he needed to talk with me about my preaching. I wondered if he would critique my delivery. When I told him I was listening, he inquired, "Why did you say *ass* this morning?" I remembered that our First Sunday liturgy includes repetition of all Ten Commandments, including the prohibition from coveting our neighbor's ass. Trying to maintain a serious composure, I explained that *ass* in this context referred to an animal, not someone's behind. We now use *donkey* in the liturgy, and those of us who know the inside story smile as we hear the new reading of the 10th commandment.

Even in ministry to the sick and depressed, appropriate humor can open people up to the hope God gives. As the Holy Spirit leads, I may share a funny story or make a funny comment just to get people to laugh. I always pray for God's leading prior to going to a sick room, and I have found that when God determines laughter is good for one's healing, the Lord will give the proper words. Our time, however, is always concluded with listening to their concerns, hearing the Word of God, and prayer for healing and restoration.

When we lighten up a bit, it also gives permission for others to find joy in the journey. At St. Stephen's, for example, one particular woman comes to mind. Sometimes she'll share a funny situation just at the right time to lift the heaviness of a difficult congregational situation. She and others teach us to enjoy God's blessings and to enjoy each other.

So may God also bless you and your people, dear friend, with the freedom to enjoy good, clean laughter.

Reveling in the Lord,

Alicia

There is a time for everything, and a season for every activity under heaven:...a time to weep and a time to laugh, a time to mourn and a time to dance.

Ecclesiastes 3:1, 4

Valuing Children

Richard L. Dresselhaus
Assemblies of God, San Diego, California

Dear Bruce,

As I have written previously, I want to admonish you again not to neglect the children who are under your pastoral care. In fact, your success in ministry might well be measured by the loving care and insightful instruction you provide for the children of your flock. Yes, I understand that most of your weekly activities will be spent with adults. But in your attitude and in your heart, and even in your schedule, I would admonish you to increasingly value children.

The status of children in some churches is alarmingly low. In some places, the children are largely ignored and treated with little honor. I have known of churches, for example, where the children meet in marginally acceptable classrooms, while their parents enjoy facilities far more appealing. This is an inequity you should not tolerate.

Not only that, but sometimes the least capable and poorly trained people are assigned to teach the children, while the more gifted and qualified teachers are asked to work with the adults. I would strongly urge you to reverse this procedure and instead be sure that the children under your care are given the very best, both in facility and in quality of instruction.

You may wonder why I speak so strongly about the status of the children in your church. Let me explain.

Most present followers of Jesus began their journey with him early on in life. In fact, if you check it out, you'll discover that very few of the people you serve have come to Christ later in life. Children have an openness to the gospel that is God-given and should be capitalized on. It is a shame to miss this wonderful window of opportunity.

Perhaps I should tell you about my own experience in this regard. Blessed by parents who loved God and a church that loved children, I, too, was introduced to Christ at a very early age and very conscious of his presence. While I know there was a point where I passed from death to life, the process of salvation for me flowed quite naturally out of the affirming, loving, and biblically instructive environment in which I grew up.

I still recall my early musings about God, his Son Jesus, the coming of Christ, the work of the church, and many other significant biblical truths as I walked through pasture paths and wooded hills of that early childhood place. As I look back, I wonder if my thoughts now are any more significant than my thoughts then. I am amazed how really good and profound those early musings were. Sure, I needed more information and training, but the germ truths were well focused and were fit beginning points for more mature reflection later in life.

That is just my point: Children must have the right start. They may not know a lot, but what they know must be right. They must have a good foundation upon which to build their spiritual house. And that cannot happen with shoddy and haphazard programs.

There is another point I want to make, Bruce. Life in our day has become hard on some children. Some kids in your church come home from school to an empty house. Some wonder what it would be like to have both parents present as a daily part of life. And, tragically, some are victims of abuse and violence.

Your church can touch these children by drawing them into a caring network of women and men who love and affirm them. Those particularly disadvantaged call for even more attention from the people of the church. Yes, you will need to step forth as advocates for victimized children. So do it with courage, Bruce. God has placed you in the protective center of these children's lives.

And I can assure you, friend, that the benefits of this care won't be unidirectional. These children will add spice to your life. For instance, on a busy Sunday morning, one little boy inquired about the location of a children's activity. I answered, "Sorry, I'm not sure where that is being held," to which he replied, "That's OK...I'll find someone who works here." He unknowingly put me in my place—but I loved it.

Or how about this letter I received: *Dear Pastor...I want to ask you a question. I want to know, can I get baptized? I've been waiting to be baptized for the longest time. If it's all right, send me a letter and tell me about it. It seems like the Lord has spoken to me and has said: "Jennifer, I think the time has come for you to be baptized."*

Bruce, the challenge is almost frighteningly demanding, but the work is filled with joyful surprises and incredible reward.

Don't forget—make it big with the children, and you'll make it big in God's kingdom...and your church will love you, too!

Grace and peace,

Richard

Jesus said, "Let the little children come to me, and do not hinder them, for the kingdom of heaven belongs to such as these."

MATTHEW 19:14

How a Servant Leads

Darryl DelHousaye
Scottsdale Bible Church and President of Phoenix Seminary, Scottsdale, Arizona

Dear Mark,

As pastors we are called servants of Jesus Christ, and yet we are told to be leaders as well. Well, which is it, servants or leaders? It may sound like an oxymoron, but the truth is that we are both, and our role is called *servant leadership*! But how can a servant lead and a leader serve? When Jesus said, "Whoever wants to become great among you must be your servant" (Matthew 20:26), what was he talking about?

As a young minister, I was told that a servant knows when he is leading by looking over his shoulder and seeing if someone is following. Leadership is influence. A good leader influences for good, and a bad leader for bad.

What is it exactly that influences people? The corporate world tells us it's power and authority. Many of those we call strong leaders are also strong personalities with much personal drive and ambition. Many of these models are aggressive, take control, get-out-of-my-way-or-get-run-over types of people. For those of us who did not have Attila the Hun for a hero, we're left quite discouraged about our own leadership potential. And yet the words of Jesus still echo in my mind, "Whoever wants to become great among you must be your servant."

The Apostle John warned us of those among us who "[love] to be first" in 3 John. And it seems to be a natural human drive to desire to exert power over others. It's human to want to drive others, yet we were called to be shepherds, not ranchers. People don't like to be driven.

If fear and intimidation are tools used to create followers, people may yield to our influence for a season, but with the residue of resentment. When people begin to feel used, we have lost them and any influence we had on them.

Reflect on what the word *servant* means. It speaks of one who lives for the benefit of another. Take a good look at Philippians 2:3-4: "Do nothing out of selfish ambition or vain conceit, but in humility consider others better than yourselves. Each of you should look not only to your own interests, but also to the interests of others." Whose interest is important to you? Some leaders appear to have visions of grandeur, desiring a reverence and allegiance belonging only to God. But servants following the pattern of our Lord come to *serve* not to *be served.* They seek to benefit others, not themselves.

Servant leadership begins, therefore, with an understanding that people have been given to us to steward. People are to be stewarded, not used. When people feel used by you, they don't feel served. When people feel valued, trusted, supported, respected, advised, challenged, rewarded, and appreciated, they feel served. In other words, when people feel loved, they feel served.

Servant leadership comes down to understanding authority. The essence of authority is the right to make decisions that affect the lives of others. With formal authority, people respond to what you say because of your position. But this is not the goal of the servant leader. The goal is to have people respond to what is said because of who he or she is—a servant.

The ultimate question, then, is how to best serve those who are under our authority. Initially, the word *authority* is a bit repellent to many because it reminds them of dictatorship. But according to the Scriptures, authority implies headship—which isn't lordship. Our people have only one Lord they worship, and we aren't him.

Headship refers to the responsibility of providing something. Loving headship provides two things: protection and honor. As the Father provided protection and honor for his Son, so we are to provide them for those under our care. When our people feel protected and honored by us, they feel loved. When we protect our people from anything that could harm them, whether it's false doctrine or any kind of deception, they feel loved. When we recognize the giftedness that God has given them and employ them into ministry, we honor them.

Mark, when our people see us approaching, the first thing that should come into their minds is our love and that we are there to help them become everything God created them to be. It comes down to this: We as pastors exist to glorify God by helping his children become great in his kingdom. Remember these believers are not there for you...you are there for them. It is the powerful influence of serving people that changes their lives for usefulness to the kingdom. This is how a servant leads, and this is how a leader serves!

Under the same wings,

Darryl

Not so with you. Instead, whoever wants to become great among you must be your servant, and whoever wants to be first must be your slave—just as the Son of Man did not come to be served, but to serve, and to give his life as a ransom for many.

Matthew 20:26-28

PERSONAL REFLECTIONS ON

The Congregation

The Community

The Sermon Offstage

H.B. London Jr.
Vice President, Ministry Outreach/Pastoral Ministries,
Focus on the Family, Colorado Springs, Colorado

Dear David,

It is a privilege to have this opportunity to approach some thoughts I've been wanting to share with you for some time. Both through my own personal experience and also from what I'm learning from others, there's so much I'd like to pass on to you.

There's a statement I've long remembered and attempted to apply to my life: *The greatest sermon I will ever deliver is not the one I preach, but the one I live.* Does that make sense to you?

There were days—perhaps there still are—when I've had to look back on a deed, a word, a thought, or even a reaction and blushed at the thought of someone thinking that was really me. Does the phrase *perception becomes reality* ring a familiar bell? It should—because it's true. People will establish their opinion of you very quickly, and at times very unfairly. If you have a large ego that constantly needs feeding, people will notice, and you will have to live with their evaluation. I'm sure you get my point. Your ministry will be formed for the most part by what people see and decide about you, even more so than what they know about you.

I remember a time I made a negative impression. Perhaps if I share that experience, it will help you see just how strongly I feel about *living* your sermon.

It was late one evening, and I was hungry. I had spent nearly all day giving myself to people. It had been a steady stream of counseling appointments, a hospital visit, and encounters with members of my congregation who had tested my joy level. I spotted a restaurant I had visited before and walked in. It was about 8:45 p.m., and as I entered, I noticed on the door that closing time was 9:00. Plenty of time.

I went up to the proprietor with every intention of placing my order, but rather than receiving a friendly greeting, I was told they were closed. "What do you mean *closed?*" I countered. "The sign on the door says 9:00 p.m., and it's certainly not 9:00." He explained that business was slow, the weather was bad, and they just thought it might be OK to close early. I recall saying something like, "This is the last time I will be coming into this place. If you post 9:00 p.m. as closing time, then that's when you should close—and not a minute before." My body language showed disgust, and as I left the restaurant, I made sure the door shut quickly and loudly. That was it. But it really wasn't. My sermon continued.

The next day I received a telephone call from a lady who asked, "Are you Pastor London, and were you in a certain restaurant last evening, and did you show great displeasure at not being served as you expected?" Sheepishly I responded, "yes." She then proceeded to tell me a scenario that I would regret forever.

You see, the lady was the wife of the man I had offended the night before. He had been watching my weekly television program and had even attended our worship service a few times. He had been a religious skeptic most of his life, but had seen in me—from a distance—someone he could trust. I will never forget her words, "Pastor, my husband said if that was you he waited on last night, not only would he never enter your church again, he would never attend any church again."

I had easily forgotten that we are to let our "gentleness be evident to all" (Philippians 4:5), that we are to "be patient with everyone"

(1 Thessalonians 5:14), and, especially, that we are not to "let any unwholesome talk come out of [our] mouths, but only what is helpful for building others up according to their needs" (Ephesians 4:29).

I have no way of knowing whether that proprietor held to his statement or not, but I do know that the man died a short time after our encounter. That restaurant experience will stay with me the rest of my life. My sermon fell to the floor with great emptiness. My heart still aches when I recall it.

David, you may be wondering, *What's the big deal; that could happen to anyone.* But I really believe that if you ponder my words, you'll get the point. There are a lot of great preachers, knowledgeable Bible scholars, and noted clergy who have the respect and admiration of the masses, but who have invalidated their sermon by a careless action or overreaction, even as I did.

Please take some time and think on these things, dear friend. There seems to be great wisdom in the pithy thought, *You never get a second chance to make a first impression.*

Still learning and still trusting,

H.B.

Watch your life and doctrine closely.
Persevere in them, because if you do,
you will save both yourself and your hearers.

1 TIMOTHY 4:16

Passion for the Story

Tony Vis

Meredith Drive Reformed Church, Des Moines, Iowa

Dear Sara,

My 4-year-old son was lost! He and I were home alone that day when suddenly I noticed that he was no longer underfoot. I had been distracted for just a brief moment, and Aaron was gone. I walked into every room of our home, but he was not there. I stepped outside into a 110-degree Arizona summer, cupped my hands to my mouth, and shouted his name. *Aaron! Aaron! Aaron!* Over and over again I shouted, but no response.

I ran frantically down the street, first in one direction and then the other. I kept running, covering every block in the immediate neighborhood and yelling his name repeatedly. I was desperate and afraid. All sorts of scenarios flashed through my mind. Had he wandered out into the dangerous desert near our home? Had someone snatched him for some perverted purpose? My son was lost, and I could think of nothing else but finding him. My son was lost; my heart was broken.

Eventually I did find him…playing with some toys in a closet in the house. And that experience has aroused within me a passion that remains to this day.

Sara, the voice of God cries out for the lives of lost people with the same feeling, passion, and desperate love that could have been heard in my voice on that day my son was lost. The biblical record is shot through-and-through with accounts of God searching, seeking, and longing for the return of his lost children.

Immediately, on the very first pages of the Bible, after Adam and Eve introduced sin and rebellion into the world, the voice of God is heard calling, "Where are you?" And the voice of the Savior has continued calling out through the corridor of time, from Adam to people today, people who are likewise lost and troubled, confused and alone. Striving to bring lost and broken human beings back into fellowship with himself has always been and will always be God's highest priority.

My prayer for you, friend, is that you will always maintain your passion for proclaiming God's good-news story. Tell it straight, tell it often, and tell it with an urgency in your voice that your hearers cannot miss! Proclaim to all who will listen that *God was in Christ reconciling the world to himself.*

Not *God was in Moses reconciling the world to himself.*

Not *God was in Elijah the prophet reconciling the world to himself.*

Not *God was in Peter or Paul reconciling the world to himself.*

Not Calvin or Luther.

Not Dr. Laura or Oprah.

Not even Billy Graham or the pope.

No! God was in *Christ* reconciling the world to himself.

This is our story, Sara! We are a people with a story to tell—a one-of-a-kind, absolutely unique story to tell—the precious, life-transforming story of Jesus Christ:

Jesus, who was with God and who was God;

Jesus, who became human and dwelt among us full of grace and truth;

Jesus, who did not consider equality with God a thing to be grasped;

Jesus, who humbled himself and became obedient unto death—

even death on a cross;

Jesus, who was buried and raised the third day and whom God exalted to the highest place and gave the name that is above every name.

This is our story; *this* is our song. There is a passion here that we need to recover and maintain. It is a passion for the story and a compassion for those who haven't yet heard the story or who haven't yet made it their story. None of us has to look long or far to find people who are hurting and lonely and lost, living with other stories that have shaped their lives in distorting ways. They are all around us! Nor does it take great powers of observation to see that the North American story is a false and distorted story that needs the transforming influence of the Jesus story if there is to be true liberty and true justice for all.

It is said that a famous violinist once happened upon a magnificent instrument in a music shop. He asked if he could buy the precious violin, but was told it had already been sold to a collector and soon would be in a showcase for display only. "But this is not a violin merely to look at," the artist shouted. "It is an instrument with which to bless the world." For weeks he pleaded with the collector to sell him the instrument, but to no avail. At last, one day, he was allowed to at least play the violin. He played that violin as one condemned to death would play to obtain ransom. When he finished playing, the collector understood and said, "I have no right to keep it. It belongs to the world. Take it into the world and let it be shared."

This Jesus story—we have no right to keep it to ourselves! It belongs to the world. And the world is waiting to hear it. No, the world is dying to hear it. Take it into the world, and let it be shared. Maintain your passion for the story!

Your fellow herald,

Tony

How beautiful are the feet of those who bring good news!
Romans 10:15b

Cracking the Culture Code

Les Magee
Teacher, Boulder, Colorado

Dear Amos,

Frequently we fail to notice things of great beauty, different perspectives, or uniqueness because of our mind-sets. Too often, we see only what we expect to see, thus missing so much around us.

Pastors and churches can also develop myopia. Regarding the lost around us, for example, experts have *prescribed* ways to reach them. Yet a limited perspective will trap us. We will never penetrate our respective harvest fields unless we widen our vision.

Fifteen years ago, my wife and I drove through the Great Salt Lake Desert of Utah to pastor a church in the shadow of the strong Latter Day Saints (LDS) culture. At the time, I didn't realize how much my 25 years of missionary experience would enhance my approach to this new ministry.

For instance, just living in another culture helped me understand what it feels like to be an outsider, to not understand the meaning of what is taking place. I know what culture shock feels like and some of the ways of dealing with it—both healthy and unhealthy. And culture shock is similar to how nonchurched people feel the first time they visit our churches. Our culture can be a foreign experience to them.

And it's good to understand a couple of things about the cultures we're encountering in order to bridge the cultural gap. It's crucial for us to *understand the words of the context in which we're working.* Since each culture has its own language, effective communication requires that we know that language. And of course, it's not just knowing words, but understanding the meaning behind each expression. We can use the same words, but they can have totally different meanings to different people. It's also important to *understand the values and assumptions of that culture.* For example, in the culture we encountered in Utah, having a good feeling about something often took precedence over knowing facts about something.

Early in this new setting, I discovered that many Christian churches in Utah were reaching out with an us-against-them attitude. A fortress-like mentality developed, and with this mind-set comes fear. The community is seen as the enemy, and walls of security are erected. The emphasis of ministry is turned inward rather than outward. After all, if someone is perceived as the enemy, it's not easy to welcome them into the fort.

I also observed that many Christians felt like second-class people. In that region, the LDS culture is predominant in every area of life—political, social, work, television, radio, and, of course, religion. They have an attractive, well-kept church building in every neighborhood. In contrast, until recent years, there were very few large, attractive Christian church campuses. As a result, many Christians felt intimidated to reach out to their LDS neighbors. Most didn't expect to see any significant growth in their churches. And, to a large extent, their expectations were fulfilled.

Rather than lament, however, churches need to seek to crack the culture code. Our church adopted a broader philosophy of reaching out to others and designed new programs to carry out that philosophy.

First of all, we were committed to the fact that God is not powerless to act in our context—that it is possible for a church based on biblical teaching and living out that teaching to flourish in this culture. It was hard to believe at first, but as God blessed us with growth, attitudes changed.

Next, we committed ourselves to building bridges (rather than walls) to the community around us. This meant no Mormon-bashing in our church, no jokes, no put-downs. And it would start from the pulpit. We wanted our people to be free to invite their LDS neighbors and friends to any of our programs and feel assured they wouldn't be embarrassed by negative comments. We wanted people investigating the faith to be able to do so freely without being put on the defensive by ridicule or any thoughtless comment.

We developed attractive programs our people would be enthusiastic about inviting their neighbors to. Some provide low-key outreach, such as our dinner theater at Christmas time. This includes a candlelight dinner, music, and a drama piece written with our culture in mind. Our Easter pageant also provides this type of opportunity. Our Sunday morning services are designed with seekers from our community in mind. Our Wednesday family night also provides us with a great tool to reach the community. It involves a prepared meal and several electives for adults, plus programs for children and youth. One of our classes during the fall quarter was called "Cross-Cultural Living in Utah." Another was "Fresh Start" for those with questions about their LDS faith.

Amos, even after many years of ministry, I need to keep studying the surrounding culture. Many important nuances are not readily apparent, and like everywhere else, the landscape keeps changing. Therefore, our vision needs continual renewal and programs need ongoing attention for greater effectiveness.

What will our churches look like in 5, 10, or 15 years? Doing business as usual? Or being part of the exciting things that God is doing? Let's embrace an expanding vision that looks for ways to reach those in our communities.

Yours in the Master,

Les

To the weak I became weak, to win the weak. I have become all things to all men so that by all possible means I might save some.

1 Corinthians 9:22

Personal Reflections on

The Community

Colleagues and Support

Brokenness

Gene Appel
Willow Creek Community Church, South Barrington, Illinois

Dear Jesse,

This is a letter I hope you can skim and never need to read again. But if you do need to, I have some great news for you. The same mercy-giving God that you passionately proclaim to others in their brokenness is also able to sustain you through the deepest valleys of your private world.

I know, because it happened to me. In the late '80s, I heard those words I never dreamed of hearing: *I'm in love with another man, and I'm leaving you.* The next morning, the woman I'd pledged my heart and life to was gone, never to return.

Suddenly, my whole world changed. As you might guess, the next few chapters of my life were filled with great pain, a lot of learning, and an extended time of healing. I wasn't just divorced. I was a divorced pastor. I wasn't just a failure. I was a pastor whose marriage failed.

I thought, *Who wants to be connected with a guy like me?* I'll tell you who—the God of amazing grace and the many mercy-extending members of his body who just wanted the chance to love me through it. Now, of course, not everybody is so loving, but I believe God has a pocket of people for each of us in our brokenness if we'll just open our eyes.

You see, I had been a ministry loner. I had bought into that old horrible advice to not get too close to anyone. And when my world fell apart, I had to face the fact that there were zero people who knew me intimately. But a letter from a brother in Christ started to crack me open. He wrote:

Dear Gene,

I cannot tell you how much I feel for you at this time, and I wish there were words to describe my sorrow. We are praying daily and thinking about you constantly. You are a dear friend and a constant source of Christian uplifting in our lives. I realize that at a time like this, time by yourself and with the Lord is most important. But don't forget that my lines are open for you. I wish I could just give you a hug and take over all the pain you are feeling in your heart. But since this is not possible, I would like to share the load with you. I'm here for you, pal, any time of day or night. I hope you will turn to me for anything you want. Our home is wide open to you; our hearts are open for you. You are like a brother to me, and I love you. When you are good and ready, please contact me any time of day or night; it doesn't matter. We won't stop praying for you, or thinking about you!

Well, I decided to take the risk and make contact. It was one of the best decisions I ever made. And over the years, God has given me crucial friends at timely moments to share unconditional acceptance, love, and confidentiality. If you wisely look for them, you'll find them, too. I'm sorry that it took a broken heart to open me up to such relationships, but I'm grateful I discovered them in this lifetime.

You'll probably tell others many times during your ministry that brokenness is one of the greatest schools of higher education they will ever attend. However, it's altogether different when you're the one enrolled in this graduate program. When this 2x4 hit me in the head and upset the whole basket of my life, I learned things about myself I'm not sure I would have learned in any other way.

First, I learned the importance of total truth-telling in relationships, even when I have to face ugly things about myself and my relationships. Second, I realized I had an unhealthy work ethic. Third, I discovered the importance of balance in my life. And fourth, I learned that when you lose everything that's important to you, you still have a relationship with Jesus Christ, and he is enough.

I remember well those awful nights feeling lonely, feeling like a failure, and wondering if this dark season would ever end. Do you know what got me through? I would often sit quietly in a dark place just singing to myself, "Jesus loves me this I know, for the Bible tells me so. Little ones to him belong. They are weak, but he is strong. Yes, Jesus loves me. Yes, Jesus loves me. Yes, Jesus loves me. The Bible tells me so." Then, afresh, I would feel Christ's deep love. And that's the love I'm committed to communicating for the rest of my life with anyone who will listen.

Jesse, never lose heart, no matter how difficult a situation may confront you. God is good. God is able. And he can use any experience to heighten your sensitivity to people and to remind you that the message you preach is the same message that saves you.

Grace and peace,

Gene

The Lord is close to the brokenhearted and saves those who are crushed in spirit.

PSALM 34:18

Being Patient With Ourselves

Dwight Perry
Great Lakes Baptist Conference, Rothschild, Wisconsin

Dear Ross,

I am sitting in my study early on a Wednesday morning rejoicing in the fact that God in his sovereignty has brought you into my life. As a midlife pastor, I can say unequivocally that in the busyness of my call, it's easy to lose sight of the fact that God's work in me is far from finished. Recently, I have been going through a rather difficult midlife reevaluation. As I look back over the past decades of ministry, I have had to ask myself some hard questions as to why, as a younger person, I was so hard on myself when I failed to meet my own expectations or the expectations of others.

As I think of you this morning and how, in just a few short days, you'll be graduating from seminary, I rejoice in all that God has done in you over the past three years. However, I pray that you realize that God is not finished with you yet, and thus you will need to be patient with yourself even as he is patient with you.

It is so easy, Ross, to fall into the trap of thinking that as God's minister your life should somehow magically fall into place. This is especially true for those of us high energy, hard-driving perfectionists. But reality has taught me that life is full of ebb and flow. At times, it seems that no matter what we do, everything comes out smelling like roses, while at other times no matter what we try, nothing goes right.

It's during these latter times that the enemy, whom Scripture calls the "accuser of our brothers," swoops down into our soul and seeks to discourage us with our obvious failures.

These times of failure not only occur in our ministries, but likewise surface in our families. For example, I recently had this type of episode with my wife. I was not connecting with her. To be honest, I was downright insensitive to her. And even after apologizing for my behavior, I still felt disgusted with myself for causing her pain.

As someone who has had the privilege of representing Christ in full-time vocational ministry for over two decades, I want to encourage you to realize no one is perfect. In fact, in those relationships that are dearest to you, you are most likely to fail. And it's especially in those relationships that you and I both need the assurance that, in spite of the blunders we make at times, God is still present, and he still cares for us and believes in us.

A few things have helped me in dealing with my predisposition to impatience with myself. Let me share these with you in an attempt to save you some anguish down the road.

The first is to reach out to friends around you. These encouragers can offer a perspective beyond the inward condemnation of our feelings. As we sense their unconditional acceptance, we can more easily feel God's acceptance. When we are going through a time of inward condemnation, the accuser wants us to not only believe his lies, but also to isolate ourselves away from those who can give us a Christ-like, balanced perspective.

This is why I strongly urge you to make sure that you are in some "rope-holding" relationships. Connect with mature friends who can hold you up even when you cannot uphold yourself. A time will also come when you are on the anchoring end for them. Remember, friend, "Two are better than one, because they have a good return for their work…But pity the man who falls and has no one to help him up" (Ecclesiastes 4:9-10).

Who are your rope-holders, Ross? If you do not have rope-holders, you desperately need to ask God to provide such persons.

Another thing that has helped me develop perspective and patience has been reading about the lives of other believers, and seeing how God has brought them through difficult periods. Being able to observe their lives and their patience (and in some cases impatience) chronicles how God instills hope even in hopeless situations.

A final practical suggestion, and the most important, is to make sure that you set aside concentrated time with Jesus. I especially enjoy reflecting in such books as the Psalms. I ask our Lord not only speak to my soul but to help me discern the source of the attacks in my mind. I seek his guidance on how I can build safeguards against the onslaught of the enemy.

Nothing—and I mean nothing—can substitute for personal times with the Lord. Gaining his perspective on our lives is so essential to our well-being. Yet, in the busyness and constant crises of ministry, we can bypass drawing close to the One who is our rock. May we never forget to listen to the One who knows us best!

I love you deeply, my brother! My prayer for you is that, as you launch your ministry, you'll remember that God is indeed in control of all things, and that He will never forsake you no matter how bleak the situation and no matter how badly you feel you have failed him. Be patient with yourself as God works out his perfect plan for your life.

God bless!

Dwight

Being confident of this, that he who began a good work in you will carry it on to completion until the day of Christ Jesus.

Philippians 1:6

Initiating Dialogue

Roger Ball
First Baptist Church, Tempe, Arizona

Dear Miguel,

Over the last six years, our many talks on marriage, theology, and the ministry have established a genuine sense of trust and respect between us. But as we've grown in our friendship, I've noticed that most of the time, I'm the one saying, "Hey, let's get together." Usually, I'm the one pushing for the time and the date to meet. Why is it that I'm the primary initiator in our relationship?

Yes, I realize scheduling *extra* meetings is a challenge for many young pastors. But the benefit of intimate dialogue with other pastors, especially with mature colleagues, is vitally important for your well-being, your marriage, and the success of your ministry. You seem a bit reluctant to be the initiator with other pastors as well. Right now, more than you realize, you need a handful of seasoned pastors who will be as open and truthful as I have been with you.

Recently, I, too, was blessed with the wisdom of fellow pastors. After serving my present congregation for 14 years, the church said to me, "You need a break from the ministry. You deserve it. Congratulations. You can do anything you want for three months but no ministry here at church. You need a sabbatical."

So immediately I began to dream and plan, and soon my sabbatical wishes were coming true. My desire was to reach out and learn from pastors from across the United States and Canada. I interviewed 20 pastors, seasoned colleagues serving faithfully in small, medium, large, and even mega-sized churches. Some were in rural churches, some in the suburbs, others in the city. They were senior pastors, youth pastors, children's pastors, executive pastors, music pastors, evangelism pastors, and teaching pastors.

To each, I offered confidentiality, and of each, I requested brutal honesty. As each minister responded to the same 10 questions, I felt like I was looking into a mirror. In their answers, I saw my own struggles and shortcomings, my successes and victories. And as I reflected on ministry priorities that surfaced, a spiritual renewal began to occur in me! Now I stand back amazed, realizing that the benefit from these contacts has far exceeded my expectations.

For example, these pastors helped me see my need for better self-care, more particularly the need for a weekly day off—a Sabbath. Not a worship Sabbath, but a restful Sabbath, a rest from work. For several years, I have failed to recognize the benefits of a weekly break from the ministry. Maybe it's because of my own expectations, or perhaps because of the expectations I feel from others. But like many ministers, I was guilty of working over 60 hours a week without a day of rest.

In my head I knew the weekly Sabbath is a principle from God, and like always, God is right. The rotting of one's soul is usually a subtle process and often goes undetected until it's too late. God created the Sabbath for that purpose—to prevent spiritual and physical burnout.

Was I out of balance? Yes! Had I fallen into the Samson syndrome? Yes! Is there more to life than ministry? Again, yes!

So be careful, Miguel, to seek your approval and affection primarily from God, not your ministry. The Proverbs say the "fear of man will prove to be a snare, but whoever trusts in the Lord is kept safe" (Proverbs 29:25). Seeking human opinion sets us on a path of self-glory and self-destruction. Remember, friend, the ministry was never meant to glorify self. It is to glorify God.

The pastors that I interviewed also encouraged me to make family care a priority. One colleague would ask himself the question, *Is my family getting the burning coals of my life or just the ashes?* He admitted, "To see the loss because of my drivenness helped me to realize that the church had become my mistress, and that a change was needed."

Ninety percent of the pastors I talked with said their ministry received far more attention than their family. And many pastors graded themselves a C- on how well they cared for their spouse. Most expressed a high degree of hopelessness regarding the well-being of their marriage and family.

I also asked each pastor, "What two things would you do differently if you could go back 10 years and start your ministry over again?" Without hesitation, they talked about really loving their families, extending more grace to others, and giving more grace to themselves. One pastor said, "I must be very careful of burnout. New opportunities excite me and can get me in trouble. I've learned to say no. Guarding personal family time is a must."

Had I not taken the time to create honest dialogue with these wise colleagues, my service could have become my ministry mistress. They reminded me to stay sensitive to God, to stay balanced, and to make adjustments needed from time to time.

So reach out, Miguel! Take the initiative to nurture open dialogue. Ask for confidentiality and brutal honesty from your colleagues, and share yourself with them. I covet this for you, dear friend.

Your brother,

Roger

Plans fail for lack of counsel,
but with many advisers they succeed.

Proverbs 15:22

Mentoring

Joey Johnson
The House of the Lord, Akron, Ohio

Dear Amy,

The best pastoral advice that I have received and that I can offer is: *Find someone to mentor you, and be a mentor to another!* This advice comes out of my decades of pastoral experience, the most profitable and enjoyable part being those spent in mentoring relationships.

It's clear from Scripture that Paul and Timothy had a special relationship (see 1 Timothy 1:2, 18; 2 Timothy 1:2). Timothy was Paul's "son in the faith," meaning Paul was instrumental in his conversion. He wrote two letters of pastoral instruction to his dear friend and ministry colleague. Paul mentored Timothy both by presence and instruction.

However, this was a two-way relationship, undoubtedly good for both Timothy *and* Paul. Paul stated that he had no one with more compassion and commitment than Timothy. When Paul faced the end of his ministry and death, Paul asked Timothy to come be with him. Timothy was in essence a co-laborer with the apostle, a partner in the gospel ministry. These two spiritual giants, who glorified God in their service to the church, seem to have been bolstered by a very special relationship.

There are other biblical examples of ministry relationships that I could cite here, the most obvious being that of our Lord and the disciples, but I think the example of Paul and Timothy should suffice. I only want to establish the fact that relationships, particularly mentoring relationships, are important and valuable to successful ministry in the gospel of Jesus Christ.

It seems a little ironic to me, as I look back over my early years of ministry, that although I knew what the Bible taught about discipleship, the thought of mentoring never entered my mind. This was probably due to my youthfulness, my individualistic nature, some "Lone Ranger" role models, and a lack of awareness concerning mentoring. And I haven't been alone. It seems like many churches have majored on discipleship rather than mentoring.

But discipleship and mentoring are different. Discipleship represents a teacher/pupil relationship. Mentoring represents a friend/advisor/coach relationship.

Amy, I shudder to think how many dark nights, painful experiences, mistakes, and near fatal falls I have faced all by myself. This was not, and is not, God's plan for us. He gives us his Holy Spirit, *and* he also gives us one another. Our God is patient, long-suffering, merciful, gracious, loving, and compassionate. And most often, he reveals these gifts through the people he sends our way. We all need friends, especially in times when support and counsel are required. This shouldn't surprise us. After all, the "one anothers" in Scripture are quite clear.

As pastors we have so much to share, and yet so much to still learn. Personally, I like to help younger colleagues with concerns, such as working with the church board, dealing with power brokers, managing the church when you don't have natural management ability, handling conflict, and building healthy congregations. I frequently address these issues individually, but our church has also established a Pastoral Mentoring Institute. At the institute, regular times of sharing and prayer are included so that pastors, prospective pastors, and church leaders can feel understood and supported.

Let me share a mentoring analogy with you. I love racquetball, and in my learning of the game, I discovered a principle that is equally applicable to pastoral mentoring. If you want to be good, you need competition at three levels. First, you need someone who is not as good as you are, so you can practice your shots and still win. Second, you need someone whose skill level is equal to yours, so you can be stretched to the limit of your ability. And third, you need someone who is better than you, so you can gauge your progress, still learn, and remain humble.

Pastoral mentoring needs the same three levels.

First, I have pastors whom I am helping. I have drawn toward me several younger, less experienced colleagues. Their questions allow me to think through and share what I have learned and am learning. This affords me the opportunity to be a big brother to other pastors and make an impact on their lives.

Second, I have friendships with pastors who are at a similar stage of development with me. Our ministry experiences and churches are similar. In these relationships, we share what God is doing without the need for bragging or trying to one-up each other. Yet we also stretch one another. These relationships allow me to compare notes with pastors who are almost exactly in the same ministerial shoes.

Third, I am developing relationships with pastors who are further down the road than I am. A number of them have been pastoring effectively for more years than I have; some have ministries that are larger. These relationships allow me to expand my vision, my thinking, and my creativity. They allow me to learn from those who have faced more challenges than I have experienced. They graciously provide help, advice, coaching, and support.

So, if I could offer any advice about ministry, it would be *don't go it alone*. For the kingdom's sake and for your well-being, develop mentoring relationships with other pastors.

Your friend in Christ,

Joey

Two are better than one, because they have a good return for their work. If one falls down, his friend can help him up. But pity the man who falls and has no one to help him up!

ECCLESIASTES 4:9-10

Personal Reflections on
Colleagues and Support

Change and Conflict

Good Tensions

Fred W. Prinzing
*Dean and Professor Emeritus, Bethel Seminary,
Everett, Washington*

Dear Philip,

Monday has always been the worst day of my week. A banner stretched over a church parking lot in Southern California clearly expressed my sentiments: "Revival Nightly, Except Monday."

In my first pastorate, Mondays usually seemed filled with stress and problems. Mondays were spent calming the troubled waters that had risen to the surface on Sundays. One of my goals was to eliminate as many problems and tensions as possible in order that my ministerial voyage would have smooth sailing.

However, the harder I tried and the more the church grew, the rockier the voyage seemed. In fact, sometimes instead of defusing tensions, I appeared to create them. And with greater diversities within the congregation, more tensions developed.

When I analyzed things, I realized either the situation had to change radically or my perspective needed to be altered. My education and experiences to that point had taught me that tensions had no place in a Spirit-controlled congregation. Tensions were viewed through a negative filter. I needed a major paradigm shift.

Tension is the balance of elements in opposition or the stretching of two opposite forces, seeking a proper balance. Positive illustrations of this tension abound in our daily lives.

A tension knob on a sewing machine allows fabric to be

stitched evenly. The tension knob on a fishing rod lets you catch fish that are swimming in the opposite direction. Most exercise bikes have a tension-adjustment knob that gives the rider the greatest benefit from a workout.

One of the best illustrations of the positive use of tension is a sailboat. Two basic elements provide resistance to moving forward—wind and water. Paradoxically, these same elements are key for a sailboat to successfully reach its objective. Eliminate the tension caused by the wind and waves, and the sailboat will remain motionless near the shore.

A pastor once wrote to me saying, "I wish I could use the advice you provided about handling tensions creatively, but we don't have any tensions in our church. I wish we had some. At least I'd know we are alive." Six months later, the pastor wrote again to inform me that the 75-year-old church had closed its doors for the final time. Good tensions, Philip, are actually a sign of life.

I've occasionally heard people say they wished they could go back to the New Testament church where they didn't have all this tension. But anyone who has read the history of the early church as recorded in Acts chapters 4 to 15 will realize the many tensions they experienced.

Many of the tensions faced by the early church resulted from opposite forces that were neither good nor bad. Tensions can have several sources. Some are caused by different cultural backgrounds, such as people's views of time and priorities. Other tensions are generational, arising from different perspectives on finances or lifestyles. Different styles of leadership, such as goal-oriented vs. people-oriented leadership can cause tension (as it did with Paul and Barnabas). Differences in doctrinal beliefs, such as the role of women in leadership and the use of gifts, are also tensions churches face. And most churches have experienced the tension that develops around worship styles.

How do you think we should respond to these tensions, Phil? What's your opinion?

Some churches attempt to eliminate one view or the other. However, what subsequently happens is the marginalization of part of the congregation. A better approach is to realize the power of the "and." When we get to the place in our thinking where it has to be this or that, we usually have eliminated the blessings of paradox.

Look for the power of the "and" regarding objectives, methods, goals, and values. Instead of trying to eliminate tensions, effort should be exerted to adjust them. Try looking for ways these tensions can actually facilitate the purpose and goals of the congregation.

I caution you, however, to watch out for bad tension in ministry as well. Just as a sailor must face destructive storms, a minister will encounter tensions that cannot be adjusted. Tensions that are sinful or divert you from achieving the goals God has helped you set require radical surgery.

Sometimes you will need to assume the role of conflict manager. This will require wisdom, discernment, and skill. If you learn, however, to be a tension adjuster, it's surprising how many conflicts can be avoided. You can't avoid the winds and waves, but as Edward Gibbon said, "The winds and the waves are always on the side of the ablest navigator."

No matter how hard we try, we cannot have a tension-free home or a tension-free church. The secret is to learn to adjust tension, not to eliminate it.

Your friend in Christ,

Fred

Keep your head in all situations, endure hardship,
do the work of an evangelist,
discharge all the duties of your ministry.

2 Timothy 4:5

The Change Agent

Randy Frazee

Willow Creek Community Church, South Barrington, Illinois

Dear Larry,

Heraclitus is known for the timeless words, "There is nothing permanent except change." The task of the change agent is ongoing. It is a vital work within the life and ministry of any congregation. And the church desperately needs change agents to rise up within it to move it forward for Christ. Today, staggering numbers of churches in America are stagnant or dying. Like never before, the church needs called and skilled innovators to stand up and be used by God.

If you feel God is calling you as an agent of change for the local church, let me offer you some time-tested wisdom and counsel that was passed down to me from effective practitioners of the past.

First and foremost, a change agent is one who inspires and competently leads the people to focus on the mission Christ gave the church, namely to guide people to an eternal and growing relationship with God. Many churches lose sight of this mission and thus lose the promised power of the Holy Spirit. The change agent's mission is to introduce (or reintroduce) the priorities that will unleash God's blessing and power in the church.

Another principle to keep in mind is that change is hard work and takes time. Nicolo Machiavelli said, "There is nothing more difficult to take in hand, more perilous to conduct, or more uncertain in its success, than to take the lead in the introduction of a new order of things." This is certainly true within the church. Helping a church make a significant turnaround usually takes around four years. Making a significant program change alone usually takes two full years from the inception of the new idea to the diffusion of that idea into the life of the congregation. Be patient, and be ready to put in the time and hard work.

The next, and one of the most important and often misunderstood principles of change, has to do with the way a leader reacts to resistance from people. We must never view the people in our congregations as the enemy of change, but rather as sheep needing a shepherd to lead them to greener, richer pastures.

Because of laggards and resisters, a change agent can wrongly conclude that people don't want to change or experience something better than they have now. But this is just not true. As American futurist Marilyn Ferguson reveals, "It's not so much that we're afraid of change or so in love with the old ways, but it's that place in between that we fear...It's like being between trapezes. It's Linus when his blanket is in the dryer. There's nothing to hold on to."

Larry, you must believe that people want a better life—that they want to be part of a more effective mission center. They are just afraid of the transition from the rung they are holding on to, to the one that is swinging out in space. Our job is to develop trust with the people in such a way that they willingly let go of what they currently have so that they may confidently grab hold of a better way.

My advice then to you is to be bold and lead the church with strength and conviction to where God wants it to go. And as you lead, do those things that help people make the transition—respect the past, communicate reasons for the change, allow people time to grieve losses, allow people the right to disagree with you without taking it personally, never surprise your governing spiritual authority, and don't get too far ahead of your people. A quote hung in my study in my early years with these immortal words: “One step ahead of the people and you are a leader; 10 steps ahead of the people and you are a martyr.”

Satan strolls about every day seeking churches that he can shoot down. If God and a church are calling you to emerge as the leader of a new day in the life of that congregation, then I urge you before God to stand up and lead with wisdom and in power.

Remember, with God’s help and guidance, not only can you keep the church alive, you can also organize a unified charge for the cause of Christ.

A fellow guide,

Randy

Then I said the them, “You see the trouble we are in: Jerusalem lies in ruins, and its gates have been burned with fire. Come, let us rebuild the wall of Jerusalem, and we will no longer be in disgrace.” I also told them about the gracious hand of my God upon me and what the king had said to me. They replied, “Let us start rebuilding.” So they began this good work.

Nehemiah 2:17-18

Handling Criticism

John Vawter
You're Not Alone, Inc., Scottsdale, Arizona

Dear Wes,

I'm so glad you've committed yourself to kingdom service. Over three decades ago when I graduated from college, I entered the vocational ministry. I have never regretted it. There is nothing I would rather do. And yet, in spite of that great sense of God's calling and job fulfillment, there have been critics along the way—and, I am sure, will be along the rest of the way. Critics are a part of life. It's how we deal with them that makes the difference between our failure and success.

It's important you realize, Wes, that pastoring is not for the fainthearted. Pastors are called to lead. Pastors are expected to set the pace. And leaders and pacesetters are always criticized. It cannot be avoided. If we don't want to live with those realities, it may be that God has gifted us instead for a support position or for another vocation. The reality is that pastors will be criticized. It's inescapable.

It's also true that we tend to become defensive when we're criticized. And the smarter we are, the better we are at avoiding the blame and ignoring criticism. Yet at times we deserve the criticism. Some pastors don't keep their word, some are perpetually late, and some overcommit. Others are overly aggressive or insensitive. Some are too dependent on the affirmation of others. And, sad to say, some pastors are criticized because they are guilty of doing stupid things.

But at times pastors are also maligned unfairly. They are criticized because they confront sin, serve as change agents, or simply work among people who act out because of personal struggles.

Enough of the reality; on to the encouragement.

Several principles for handling criticism have served me well. So, I pass them on to you with the hope that they will carry you through those rough times when the critics are out in abundance.

First, expect criticism; don't let it surprise you. It *will* happen.

Second, be careful not to let criticism, valid or invalid, control you. There are some people who will never be happy—unless being grumpy and negative makes them happy. When I left a church I had pastored for 14 years, one critic said to the elder board chairman, "Do you think the denomination could send us a good pastor this time? The last three have been lousy." Wes, do some math—I had been there 14 years, my predecessor 10 years, and his predecessor 5 years. That is 29 years. Does that tell you something about the perpetual critic? They are usually set in their opinions. Don't waste energy trying to change them, placate them, or satisfy them. And for certain, don't be controlled by them.

Third, find a soul mate to share your pain and to help you process the criticism. At times, your spouse may be the one to confide in and lean on. But realize you may also increase his or her burden. You may want to choose another ministry colleague. But make sure he or she is someone you can trust.

Fourth, recognize that criticism does hurt. Don't play the macho-man game. If it hurts, admit it, give it to God, and let him minister to you. Jesus was honest with his pain in the garden of Gethsemane. We can't afford to do less.

Fifth, don't be defensive, potentially missing the truth of helpful criticism. Sometimes valid criticism comes in an invalid manner. Overlook the manner. Remember that "love covers over a multitude of sins" (1 Peter 4:8). When the criticism is valid, be mature enough to admit it. Don't be defensive—although that is easier to say than do. Work on improving. And give thanks. If we thank God for everything (even criticism), he will find ways to conform us further into the image of Christ.

Sixth, a wise man told me early in my ministry to weigh my critics but never count them. It's important that we don't keep score. Don't get angry, don't get irritated, and don't react. Rather, recognize the criticism as an opportunity to serve those in the church by bringing them back to the biblical patterns of thinking. Also, when you do stumble and react in an improper manner, be mature enough to admit it and ask forgiveness from the one you have offended. It's not easy, but it is necessary and right. Jesus said if anyone has something against us, we are to leave our offering and go to the person. Don't fail to do this, or the negative effects will far outweigh the impact of your sin.

Finally, remember that critics often take their own struggles out on you. One time, when I was in the midst of some heavy criticism for not taking a political stand for a special interest group, a wise man told me, "I know you are under a lot of criticism, and it's unfair. But remember; only you are responsible for your spiritual life and for your godly attitudes or lack thereof." It was then that Paul's words about taking "captive every thought to make it obedient to Christ" (2 Corinthians 10:5) took on new meaning.

You *will* face criticism. You can allow it to slowly make you bitter and negative. Or you can use it as an opportunity to learn, to bring everything to the feet of Jesus, and to give thanks to God in all things.

Sincerely your friend and brother,

John

A fool shows his annoyance at once,
but a prudent man overlooks an insult.

Proverbs 12:16

Confronting Change

David C. Cooper

Mount Paran Church of God, Atlanta, Georgia

Dear Priscilla,

The one constant of these times is change. Everyday we face astounding scientific and technological changes resulting from the greatest knowledge explosion in history. Our culture is changing socially, economically, educationally, politically, and spiritually.

Let's be honest: Change is difficult for all of us. It involves the loss of position, requires cooperation, results in new roles and job descriptions, demands the acquisition of new skills and knowledge, and, therefore, threatens our comfort zones.

One of the most important aspects of change, as it affects a local church, concerns the issue of providing meaningful ministry for the diverse groups that comprise the congregation. And the world seems to be saying to the church: "Be relevant! Speak my language! Show me how Christ can make a difference in my daily life." All the talk these days about being relevant, transforming congregations, and adopting new ministry styles sounds great except to those who still prefer the old wineskins (and they usually represent the bulk of the church's financial support).

How can we simultaneously minister effectively to children with their high-tech, multimedia, visual approach to learning; baby boomers with their love of '70s-style music, involvement in political issues, and demands for quality family ministry; Generation X-ers with their struggle for recognition, and search for future security in a world that appears very insecure; nonchurched neighbors who are unaccustomed to the sights and sounds of Christian expressions of worship and can't tell the Old from the New Testament; and traditional members who love to sing the old hymns, cherish the traditional approaches to ministry, and base their weekly schedule around the events at the church?

If staying on the cutting edge demands new, innovative approaches to ministry, what would I tell you about staying relevant and leading your congregation through seasons of ministry? Let's try this:

Connect with the church's history. Study the congregation's history, including such factors as past leaders, important developments, vision of ministry, growth patterns, demographic makeup of the congregation, past struggles, and so on. New ministry approaches need to build upon the foundation of the past if possible.

Bond with the congregation. Pastors who effectively lead their congregations do so because there exists between them a strong bond of mutual love, respect, and trust developed through years of devoted service.

Earn the right to lead. Longevity in ministry is fundamental to effective leadership. Before initiating change, consider your own future commitment to the church.

Secure the support of your key leaders. Avoid making decisions in a vacuum. Use a team approach that involves both selling your ideas to your leaders and submitting to their counsel. The circle of leadership is only complete when others follow. Make sure you have key leaders on your side before initiating change.

Keep changes commensurate with the overall vision of ministry. An old adage is appropriate to this point: *The main business is to keep the main business the main business.* Avoid sporadic, impulsive changes that fail to compliment the central thrust of your ministry.

Learn to live with certain imperfections and frustrations in the ministry. We all know that no perfect churches exist, yet pastors seem obsessed with the idea of creating them. Before making changes ask, "Will this new approach result in any measurable accomplishment in the kingdom of God?" Constant change of nonessentials can typecast the pastor as being preoccupied with the trivial and unsatisfied with the congregation.

Be sensitive to the different dynamics involved between pastoring a newly formed congregation and an older, more established one. The former is seeking a ministry vision; the latter has operated from a ministry vision for a long time. Trying to impose a new vision on an established congregation can appear as a criticism of their ministry as it currently exists.

The agenda for change must come from the leadership of the Holy Spirit accompanied by effectual prayer. There exists no virtue in change for the sake of change. Change needs to be Spirit-led in order to be effective.

Follow through. Take the risk. Implement the change. Leadership transcends the fear of failure, takes the leap of faith, and implements change when it is needed.

So Priscilla, as you face the challenges of tomorrow, remember the words of Adoniram Judson, missionary to Burma: "The future is as bright as the promises of God." Go for those Spirit-led, kingdom-impacting innovations, and warmly bring your people along on the journey.

God's blessings!

David

Dear Pastor,

Be shepherds of God's flock that is under your care…
not lording it over those entrusted to you,
but being examples to the flock.

1 Peter 5:2-3

PERSONAL REFLECTIONS ON

Change and Conflict

Preaching

Preaching Priorities

Haddon Robinson

Gordon-Conwell Theological Seminary, Hamilton, Massachusetts

Dear Michael,

So God has tapped you on the shoulder, and you are going to pastor. That's great! I can't think of a greater privilege than to teach the Word of God to the people of God. But let me caution you that being a pastor isn't all it is made out to be. One cynic scoffed, "Pastors don't get paid much, but you can't beat the hours—11:00 to 12:00 on Sunday." Of all the sick jokes I know, that one is the most anemic! Being the successful pastor of a growing congregation may be the most demanding calling in Christ's entire kingdom.

All you have to do is glance at a minister's schedule to see the dimensions of the assignment. In the morning, a pastor sets aside time for study. He has to be a scholar. People in the congregation expect a minister to know the Scriptures and to know how to apply them to their daily lives. On a couple of afternoons, the pastor schedules time to visit in the hospitals. Now she is expected to be a member of a healing team. On other afternoons, the minister maps out some time for counseling. People in the church and in the community come to him with broken hearts, broken homes, and broken lives, and they expect him to have the glue to put them together again. Added in on short notice are funerals. (People don't die according to schedule.) Now the pastor serves as a grief therapist. Her presence gives comfort to people torn by grief.

On one evening, the minister meets with the Christian education committee. As an educator, he helps plan a program to teach everyone from womb to tomb. On another evening, the pastor meets with the trustees. Now she serves as a CEO planning a budget. And, of course, the pastor is expected to be a communicator. A couple of times a week, people expect him to deliver a relevant message from Scripture that will hold their attention and touch their lives. Then, like any Christian, the pastor is expected to be a loving spouse, a devoted father or mother, and a contributing member of the community.

Michael, if you are going to survive in ministry, you must establish priorities. You can't be all circumference. You have to have a center.

God always puts "to be" ahead of "to do," and you should, too. Make your *self* your first priority. Your character comes before your service. Since your ministry defines your life, you will tend to believe that if your church is successful, you are successful; if your church fails, then you have failed. That is a myth. I have known pastors who have built large, thriving congregations whose spirits shriveled up in the process. You are a human being who needs to cultivate a lively friendship with God. It's hard to introduce your people to someone you don't know very well yourself. Put yourself and your own inner life first. Regularly schedule time for reading, reflection, relaxation, and prayer.

Your second priority should be the public ministry of the Scriptures. People expect you to preach. In fact, they refer to you as "the preacher." A preacher who doesn't preach, therefore, resembles a clock that doesn't run. The clock sits there on the mantle. It looks like a clock, and people call it a clock. But it fails in the function for which it was made.

Don't let anyone talk you out of this. Don't believe the trendy lie that preaching doesn't work anymore and that we need new methods for a new day. Poor, dull, insipid preaching has never accomplished anything at any time. The remedy for poor preaching isn't the elimination of public discourse. The only remedy for bad preaching is good preaching. Make preaching your magnificent passion. Give yourself to it. Read a couple of books on homiletics each year. Study tapes of other preachers. Listen and critique your own sermons. Ask thoughtful listeners in your congregation to evaluate you.

Finally, Michael, let me suggest a project. Since a great deal of preaching is more caught than taught, pick out one skilled preacher each year, and study him. Read or listen to his sermons. If he has a biography, read it. If he is still alive, try to interview him in person or over the phone. Good models will mold you into being the preacher God has summoned you to be.

Michael, you can't be all things to everybody without ending up being of no good to anybody. Establish your priorities, and stick with them. And among those priorities keep the communication of God's message high.

Today as you look forward to ministry, you'll say, "I will." In years to come when you look back on your ministry, may you be able to say, "I did."

An object of grace,

Haddon

Devote yourself to the public reading of Scripture, to preaching and to teaching. Do not neglect your gift, which was given you through a prophetic message when the body of elders laid their hands on you. Be diligent in these matters; give yourself wholly to them, so that everyone may see your progress.

1 Timothy 4:13-15

Common Ground

Bill Hull
Author and Teacher, Long Beach, California

Dear Justin,

What has been the greatest change in the church in the last 10 years? What are those things that remain constant? These are the questions I'm most frequently asked by friends. The reason they ask is that a decade ago I left the pastoral life for a fast-paced global teaching ministry. But now I have returned to church ministry, and they want to know what has changed.

Some expect me to say something like, "the continued decay of absolute truth, the evaporation of discretionary time, a growing unwillingness on people's part to make long-term commitments," or ye ole faithful, "the continuing challenge of ministry in a post-Christian, postmodern milieu."

Others are convinced the biggest change is the area of church music—the conveyer belt of what is contemporary continuing to roll into the future. It's humorous that 50-year-olds are now arguing to keep the music they fought to get 20 years ago. The now 30-somethings will do the same in two decades.

These are all changes, Justin, but I think they pale in comparison to the biggest change. The biggest change is the colossus of communication and its related partner, technology.

Presently I am the senior pastor of a congregation with eight pastoral staff, and I have no secretary. In fact, there are only two secretaries for the entire church. Twenty years ago, I was the only pastor in a church of 150, and I had a full-time personal secretary. In the past nine months, I have written zero letters and a thousand e-mails. My secretary is my Palm Pilot; I communicate to the elders and many church members via e-mail. I must have my sermon outline complete by Thursday noon for our computer tech to prepare the media presentation for Sunday. And our church, like so many others, displays its philosophy of ministry, service information, and discipleship resources on our Web site. Yes, technology has changed communication and in many ways improved it.

However, within this expanding area of communication and technology, the greatest challenge of change is in those minutes I stand to speak before the congregation—that vital communication we call the sermon.

Are you aware that the word *communication* comes from the Latin *communis*, meaning "to have in common"? Even in our preparation for preaching, we must start from common ground when attempting to reach others.

Twenty years ago a pastor could assume his hearers possessed some information about the Bible. Today, however, the common ground of secular culture far overshadows that of the church and its biblical worldview. We can lament this fact, but what would be the point? Let's view the common ground of culture as an ally in presenting the gospel.

When I prepare the Sunday message, I must ask myself what the common ground is. I know that most of my hearers will know a popular movie actor, but will have almost zero knowledge of Søren Kierkegaard, the Danish philosopher who did much to form a Christian view of man's immaterial nature. This past Sunday I quoted both an actor and Kierkegaard.

The common ground for communication then must be both

popular culture and biblical history. Thus the backdrop of my presentations is very different. Ten years ago, I may have started a message on self-sacrifice based on Luke 9:23-25 with an illustration from the life of Jesus or my own life. I still would do that from time to time, but now I have new weapons in my arsenal. With the advent of media tools, we can launch out and find interesting starting points for communication. I started a recent sermon with a slide of "The Metamorphis of Narcissus" by Salvador Dali and told the story of the Greek tragedy. It powerfully illustrates the futility of a selfish life. The people to whom I preach are not ignorant; in fact, they're highly educated in art, literature, and music. But many lack biblical background. I try to find common ground as a starting point to teach them the Bible.

What has not changed, Justin, is the truth of the Bible. In fact, interest in this ancient book is up. The smartest marketing technique any pastor could choose is simply to teach the Scriptures in a clear and interesting manner. So don't be afraid of history and important biblical words. Take time to explain them to the people. But remember to start where they are and bridge them to the reality of the message in the text.

What also hasn't changed is that people still need to be encouraged, exhorted, comforted, and confronted. What hasn't changed is the basic nature of people and their needs. What hasn't changed is the supernatural nature of a person filled with the Holy Spirit explaining the truth about God, the world, and ourselves. If anything has changed at all in this regard, it is that people are hungry for the truth *straight up*. They yearn for authenticity, vulnerability, and a person willing to shoot straight with understanding and wisdom. I find the more I teach the Scriptures in a clear and interesting way, the more they come and the more they want.

So, dear friend, give them some contemporary connecting points, and then lay some Scriptures on them. Find some common ground in the midst of their changing world—they will love it.

Yours in him,

Bill

Let your conversation be always full of grace, seasoned with salt, so that you may know how to answer everyone.
COLOSSIANS 4:6

Maintaining High-Level Preaching

Timothy Chan
Gaithersburg Chinese Alliance Church, Gaithersburg, Maryland

Dear Jim,

Sunday *after* the sermon is a time of great relief for me. Come what may, I always enjoy the afternoon, feeling that I have done a great service for God in faithfully delivering his truth. I feel accomplished, contented, and well. Then comes Monday morning, when I face a desk full of work and the reality that in six days I have to preach another sermon. The thought makes me sweat. Having been a pastor for over 11 years, I still have to cast out the demon called fear in the name of Jesus Christ.

A time comes for most preachers when our fountain of ideas is dry and we seem to preach the same truths under different titles or contexts. We have tried enriching the content by using illustrations from the media. But we have learned that this cannot cure an anemic message. Maybe we've even tried to adapt a message from another preacher. Likewise we learned that borrowing from world-class preachers doesn't guarantee success because they have different congregations and contexts.

What is worse is that people from the congregation may have come across your borrowed idea and come up to you after the service saying, "So, pastor, you preached a great sermon today. Will you be preaching Chuck Swindoll's Moses Part III sermon next Sunday?"

On the other hand, the right message, in the right context, at the right time is a winner every time. Your message, for your people, at their time of need guarantees receptivity. And I've found that high-level preaching is facilitated by maintaining three related practices.

First use *personal enthusiasm* to connect the Bible to life situations. Speak from your heart. Share your experiences in the light of the biblical message. Use Joshua 24 to explain how you struggle to become a person of calling. Or try Ephesians 4:29, and describe your first personal evangelism experience in a gas station with some wild-looking teens. Remember, enthusiasm is the fuel of your preaching.

Second, *contextualize* all of your preaching. If you find that preaching ideas and themes from other preachers opens your horizons to possible messages, then be sure to translate any ideas first into your own personal experience. Communication is a process of transmitting a *felt* concept. It is not merely words or ideas. It is an emotional and intellectual association between you and the congregation. The resonance derived from your experiences together is important because your people have to feel connected with you before effective communication begins.

Instead of using a well-known speaker's messages on world evangelism, find the implications *behind* the message. Extract the ideas out of the incidents, and then apply the biblical idea in your own context. If the idea is about sacrifice, share a few experiences of those in the congregation who have gone on missions—unfiltered water, a shower every four days, sporadic electric outage, yet lives touched. When people identify with these experiences, you have a better chance to communicate effectively.

Third, *speak from your conviction*. Speak the truth as you have perceived it in the light of the Scripture. Truth is felt by the audience through your person. When you articulate what is deep in your soul, your voice will be firm, your posture will be strong, and your gestures will be powerful. You won't need a mirror for rehearsals. Just speak out with passion like Moses, like Joshua, or like Paul. When we speak from what is inside us, fleshing out the biblical truth, we bring each message home.

There are many skills we can learn to become stronger preachers. But remember our purpose is never to impress people with our preaching skills. Our purpose is to communicate life-changing truth to each and every person. Our goal is to motivate our congregations to grow into Christ-likeness.

So, Jim, avoid carrying a business card that does not belong to you. Avoid short cuts. Your sermon jar may not be full, but it can be filled. Let the Potter work on you. Give God a chance to use your simple faith and straight-forward enthusiasm as clay to mold you into a piece of artwork—a unique preacher.

Your fellow craftsman in Christ,

Timothy

Unlike so many, we do not peddle the word of God
for profit. On the contrary,
in Christ we speak before God with sincerity,
like men sent from God.

2 CORINTHIANS 2:17

PERSONAL REFLECTIONS ON

Preaching

Self-Care

Dealing With Our Dents

Alan Nelson
Executive Editor of Rev! Magazine, Fort Collins, Colorado

Dear Wil,

During the Oklahoma City bombing, I served as a clergy member on the notification teams that informed the families when a victim had been identified. The team consisted of a member of the coroner's office, a counselor, and a pastor. The family would be led into the room on the fourth floor of the Christian Church, and the coroner would inform the family that their loved one was dead. The counselor and clergy members were available to assist in whatever way seemed appropriate. After each meeting, the support team debriefed with another counselor. I remember thinking at the time, *This is unnecessary. Don't they know that pastors deal with death and dying all the time? Why do we need to talk with anyone?*

Looking back over a couple decades of local church work as a staff member, planter, and senior pastor, I can think of a number of things I'd do differently. Fortunately or unfortunately, that's how we learn most—from our mistakes. But if I was pressed to target one thing I'd change, I know what it would be.

I've always believed in the benefits of psychology appropriately applied. Like most pastors, I've done a fair share of pastoral counseling and referred a lot of people to professional counselors over the years. While I've been a fan of therapy as part of a person's holistic growth, I never practiced what I preached. For whatever reason, I did not see myself as a candidate for needing counsel in that format.

Occasionally I heard pastors, even a few well-known, who mentioned being in counseling. A small voice in me whispered, "Whew, wonder what *that* guy's problem is? How can a pastor like that need a shrink?" But after decades of wrestling with a low-grade anger that would sometimes manifest itself as impatience, defensiveness, and shutting people down, I went for help. My journey of counseling was nothing short of a second conversion experience for me. Things stemming from my family of origin and childhood issues emerged and were addressed. I felt flayed open and humiliated, but also deeply relieved and healed.

Even mentioning this now, I feel a cringe of reticence because it's always bugged me when people seem to blame their problems on childhood or family issues. But it's not about shirking responsibility as much as it is owning one's baggage. We're all dented. The question is to what degree and how our dents affect others. Pastors' emotional health is important, not only for our sakes and our families' sakes. Our shape affects those we serve. A pastor's dents influence everyone in his or her congregation.

My oversight involved degrees of ignorance and pride. I didn't read the signs. What I chalked up to as temperament was quite often dents. There's a difference. Learn the signs and symptoms. If in doubt, talk to a good counselor. It can only help. Are there relational issues that pop up more often than you'd like? Do you struggle with addictive or obsessive yearnings? Is there a nagging compulsion to overreact or flee certain situations? Are you defensive, angry, or offensive? Are you harboring a secret behavior? Do you wrestle with depression, perfectionism, or a martyr complex? These are sometimes hard to identify when you're on the inside looking out, but don't pass them off as superficial life matters.

The other issue that prevented my pursuit of healing was pride, in part because my particular dents prompted me to try to project myself as better than I was. But then there was the pressure most of us pastors feel to live up to people and God's expectations of our role. After all, we're "God's anointed." What will people think if we're in therapy? We're the ones who give counsel, not receive it. My first two counseling sessions were spent admitting my awkwardness at being the one "on the couch." The counselors told me, rather bluntly, "Get over it!"

If I could change ministerial preparation in just one way, it would be to require every pastoral candidate to go through a battery of counseling sessions—a proactive procedure to identify and diagnose the scale of his or her dents. I wonder how my ministry would be different had I discovered the extent of my dents earlier. If nothing else, I'm confident that I'd have been more fulfilled serving God, instead of feeling perpetually dissatisfied and restless.

Sometimes I shake my head, wondering why someone hadn't come alongside me, put an arm around me, and said, "Pastor, I'm wondering if you might want to talk to someone, just to see if there's something you need to unpack." They would have become my best ally, whether I knew it at the time or not. So in case you've never had someone do that in your life, let me be the one. I can't do my mistakes over, but I can wave the flag for others in ministry to check their dents—earlier rather than later. Every pastor has them, hidden or not. They *will* affect your ministry. There's no shame in asking yourself the tough questions up front. Don't let the price tag of professional counseling or the stigma of "being in therapy" diminish your ministry over the years. Your wife, friends, staff, parishioners, and Lord need the best you possible.

In faith,

Alan

Your attitude should be the same as that of Christ Jesus…
he humbled himself.

Philippians 2:5-8

Self-Awareness

Pete Scazzero
New Life Fellowship, Elmhurst Queens, New York

Dear Jay,

When I began pastoring, at least for a few months, I believed that I could do just about anything—manage a megachurch, counsel, teach, pray, lead, and build a leadership team. There was a subtle grandiosity that marked my humility!

I had served on InterVarsity staff at Rutgers University and surrounding New Jersey colleges and universities for three years. This was followed by three years at seminary. My mind was filled with the likes of Hudson Taylor, David Brainerd, Jim Elliot, Willow Creek, and Paul Yongii Cho. I, too, would do a great work for God.

Following seminary, my wife of six months, Geri, and I spent an additional year in Costa Rica learning Spanish to prepare for pastoring in New York City. Then finally, we moved into Queens, New York to get the lay of the land prior to planting a church that would plant other churches in both English and Spanish. Thus another year was spent preparing, serving as an associate pastor, and seeking God's face two to three hours a day in prayer about the future.

I was a rocket ready to be launched, seasoned (at least I thought so), 31 years old, full of fire. I had been well trained and mentored. Who would ever have imagined that six years later I would be on a therapist's couch, depressed, angry at God for my horrible life, and thoroughly confused as to why Geri felt she would be happier separated than married to me! What do I wish someone had told me?

Three simple principles:

1. Be yourself. I tried to be a good pastor, at least, what others thought I should be. The problem was that I was trying to be somebody else! And that ran against the grain of my soul.

Thomas Merton has spoken of the "true self" in his writings. It's a composite of your personality, your story, and your limitations. To live another person's life is a great burden. I didn't explore the story of my life and its influence in shaping me until my life and ministry were crumbling. I thought, *Why bother? I'm a new creation in Christ empowered by the Holy Spirit!*

Don't make the same mistake, Jay. Know your story. Take time to explore your family of origin. What critical events have shaped you today? What limps has God given you as a result? How do they impact the way you relate to people today?

2. Be truthful. By year six of our ministry, we had started two churches—one in English with about 450 people, another in Spanish with almost 300. I was senior pastor of both. I was proclaiming our vision of churches all over the city and overseas. (No, I didn't understand my limitations.)

I was so committed to doing a good job that I lied. Not consciously, but I lied to myself. I didn't embrace my limits and weaknesses. I looked at only the good side of others, myself, and the ministry. I lied to others. I made promises I couldn't keep. I would take responsibility and blame for things to ease over tensions and resolve conflicts. I wouldn't tell people hard things about their lives for fear they would leave. I lied to God. Much of my work for him was for me. My low level of awareness made it difficult to discern the two. And it was too painful to seriously address.

You can't build a church, the pillar and foundation of the truth, upon lies and half-truths. The material is too flimsy.

3. Be Loving. First Corinthians 13 makes clear that it's possible to move in the gifts of God and not be loving. It's true—I did it. I was too busy working to be loving. I thought I loved my wife, children, staff, and friends. I couldn't understand why they didn't feel it, why they didn't feel valued. I rationalized that it was their problem. It wasn't. When our Spanish congregation had a split, I found myself descending, against my will, into the reality of who I was—a person who didn't really love well.

Jay, I have learned a lot from this experience. In fact, I believe that failure, depression, weakness, loss, sorrow, and closed doors are integral parts of God's work in our lives. I've also learned a lot from Mother Teresa. She taught me the value of loving one person—just one. I continue to work at growing in my ability to listen deeply to people's stories, to be present, to value the unlovely, and to see the image of God in each person I meet.

I believe this is the order God has for our love: Love God (take the time you need to enjoy him); love yourself (self-care is not a selfish act. It is good stewardship of the only gift you have, the gift you are to give others); love your spouse (if applicable); love your children (if applicable); and finally, with what is left, love the church.

Everything in hell and on earth will come against these priorities. But this is the pathway to joy and long-term fruit both for you and those you serve.

Warmly yours in Christ,

Pete

Mary…sat at the Lord's feet listening to what he said.

Luke 10:39

Getting Help

Douglas J. Brouwer
First Presbyterian Church, Ann Arbor, Michigan

Dear Dan,

If I've learned anything in my years of pastoral ministry, it's that I sometimes need help. Wait a minute. Let me rephrase that. I need help all the time. In fact, hardly a day goes by when I don't need some type of assistance.

I'll be honest, though. Asking for help isn't something that comes naturally to most of us in pastoral ministry. Personally, I would rather try and fail before admitting that I need another's advice or support.

But when I don't ask for the help I need, I get myself into trouble. You see, none of us have all the skills, gifts, and wisdom needed for ministry, let alone for daily living. So, by all means, *learn to get the help you need.* Find a way to get past your stubborn self-reliance or whatever holds you back. Seek guidance in whatever area it is needed.

More particularly, Dan, pursue the support that's needed in three critical areas of life.

Get help in your relationship with God. A pastor's relationship with God is *the* most important key to his or her effectiveness in ministry. Very few relationships are rock-solid all the time. Most relationships, even the best of them, need help occasionally. Our relationship with God is no different. If there's a problem, we need help. But where does a pastor turn for help?

Many of us have found accountability to a spiritual leader quite beneficial. This spiritual director is someone who knows how to ask us the all-important question, "Where is God right now in this thing?"—no matter what it is you are going through. So ask God to introduce you to a spiritual guide and friend, someone who will ask you the hard questions.

Get help in your marriage relationship. Not all pastors are married, but many of us are. The health of our marriages, I have come to see, is critically important in the effectiveness of our ministries. When my wife and I are out of sync, my service suffers.

A while back, my wife and I sought help to work through some tough issues in our own marriage. Unexpectedly, we later found ourselves able to encourage others who were struggling in similar areas. We could say, "Look, it works. We're happier now than we've ever been. We got the help we needed. It wasn't easy. Those first few meetings with our therapist were as hard as anything we had ever done, but today we know we did the right thing. Would you like the name of the person we saw?"

Be smart. Choose a person with the right credentials, as you would choose any other professional. But do it. Get the help you need, and then make the wonderful discovery that your vulnerability and willingness to get help can even be the occasion for healing in the marriages of others.

Get help in your relationship with the church. I am always surprised by how few of my friends in ministry ever ask for help with their churches. Very few pastors I know ever think to ask someone outside the church for help with a tough problem. With so many resources to choose from, it sometimes boggles my mind that so many pastors choose to suffer alone.

First, we can seek assistance from specific colleagues we deeply respect. My experience is that most pastors welcome calls from their colleagues and are genuinely eager to offer their wisdom and caring concern. I have called pastors at churches larger than mine, not really expecting to get through to them, only to find warm and caring voices at the other end, asking how they could be of help.

Secondly, I have also turned to former seminary professors. The further away I get from my graduation date, the fewer faculty members I seem to know, but often there is someone there ready, willing, and eager to talk. One time I called a professor and he surprised me by inviting me to come over *that same day* to talk things over.

Third, we can participate in a ministry support group. When I first came to my present congregation, I called a local pastoral-counseling center and asked if they had a clergy support group. They did, and I joined. For several years I attended their meetings every week and genuinely looked forward to our time together. They listened to me, I listened to them, and together we felt encouraged in our ministries. I'm a strong believer that pastors need to find groups of peers—outside of their own staffs—for friendship, honest sharing, and support.

Is there anything else I could add about getting help? Sure. There are far more possibilities than I have mentioned here. I guess my bottom-line advice is to be creative. If one source of help doesn't work, try another. Be like the persistent widow in Luke 18, and God will hear you.

Your friend,

Douglas

Ask and it will be given to you; seek and you will find; knock and the door will be opened to you. For everyone who asks receives; he who seeks finds; and to him who knocks, the door will be opened.

Matthew 7:7-8

Keeping in Shape

Richard P. Camp Jr.
Chaplain, United States Military Academy, 1973-1996
Director, A Christian Ministry in the National Parks,
Freeport, Maine

Dear Kurt,

I was happy to bump into you in the weight room this afternoon. It's good to be able to lift weights and enjoy time with you and fellow athletes who are agonizing under the discipline of growing stronger. I'm not sure why, during the sixth decade of my life, I am subjecting myself to this physical torture. I guess intellectually I know that it is good for my body to be strong, both for physical vitality and as a means of resisting the frequent maladies that attack the body's immune system. There is also a psychological well-being that comes from being physically fit rather than sluggish and flabby. Perhaps the most important benefit of this effort for me comes from the sheer discipline of doing what is profitable. You might be wondering where I'm going with this. Believe it or not, for me, physical discipline helps me develop my relationship with God!

I see faith as a spiritual muscle. Communication with an invisible God is a spiritual muscle that grows stronger with regular exercise. Enduring values like faith, hope, and love are spiritual muscles that become flabby without regular and disciplined exercise. To be spiritually out of shape and think you can be at your best for Christian witness is like running a marathon without training and thinking you'll win. It just won't happen! God wants us to run to win! So to that end, we must pay the price of tough spiritual training.

You know the thrill of a critical play in a game. The team needs three yards to keep the winning drive alive, and the ball is handed to you. All your hard work in preparation for this game—strength training, running, conditioning, and mental commitment—comes into play at that moment. You are prepared, and you make it happen!

Now carry that over to your relationship with God. In life's critical situations—temptation, disappointment, tough decisions—your regular exercise of spiritual muscle will help you to stand tall for what is good and right, even under the pressure of adversity.

God's grace in our lives enables us to grow stronger. Just because grace is God's work, however, doesn't mean that growth is painless. Growth calls into action new parts of our minds, emotions, and bodies. What we experience at these times often feels like pain. We are not used to stretching ourselves in these ways, but that comes as no surprise to you. Remember how sore you were after two practices that day back in August? A commitment to Christ and obedience to his commands stretches us beyond ourselves, and that hurts! But in the big picture, this growing pain leads to health and strength.

There is another important lesson I learned in the weight room, and that's the benefit of working with a partner. I know you understand the role of the spotter: First, he coaches and encourages you to get the best out of your workout. Second, he assists physically when certain muscles have become exhausted, again, so you can get the most out of your workout.

Likewise, it's important to understand that the development of your spiritual muscle will also be enhanced by working with a partner, a spiritual spotter who can help with accountability and motivate you to grow strong in grace. There is a time and place for personal intimacy with God. Jesus taught his disciples the importance of a quiet solitary retreat for prayer and communion with the Father. But he also guided them into shared intimacy. Two and three getting together in his name adds impetus for building the spiritual muscle of commitment, fellowship, and service.

On Saturday, you and your teammates will compete on the "fields of friendly strife." You have been taught to play the game to win. The prize will be another win on your season record or, at least, the knowledge that you gave it your best.

As a follower of Jesus, the battle in which you are engaged is a much more significant contest, the reward of which is an eternal prize that will not fade in its significance. The disciplines and sacrifices that you make in your daily life will be investments for eternity.

My prayer for you, Kurt, is that you will make the time and effort to keep yourself spiritually fit. Physical fitness has great value—you know that. But spiritual fitness is valuable in every part of life, both here and beyond. I place you in God's care.

Your friend,

Richard

Do you not know that in a race all the runners run, but only one gets the prize? Run in such a way as to get the prize. Everyone who competes in the games goes into strict training. They do it to get a crown that will not last; but we do it to get a crown that will last forever. Therefore, I do not run like a man running aimlessly; I do not fight like a man beating the air. No, I beat my body and make it my slave so that after I have preached to others, I myself will not be disqualified for the prize.

1 Corinthians 9:24-27

The Emotional Health of a Leader

Carol A. Travilla
Pathfinders, Tempe, Arizona

Dear Rick,

Why would the senior minister of one of the world's most dynamic churches confess that he was full of anxiety and feelings of frustration? Why would he admit that he was extremely vulnerable to temptation in areas he hadn't felt vulnerable in before? Why had joy abandoned him? Why couldn't he bear the thought of 20 more years of this? As Bill Hybels related his story, he said, "I was only checking two gauges on my dashboard of life." While his physical gauge and spiritual gauge were full, he realized that a third gauge, his emotional gauge, was approaching empty.

I can identify with this colleague's story. My husband and I have worked in pastoral ministry for over 30 years. From the beginning, we genuinely desired to serve the Lord and minister to people's needs. But we knew nothing about the world of our feelings. Both of us were taught that anger was sin, and that life must be lived peacefully *at any price*. We had no tools for resolving conflict, no instruction for being honest about hurt, anger, or feelings of inadequacy. Our value came from what we were able to produce or perform. These faulty internal messages pushed us both to near crashes when we were in our late 30s.

As a result of our experience, I began to search the Bible for the truth about expressing and dealing with human emotions. I studied

Jesus' life for clues about developing emotional health. My findings led me to the conclusion that God created us with a whole range of feelings—for our own good. My first step toward developing emotional health came when I admitted this reality and resolved to monitor consistently all of the diagnostic signals in my life.

Regularly, I check my emotional health by asking myself a few questions: *Am I irritable with the people I love most? Am I becoming more vulnerable to temptation? Do my anxious thoughts stem from hidden perfectionism or unrealistic expectations? Have I directly and positively communicated my needs? Am I wallowing in self-pity, causing me to feel helpless and misunderstood?*

When our emotional gauges are in the green, a personal sense of well-being frees us to experience all of our feelings without judgment and to express them without defenses. But when we find we are not interacting with openness, freedom, and confidence, we should sense a warning that something is wrong, that our emotional reserves are probably running out. The key to avoiding a crash in ministry is maintaining a balance between *self*-care and *other*-care. Unfortunately, too often some mistakenly view self-care as selfishness.

Think about this: Jesus' life verifies that the Son of Man valued self-care. He went away alone to pray often, to be renewed in spirit, and to gain perspective on his purpose. Sometimes he said no to a person's request. Several times the Gospels tell us that Jesus sent the crowds away. We read that he was tired, hungry, sad, angry, lonely, even disappointed. He admitted it. How else would the writers of the Gospels have known?

We also observe that he guarded hang-time with his ministry team of 12. He had no unrealistic expectations about others or his work. He knew the hearts of people. Still, he communicated God's love and the people's need to believe and make positive change. Jesus was the master of other-care, yet, he didn't ignore his human need for self-care.

It takes courage to set limits, to move beyond our need for approval, and to examine our own emotions. My husband and I have learned that sometimes our beliefs are not grounded in facts. These beliefs include: *If we just do more, the situation will get better; we have the power to change the people in our care; we ought to be available at all times; there must never be any limit to what we can do;* and *we should not have problems like the people in our congregation.* Perhaps you would like to check out your own beliefs. Do any of yours resemble ours?

So, friend, learn to recognize your own wearing and warning signs. Try not to minimize what is going on for you personally, in your family, in your church, and in your culture. Remember, the secret to maintaining emotional health in your role as a Christian leader is learning to balance self-care and other-care. Be lovingly gentle with yourself, as well as others.

When we keep a close eye on all our life gauges, being loving, merciful, and kind to ourselves, we become emotionally healthy Christian leaders. Only then do we have the resources to joyfully give God's faithful love, quiet mercies, and unknown kindness to the people around us.

Sincerely,

Carol

He has showed you, O man, what is good. And what does the Lord require of you? To act justly and to love mercy and to walk humbly with your God.

Micah 6:8

Patience and Persistence

Vernon Grounds
Denver Seminary, Littleton, Colorado

Dear Cody,

Often I'm asked for my favorite text. That question is just about impossible to answer. One text out of the tens of thousands in Holy Writ! But if the inquirer wants to know my number-one guideline for ministry, I can reply without hesitation—it's Paul's admonition in 1 Corinthians 15:58 to be steadfast in the Lord and abounding in his service. Steadfastness—not an obtuse, self-righteous rigidity, but a sort of sanctified stick-to-it attitude—is what I have found to be an indispensable element in effective Christian service. So take a moment, friend, and reflect on how patience and persistence are foundational in three areas of our lives.

First, we must have patience and persistence *in our service to others.* Honestly, as I look back across the years, too often I have observed a pastor abandon a post prematurely that was initially accepted with enthusiasm as the place of God's assignment. To be sure, I don't walk in another person's shoes, and perhaps in the same instance, I would have thrown in the towel as well. Yes, Spirit-guided wisdom is definitely necessary to know when and if one should leave a certain charge. But I wonder at times whether a white flag was prematurely raised because the work was stagnant, the critics vituperative, or the battle too uncomfortably hot.

Even in the best of ministries, in which conflict is minimal, patience and persistence are needed. The people who make up our congregations or who inhabit our mission fields require us to exercise patience again and again and still again. A pastor, for example, may be blessed with mostly supportive, appreciative people who encourage him or her and kindly overlook shortcomings. However, in almost every church there are also problem members who create difficulties. Faithful in attendance, generous in stewardship, they are nevertheless like tiny thorns that gnaw into one's toes on a long walk.

They delight to engage in protracted telephone monologues. After services on Sunday morning, they buttonhole the preacher and carry on a one-sided conversation. Each acts as if he or she were the sole church member entitled to the pastor's endless attention. Yet these are the very sheep whose insistent bleating signals their need for shepherding care. Only with patience and persistence can we redirect these challenging sheep.

Second, dear friend, patience and persistence are loudly called for *in honestly facing the blemished reality of our own characters*. If I am to exercise a Christ-like patience with other inch-by-inch pilgrims, what about patience with my own still-conflicted person? Yes, we need patience with ourselves.

Now, I'm not suggesting that we indulge in a bland self-acceptance that makes us indifferent to entrenched sins, excused as inborn traits incapable of change. Granted, our temperament is genetically given, but I dare not use it to sanction morbidity, laziness, or egocentricity. Nor can I relax my efforts to overcome pride, anger, and gluttony. Not in the least! The biblical ideals and imperatives motivate an ongoing struggle against the flesh, to say nothing of the struggle with the world and the devil. At the same time, my snail-like growth in grace requires patience and persistence.

Have patience and be grateful for God's unconditioned acceptance of yourself in Christ as you continue the ascent like a climber inching up Mount Everest. Have patience and persistence to prevent inching growth from driving you to despair or from inducing a mood of self-disparagement and self-disgust. Patience and persistence! Acknowledge those fleeting feelings of weary defeat that assail the soul, yet refuse to yield. Resolutely refuse to give up even if there are months of self-despair and self-disgust interspersed with days of harsh self-discipline. Relax! Reckon on your God-bestowed, unchangeable self-identity in his Son, and move ahead in your faith journey with confident persistence.

Finally, Cody, according to no less an authority than Jesus Christ, I must have patience and persistence *with God*. With God? Doesn't the mere thought of that verge on blasphemy? Not in view of our Lord's two parables about stubbornly insistent intercession, the stories of the man who keeps knocking on his friend's door at midnight and the widow who with dogged shamelessness pursues the unjust judge (Luke 11:5-7; Luke 18:1-8).

Sometimes God is silent as we cry for his help, he delays in granting a fervent plea repeated and repeated. The mystery of why he is forcing us to show the depth and sincerity of our request and compelling us to develop a total trust in his camouflaged wisdom and love is indeed a hard lesson in persistence. And this lesson, let me confess, I have by no means mastered. Yet these tough assignments in the curriculum of spirituality cannot be sidestepped.

Well, there you have the candid advice of a pilgrim-pastor-professor who has taken 1 Corinthians 15:58 as his guideline in ministry. May our Lord bless your faithful, persistent service!

Your friend,

Vernon

Therefore, my dear brothers, stand firm. Let nothing move you. Always give yourselves fully to the work of the Lord, because you know that your labor in the Lord is not in vain.

1 Corinthians 15:58

Personal Reflections on

Self-Care

The Journey

The Balancing Line

Jill Briscoe
Elmbrook Church, Brookfield, Wisconsin

Dear Rachel,

When I was little, my father took me down to the Liverpool docks. It was at the height of the World War II, and he wanted me to see the ships from allied countries that had brought life-sustaining food to Britain. "There's so many boxes, Daddy," I said in awe. "It's a wonder the boat didn't sink!" My father pointed out the Plimsoll line painted around each boat. "See that line?" he asked me. "That's put there by the boat maker. He alone knows how much cargo the boat can carry. The secret is to load and reload with just as much cargo as the maker intended it to carry." The Plimsoll line was in fact the balancing line.

From time to time, I find myself thinking about that incident and musing that Christian ministers and missionaries are like boats. We all have a Plimsoll line around our souls put there by our Designer and Maker. He has charted the water we sail and chooses the cargo for each of our journeys.

In my long ministry experience, I have found that the secret of arriving in one piece at the planned port of call is the degree to which I understand who he says I am, where he says I'm going, who's going with me to help carry the load, and just what burdens he has determined I must carry. To carry a weight far too great is to risk sinking without a trace, while to carry a load too little is to feel somehow disappointedly unfulfilled.

For example, when I first began to work with young people in Britain, I accepted many invitations to help. The cargo of endless hours of listening, loving, playing, chasing, counseling, and teaching was a happy burden that appeared easy to carry. But I had to learn early on that some burdens belong to others, and I would do them a disservice by taking them onto my ship.

After our boats (Stuart's and mine) had steamed across the Atlantic and landed in the States, I was asked to write and write, as well as teach and teach. Soon I was sinking under the weight of too many commitments. My primary responsibility was to our three teenagers and our burgeoning church. How much more could I take on?

Then I reflected on our Lord's ministry. He didn't do everything. But he did set about his Father's business. And loaded onto Christ's ship was a cross.

The *cross,* Rachel, is one type of cargo that God also asks us to carry on every ministry journey. Whatever ministry boxes are loaded onto our ships, the cross is always among them. For me, for example, it was in the form of meetings and periodic absences from my family. Yet I have discovered there is no sense of completion or fulfillment without willingly embracing it. If ministry costs me nothing at all, it will achieve nothing at all! It is the Lord who makes sure the cross is aboard. What blessings I would miss if I left it behind!

Another piece of cargo he lovingly loads onto our lives is the cargo of *crisis*. Thinking back over the major journeys of my life, none have been undertaken without some pretty heavy crisis cargo. Often I have complained, "Lord, we could make so much more progress without *this* piece of baggage!" Yet again and again, I have realized that it has been this very piece of baggage that has kept the ship balanced in the waves and has given me the joy of accomplishing that particular voyage.

A third type of cargo that the Lord seems to load on every ministry journey is *compassion*. The Lord wants us to travel with a contrite heart—one that is sensitive to the things that break his heart. He is pained by pride, stubbornness, self-will, and a self-inflated ego. We need to leave the boxes of egocentricity on the dock. Then we have more capacity to carry compassion.

Many times I have misread his instructions. Occasionally, I have sunk myself, with all the unrealistic expectations that he never asked me to carry! At times, he has guided me into dry dock for repairs. At other times, he has allowed me to cruise without a storm in sight. But mostly he mends me and balances me as I sail, keeping me stable however hard the winds blow.

In ministry I have struggled with loneliness, a low self-image, meager resources, people's expectations, separations, and even criticism from my husband, kids, and myself. Yet I have discovered each one of these burdens is on my boat by divine plan and by permission of the ship's Owner. He knows me so well; he made me. Balance is simply being in tune with the Maker of my ship.

Dear Rachel, we each sail into enemy territory loaded just right with the cargo of life-saving food for a world at war. What a privilege. There is no greater joy, exhilaration, or satisfaction than travel like this. And the best thing about being God's boat is that the Master goes along on each trip!

Bon voyage!

Jill

So, if you think you are standing firm, be careful that you don't fall! No temptation has seized you except what is common to man. And God is faithful; he will not let you be tempted beyond what you can bear. But when you are tempted, he will also provide a way out so that you can stand up under it.

1 Corinthians 10:12-13

Being an Elder When You Are Really a Younger

Jerry Sheveland
President, Baptist General Conference, Arlington Heights, Illinois

Dear José,

A number of years ago, I celebrated my 40th birthday, or as we self-absorbed baby boomers like to say, the big four-O. I was the center of surprise parties, middle-age jokes, and cards that in one way or another explored the theme of being over the hill. I didn't mind the celebrations. In fact, I rather like this side of the hill. Now I have really become what for years I had been pretending to be—a senior pastor. I first received the title at age 26. It didn't fit.

It's hard to be an elder when you're really a younger. Like a little boy shuffling along in daddy's shoes, I often played the part. I found that the secret to pulling it off is summed up in one seven-letter word—*dignity.* Even if you're doing something for the first time, you act as if you were born doing it. When it works, it's great. When it doesn't, well, it will make a wonderful story years later when you're secure enough to tell it.

This is where the story about my first baptism fits in. You can imagine my pride and nervousness the evening I stood at the top of the steps leading down into the baptistery tank. As I was about to step down, something went wrong. I don't know if I slipped or if I tripped over my long robe. What I do know is that the first thing the congregation saw was their young pastor tumbling into the baptistery.

The fall triggered a small tidal wave that spilled over the edge onto the organist who was seated below. So much for dignity!

The congregation enjoyed the mishap immensely. They laughed and kidded me about it following the service. For many Sundays thereafter, I caught different ones smiling in the middle of my sermons, and I knew what they were thinking about. But I also knew that they were seeing my heart, and that they were respecting my calling.

Whether you are young in age or young in experience, gaining credibility is a crucial leadership issue. So how does a pastor overcome the perception of inexperience and earn the trust of the congregation? I have found that several disciplines affect one's strength of influence.

Model personal credibility. Effective leaders demonstrate by their actions and demeanor that they are worthy of trust. They make every effort to consistently display integrity, graciousness, dependability, enthusiasm, and a willingness to assume responsibility. They don't demand trust. They strive to be trustworthy. This is why Peter admonished us to be examples to our congregation. If we are going to lead, then our lives need to be worthy for others to follow.

Invest in relationships. Loving leadership begins with a heart check—making certain that our genuine desire is to serve people not use them. The more we care for people, the more they will respond to our leadership. Several skills will help: listening, laughing, playing, peace-making, patience-practicing, and time-giving. Love is the most powerful motivator in the world.

Magnify God's power and glory. The authority to lead God's people resides in Jesus Christ. He is the head of the church, and we serve his desire. This means that the beginning point for us is profound humility. It also means that we must exalt the sovereignty of God, the authority of Christ, the power of the Holy Spirit, the centrality of prayer, and the infallibility of God's Word. True believers long to be led by spiritually empowered leaders.

Lead by following. Building credibility involves our willingness to follow as much as our willingness to lead. Servant leaders evidence a sincere desire to be accountable to their governing boards. It is seen in their graciousness when decisions don't go their way. You will hear other pastors gripe and joke about ornery elders or domineering deacons. Please don't follow their lead. Modeling accountability will help you nurture a leadership team that practices mutual submission and servanthood.

Earn the right to fail. Most pastors want to serve in an environment where there is a freedom to fail, one where risk-taking is valued. Such an environment is developed by building a history of successes. It is unwise to begin our ministries with high-risk and high-conflict attempts at change. Two years into my previous pastorate, I attempted to change the governance structure of our 100-year-old congregation. I should have known better.

Be patient. When I moved to a new ministry, I was surprised by how little credibility I brought with me. After nine years of building trust in a previous pastorate, I found myself starting all over again. After a while, one of our members confided to me, "I didn't know what to think about you at first, but you have really grown on me." This comment caused me to reflect that building trust often takes longer than we would like to believe. The formula for trust is T+F=C. *Time* plus *faithfulness* equals *credibility*. It is the reason why effective leaders take longevity seriously.

José, I could tell you other great baptism stories. I could also share many precious highlights, ways that God has chosen to use me to touch his flock. However, for now let me just conclude by admonishing you to let the Lord widen your circle of influence as you deepen your commitment to be his faithful servant. Oh—and do it with dignity.

A fellow elder,

Jerry

Don't let anyone look down on you because you are young,
but set an example for the believers in speech, in life,
in love, in faith and in purity.

1 Timothy 4:12

Only You

John R. Cionca
Ministry Transitions, Inc. and Bethel Seminary,
St. Paul, Minnesota

Dear Beth,

We live in an era of church-growth experts, pastors' conferences, consultants, teaching churches, resource Web sites, and pastoral ministry helps. New voices and role models arise each year, and ministry advice abounds. But just when you're ready to clone the preaching style of one megachurch pastor and the leadership style of another, George Barna comes along with a research report that says both styles will be obsolete in five years. So what's a pastor to do?

Perhaps the best advice I've ever heard is: *First, always remain a student of the Scriptures, and second, always be a student of the culture.* But let me add one more area of focus—*always be a student of yourself!* In other words, you'll make the most impact with your congregation if you operate out of the unique composite of what God has woven together in your life. Let me pass on three thoughts along this line. I believe they can ease the pressure you may place upon yourself.

First, *recognize your uniqueness.* Look at any group of people, and you will realize that you are *physically unique.* Even identical twins have their subtle differences. No one else has your fingerprints; no one else has your DNA. That should tell you something.

You are also *psychologically unique.* Millions of people may be extroverts or creative or reflective. Nevertheless, if you were to take the TJTA, CPI, 16PF, MMPI, or the Meyers-Briggs, no one would match your personality across those instruments. Again, Beth, that should tell you something.

And *experientially you are unique.* The family you entered was a different family than the one your brother or sister entered. While many people have had similar experiences, you have had a series of experiences that have imprinted your interaction with life. Some of those were great, some difficult, and some painful. And Paul assured us that, no matter what the experience, God uses it in our lives (Romans 8:28). Again, that should tell you something.

If nobody else looks like you, no one else is psychologically wired like you, and no one else has had the same life experiences as you, I think it's safe to give up the pastoral cloning game and just be yourself.

So let me offer the following suggestions. First, *recognize your uniqueness.* Become a student of yourself. Benefit from a personality inventory such as *ProScan* by Professional DynaMetric Programs (PDP) to understand your basic natural self, your priority environment, and your outward self (how you come across to others). Also use an instrument such as Leadership Effectiveness & Adaptability Description (LEAD) by the Center for Leadership Studies, Inc. to help you understand your primary leadership style and know how you can adapt that style to fit particular situations. And work through a book such as *Creating You & Co.: Learn to Think Like the CEO of Your Own Career* to get a holistic picture of ministry/career direction and possibilities. Take advantage of the good resources out there to help you get a more complete picture of yourself.

Second, *respond to your giftedness.* God has blessed you with many gifts and abilities. Some of your colleagues are musical, others great with their hands, some are coordinated, and others funny. You have been given many natural abilities, you have acquired some skills, and

God has endowed you with spiritual gifts. It matters little how or when a particular talent was added to your gift mix. The bottom line is that whatever we do, we're to "do it all for the glory of God" (1 Corinthians 10:31). So look for ways to maximize not only the personality and background that God has provided, but also the many talents that he has woven into your life.

Career counselors tell us that a good job fit is one that utilizes 60-70 percent of our natural wiring. Yes, every job has some dimensions to it that we don't enjoy. But as you grow in your understanding of how God has endowed you, it will be easier for you to discern where to give your primary attention and where to delegate.

Third, *refuse comparison.* A woman came up to me after one of our services and said, "John, you know that I'm in this church because of your preaching, but you're not my favorite preacher...Charles Stanley is." I responded, "Eleanor, that's OK. If God wanted me to be Charles Stanley, he would have had me born to Mama Stanley. Instead, he had me born to Mama Cionca. And that's just fine."

When I hear the poor preaching of some pastors, I wish their congregations could have me instead. However, when I hear the preaching of communicators like Chuck Swindoll, I think, *my poor people,* and I want to mail back my ordination certificate! The comparison game can kill us.

Do you remember when Peter asked Jesus, "Lord, what about him?" Jesus responded, "What is that to you? You must follow me" (John 21:21-22). It really doesn't matter how many talents you have—10? 5? 2?—but how faithful you are in utilizing what God has given to you. Yes, some pastors have comfortable salaries, while some receive meager support. Some preach to thousands, while some to just a handful. God is responsible for how he has gifted our colleagues. So let's just focus on how he's wired us and how he leads us.

So there you have it, Beth! What an incredible privilege we have—pastoring the flock of God. Just let the sovereign God, who designed you and brought you this far, continue to work through your unique personhood. Enjoy the adventure, dear friend!

God's best!

John

For we are God's workmanship, created in Christ Jesus
to do good works, which God prepared
in advance for us to do.

Ephesians 2:10

Enjoy the Journey

David C. Fisher
Plymouth Church of the Pilgrims, Brooklyn, New York

Dear Ben,

This summer I discovered something about myself. I learned it driving across Wisconsin, of all places. I suppose I've driven through Wisconsin 25 times. My wife and I live in Minneapolis, both our families live in Ohio, and you have to go through Wisconsin to get to Ohio. In addition, our daughter lives in Chicago, requiring another two trips through Wisconsin per visit.

For years, Wisconsin was an obstacle between our destinations and us. I was always in a hurry to get to the other side of Wisconsin. It seemed so long and (dare I say it?) boring. But right smack in the middle of my last trip, something strange happened. For the very first time, I noticed that Wisconsin is a very pretty place. I was so amazed I slowed down to get a better look. I saw rolling hills and picturesque farms that I had missed for years. In my hurry to get to the other side of Wisconsin, my vision narrowed to the width of a concrete highway, and I just plain missed 300 miles of God's good creation.

I was so impressed with the new discovery that early the next Saturday morning, a friend and I rode our motorcycles to Chippewa Falls where another friend lives. The three of us spent the rest of the day meandering down back roads through the lake country of western Wisconsin. I had no idea all those rivers, lakes, woods, and small towns were there. And all of it so pretty. Why didn't I ever slow down long enough to see it before?

I guess most of my adult life has been dominated by destinations. I'm always going somewhere, completing some goal, fashioning some future, doing some task. Because I'm so preoccupied with destinations, I don't even know what I've missed along the way. But very likely I've missed lots of wonderful days and delightful experiences. Head down, vision narrowed to the path before me, God only knows what I've sped by on the way somewhere.

In a similar way, pastoral life is full of destinations, tasks, and other narrow highways through life, and I've learned to move fast through all of it. I seldom sit down in a hospital room or a living room and just listen. I have a list in my pocket: more people, another hospital, another place to go or something else to do.

My mind never stops moving. It's filled with information and continually sorting it out, sifting through it, and moving on to the next thought. How rare to sit in silence before God, to be still and know anything but tumbling thoughts working toward a sermon, a meeting, a strategy, a writing assignment. And how very bad for my soul!

And bad for ministry, too. Do the people sense I'm always in a hurry? How can they miss it? I've learned how to move swiftly and, I trust, graciously from person to person in public settings. Yet the times I do slow down enough to really listen, I invariably receive a blessing.

I've traveled down the pastoral road quite a few miles in my many years of ministry. Like the saying goes, *I've been there, done that.* But since that trip through Wisconsin, I've worked hard at slowing down enough to see what's beside the highway of my life. Honestly, I'm still not very good at it. And I can't sit still very long. But I'm learning to enjoy more of the vistas in each day's journey.

Now, for example, I stopped scheduling breakfast meetings. Each morning I get up early and make coffee for my wife and me. We spend the first hour of each day together with no agenda except being together. Our relationship is foundational and infinitely more important than any breakfast meeting I've ever attended.

I've also re-established a habit from my early ministry. I arrive at the office before anyone else, shut the door, and spend two hours in quiet reading and reflection. Only an emergency alters this discipline. I read from my Greek New Testament followed by systematic reading through books of devotion, theology, biography, and pastoral helps. I don't take phone calls, and the staff knows not to interrupt. It's a matter of feeding my soul, making space for God, and creating a pace for that day and all of life. Then when I hit the road about 10:00 a.m., my heart is full, and I'm ready for ministry. No matter what happens the rest of the day, I've had a good day already.

After years of thinking about it, I decided to work at home one day a week. Friday works for me. It is a day for reading, writing, and thinking. Sometimes I finish my sermon, though ordinarily that task is finished Thursday evening. I don't answer the phone, and my staff respects my day alone. When the weather permits, I ride my motorcycle through the countryside in the afternoon and into the evening. Friday at home is the most refreshing and pacing experience I've known. I'm a better man, husband, father, and pastor because of it.

When my life ends, I hope my family and my church say of me, "He loved us." Honestly, people won't really see how many balls we juggled or how fast we could move about. They'll only know how we loved them. And this requires that we slow down and take the time to love God, love life, and love them.

Your fellow traveler,

David

"Martha, Martha," the Lord answered,
"you are worried and upset about many things,
but only one thing is needed."

LUKE 10:41-42A

Personal Reflections on

The Journey

About The Editor

John R. Cionca,

MRE, MA, PhD, is the executive director of Ministry Transitions, Inc. He is also the professor of ministry leadership at Bethel Theological Seminary in St. Paul, Minnesota. Dr. Cionca has served as a youth pastor, discipleship pastor, senior pastor, interim pastor, seminar leader, and ministry advisor. Author and co-author of seven books, his most recent resources are *Before You Move: A Guide to Making Transitions in Ministry* and *Search Counsel: A Devotional Coaching Guide for Call Teams.* John and his wife, Barbara, have two adult children and live in the Twin Cities.

RISING TIDES

John R. Wennersten
and Denise Robbins

RISING TIDES

Climate Refugees in the Twenty-First Century

INDIANA UNIVERSITY PRESS

This book is a publication of

Indiana University Press
Office of Scholarly Publishing
Herman B Wells Library 350
1320 East 10th Street
Bloomington, Indiana 47405 USA

iupress.indiana.edu

The paper used in this publication meets the minimum requirements of the American National Standard for Information Sciences—Permanence of Paper for Printed Library Materials, ANSI Z39.48–1992.

Manufactured in the
United States of America

Cataloging information is available from the Library of Congress.

ISBN 978-0-253-02593-7 (cloth)
ISBN 978-0-253-02588-3 (pbk.)
ISBN 978-0-253-02592-0 (e-bk.)

1 2 3 4 5 22 21 20 19 18 17

This book is dedicated to my wife, Ruth Ellen,
and our global family

John R. Wennersten

To my mother

Denise Robbins

CONTENTS

PREFACE

Climate change has been on the public radar for years, thanks in part to documentaries and news reports like Al Gore's *An Inconvenient Truth*. The most crucial element of this problem, however, extends far beyond the natural environment; it affects all of the people on this earth. There is little public concern about the people who will be displaced and cast asunder on the planet as the result of climate change. In developed countries many do not see climate refugees as a pressing issue; others see climate change and refugee populations through the national lens of homophobia and nativism. The fate of the polar bear in an age of global climate change generates more public concern than the fate of millions of lives.

In writing this book we have sought to offer a critical survey of climate refugees in the twenty-first century and to discuss the problematic and hopeful aspects of the issue. The most difficult problems in the future will be not only getting the public to accept climate change as a rationale for massive population displacements but also to convince governments to thoroughly address the issue. The world has a moral duty to protect those who are forced to flee, whether by war, famine, or climate change.

Global climate change and global refugee crises will soon become inextricably interlinked. The climate is changing and the pace of that change has been increasing at rates that have startled geophysicists, demographers, and the general scientific community. A new tsunami of climate refugees flows across the earth. We are now at the moment of truth.

RISING
TIDES

PART ONE
Climate Refugees in the Twenty-First Century

Introduction

> The issue of environmental refugees is fast becoming prominent in the global arena. Indeed it promises to rank as one of the foremost human crises of our times.
>
> *Norman Myers, "Environmental Exodus"*

THE MAN IN THE TUNNEL

On August 6, 2015, a misty gray day, an illegal migrant was arrested in Britain after he had walked the entire thirty-one-mile length of the English Channel Tunnel. His name was Abdul Tahman Haroun, a forty-year-old Sudanese illegal immigrant who walked the tunnel to Britain from Calais, France. He was charged with malicious obstruction to a railroad carriageway. The fact that he succeeded in walking under the channel to Folkstone, England, underscores the desperation of people like him fleeing the impoverished dry lands of Sudan. On that same date there were at least five hundred other attempts to reach Britain from Calais through the tunnel. The net effect of this development has been that Britain has posted one hundred more guards in the Eurotunnel terminal and announced new measures to deter asylum seekers, with possible prison sentences of up to five years.[1]

The tunnel is part of a larger issue of the number of people illegally trying to get into Europe from the Middle East and North Africa. Because of war and worsening environmental conditions, a constant flow of humanity is coming across into Europe, and there is no sign that it will be slowing down. Whether attempted by tunnel entry or in boats, which frequently capsize in the Mediterranean, this migration is part of humanity's distress call.

Climate change is with us and we need to think about the next big, disturbing idea—the potentially disastrous consequences of massive numbers of environmental refugees at large on the planet. As early as 1990 the Intergovernmental Panel on Climate Change reported that "the greatest single impact of climate change could be on human migration with millions of people displaced by shoreline erosion, coastal flooding, and agricultural disruption," writes the United Nations Development Program in its 2015 Human Development Report.[2] These people will be left to seek new homes in an era where "asylum" has increasingly become an unwelcome term. In a recent book entitled *Constant Battles*, Steven LeBlanc of the Peabody Museum of Archeology argues that environmental changes such as population growth, droughts, and crop failures in the ancient Middle East resulted in higher levels of warfare. Anthropologist Jared Diamond describes similar developments among the ancient Mayans of Mexico and the Anasazi culture of New Mexico in *Collapse: How Societies Choose to Fail or Succeed*.[3] In addition, as Michael Klare observes, "Many experts believe that the fighting in Darfur and other war-ravaged areas of North Africa has been driven, at least in part, by competition among desert tribes for scarce water supplies, exacerbated in some cases by rising population levels."[4]

THE RESEARCH OF CAMILO MORA

University of Hawaii biogeographer Camilo Mora and colleagues have recently published a disturbing analysis of what lies in the global future.[5] They call it the era of "climate departure," a point at which, as Diane Toomey of Yale's *Environment 360* puts it, "the earth's climate begins to cease resembling what has come before and moves into a new state, one where heat records are routinely shattered and what was once considered extreme will become the norm."[6] Mora and his coauthors examined millions of data points from various regions to determine what climate departure will mean for our planet. Interviewed by Toomey, Mora pegs the date of climate departure as 2047: "At the broadest scale, we calculate that year, under a business as usual scenario, is going to be 2047. Basically, by the year 2047 the climate is going to move beyond something we've never seen in the last 150 years."[7] The scientific models cover 200-year periods from sixty thousand locations around the world. The biggest climate changes, Mora's team predicts, will actually occur sooner in the tropics, where species have long adapted to a stable climate and will suffer dramatically if the average temperature increases by just one or two degrees Celsius. This is already happening in some places in the world's oceans, with massive bleaching of coral reefs.[8]

What scares Mora as a scientist and as an earth dweller is that changes are already happening around the world and that "people can't appreciate the magnitude of these changes until it is too late," but "when we start damaging physical systems and the carrying capacity of physical systems to produce food, people will react to this in a terrible way."[9] Climate departure will take place in a world of limited food. People need about two hectares each to provide the food to sustain them. Since there are some seven billion people on earth at present, and Mora's team has estimated that the planet has only eleven billion hectares that can be sustainably harvested, "every year we consume three billion hectares." The only remedy for the future, Mora notes, is to alert the public consciousness and embark on a concerted effort at reducing population growth.[10]

Most potential climate change consequences are described are in terms of weather extremes such as heat waves, floods, and severe storms. If we can extrapolate Mora's data well into the future, we can anticipate greater and more damaging tropical storms and extreme heat waves that will transform moderate climate zones in the hemispheres into tropical environments or deserts. According to a data analysis published by the US Climate Change Science Program, there have been three distinct periods in the twentieth century in which the average number of tropical storms increased and then continued at "elevated levels." The level of tropical storms globewide remained relatively stable until the close of the century, but in the ten-year period from 1995 to 2005, the number of extreme cyclones and hurricanes increased from an average of ten to fifteen: eight hurricanes and seven tropical storms.[11] And as the Climate

Institute notes, "It is important to consider that two of the driving forces behind hurricane formation (sea surface temperature and humidity levels) have been influenced by climate change."[12] Heat waves are another extreme weather event that will increase in number as greenhouse gas emissions continue, driving global temperatures caused by climate change increasingly higher. India and a number of other countries have seen their summer temperatures increase to over one hundred degrees Fahrenheit. The summer of 2003 saw one of the highest weather-related death tolls in European history as fifty-two thousand people died as a result of heat extremes.[13]

With increased temperatures comes increased capacity of the atmosphere to hold moisture, resulting in heavier rainstorms. An increase in the intensity of floods in low-lying areas would be catastrophic around the world. In Bangladesh, for example, over seventeen million people live in elevations of less than three feet above sea level, and millions inhabit the flood plains and flat banks in the subcontinent along the Ganges and Brahmaputra rivers.[14]

Environmental factors are almost invariably linked with economic factors in the push and pull of everyday existence. In developing countries it is the impoverished who often bear the brunt of the most environmental damage, which in turn sets off migration events. Because people often become climate refugees as the result of multi-causal factors, it is not easy to quantify their displacement as a social science problem. But it should also be recognized that sometimes environmental decline has nothing to do with political economy. As Norman Myers has pointed out, "Not all factors can be quantified in comprehensive detail, nor can all analyses be supported with across-the-board documentation."[15] As we have seen, however, the links between climate and human migration are not new. The droughts of the 1930s in the plains of the American Dust Bowl forced hundreds of thousands of migrants toward California, and those that struck the Sahel region of Africa between 1969 and 1974 displaced millions of farmers and nomads toward the cities.[16] If future changes in the climate continue to force mass levels of migration, it raises the question of when these victims will be granted rights to a form of protection.

FROM "*REFUGIE*" TO "REFUGEE"

The world has seen massive influxes of refugees before. The term "refugee" was first applied to Protestant Huguenots of France who were forced to leave the country by edict of King Louis XIV in 1685. (Revocation of the Edict of Nantes allowing religious toleration.) It was adopted from the French word "refugie," originally meaning someone seeking religious asylum. Today, the term applies to those who flee to safety in a foreign country away from political upheaval.[17] Neither the term "refugee" nor "migrant" seemed at all popular then or now, as it seems to confer a stigma on the persons involved. There is an intriguing body of literature on past refugee problems from the eighteenth through the twentieth centuries. In the past, refugees were often by-products of state-building processes. Nation-states excluded unwanted minorities much as the newly unified German state after 1864 excluded Poles. Turks excluded Armenians, and Balkan countries excluded Muslims. Relocation of refugees was seen as a preemptive measure to deal with problems of overcrowding and resource scarcity.

World War I created the first refugee crisis. The victorious nations at the Paris Peace Conference created the League of Nations, part of whose task was to deal with the repatriation and resettlement of 9.5 million refugees. The League of Nations was scarcely prepared to deal with the situation. The victors as well as the vanquished were in dire financial straits. The League of Nations' High Commission for Refugees (1921) did meritorious work in repatriating prisoners of war, and under Commissioner Fridjhof Nansen the league was able to initiate identification papers for homeless or stateless refugees. But as historian Michael Marrus has pointed out, dealing with the refugee problem in the 1920s and 1930s was like "using bedroom sheets to block a hurricane."[18]

Like the previous world war, World War II produced a tsunami of refugees. Allied military officials in 1945 quickly divided the vast hordes of people, over nine million, who had been either prisoners of war or enslaved by Nazi Germany, into two groups: refugees, who could be repatriated to their home countries, and "displaced persons," who had no homeland. As Marrus describes it: "Millions of refugees moved through the wreckage of Eastern Europe: Germans expelled by the Russians and various governments, thousands of forced laborers released by the Nazi collapse, some 2.5 million Poles and Czechs returning from the Soviet Union . . . cast out of their homes by the conflagration of war." Late in the war the International Refugee Organization was started by the United Nations to deal with the twin issues of refugee repatriation and resettlement. Across Germany and Eastern Europe "displaced persons camps" were organized to safeguard the mass of refugees from starvation and neglect. By 1949 the refugee horde had been reduced to what the High Commission on Refugees called "the final million."[19] There was no home for these people in Europe, and the bulk were taken by ship to the United States, Australia, and Canada. England and France took in fewer than one hundred thousand each. When future refugee crises erupted after the turn of the twenty-first century, these gates of resettlement and rehabilitation would be closed.

The United States, meanwhile, had been pursuing its own migration strategies. As Jane McAdam explains, during World War II President Franklin Roosevelt "created a covert research initiative known as the 'M Project' (M for 'migration'), appointing a small team of experts to study possible resettlement sites across the world" for upward of ten to twenty million refugees in the postwar period. At its conclusion in 1945, the M Project had compiled more than six hundred land studies.[20] This secret study, led by geographer Henry Field,[21] was considered political dynamite during the war. According to McAdam, "Argentina, Brazil, Bolivia, Australia's Northern Territories, Canada and Manchuria were identified as possible areas for refugee resettlement."[22] Strangely the vast unpopulated landscape of Alaska was not mentioned.

The Holocaust of World War II had created a problematic world of refugees, displaced persons, and embittered national populations but until 1944, President Roosevelt was disinclined to do much about saving Jewish refugees in Europe, who were perishing by the millions. It was only through the determined intercession of Henry Morgenthau Jr., the secretary of the treasury and sole Jew in Roosevelt's cabinet, that the president was forced to confront the reality of the Holocaust. The report of the secretary of the treasury marked the transformation of American policy toward refugees. Roosevelt created the War Refugee Board, and its operatives were credited with rescuing two hundred thousand Jews from the Holocaust. This was an impressive feat but amounted to only a tiny fraction of the millions of innocent people who ultimately perished.

At this writing, Europe is under siege by Syrian war refugees who represent one of the largest war-induced migrations in history. The war has dragged on for over four years now, taking more than two hundred thousand lives and causing untold destruction to the Syrian environment. Well over a million refugees have entered Europe, adding a complex religious and cultural mix to the already complicated issue of climate refugees. These streams of migrants may literally change the face of the continent in a generation. Optimists hope that through resettlement and education the issues can be resolved. Others believe that this might be the time when things begin to fall apart in our global system. At present, while a dangerous situation unfolds, many world leaders have chosen paralysis and mutual recrimination. At this juncture members of the EU nations of Europe are discussing ways to keep further immigration limited to "documented" refugees.

In 2009 only 30 percent of Americans believed that the world climate was changing. By 2012, surveys revealed that 70 percent of the American people had come to believe that greenhouse gases had altered the planet. A new age of environmental change—and subsequently refugees—had dawned.[23]

Environmental refugees in an age of sectarian violence, civil war, and economic recession are not a flashy public policy project. Most policy makers wish the subject would go away. But in an age when the world is being forced to bear witness to the fact that millions are fleeing their homes owing to sea rise, desertification, drought, unprecedented hurricanes, tsunamis, and war, the topic is stubbornly resistant to the kinds of public amnesia so often in effect in the world theater of nations.

We do not know how soon reality will trump ideology. At present there are lots of back-and-forth discussions between national and international leaders that have not been very productive. What is certain, however, is that climate change is not just changing the planet; it is changing human lives. In a 2007 essay for the *Financial Times*, David

Cameron points out that "as early as 1971, Richard Falk [a professor of international law at Princeton University,] argued that environmental change was a security issue and outlined what he called his 'first law of ecological politics': the faster the rate of change, the less time to adapt, the more dangerous the impact will be."[24] We are now living in an age of resource shocks. Unbridled world consumption of food and water and other resources combined with the advent of climate change may produce a global explosion, writes Michael Klare in his book *The Race for What's Left*. Different nations are coming up with different strategies on migration. Ultimately, climate refugees present us with a troublesome issue of human rights in an age of climate change, violence, and technological transformation.[25]

THE BIG PUSH

Extreme weather events in North Africa and elsewhere may become the norm rather than the exception. Certainly desertification has put large populations on the move in search of water, livelihood, and security. A rise in sea level will create serious situations considering that a quarter of the world's population lives on or near coasts and that the majority of our own megacities are situated in coastal areas. A Pentagon memo notes: "Picture Japan's coastal cities flooded, with their freshwater supplies contaminated. Envision Pakistan, India, and China—all nuclear powers—skirmishing at their borders over access to shared rivers and arable land with older coastal areas now submerged under rising seas."[26]

It is often difficult to differentiate between those refugees driven by environmental factors and those driven by other factors. Economics, politics, culture, and climate intertwine like some sociological double helix. What refugees have in common, however, is that they are suffering, and often they are impoverished by the environmental degradation of their homeland, affected by tsunamis, desertification, water scarcity, and disease.

There is considerable uncertainty as to where these streams of global environmental refugees will flow. But it is a safe bet that they will lap up on the shores of prosperous developed Western nations, which are already becoming increasingly xenophobic. The Office of the United Nations High Commission for Refugees (UNHCR), with a lean staff of ten thousand seven hundred workers, is already stressed by refugee crises of some twenty-one and one-third million.[27] Add millions of people displaced by climate change, and you have a crisis of governance and management that will sorely tax the wisest solons at the UN and other governmental agencies.

It is not rocket science to conclude that as the century progresses there will be a glaring need for more farms and farmers to feed the planet's burgeoning population. Meanwhile, major countries like China are buying farmland in whatever country they can find it, and food stocks on Wall Street such as ConAgra and General Mills are soaring. Access to supplies like water and grain will become major concerns to countries with diminished rainfall. By 2020, warns Chatham House in its *Resources Futures* report, "yields from rain-fed agriculture could be reduced by 50 percent" in some countries. The highest rates of loss are expected to be in Africa, where reliance on rain-fed farming is greatest, but agriculture in China, India, Pakistan, and Central Asia is also likely to be severely affected.[28] Heat waves will diminish the flow of rivers, which will mean diminishing supplies of water for irrigation and hydroelectric power. Long range, in addition to setting waves of population migration in motion, a changed environment in the future will transform infrastructures of government out of recognition from their older patterns.

Presently, in the safe, affluent confines of our homes, we watch on our television or read in our newspapers or on the Internet of the relentless march of hundreds of thousands of refugees out of Africa and the Middle East bound for the sanctuary and prosperity of England and Western Europe. They are people who cannot hold on to a livelihood in their forsaken homelands because of drought, soil erosion, desertification, floods, and war. They are desperate people who are willing to risk the violence of nativist Europeans or drowning in a tempest of the Mediterranean Sea. Unlike other refugees of yesteryear, these people have abandoned their homeland with little hope of a foreseeable return.

Environmental refugees are a problem of development policy beyond the scope of a single country or agency. The problems are fraught with emotion, human agency, and political controversy. How will people be relocated and settled? Is it possible to offer environmental refugees temporary or permanent asylum? Will these refugees have any collective rights in the new areas they inhabit? And who will pay the costs of all the affected countries during the process of resettlement?

Developed Western nations like the United States also have begun to feel the shock of environmental stresses and catastrophes. A decade ago Hurricane Katrina put the proud Southern city of New Orleans underwater, and more recently Hurricane Sandy decimated the Middle Atlantic coast and flooded New York City. Today the Southwest languishes in one of the worst droughts in recent memory while environmental historians point out similarities with the Dust Bowl of winds that roared across the drought-ridden plains of Kansas, Texas, and Oklahoma in the 1930s and covered distant cities like Washington and Philadelphia in a choking mantle of dust and dirt. California worries about its San Andreas Fault, and seismologists of the Pacific Northwest fear the coming of what they call "The Big One"—sliding tectonic plates of the "Cascadian subduction zone" resulting in a major earthquake followed by tsunamis whose impact will cover some 140,000 square miles, render seven million people homeless, and destroy and flood Seattle, Tacoma, Eugene, and Salem, the capital of Oregon.

Comprehending the scale of our looming climate crisis is difficult. And absorbing climate refugees or their war-torn brethren is burdensome and fraught with controversy. It is easy to welcome them at the airport but more complex to provide them with sustenance and jobs. Thus, when we contemplate the subject of refugees and the future, we might do well to look in a mirror and recognize that every one of us is or could be a migrant.

NOTES

http://climate.org/archive/PDF/Environmental%20Exodus.pdf

1. "Channel Tunnel: Man Accused of Trying to Walk to UK," *BBC News*, August 7, 2015.

2. "Human Development Report 2015," United Nations Development Programme, 2015.

3. Jared Diamond, *Collapse: How Societies Choose to Fail or Succeed*, rev. ed. (New York: Penguin, 2011).

4. Michael T. Klare, "Entering a Resource-Shock World: How Resource Scarcity and Climate Change Could Produce a Global Explosion," *TomDispatch.com*, http://www.tomdispatch.com/blog/175690/

5. Camilo Mora et al., "The Projected Timing of Climate Departure from Recent Variability," *Nature* 502 (October 10, 2013): 183–87.

6. Diane Toomey, "Where Will the Earth Head after Its 'Climate Departure'?," *Yale Environment 360*, July 2, 2014, http://e360.yale.edu/feature/interview_camilo_mora_where_will_earth_head_after_its_climate_departure/2783/

7. Ibid.

8. Ibid.; Juliet Eilperin, "More Frequent Heat Waves Linked to Global Warming," *Washington Post*, August 4, 2006.

9. Toomey, "Where Will the Earth Head?"

10. Ibid.

11. Greg J. Holland and Peter J. Webster. "Heightened Tropical Cyclone Activity in the North Atlantic: Natural Variability or Climate Trend?" *Philosophical Transactions of the Royal Society A: Mathematical, Physical and Engineering Sciences* 365 (2007): 2695–2716.

12. Quote and analysis from the Climate Institute, "Topics/Core Issues: Extreme Weather," accessed October 26, 2016, http://climate.org/archive/topics/extreme-weather/index.html

13. Janet Larson, "Setting the Record Straight: More than 52,000 Died from Heat in Summer 2003," Plan B Updates, Earth Policy Institute, July 28, 2006.

14. Government of Bangladesh and the European Commission, "Damage, Loss, and Needs Assessment for Disaster Recovery and Reconstruction," pp. 14–16.

15. Norman Myers, *Environmental Exodus: An Emergent Crisis in the Global Arena* (Washington, DC: Climate Institute, 1995), 32.

16. UN High Commissioner for Refugees, "Climate Change and Forced Migration," January 1, 2008, http://reliefweb.int/report/world/climate-change-and-forced-migration

17. Ben Zimmer, *The Wall Street Journal*, "The Burden Carried by 'Refugee,'" September 4, 2015

18. Michael R. Marrus, *The Unwanted: European Refugees in the Twentieth Century* (New York: Oxford University Press, 1985), 52.

19. Ibid.

20. Jane McAdam, "Lessons from Planned Relocation and Resettlement in the Past," *Forced Migration Review* 49 (May 2015), 30–33, http://www.fmreview.org/sites/fmr/files/FMRdownloads/en/climatechange-disasters.pdf

21. Henry Field, *M Project for F. D. R.: Studies on Migration and Settlement* Literary Licensing, LLC, 2013

22. McAdam, "Lessons," p. 31.

23. "Polling the American Public on Climate Change," Environmental and Energy Study Institute, *EESI Reports*, October 2014.

24. David Cameron, "A Warmer World Is Ripe for Conflict and Danger," FT.com, January 24, 2007, http://www.ft.com/cms/s/0/49bca770-ab4f-11db-b5db-0000779e2340.html?ft_site=falcon&desktop=true#axzz4WGfG9J3i

25. Michael Klare, *The Race for What's Left: The Global Scramble for the World's Last Resources* (New York: Picador, 2012).

26. Dan Brook and Richard H. Schwartz, "The Warming Globe and Us: It's More than Co2," *Dissident Voice,* May 1, 2007

27. UNHCR, "Figures at a Glance," http://www.unhcr.org/figures-at-a-glance.html

28. Bernice Lee, Felix Preston, Jaakko Kooroshy, Rob Bailey, and Glada Lahn, *Resources Futures: A Chatham House Report* (London: The Royal Institute of International Affairs, December 2012), 76.

1

Seeking Shelter from the Storm

The costs and consequences of climate change on our world will define the twenty-first century.

Michael Werz and Laura Conley, Center for American Progress

In its 2007 report, the United Nations Intergovernmental Panel on Climate Change (IPCC) warned that warming of the global climate system from fossil fuel emissions is unequivocal, as is now evident from observations of increases in global average and ocean temperatures, with widespread melting of snow and ice and a rising average global sea level. Given rising temperatures and increases in precipitation, the availability of freshwater will shift. Some areas of the planet will be much wetter, some much drier. Both drought and flooding will increase. Water stored in glacier snowpack will decline, reducing water supplies to more than a billion people. Global changes in land use patterns and the overexploitation of resources will set populations in motion. The conclusion today is inescapable: humans have emerged as a major force in nature and are altering the structure of the planet. We are now witnessing the human devastation of the earth.[1]

The United Nations High Commissioner for Refugees, António Guterres, declared climate change to be "the defining challenge of our times."[2] Today there is a new awareness that environmental factors—worsened in an atmosphere heated up by massive worldwide carbon dioxide emissions—can be triggers for major population movements. As the planet continues to warm, it will foster extreme weather events like tropical cyclones, and floods will increase in intensity due to warmer

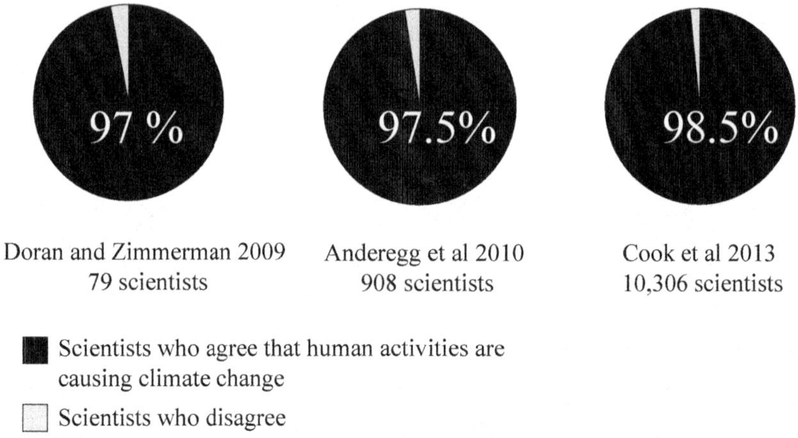

Figure 1.1: The scientific consensus on climate change has grown stronger with each examination.

sea surface and atmospheric temperatures. Rising sea levels in the South Pacific and elsewhere will destroy small island states. In other areas, glacier retreat will lessen available supplies of freshwater. Areas vulnerable to water stress and drought will be at high risk.

No one can wait to act until 100 percent scientific proof that human-caused climate change is in place, especially when the lives and livelihoods of considerable numbers of people are at risk,[3] but for all intents and purposes we are already there. Scientists have concluded that fossil fuels are driving global warming with 95 percent certainty—the same degree of scientific certainty as the consensus that cigarettes can kill and that HIV causes AIDS (see figure 1.1).[4]

Though many predictions about future impacts of climate changes come in ranges, there is "little doubt" that parts of the earth are becoming less habitable due to factors related to climate change, argues the International Organization for Migration.[5] Already, warmer surface temperatures have brought changes to the global climate at rates unseen over previous millennia. With global temperature predicted to rise two to five degrees centigrade by century's end, migrations will become larger and more problematic.[6] Thus, climate or environmental refugees could become one of the foremost human crises of our times. As UN Undersecretary-General Achim Steiner has argued, "The question we must continually ask ourselves in the face of scientific complexity and uncertainty, but also with growing evidence of climate change, is at what point precaution, common sense, or prudent risk management demands action?"[7]

SEA LEVEL RISE AND MIGRATION

Lester Brown, in his book *World on the Edge*, writes that "over the longer term, rising-sea refugees will likely dominate the flow of environmental refugees."[8] How far might sea levels rise? The most conservative projections estimate between one and three feet. The ever-practical and forward-looking Dutch, for planning purposes, are assuming a two-and-a-half-foot rise by 2050.[9] Maybe the Dutch can withstand two and a half feet, but this is enough to obliterate large portions of island nations like the Maldives. Yet scientists now think we are locked in to a sea level rise of *at least* three feet, and that is only with aggressive worldwide reduction of fossil fuels. Without climate action, sea levels could rise six feet by the end of 2100 and as much as ten feet within two centuries, creating a huge threat to coastal communities around the globe.[10]

Ten percent of the world's population currently lives in low-lying coastal zones, and this population sector is growing rapidly. Sustained global warming of about three degrees centigrade, experts agree, will result in sea level rise of one-quarter meter by 2040 that will damage coastal wetlands, impair fisheries, and disrupt fresh groundwater supplies, with saltwater intrusion ruining farmlands and affecting drinking water supplies. Large urban centers such as Shanghai, Manila, Bangkok, Dhaka, and Jakarta, are already vulnerable to subsidence. Rising tides and storm surges are already putting areas of land underwater—places as diverse as neighborhoods in Norfolk, Virginia; major parts of southern Louisiana; and island republics like Tuvalu and the Maldives in the Indian and Pacific oceans. In the Western Hemisphere, Americans may find themselves struggling to resettle tens of millions forced to migrate because of rising tides along the Gulf of Mexico, South Florida, and the

East Coast, reaching nearly to New England. While scientists cannot predict the details of short-term human history, there is little doubt that changes will be momentous. Renowned climatologist James Hansen argues that China will have great difficulties despite its growing economic power as "hundreds of millions of Chinese are displaced by rising seas. With the submersion of Florida and coastal cities, the United States may be equally stressed." With global interdependence, he notes, "there may be a threat of collapse of economic and social systems."[11]

On the northern Atlantic coast of the United States, sea levels are rising about four times faster than the global average, conservatively predicted to rise six feet by 2100. New York, Norfolk, and Boston are particularly at risk and already experience damaging floods from even minor storms.[12] On a small inlet off the coast of Virginia called Chincoteague, a wildlife haven of wild beaches and feral ponies, beaches are losing about twenty feet of coastline a year.

In July 2013 a *Rolling Stone* article headline blared: "Goodbye, Miami." Writer Jeff Goodell predicted that due to the rising tides Miami would be uninhabitable by 2030 and completely underwater by the end of the century, when it would essentially transform into a snorkeling spot, "where people could swim with sharks and sea turtles and explore the wreckage of a great American city."[13] Goodell's article sparked some controversy, but it was not unreasonable. In fact, of all the people in the United States who will be affected by sea level rise, at least 40 percent live in Florida, according to analyses by the news organization Climate Central. And Miami faces a unique risk: its precarious foundation. Miami, and much of South Florida, is built on a foundation of porous limestone. Any levees or seawalls would be ineffective against floods. Ocean water would simply leach through the bedrock instead. The effects of this are already taking place, with seawater seeping onto the streets through the drains, flooding outdated sewage systems. According to the Florida Department of Transportation, the rising seas will flood major coastal highways after 2050 and cause them to deteriorate, saturating and eroding the limestone beneath them. Scientists and experts are already warning the state government of a future mass exodus as people move away from flooded Florida.

The latest research shows that it will not be just Floridians who need to flee. Sea level rises could force between four and thirteen million people in coastal American communities from their homes by 2100.[14] It is not clear where they will go.

The good news is that not all cities are locked into an unlivable sea level scenario. Strong action on climate change would make all the difference for fourteen major US cities, including Jacksonville, Florida, and a handful of cities in Virginia and California.[15]

FRESHWATER SCARCITY AND CONFLICT

As Andrea Appleton notes in the *Johns Hopkins Health Review,* "With climate change comes uncertainty about water resources." Further, she adds that "a real water scarcity could require a fundamental thinking of how we manage water."[16] We take water for granted now, but that attitude will undergo radical change as the century progresses. A lot of what people believe about water is nonsense. People think there will always be water and when they turn on their taps water will flow. This will not necessarily be true in the future, though there will always be water for the wealthy. The quotidian work of water over the centuries, however, is not the stuff of the popular media. We fill our baths and hot tubs with the expectation that we can discard the wasted water when we are finished. That there will always be water is an idea deeply rooted in our subconscious. It is the major selfish conceit of the affluent West.

Awareness of water as an ecological concept is fairly recent, dating for the most part from the mid-twentieth century. The growing desertification of the planet and the disappearance of wetlands of the world have helped to give us a stronger environmental focus. It is only now in the twenty-first century that we are beginning to realize that water is the key component of climate change. For some time, experts have argued about the earth's carrying capacity to support ever-larger populations. For example, will there be enough food and water on the planet to support a population of eight to ten billion people? Meanwhile, in developing nations, water issues intensify every day between rich residents of overcrowded cities and their poorest neighbors. The World Water Forum, at its third triennial meeting, in Istanbul in 2009, offered a grim assessment in its "Water in a Changing World" report. It was still business as usual for the five billion people, or two-thirds of the planet, who do not have access to safe water, adequate sanitation, or enough food to eat.[17] Each year, the World Water Forum reported, the world increases by eighty million people, continually stressing our global freshwater resources.

Looking at water through the critical lens of the twenty-first century, we see our rivers drying up. Some of the world's largest rivers, including the Yellow, the Niger, and the Colorado, are drying up as a result of climate change with potentially disastrous consequences for many of the world's populous regions and cities of the world.[18] Water in the Rio Grande evaporates before reaching the Gulf, the flow of the Nile has choked by a dam, and reservoirs lose millions of gallons of water through evaporation. In many parts of India, farmers desperate for irrigation water plunder their aquifers faster than rainfall can replenish the withdrawn water. Scientists also predict that those rivers that have seen stable or increased flows, such as the Brahmaputra in South Asia and the Yangtze in China, could wither as inland glaciers melt and rainfall patterns are altered as a result of climate change.[19]

More than half the world's wetlands have disappeared, and climate change around the world has altered weather patterns and led to water shortages.[20] Such developments may unleash conflict and major out-migrations in developed countries as well. In the United States hydrologists fear that as water as a commodity becomes increasingly scarcer, conflicts will arise between the United States and Canada over access to the Great Lakes. As the Southwestern states and California swelter under the onslaught of a multiyear drought, governments increasingly turn a hungry eye toward tapping Lake Superior and bringing the "blue gold" to irrigate their parched lands. Consider the Colorado River, a major water source for seven states and parts of northwestern Mexico. Currently the Colorado River barely meets the needs of the many millions who rely on it. If water levels drop further, Peter Gleick of the Pacific Institute in Oakland, California, said to *Newsweek*, it could "derail the system altogether."[21] Additionally, drought-induced population out-migration may strain state and federal budgets with relocation costs and the attendant problems of community upheaval.

When profound water shortages or ravaging floods put populations on the move, they must go somewhere, and this migration can create conflict in the area receiving migrants. The arrival of migrants to areas that already are experiencing water shortages, such as parts of India, can burden the economic and resource base of the receiving area.[22] And when these migrants belong to different ethnic or religious groups, residents may feel threatened and respond aggressively. No matter how peaceful climate refugees may be, in most cases their arrival will generate significant levels of public suspicion and mistrust. As Rafael Reveny notes, sudden drastic environmental changes can push many people to migrate quickly. The arrival of Bangladeshi climate refugees in India led to violence in the 1980s.[23] Similarly, the absorption of Dust Bowl migrants in California during the 1930s depression had more than its share of conflict. "Okies" from the Oklahoma plains faced slurs, discrimination, and beatings. Their shacks were burned, and police manned the California border to block their entry into the state.

The main crisis to come, however, will be the water rivalry between India and China, which undoubtedly will produce an anguished flow of climate refugees. China's unique water power status stems from its control of the headwaters of the Ganges and Brahmaputra Rivers that flow into India and other Southeast Asian countries. As both China and India have nuclear weapons, hydrologists worry that water conflicts between India and China may result in nuclear attacks on dams and other riparian systems. China's aggressive dam construction of India's headwaters in the high Himalayas is a constant irritant to India As the Carnegie Foundation points out in its report, "A Crisis to Come," China now has hydrohegemony over key headwaters that flow into much of South Asia and more dams "than the rest of the world combined," yet has historically poor environmental practices over these waters, "which has had devastating consequences for the environment":

> Headwaters—China is the largest source of transboundary river flows, including many, such as the Brahmaputra River, that flow from the Tibetan plateau to much of South Asia.
>
> Dams—No country in history has built more dams than China, which has built more dams than the rest of the world combined.

Environmental practices—China's use of rivers has been ecologically unsafe, which has had devastating consequences for the environment.

The Carnegie Foundation offers this perspective: "After many years of denying plans to build a mega-dam on the Brahmaputra River, one of the major rivers of Asia, China recently announced plans to begin construction. This river is one of India's and Bangladesh's largest sources of water, and any water diversion could be devastating to both countries." Water conflict between China and its neighbors has real national security implications, a problem that will only become worse.[24] Water issues in this part of the world involve the fate of the Tibetan Himalayan plateau and rivers that flow from there to serve the water needs of a billion people. Currently, glaciers in Tibet are melting as a result of increased temperatures. After an initial burst of too much water, there is going to be a shortage. Climate models suggest "peak meltwater" could be reached by the 2050s, with major rivers losing up to 20 percent of their flow. China will monopolize what's left of the water resource, and that will lead to major problems. With China and India attempting to store water for their combined four hundred dams, water shortages will create instability in the region. Clashes along the border between Chinese and Indian troops over the past five decades have resulted in deep mistrust on both sides. Both countries have memories of a short but brutal war between them in 1962.[25]

AGRICULTURAL CRISES AS MIGRATION DRIVERS

Agriculture has become the modern Agasthya, the mythical Indian giant who drank the seas dry.[26] Unless careful provisions are made, the expansion of agriculture, with its immense need for irrigation water, may gobble up what is left of the planet's groundwater in virgin lands and wilderness. To deal with "Agasthaya," research into new crop yields that produce seeds tolerant of increasing temperatures and water scarcity is increasingly a part of a survival agenda. One should mention, however, that the technological innovations of the Green Revolution have largely run their course, and there is little prospect in agricultural yields increasing at the exponential rate they have in the past as a result of new farming techniques.[27] Despite manifold technological innovations, agriculture appears to have plateaued. According to world climate expert Lester Brown, the world agricultural harvest in 1993 was only 4.2 percent higher than that of 1984 while world population increased by 16 percent. During this time, grain output per person declined by 11 percent. The Food and Agricultural Organization (FAO) of the United Nations reports that about 793 million people were estimated to be chronically undernourished in 2015.[28] If projections of world population growing to 9.8 billion by 2050 come true, farms will have to produce three times as many calories as today. Further, there are few new areas remaining that can be opened up for agriculture around the globe. The problems are compounded in a number of countries by inadequate government. As UN observers have said, in certain countries it is not so much faulty as failed governments or no government. Only a few countries in this area seem capable of remaining self-sufficient in food—Kenya, Botswana, and Zimbabwe.

At present, droughts top the list of worst global disasters. Since the beginning of the twentieth century, droughts have been responsible for the deaths and uprooting of millions of people—China in 1907, with a toll of twenty-five million; Ukraine in the Volga region of the Soviet Union in 1921–1922, 5 million; and droughts in India in 1965 caused a death toll of 1.5 million. In addition, storm surges in Bangladesh routinely kill thousands.

Throughout Africa, desertification has become so pervasive that whole villages and farms are overtaken by sand. The 1982–1984 droughts in Africa, for example, left 184 million people in twenty-four African countries on the brink of starvation. Ten million left their homes in search of food with two million displaced persons winding up in refugee camps in five countries. Many who waited too long to migrate died. As a result of these disasters owing to climate change, more people are being killed or displaced by landslides, cyclones, and floods than ever before.[29] The *Stern Review*, a British government report on the economics of climate change warned: "As temperatures rise and conditions deteriorate significantly, climate change will test the resilience of many societies around the world. Large numbers of people will be compelled to leave their homes when resources drop below a critical threshold. China, for instance, could see three hundred million of its people suffer from the wholesale reduction in glacial meltwater."[30]

Landlessness derives from environmental factors as much as economic ones. Experts point out that this problem is particularly acute in Mexico, Central America, Pakistan, India, and Bangladesh. Where people own little or no land in agriculture communities, the productive value of farmland is degraded, as too much pressure is placed on too little to obtain a livelihood. Meanwhile, the United Nations estimates that we will have to feed an extra 1.3 billion people in this decade alone and 4.1 billion by 2050. In Malaysia and other countries, deforestation has resulted in a decline of rainfall, with disastrous impact on local rice production. Recent studies have pointed out that the deforestation of the Himalayan foothills has had a multibillion-dollar negative impact on agricultural systems in the Ganges Valley of India.[31]

Whatever the cause of deforestation, it eliminates the homelands and livelihoods of large numbers of people in the developing world. Desertification is now at work on over one-third of the world's surface—some forty-five million square kilometers drying out to a state of severely depleted productivity. Desertification is leading to burgeoning catastrophe in sub-Saharan Africa, a region with some of the world's greatest population pressures. As early as the 1980s scientists pointed to the Sahel region, the Horn of Africa, and a dry corridor from Namibia through Botswana and Zimbabwe to southern Mozambique. By 1987 an estimated ten million people had become environmental or climate refugees in semiarid lands. Today a total of 900 million people are at risk in areas undergoing desertification. At the same time, these areas also have populations growing at rates of over 3 percent a year. Drought in Africa is now different. Areas in the Sahel, Somalia, and elsewhere face untold calamities because there is less water and more people. Water shortages cause major problems for health, agriculture, and industry. What is especially relevant is that in 90 percent of the developing world there is a lack of clean water for domestic use, which results in various diseases and maladies like cholera and intestinal parasites.

Meanwhile, much of the region suffers from a food deficit. The region's hopes of purchasing food from outside are meager because of its adverse trade relations and deficiencies in technological innovation and political will. In sum, United Nations experts believe that sub-Saharan Africa's outlook provides abundant scope for rapidly growing numbers of climate refugees. Food shortages are already largely responsible for driving people out of Egypt and Tunisia.[32]

Recently there has been a major falloff in Russian wheat harvests, because temperatures in the heartland have risen to 100 degrees Fahrenheit. Elsewhere, in another major grain belt, Australia's Murray River and Queensland areas, harvests have been severely diminished. The Murray River has been plagued for years by crop-killing drought, and the recent floods in Queensland have severely diminished Australia's agricultural productivity.

The Wall Street Journal summed up the problem: "China's farmers need water because China needs food. Production of rice, wheat, and corn topped out at 441.4 million tons in 1998 and has not hit that level since. Seawater has leaked into depleted aquifers in the north of China, threatening to turn land barren"[33]. Similar developments have already happened on the Great Plains of the United States. Genetic research into more hardy grains for an uncertain future proceeds apace with the problem. The real project ahead is to get people into actually valuing water in a realistic manner, says water expert Peter Rogers. "We do not have to experience a water crisis," said Rogers, "but we could have a really serious one if we ignore the warning signs and do not provide the leadership and the social determination required to avoid it."[34] Meanwhile, 2011 unfolded as a year of food crisis. Prices for food reached record global levels, driven by increases in the price of wheat, corn, sugar, and oils.

Nobel Prize–winning economist Paul Krugman has argued that rising concentrations of greenhouse gases are changing our global food system. Responding to assertions that climate change has no bearing on the problem, he admits that changing patterns of consumption and population growth have their influence on high food prices. But with climate change he argues that this is just a beginning. We may have had a few bad winters, but "don't let the snow fool you." In a warming world, "there will be much more and much worse to come."[35]

MIGRATION DRIVERS

Migration is driven by a number of factors that are interrelated and often conjoined with the problems of social and economic privilege. Listed below are the principal drivers of climate refugee populations:

1. Natural disasters such as earthquakes, hurricanes, floods, and droughts.
2. Development projects that involve changes in the environment. Specifically, this refers to dam and irrigation projects, nuclear power plants, and industrial accidents.
3. Environmental problems caused by population growth.
4. Slow climate changes: agricultural failure, deforestation, and desertification.
5. Conflicts or wars caused by environmental change.
6. Economic distress.

Natural Disasters

Of these drivers, droughts, floods, and rising sea levels could drive many millions of people to migrate. Recent studies point to the fact that at least twenty million people were displaced by sudden-onset disasters in 2008 alone. The floods in New Orleans in August, 2005 caused by Hurricane Katrina forced the evacuation of thousands of the city's inhabitants while tens of thousands of African Americans were left behind in a flooded water trap because of a lack of transportation out of the city. On average worldwide, about 106 million people have been affected by flooding between 2000 and 2005 and 38 million affected by hurricanes. It is well known that even today with our advanced technological apparatus, no climate model is able to predict with accuracy the damage of storms and floods to densely populated areas and whether the damage will have tragic consequences. Frequent storms and floods are destroying the Bangladeshian landscape. Largely due to this, 12–17 million Bangladeshis moved to India and a half million moved internally in the 1990s.

Starting in the 1990s, a number of extreme weather events have occurred with sharp weather shifts, which have a capacity to generate large

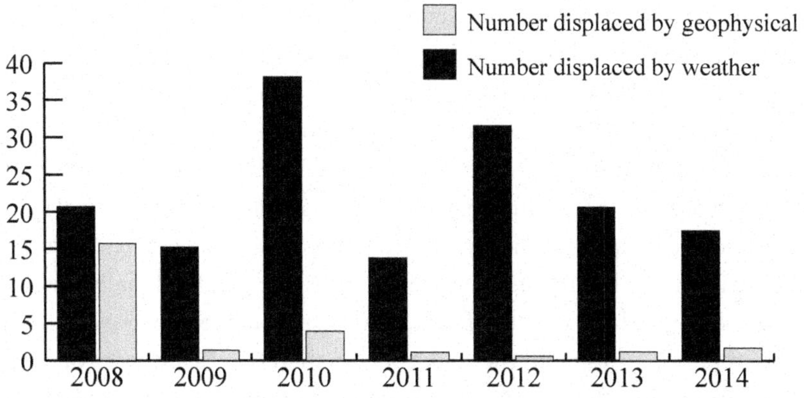

Figure 1.2: Displacement from weather events far outpaces displacement from geophysical events. Source: Internal Displacement Monitoring Centre.

numbers of climate refugees. As the atmosphere slowly but steadily warms up, global warming models predict more violent weather in many parts of the world. The number of natural disasters has more than doubled in recent years. This increase is due to a sharp rise in the number of weather-related disasters, and these disasters are happening in developed countries too. Superstorm Sandy on the eastern coast of the United States cost $50–$80 billion in damages in 2012.

Climate disasters like hurricanes and droughts have caused profound economic losses in recent times. From 1970 to 2012, there were over 8,835 climate disasters that resulted in US $2.4 trillion of economic losses with corresponding health epidemics, according to a report from the World Meteorological Organization. Africa offers an arresting case in point. African states are likely to be the most vulnerable to multiple stresses, with up to 250 million people projected to suffer from water and food insecurity and, in low-lying areas, a rising sea level.[36]

Development Projects

An excellent example of this driver involves the town of Chernobyl in the Ukraine. After the explosion of a nuclear reactor nearby, Soviet officials announced plans to demolish Chernobyl. The Chernobyl accident, with a radioactive fallout fifty times that of Hiroshima, and irradiating an area of 200,000 square kilometers, caused 116,000 people to evacuate within 30 kilometers of the nuclear station. The city's death warrant extinguished any hope of returning for the ten thousand former residents. Thus, these people have become part of a growing class of displaced persons—environmental refugees. Similarly, the Bhopal spill of toxic chemicals in India laid waste to the countryside, forcing major population displacements. The gradual poisoning of land and water by toxic waste and the effects of natural disasters made worse by human efforts are also adding to the ranks of climate refugees. Other proposed disruptions, like the building of hydroelectric dams, can set populations in motion, though for supposedly benign reasons. Dam projects have already resulted in the resettlement of twenty million people in India and thirty million in China, and they currently uproot more than ten million people in developing worlds every year, according to the World Bank. The Three Gorges Dam on the Yangtze River has uprooted over one million people. In developing countries more than one thousand large dams are currently under construction. These dams, when operational, will have a profound impact on local communities.

Population Growth and Urbanization

Global population pressures are further compounded by rapid urbanization in developing countries. In 1950 only 18 percent of humankind lived in urban communities, whether of the developing or developed worlds. By 1993 the overall total of developing-world urban population had expanded from 285 million in 1950 to 1.4 billion in 1990. Just three countries—India, Nigeria, and China—are expected to account for 37 percent of the projected growth of the world's urban population between 2014 and 2050. India is projected to add 404 million urban dwellers; China, 292 million; and Nigeria, 212 million.[37] It is daunting to contemplate Mexico City's urban population of seventeen million, the equivalent of the national populations of Sweden, Norway, and Denmark combined. Developing cities like Jakarta and Lagos have populations exceeding ten million, greatly straining an infrastructure that has been little improved since Indonesia and Nigeria were colonial dependencies.

Urban planners point out that the ideal size for a typical city is one million people! Beyond that number, pollution, health problems, and the overloading of housing and other cities begin to negatively impact the environment.

In developing-world cities, generally more than one billion people are believed to be living in conditions so polluted that the air is not fit to breathe.[38] Most of them live in squatter settlements, shantytowns, and slums. Nigeria seems to symbolize a host of negative factors leading to a perfect future storm of refugees. Soil erosion, desertification, deforestation, widespread water pollution, and outright water shortages point to a less than hopeful future for that country and its conurbations.

How far does urban population growth tie into the overriding issue of climate refugees? In most cases population growth is not the sole factor. But it is that growth that puts tremendous strain on environments. It is worth pointing out that those areas of the world with the most rapidly expanding urban populations are those with the most land degradation, water deficits, agricultural stresses, unemployment, and poverty. Sub-Saharan Africa appears to be caught in a demographic trap where population in the countryside and towns and cities has already exceeded environmental carrying capacity.

Deforestation, Agriculture Failure, and Desertification

Extreme environmental events like tsunamis and cyclones tend to capture media attention, but it is gradual changes in the environment that are likely to have a much greater impact on the movement of people in the future. The International Organization for Migration (IOM) noted that twice as many people have been affected by droughts as by storms over the past thirty years—1.6 billion people and approximately 718 million, respectively.[39]

Many lesser-developed countries today share experiences similar to that of the 1930s American Dust Bowl. Access to freshwater and arable land continue to be points of social friction and conflict. "The smallest amounts of arable land per capita are in Africa and Asia, particularly East Asia, South Asia, and the Middle East," writes Rafael Reuveny. "About one billion people in the world lack access to drinkable water, including about half the population in sub-Saharan Africa and one-third in Asia."[40] The migration examples of the US Great Plains as well as the more recent example of 2005's Hurricane Katrina exemplify how people leave areas due to intense weather-related disasters. But as social scientists like Reuveny and others have pointed out on the matter of migration, "The key issue is not how strong a disaster is per se, but rather how strong it is relative to the ability of people to withstand it."[41]

Wars and Conflicts

When it comes to discussion of climate change and migration, researchers can easily identify conflict hotspots. The problems of sub-Saharan Africa are so severe in terms of water, desertification, and conflict that it is hardly surprising that the new terminology for climate refugee should be coined there. Jeffrey Mazo of the Institute for Strategic Studies argues that the ongoing civil war in Darfur represents the "first modern climate-change conflict,"[42] a position partly supported by UN Secretary-General Ban Ki-moon.[43] Darfur's violence has taken place in a drought that began in the 1980s. The drying climate disrupted traditional patterns of coexistence between farmers and herders and led to scarcity, which contributed to fighting, and "by 2003, it evolved into the full-fledged tragedy we witness today."[44] In a growing number of nations such as Ethiopia, Chad, Sudan, Liberia, Somalia, Mozambique, and Haiti, normal state services, even boundaries, have disappeared. Armed conflict in the semiarid regions of Africa has been exacerbated by drought. In these regions people displaced by climate-related disasters and conflict face many challenges in terms of food, water, shelter, health care, and gender protection.

One of the area's greatest challenges is that automatic weapons have become cheap and are widely dispersed, giving rise to warlords who are shoving aside chiefs and clan elders. Climate migrants in northwest Africa, for example, are causing unsettling developments in terms of economies and international security.[45] Unfortunately, the existing global institutional framework cannot address a problem as gigantic in scope as northwest African countries and their climate problems. Nations are jealous of their hegemony and do not wish to cede authority to collective international action. Finally, nations have problems understanding why they have to take action to facilitate migration of peoples who are not being helped by their own governments.

Economic Distress

When people are forced to work agricultural lands of diminishing economic value or to survive working at very low wages, they become part of a driving migratory force that rationalizes "anyplace but here." Essentially the global trade system of the modern era allows multinational corporations to scour the planet in search of the cheapest and most exploitable labor force. Rather than chain the worker in place, however, the global system makes populations restive. Capital moves freely around the planet, and soon large migratory populations will move as well. These people know of a better place—the Western European nations and the United States—and they see it on television and the internet.

Low-wage societies are essentially polluting societies as corporations in their midst extract commodities with little thought to the environment. When coupled with the other drivers that we have identified, economics is probably an igniting force equal to natural disasters and war.

The potential for migration when linked to a rise in sea level is considerable. Populations living at an altitude of less than one meter will be directly vulnerable as the century unfolds. Flood zones in highly populated South Asia (near the Indus, Ganges-Brahmaputra, Yangtze, and Pearl Rivers) will pose great risk for resident populations. Drought will also force populations to move. For example, in the Sahel between 1973 and 1999, desertification displaced nearly one million people in Niger. The periodic drought and desertification that plagued northeast Brazil between 1960 and 1980 prompted 3.4 million people to emigrate. Bangladesh, already known for its disastrous floods, faces rising waters in its future from climate-driven glacial meltdowns in neighboring India.[46] Also, in the Andes region of South America, water shortages caused by melting glaciers will drive climate, migration, and security concerns. Finally, China is in the midst of highly problematic environmental change with water shortages and atmospheric pollution. China's water stresses affect millions of people who in the future will become internally displaced migrants and transborder refugees.

THE FORCE OF CLIMATE CHANGE

As we now see it, climate change will fundamentally affect the lives of millions of people who will be forced over the next decades to leave their villages and cities to seek refuge in other areas. The United Nations has projected that in 2020 we will have fifty million environmental refugees. While scholars debate the magnitude of this refugee flow and argue that these assumptions are built upon formulations of human behavior that are too generalized, current research by Norman Myers of Oxford University and others identify twenty-five million people on the planet as environmental refugees.[47] Currently, there is little real research on environmental refugees from the standpoint of national initiatives for amelioration or global governance. While research slowly enters public consciousness in the coming decades, experts like Camilo Mora argue that climate change will increasingly threaten humanity's shared interests and collective security in many parts of the world, disproportionately affecting the globe's least-developed countries.[48]

The conclusion today is inescapable: humans have emerged as a major force in nature and are altering the structure of the planet. We are now witnessing the human devastation of the earth. Climate refugees, once thought to be a problem confined to segments of the developing world, are on the verge of becoming a global problem. How we respond to this problem will dictate how well we can sustain ourselves in what we call civilized human society.

NOTES

Michael Werz and Laura Conley, "Climate Change, Migration, and Conflict," https://www.americanprogress.org/issues/security/reports/2012/01/03/10857/climate-change-migration-and-conflict/.

1. United Nations Intergovernmental Panel on Climate Change, *IPCC Fourth Assessment Report: Climate Change 2007*, https://www.ipcc.ch/publications_and_data/ar4/syr/en/spms1.html.

2. António Guterres, "Maintenance of International Peace and Security: New Challenges to International Peace and Security and Conflict Prevention," United Nations High Commissioner for Refugees Security Council Briefing, http://www.unhcr.org/.

3. Achim Steiner, "Climate Migration Will Not Wait for Scientific Certainty on Global Warming," *Guardian*, May 11, 2011, https://www.theguardian.com/environment/2011/may/11/climate-change-scientific-evidence-united-nations.

4. See figure 1.1: Peter T. Doran and Maggie Kendall Zimmerman, "Examining the Scientific Consensus on Climate Change," *EOS Transactions: American Geophysical Union* 90, no. 3 (2009): 22–23; William R. L. Anderegg et al., "Expert Credibility in Climate Change," *Proceedings of the National Academy of Sciences* 107, no. 27 (2010): 12107–12109; Cook et al., "Quantifying the Consensus on Anthropotenic Global Warming in the Scientific Literature," *Environmental Research Letters* 8 (2013): doi:10.1088/1748-9326/8/2/024024.

5. "Migration, Environment and Climate Change: Assessing The Evidence," International Organization on Migration, edited by Frank Laczko and Christine Aghazarm, 2009, http://publications.iom.int/system/files/pdf/migration_and_environment.pdf.

6. United Nations Intergovernmental Panel on Climate Change, *Climate Change 2013: The Physical Science Basis*, http://www.ipcc.ch/report/ar5/wg1/.

7. Steiner, "Climate Migration."

8. Lester Brown, *World on the Edge* (New York: W. W. Norton, 2009), 73.

9. Rob Young and Orrin Pilkey, "How High Will Seas Rise? Get Ready for Seven Feet," *Yale Environment 360*, January 14, 2010.

10. Brandon Miller, "Expert: We're 'locked in' to 3-Foot Sea Level Rise," CNN.com, last modified September 4, 2015.

11. James Hansen, *Storms of My Grandchildren* (New York: Bloomsbury, 2009), 259. Hansen believes the beginning of these storms is at hand. See James Hansen et al., "Ice Melt, Sea Level Rise and Superstorms: Evidence from Paleoclimate Data, Climate Modeling, and Modern Observations That 2 °C Global Warming Could Be Dangerous," *Atmospheric Chemistry and Physics* 16 (2016): 3761–3812.

12. Melanie Gade, "Sea Level Rise Accelerating in U.S. Atlantic Coast," *US Geological Survey*, June 24, 2012, https://soundwaves.usgs.gov/2012/10/research.html.

13. Jeff Goodell, "Goodbye, Miami," *RollingStone.com*, June 20, 2013.

14. Chris D'Angelo, "Sea Level Rise Could Displace 13 Million Americans," *Huffington Post*, March 16, 2016.

15. "Sea Level Rise Will Swallow Miami, New Orleans, Study Finds," *Phys.org*, October 12, 2015.

16. Andrea Appleton, "Thirsty Planet," *Johns Hopkins Health Review* Spring/Summer, 2015, 2: no. 1.

17. "Water in a Changing World," *UNESCO Forum*, Istanbul, Turkey, March 16, 2009.

18. James Murray, "Study Warns Global Rivers Are Drying Up," http://www.businessgreen.com/bg/news/1801434/study-warns-global-rivers-drying

19. Murray, "Global Rivers Are Drying Up."

20. Shane Harris, "Water Wars," *Foreign Policy*, September 18, 2014, http://foreignpolicy.com/2014/09/18/water-wars/.

21. Peter Gleick quoted in Michael Klare, "Wars for Water?" *Newsweek*, April 15, 2007.

22. Rafael Reuveny, "Climate-Induced Migration and Violent Conflict," *Political Geography* 26, no. 6 (2007).

23. Reuveny, "Climate-Induced Migration."

24. Brahma Chellaney, Ashley J. Tellis, "A Crisis to Come? China, India, and Water Rivalry," the Carnegie Endowment for International Peace, September 13, 2011, http://carnegieendowment.org/2011/09/13/crisis-to-come-china-india-and-water-rivalry-event-3362.

25. Ed King, "Climate Change Could Lead to China-India Water Conflict," *Climate Home*, http://www.climatechangenews.com/2014/06/11/climate-change-could-lead-to-china-india-water-conflict/.

26. *Economist*, "Sin Aqua Non," April 8, 2009, http://www.economist.com/node/13447271.

27. Lizzie Collingham, *The Taste of War: World War Two and the Battle for Food* (London: Allen Lane, 2010), quoted in "Marching on Their Stomachs," *Economist*, February 3, 2011, http://www.economist.com/node/18060808.

28. Food and Agriculture Organization of the United Nations, *The State of Food Insecurity in the World 2015*, http://www.fao.org/hunger/key-messages/en/.

29. Jodi L. Jacobson, "Environmental Refugees: A Yardstick of Habitability," *Bulletin of Science, Technology and Society*, 8 (1988): 257–258.

30. Nicholas Stern, *Stern Review on the Economics of Climate Change* (London: HM Treasury, 2006).

31. James Owen, "Himalayan Forests Vanishing, Species May Follow, Study Says," *National Geographic*, May 30, 2006.

32. Joanna Zelman, "50 Million Environmental Refugees by 2020, Experts Predict," *Huffington Post*, May 25, 2011.

33. Justin Lahart, Patrick Barta and Andrew Batson, "New Limits to Growth Revive Malthusian Fears," *The Wall Street Journal*, March 24, 2008.

34. Peter Rogers, "Running Out of Water: Or Just Another Six-Point Plan to Resolve the Water Crisis?" Oxford Martin School Seminar, December 3, 2010. Archived at the London Water Research Group: https://lwrg.wordpress.com/news/archived/.

35. Paul Krugman, "Droughts, Floods, and Food," *New York Times*, February 6, 2011.

36. UN Intergovernmental Panel on Climate Change Report, *Climate Change 2007: Impacts, Adaptation, and Vulnerability. Contribution of Working Group II to the Fourth Assessment Report of the Intergovernmental Panel on Climate Change*, M. L. Parry, O. F. Canziani, J. P. Palutikof, P. J. van der Linden, and C. E. Hanson, eds. (Cambridge, UK: Cambridge University Press, 2007).

37. United Nations Department of Economic and Social Affairs, *World Urbanization Prospects: The 2014 Revision*, 2014.

38. Norman Myers and Noel Brown, "The Role of Major Foundations in the Implementation of Agenda 21: The Five-Year Follow-Up to the Earth Summit," report to the Earth Council, n.d., http://www.grida.no/geo/GEO/Geo-1-019.htm.

39. International Organization for Migration, *Migration, Environment, and Climate Change: Assessing the Evidence* (Geneva: International Organization for Migration, 2009), 17.

40. Rafael Reuveny, "Climate-Induced Migration Migration and Violent Conflict," *Political Geography* 26, no. 6 (2007).

41. Reuveny, "Climate-Induced Migration," 661.

42. Jeffrey Mazo, "Darfur: The First Modern Climate Change Conflict," *Climate Conflict: How Global Warming Threatens Security and What to Do about It* (New York: Adelphi Books, 2014), 73–74.

43. *Economist*, "Cimate Wars," July 8, 2010.

44. Mazo, "Darfur." 73–74.

45. Michael Werz and Laura Conley, "Climate Change, Migration, and Conflict," https://www.americanprogress.org/issues/security/reports/2012/01/03/10857/climate-change-migration-and-conflict/.

46. Ibid.

47. Norman Myers, *Environmental Exodus: An Emergent Crisis in the Global Arena* (Washington, DC: Climate Institute, 1995).

48. Camillo Mora et al., "The Projected Timing of Climate Departure from Recent Variability," *Nature* 502 (October 10, 2013): 183–87.

2

Refugeedom

We are witnessing a paradigm change.

António Guterres, UN High Commissioner for Refugees

GLOBAL GOVERNANCE AND THE PROTECTION OF CLIMATE REFUGEES

Until now mankind has weathered environmental crises over the millennia. The question, however, is whether human behavior in the present may be adequate for survival in the future. For 2.7 million years, humans lived within the framework of alternating ice ages and warming periods. But until the industrial age, the rate of global climate change was slow. In the past, mobility was the key to surviving climate change. That strategy is severely restricted today as the pace of climate change is breaking all records. The problem is serious, and there is no established method of dealing with such challenging phenomena.

Refugee literature often distinguishes between "temporary" or "permanent" migrations, but these distinctions provide little help in the aftermath of environmental disaster. International support is required in all disaster situations whether the displaced climate exiles are permanent or not. As Biermann and Boas note, the main institution dealing with refugees is the United Nations, acting through the 1951 Geneva Convention Relating to the Status of Refugees and its 1967 Protocol Relating to the Status of Refugees.[1] The UN is restricted to helping individual political refugees who flee their countries because of state-led persecution, and this does not cover climate refugees. At best, the UN refers to climate refugees as "internally displaced persons" and offers some programs for them under the Office of the High Commissioner for Human Rights. But it is more of a Band-Aid program than a major corrective. The current international regime embodied in the United Nations provides only marginal protection, with no specific mandate, to climate refugees. This is a problem that strikes at the core of Western development policy toward poorer nations, especially the very poorest. Nothing positive can happen with United Nations leadership until an independent regime for the protection and resettlement of climate refugees is established.

World War II created the largest population displacement in modern history. At the end of World War II, notes Christian Aid, some sixty-six million people were displaced across Europe, with millions similarly displaced in China. The victorious nations were optimistic that the "displaced person" problem could be solved.[2] When the United Nations wrapped up its initial European refugee efforts after 1950, however, large numbers of people remained uprooted. To a large extent, global history since World War II has been the history of international migration. In sheer size, the waves of people displaced by environmental and political calamities have been greater than the world has ever seen. Admittedly, war has been the prime mover in the refugee world, creating precedents and circumstances that would affect millions in an era of climate change.

In the 1930s and 1940s millions of people became uprooted, homeless, and often stateless. Europe has a refugee history that it seldom wishes to acknowledge. Here are some figures that show the incredible European migratory stream of the World War II era:

MIGRATION IN WAR-TORN EUROPE, 1944–1947

1940–1945	5 million Jews from Germany to extermination camps in Poland and elsewhere
	4 million Reich Germans from Soviet Zone to US and British zones
	2.7 million ethnic Germans from Czechoslovakia

1944–194	51 million ethnic Germans from old Poland to Germany
1946–1947	6 million Reich Germans from New Poland to Germany[3]

In the case of Jews and Germans alone, we see a tremendous demographic upheaval. Add to it the millions of homeless on the European continent. Some of these fled from war zones; others were removed at the behest of government. The Holocaust of World War II created a problematic world of refugees, displaced persons, and embittered national populations. Until 1944, for example, President Roosevelt was disinclined to do much about saving Jewish refugees in Europe, who were perishing by the millions. It was only through the determined intercession of Treasury Secretary Henry Morgenthau that the president was forced to confront the reality of the Holocaust. Morgenthau's report marked the transformation of American policy on refugees. Roosevelt created the War Refugee Board, and its operatives were credited with rescuing two hundred thousand Jews from the Holocaust. This was an impressive feat but comprised only a tiny fraction of people compared to the millions who perished. Neither the term "refugee" nor "migrant" were at all popular then or now, as both seemed to confer a stigma on the persons involved.

Refugees sometimes wandered for years, largely because governments could not account for their nationality—a technical question of often bewildering complexity. Since that time the world has lurched from one crisis to another: the partition of India, the creation of Israel, the Hungarian uprising, the Korean and Vietnam Wars, and the current ongoing conflict in the Middle East, as well as severe droughts in Africa. Census takers have been hard pressed to enumerate the exact number of the hordes of men and women wandering across national frontiers.

Since the 1950s the global refugee problem has accelerated far beyond anyone's expectations and, increasingly, older refugee definitions do not apply well to current realities. In 1951 there were 1.5 million refugees worldwide. On January 1, 2000, the UN High Commission for Refugees (UNHCR) considered 22.3 million people to be "of concern." Add to that the 13–18 million internally displaced persons as a result of war and en-

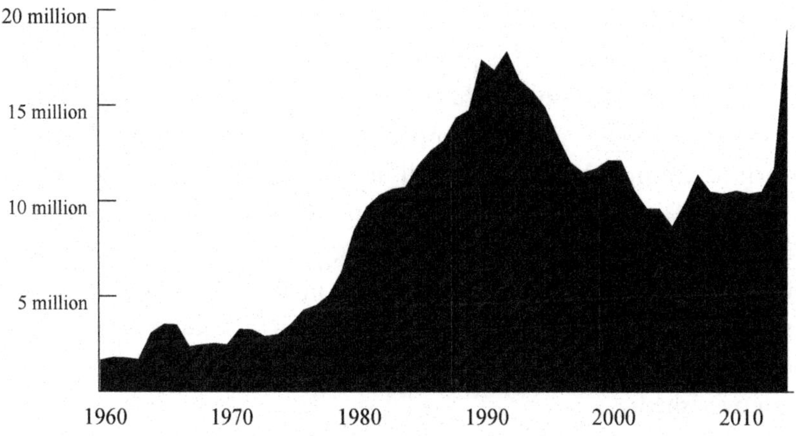

Figure 2.1: Number of refugees since the 1960s. Source: UNHCR Statistical Online Population Database.

vironmental disaster, and you have a total of over 50 million. According to the UN's Women's Commission for Refugees, Women, and Children, the overall total of refugees by 1994, whether officially recognized or not, was some 57 million.[4] Although this number amounts to a best-judgment assessment, it is a number well worth pondering.

The increased demand for asylum and resettlement occurs at a time of unprecedented globalization of the world economy. As a driver of climate migration, economic change is often ignored largely because people in today's crisis-stricken Europe forget how much richer Western Europe is than most of Asia and just about all of Africa. Using new immigrant surveys, Yale economist Marc Rosenzweig noted that "the poorest 1 percent of the population of Denmark has an income higher than 95 percent of the population living in Mali, Madagascar or Tanzania."[5]. Ten African countries comprising some 150 million people have lower per capita gross national product (GNP) than they did at the time of independence. Add climate change or natural disasters to the equation, and people will readily head toward areas like Europe where living conditions are better.[6] The computer has revolutionized communications, and better parts of the world are now more knowable to asylum seekers. Furthermore, migration scholar Michael Head has noted, "The ever widening gulf between the capital-rich, technologically advanced and militarily powerful states and the rest of the world has fueled the demand for the right to escape poverty."[7]

The number of climate refugees appears to be expanding more rapidly than others as environments of all types around the globe have been declining. Their number will increase greatly, say experts at the National Academy of Sciences, as global warming accelerates, sea levels rise, and flooding and drought disrupt agricultural systems in developing nations.[8] And we are now seeing that people who migrate often do so because of the environmental degradation of their home region. Environmental factors as much as any other factors make them economically impoverished.

REFUGEE FLOWS

There is considerable uncertainty as to where these streams of global environmental refugees will flow. But it is a safe bet that they will lap up on the shores of prosperous developed Western nations, which are already becoming increasingly xenophobic. The UNHCR, with a lean staff of 7600 workers, is already stressed by refugee crises of some 37 million in Africa and the Middle East. Add millions of people displaced by climate change, and you have a crisis of governance and management that will sorely tax the wisest solons at the UN and other governmental agencies.

Already Western nations are feeling the pain of including refugee populations in their midst. Australian immigration minister Philip Ruddock urged the fiftieth-anniversary meeting of the UNHCR to curtail the rights of those seeking asylum because of either political or environmental causes.[9] Ruddock and others have pointed out the enormous increase in the flight of people from the states of their birth in the final decades of the twentieth century and are fearful that this mass movement is likely to grow exponentially in the twenty-first century. Increasingly migrants "are resorting to unauthorized methods of entry, often at great risk to their lives."[10]

Climate refugees are a problem of development policy beyond the scope of a single country or agency. The problems are fraught with emotion, human agency, and political controversy. How will people be relocated and settled? Is it possible to offer environmental refugees temporary asylum? Will these refugees have any collective rights in the new areas they inhabit? And, lastly, as currently vast areas of the world are being rendered unfit for human habitation, who will pay the costs of all the affected countries during the process of resettlement?

The need for planning for climate refugees comes at a time when many countries are devoting little thought to this emerging issue. Indeed some critics point out that nations have yet to challenge the concept of economic growth itself. The problems of climate refugees cannot be addressed without confronting the socially acceptable definitions of growth and the largely unquestioned faith in its benefits. Limits to growth are actually emerging, notes Richard Heinberg, an expert with the Post Carbon Institute and author of *The End of Growth: Adapting to Our New Economic Reality*.[11] Fossil fuels like oil are nonrenewable, and they are finite; as the world's primary sources of oil and gas run out, fossil fuel companies are turning to increasingly risky and expensive methods of extraction. Wind and solar power can help generate electricity, especially in rural communities, but they are not good options for dealing with issues like urban crowding, the transportation of populations, and expanding food supplies. Preserving and protecting green areas of countries coupled with stabilizing urban growth may be one key to preparing for future problems. Even before countries can deal with the onslaught of climate refugees, they will have to power down the ways they pollute and use up the landscapes and open places. Adds Peter Victor, an economist at Ontario's York University, the idea of progress once had many measures but now relates only to the economy.[12] If we are to deal with large-scale exchanges of population around the planet, we have to recognize that economics does not dominate the larger ecosystem. The limits of the natural world come into play. Ideas such as these need to be kept in perspective as nations debate what to do with climate refugees.

Hopefully, the current attitudes of northern developed countries will change from self-interest to financial support of climate change adaptation programs in the poorer nations in the south.[13] We are now seeing the decoupling of economic growth and greenhouse emissions. Nearly two dozen countries increased their GDP since 2000 while their emissions have stayed flat or gone down, including developed and developing countries alike, the World Resources Institute reported in 2016.[14] This is the result of larger consumption of alternatives to high carbon energy like coal and oil. Articles abound in economic journals about the success of wind and solar power in this regard.

Such optimism may be premature, however. Bill McKibben, journalist and cofounder of the climate advocacy organization 350.org, notes that while one greenhouse gas decreased in the United States, another, far more nefarious one may have increased. Methane, the by-product of natural gas, is a much more potent greenhouse gas—it captures more of the sun's rays. And the boom of hydraulic fracturing (or "fracking") for natural gas in the States and around the world has led to concerns that methane emissions may be the new culprit of climate change.[15]

Regardless, the global economy has largely been running business as usual—as of April 2016, countries around the globe were still planning to build hundreds of new coal-fired power plants.[16] Without more aggressive action to reduce fossil fuel usage, including preventing new sources of fossil fuel emissions, the reductions we have seen thus far will not be enough to prevent catastrophic climate changes. And the decoupling process will require much more effort in poor countries with large populations living in energy poverty. Under "business as usual," coal companies are trying to build new coal plants in a misguided effort to lift developing nations out of poverty. Yet often the coal plants require massive, and expensive, new distribution infrastructure and pollute the communities they intended to help. The idea that petroleum and coal is "cheap" in these communities is not only a farce, but it also ignores the larger problems that emissions bring.[17]

THE UNITED NATIONS' POSITION ON CLIMATE CHANGE REFUGEES

The 1951 UN Convention Relating to the Status of Refugees remains the main plank of legal protection of refugees today. According to the UNHRC, refugee status entitles a person to safe asylum in another country or, barring this possibility, aid and assistance such as financial grants, food, shelter, tools, clinics, and shelters. Neither the Geneva Convention nor the UNHRC protocol of 1967 regard environmental displacement as a determinant of refugee status. A refugee is considered by the United Nations to be a person who is fleeing persecution due to his or her race, religion, nationality, politics, or sectarian origins.[18] In the legal proceedings of the UNHRC, there is no mention of environment as a reason to flee. Nevertheless, environmental migrants are refugees, many of whom have abandoned their homelands on a semipermanent or permanent basis, with little anticipation of return.

Refugee movements within the purview of the United Nations have been generally regarded as unruly and unpredictable, and refugee flows are beyond the control of individual states. Since the 1967 protocol, the United Nations makes the status of the refugee "exceptional" so as to preclude dealing with overwhelming numbers. It also focuses on individuals rather than groups. Unlike traditional refugees, environmental refugees do not have the same legal standing in the international community.

Given the stresses in the international community from war and other worldwide tensions, it will be difficult for nations to add "climate refugee" to the approved asylum list. Some officials in the United Nations fear that by including environmentally displaced persons in the recognized refugee status, the current protection for refugees recognized by the Geneva Convention would be seriously devalued. For the UNHCR the phrase "climate refugee" is a misnomer. According to a recent article in the *Guardian* "there are a number of reasons why 'climate refugee' status does not make sense for people who might have to move."[19] The term is legally contentious and culturally insulting to many migrants.

"Across the world refugees encounter racism and discrimination. Host governments often do little to challenge this [poor treatment]." Thus "the prospect of becoming a refugee comes with a lot of baggage. . . . It explains why many people do not like the term 'climate refugee' and why they do not see the creation of climate-refugee status as a good solution." Media stories of fetid refugee camps and photos of people huddled in small boats condition all too often popular conceptions of refugees.[20] For the UN, people affected by environmental disruptions are matters of "concern." But funding of refugees and politics rests at the heart of the problem. The UNHCR is fearful that it will be overwhelmed by a tsunami of refugees.

In a 2001 article written by sociologist Richard Black of the University of Sussex and funded by the UNHCR, the problem was explored in a manner calculated to reframe the problem as a nonissue. According to Black, "The strength of the academic case [regarding the existence of climate refugees] is often depressingly weak." Hard evidence, argued Black, is a necessary component of an increase in migration at times or in places of more severe environmental degradation that would turn people into international migrants or permanent refugees in their own country. "Moreover," Black concluded, "there remains a danger that academic and policy writing on 'environmental refugees' has more to do with bureaucratic agendas of international organizations and academics than with any real theoretical or empirical insight."[21] Finally, critics of the term "climate refugee" or "environmental refugee" wonder if protection is morally necessary—more a matter of home governments to deal with. As they are quick to point out, a refugee is someone who flees political, ethnic, or religious persecution. So-called environmental or climate refugees do not fill the bill in this regard.

DEFINING "CLIMATE REFUGEE"

The field of refugee studies has grown dramatically since the latter part of the twentieth century.[22] Yet trying to put a starting date on a term of academic inquiry that has no specific organizational history is difficult. However, it is safe to say that the terms "environment" and "refugee" have been linked since 1948, when the term was first used to discuss various aspects of the Palestinian refugee problem. The term "ecological refugee" in official terminology was first used by Lester Brown of Worldwatch Institute in 1976.[23]

Since then, other terms such as "environmentally displaced persons" and "environmental migrants" have also come into popular usage. The term "environmental refugee" has been around for a long time, but it has been sufficiently emotionally and politically charged to sink into the

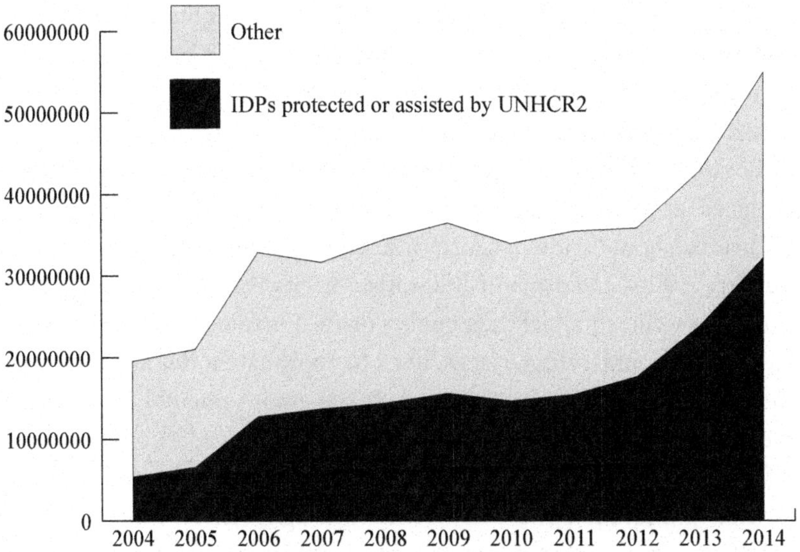

Figure 2.2: Proportion of IDPs increased in past decade. Source: UNHCR.

public consciousness. Recently, however, "climate refugee" has gained traction because of increased media attention and the proliferation of documentary films like *Sun Come Up* (2010), the story of Carteret Islanders in the South Pacific who are forced by climate change to leave their ancestral land to migrate to politically unstable Bougainville in New Guinea's Solomon Islands.[24]

The term "environmental refugee" came into usage in the United Nations in 1985 as a report title for the United Nations Environment Programme.[25] This growing concern of the international community about the consequences of migration resulting from environmental deterioration was reinforced in 1990 by the publication of the first UN Intergovernmental Panel on Climate Change, which stated that the "gravest effects of climate change may be those on human migration as millions will be displaced."[26]

At this writing the UNHCR has moved toward the term "environmentally displaced persons" to keep out of the "refugee" legal thicket. "Refugee," as we have seen, refers to persecuted people whose human rights have been violated. Earthquakes, floods, droughts, and so on may be harmful, but they do not constitute "persecution" as it is currently defined. The term "refugee," in its technical definition, implies persons who have already crossed an international border.

For the purpose of this book we define "environmental" and "climate refugees" as persons who can no longer gain a secure livelihood in their traditional homelands because of events like sea level rise, extreme weather events, and drought and water scarcity that jeopardize their existence or seriously affect their quality of life. Further, after defining *what* an environmental refugee is, we need to apply categories as to whether their flight is forced or anticipatory. Is the environmental degradation the primary cause of their migration or merely an additional cause of refugeedom? Or is the term merely a politically correct one for "undocumented immigrant"? These terms shed little light on how climate change creates refugees within national borders. Yet the number of "internally displaced persons," or IDPs, has been increasing exponentially in recent years (see fig. 2.2). Therefore, our position is that we reject the narrow term of "refugee" currently used by the UN in favor of a more inclusive one that takes environmental factors into consideration.

In a changing world we may have to alter our traditional understanding of the term "refugee" in order to accommodate our awareness of new situations and circumstances that may arise. As late as 2003, researchers at Deutsche Bank in Frankfurt dismissed a future migration flood of political and environmental refugees into Europe as a "fairy tale." In its report the bank argued that concerns in European industrial countries about a major increase in migration were unfounded.[27] Thus as the twentieth century waned, Deutsche Bank reflected the opinions of many Western leaders. Few were prepared for the storm that was to come. While political or religious refugees are protected by international law, it is unclear what conventions and policies protect people displaced by extreme weather events.

Though people in Western developed countries are less likely to become climate refugees, sudden climatic events like Hurricane Katrina in New Orleans can catapult a large population into a realm of environmental refugeedom. In fact, the plight of Hurricane Katrina survivors provoked an interesting discussion in the media over whether it was appropriate to deem them "refugees." The term was criticized by Rev. Jesse Jackson, who said it was "racist" to "call American citizens refugees." Multiple news organizations banned the word in response to this criticism, including the *Washington Post* and the *Boston Globe,* but others argued that the alternative terms—"evacuees" or "displaced people"—were not good enough, not dramatic enough to convey the situation. *New York Times* spokesperson Catherine Mathis said, "Webster's defines a refugee as a person fleeing 'home or country' in search of refuge, and it certainly does justice to the suffering legions driven from their homes by Katrina."[28] *New York Times Magazine* "On Language" columnist, William Safire, said he believes the word "refugee" is "neither racist nor ethnic nor in any way demeaning." The bigger issue, Safire thinks, is that it implies people who have crossed borders because "they do not have the protection of their own country," citing Brookings Institution senior fellow Roberta Cohen. He preferred the terms "Katrina survivors" and "flood victims."[29]

However, it is primarily people in poor, developing countries that have high population density, marginal food stores, health problems, and political instability who will become environmental refugees. As the future unfolds, these climate refugees will be on the move in Africa, Asia, Latin America, and Oceania. Today the greatest numbers of environmental refugees are living in sub-Saharan Africa, the Indian subcontinent, China, Mexico, and Central America. Of the 150 million facing food deficits or famine, 135 million have been affected by severe desertification, with untold millions of farmers in this region who have abandoned traditional farmlands for tropical forest areas.

As the International Organization for Migration has noted, migration, especially a mass influx of migrants, can affect the environment in places of destination as well. Camps and temporary shelters in urban areas can produce strains on public health and water supply and generally degrade local ecosystems.[30] Also, these migrants with their different culture and languages may become a permanent part of urban centers—mostly marginalized groups of the old and the poor and women and children. Not all migrants will be able to cope with new and stressful environments. As information chains become available among affected peoples, many will elect not to migrate at all and will remain internally displaced climate refugees.

As the *Huffington Post* put it, "Xenophobes warn that Europe's cultural identity is at risk, and yet the founding treaty of the EU calls for societies characterized by pluralism, nondiscrimination, tolerance, justice, solidarity, and equality between women and men. That means welcoming refugees and taking steps to integrate them in a way that respects these values and their identity."[31] In 2004, filmmaker Roland Emmerich dramatized the potentially ironic consequences of xenophobia in a scene from *The Day after Tomorrow*: American citizens flee en masse from lightning and a terrible climatic disturbance from the north only to find themselves running up against the very fences they had constructed to keep Mexican migrants out.[32] In Europe a tsunami of displaced Muslims is already producing public outrage over governments' inability to deal with the invasion of local cultures and landscapes. This is coming about largely because people generally have difficulty dealing with sudden unpredictable crises. The net result may be significant increases in violence toward migrants and minority groups.

NATIONAL SECURITY AND INTERNATIONAL EQUITY

The climate refugee issue is fraught with questions about national security. Along with changing climate come internal and cross-border tensions stemming from large-scale migrations. Radical changes in the environment result in resource scarcity and this intensifies social conflict. Weak and failing states in Africa, for example, may suffer from numerous public health problems caused by toxic water supplies.

All of this points to the simple fact that climate debate is rooted in a monstrous problem of national and international inequities spawned by the reluctance or resistance of developed nations to assist developing countries to manage the challenges of climate change. This could result in a rift in north-south relations. Further, climate change could have deep implications for the effectiveness and viability in even stronger existing governments. China, experts argue, will have to play a critical role in all climate change discussions. According to the World Bank, sixteen of the world's twenty most-polluted cities are in China—the air is so polluted that it leads to 400,000 premature deaths every year.[33]

The UN General Assembly is beginning to pay more attention to population displacement and involuntary migration in relation to environmental change. However, the UN is currently more preoccupied with the international security aspects of climate change in terms of loss of physical territory, statelessness, and cultural survival rather than the everyday human impact of environmental changes. Developing policies that will allow the United Nations to adapt its work to the problems of climate change and vulnerable affected populations proceeds at a snail's pace. Meanwhile, climate or environmental refugees could become one of the foremost human crises of our times.

Thus, despite debate over terminology, displaced peoples are on the move. They live in countries wracked by conflict and environmental disasters. They have no special laws to protect them, and their plight until recently has garnered little public attention. They appear in the jargon as IDPs (internally displaced persons), but IDPs hardly make their way into the mainstream news. They are at the mercy of their own governments, which are often either unable to help, actively hostile, or reluctant to admit outsiders who might interfere.

The more complex society becomes, the more vulnerable it is to changes inside and out. Issues like how to handle an influx of climate refugees are not easily resolved. In addition, in the arena of international politics, large amounts of spending are for weapons that can provide military solutions to problems that might be addressed otherwise. Looking out at the world from the safe, prosperous confines of the United States, it is evident that America, just by itself, is neglecting many international environmental problems.

The struggle for access to natural resources will accelerate. Conflict over valuable resources—and the power and wealth they confer—has become part of the matrix of climate migration. This conflict intersects with ethnic, religious, and tribal antagonisms. The struggle over access to oil and other natural resources on the planet is well known. But as Michael Klare has noted in his work *Resource Wars: The New Landscape of Global Conflict*, "Struggles over access to energy sources are likely to break out in other parts of the globe as well." Water and access to it will most likely provoke the most intense conflicts in the future, and these conflicts will force many people to seek sanctuary elsewhere.[34]

In a worst-case scenario some nations that are already failing, like Libya and the Sudan, may collapse, leaving them open to terrorist rule. Outmigration of populations may involve millions. The arrival of migrants in host countries from different ethnic and cultural backgrounds may be the source of great social and class conflict on the continent. As World Bank economist Nicholas Stern and others have forcefully argued, the potential for conflict is greater if the host country is either underdeveloped or experiencing economic problems.[35] Greece, Pakistan, Lebanon, and India are good examples.

The institutional frameworks for addressing migration, displacement, and relocation in the context of climate change at regional and global levels do not exist outside of the usual refugee cant. No right to admission to a foreign state in the case of displacement due to environmental hazards or disasters is enshrined in international law. In West Africa, for example, a region with more than its share of environmental woes, there is currently no consensus internationally or in the West African region on procedures to admit or protect peoples crossing borders in disaster contexts. Rural renewal, through advanced agricultural practices and introduction of better strains of seeds, faces a major challenge because populations in West Africa often opt for migration rather than farming as environmental degradation continues apace.

Global governance of international migration of climate and political refugees has been much more controversial than has been the case regarding most transnational issues. For example, notes Susan Martin of Georgetown University, there is not a single country today that is not affected by the movement of some 232 million international migrants with a world of personal agendas and ambitions.[36] Management of climate refugees, specifically, cannot be handled by unilateral action.

In a world of work and settlement, placing climate refugees involves working not only with nations but also with unions, humanitarian organizations, multinational corporations, and labor recruitment agencies. Most states are unclear as to what they want to achieve through their immigration/refugee policies. And many people have difficulty seeing either the short-term or long-term benefit of having large numbers of migrants in their midst. As Martin notes, "Public opinion also is often ambivalent, at best, about immigration." Martin is more realistic than some scholars on the subject of climate refugees, other refugees, and international governance. According to scholar Susan Martin, "the immigration policies of most destination countries are not conducive to receiving large numbers of environmental migrants unless they enter through already existing admission catgories."[37]

While we are aware that large numbers of refugees suffer in the world because of ethnic conflicts, war, and totalitarian regimes, that does not detract from the fact that we see refugees as victims of undisputed climate change impacts. Similarly, because of these very significant environmental disruptions on the planet, we do not see much value in speculations about whether or not climate refugees are a temporary or permanent phenomenon. Climate refugees are with us because our climate is undergoing major transformations. The response of the international community to these transformations is not adequate and is still at its early stages. One of the significant consequences of the end of the Cold War is the diffusion of power. The United States remains a dominant player on the world stage but has neither the moral influence nor the political clout that it enjoyed in earlier years. The ability of the United States to address these issues is further complicated by climate skeptics in the media and Congress who reject the overwhelming consensus of the global scientific community. Meanwhile, terrorism is a horrible counterfoil to the actions of all responsible nations. Currently there is no body of government and no international authority mandated with responsibility for climate-induced displacement. Therein lies the problem. Yet, too many elected officials appear determined to either ignore or refute the facts about climate change—even where global warming is already hurting their communities and their constituents.

Until now, although population displacement by war and nationalism has been a common development in the modern era, refugees have been on the margins of our historical thinking. Opportunities for resettlement were often so limited that the modern era saw the rise of the refugee camp. In recent years the largest groups of global refugees have been internally displaced by either sectarian violence or environmental change. They have not been forced out of the nation in which they claimed citizenship. Thus in the modern era we see the emergence of international climate migrants and the internally displaced by natural disasters—a new kind of "refugeedom."

NOTES

UNHCR, "Worldwide Displacement Hits All-Time High as War and Persecution Increase," http://www.unhcr.org/news/latest/2015/6/558193896/worldwide-displacement-hits-all-time-high-war-persecution-increase.html.

1. Frank Biermann and Ingrid Boas, "Climate Change and Human Migration: Towards a Global Governance System to Protect Climate Refugees," http://www.globalgovernancewatch.org/library/doclib/20160205_ClimateChangeandHumanMigration.pdf.
2. "Human tide: the real migration crisis," Christian Aid, May 2007, https://www.christianaid.org.uk/Images/human-tide.pdf.
3. Michael Marrus, *The Unwanted: European Refugees from the First World War through the Cold War* (Philadelphia: Temple University Press, 2001), 299.
4. Report of the United Nations High Commissioner for Refugees, New York: United Nations, January 1, 1995.
5. Branko Milanovic, "The Economic Causes of Migration," *The Globalist*, October 22, 2013.
6. Guillermina Jasso, Douglas S. Massey, Mark R. Rosenzweig, and James P. Smith, "The New Immigrant Survey in the US: The Experience over Time," Migration Policy Institute, January 2003.
7. Michael Head, "Refugees, Global Inequality, and a New Concept of Citizenship," *Australian International Law Journal* (2002): 59.
8. Colin P. Kelly, Shahrzad Mohtadi, Mark A. Cane, Richard Seager, and Yochanan Kushnir, "Climate Change in the Fertile Crescent and Implications of the Recent Syrian Drought," *Proceedings of the National Academy of Sciences* 112, no. 11 (2015).
9. See Paul Daley, "How Ruddock Urged Europe to Get Tougher," http://www.theage.com.au/articles/2002/07/20/1026898930680.html.
10. Bruno Rego, "Environmental Citizenship as Anthropology of Hope: A Tale of a Realistic Utopia," Transaction Papers, 13th Annual Conference, Environmental Justice and Citizenship, Mansfield College, Oxford, July 2014.
11. Richard Heinberg, *The End of Growth: Adapting to Our New Economic Reality* (New York: New Society Publications, 2011).
12. Peter Victor, "Questioning Economic Growth," *Nature* 468 (November 18, 2010): 370.
13. Heinberg, *End of Growth;* Eben Fodor, *Better Not Bigger* (New York: New Society Publishers, 2007); Peter Victor, *Managing without Growth, Slow by Design* (Northampton, MA: Edward Elgar Publishers, 2008).
14. Nate Aden, "The Roads to Decoupling: 21 Countries Are Reducing Carbon Emissions While Growing GDP," World Resources Institute, April 5, 2016.
15. Bill McKibben, "Global Warming's Terrifying New Chemistry," *The Nation*, March 23, 2016.

16. Brad Plumer, "Hundreds of Coal Plants Are Still Being Planned Worldwide—Enough to Cook the Planet," Vox, updated April 5, 2016.

17. Denise Robbins, "Experts Debunk the Coal Industry's 'Energy Poverty' Argument against the Pope's Climate Action," Media Matters, July 6, 2015.

18. UNHCR, Convention and Protocol Relating to the Status of Refugees (1952), chapter I, article 1, section A, subsection (2).

19. Alex Randall, "Don't Call Them 'Refugees': Why Climate-Change Victims Need a Different Label," *Guardian*, September 18, 2014

20. Alex Randall, "Don't Call Them 'Refugees'; Michael Werz and Laura Conley, "Climate Change, Migration, and Conflict: Addressing Complex Crisis Scenarios in the 21st Century," Center for American Progress, January 2012.

21. Richard Black, "Environmental Refugees: Myth or Reality," New Issues in Refugee Research, Working Paper No. 34, UNHCR, March 2001.

22. Richard Black, "Fifty Years of Refugee Studies," *International Migration Review* 35, no. 1 (Spring 2001): 57.

23. Lester R. Brown, Patricia L. McGrath, and Bruce Stokes, *Twenty-Two Dimensions of the Population Problem*, Worldwatch Paper 5 (Washington, DC: Worldwatch Institute, March 1976).

24. http://redantelopefilms.com/project/sun-come-up/

25. Essam El-Hinnawi, *Environmental Refugees* (Nairobi: United Nations Environment Programme, 1985)

26. Intergovernmental Panel on Climate Change (IPCC), *Policymakers' Summary of the Potential Impacts of Climate Change*, 1990, (Geneva: IPCC Secretariat, 1990), 20.

27. Deutsche Bank Research, "International Migration: Who, Where, and Why?," *Current Issues*, August 1, 2003, 4.

28. "Calling Katrina Survivors 'Refugees' Stirs Debate," Associated Press, September 7, 2005.

29. William Safire, "Katrina Words," *New York Times*, September 18, 2005

30. international Organization for Migration, "Migration, Climate Change, and the Environment," https://www.iom.int/sites/default/files/our_work/ICP/IDM/iom_policybrief_may09_en.pdf.

31. Judith Sunderland, "Fear and Loathing of Refugees in Europe," *Huffington Post*, February 9, 2016, http://www.huffingtonpost.com/judith-sunderland/fear-and-loathing-of-refu_b_9188204.html.

32. Etienne Piguet, "Climate Change and Forced Migration," New Issues in Refugee research, Research Paper No. 153 (UNHCR, 2008).

33. Christine Lagorio, "The Most Polluted Places on Earth," CBS Evening News, June 6, 2007

34. Michael T. Klare, *Resource Wars: The New Landscape of Global Conflict* (New York: Henry Holt, 2001), xi.

35. Nicholas Stern, *The Stern Review on the Economics of Climate Change*, (London: London School of Economics, 2006).

36. Susan Martin, *International Migration: Evolving Trends from the Early Twentieth Century to the Present* (Cambridge, UK: Cambridge University Press, 2014).

37. Susan Martin, "Climate Change and International Migration," Institute for the Study of International Migration, June, 2010, p.3.

PART TWO
Pressure Points and Regional Analysis

3

What Happens When Your Country Drowns?

> If you were faced with the threat of the disappearance of your nation, what would you do?
>
> *Enele Sopoaga, prime minister of Tuvalu, at the United Nations climate summit in Lima, Peru, December 2014*

For those familiar with the term "climate change refugees," Pacific islands may be the first thing that come to mind. There are hundreds of small, low-lying island nations in the Pacific Ocean, with pristine beaches surrounded by endless seas. They are magnificently beautiful, and a prime tourist destination, but it is easy to see how global warming imperils their existence. As the seas slowly rise—slowly but at an inevitable and increasing pace—their land disappears inch by inch. Sea level rise is a clear, inarguable result of climate change, and if it continues unabated, ocean tides will keep encroaching farther on island shores, potentially wiping out hundreds of islands from the map. It settles the question of whether, in the future, will we need to make new maps and globes.

THE RISING SEAS: SLOW-MOVING CRISIS WITH DRASTIC CONSEQUENCES

The sheer variance of impacts from climate change can be difficult to grasp. Some regions will see severe, unabated drought while others will face floods and storms intense enough to wipe out entire industries. While the average temperature rises, cold winter weather will also become more extreme in some areas due to a weakened polar vortex. Scientists have connected global warming to monsoons, heat waves, storms, coral bleaching, snowstorms, and even increased shark attacks. The science is more settled on some predictions than on others, but one impact is a constant throughout the world: global warming is causing the oceans to rise.

Slowly but surely, the global sea level is rising approximately one-tenth of an inch each year.[1] The National Oceanic and Atmospheric Association (NOAA) has calculated sea level rise at a rate of 0.12 inches per year, more than twice as fast as the preceding ninety years.[2] Every increase in sea level rise causes the tide to encroach much further onto the shore, threatening coastal homes and communities around the world. In 2013 conservative estimates projected between one and three feet of sea level rise by 2100, but now those projections are outdated, and sea levels are expected to rise between three and six feet by the end of the century.[3] It seems every new study about melting ice caps and sea level rise paints a more dire picture than the last.

Two major factors are causing the seas to rise at such an unprecedented rate, both of which are connected to warmer global temperatures. The first is the melting of the ice sheets. Glaciers, polar ice caps, huge ice sheets, are heating up and releasing more water each year. Standard depictions of global warming tend to include images of glaciers disappearing—from the Himalayas in India, to Mount Kilimanjaro in Africa, to Glacier National Park in the Rockies. The glacier melt is leading to a surplus of runoff that eventually leads to the ocean and causes sea levels to rise. The giant ice sheets in the Antarctic and on top of Greenland are melting at an accelerated rate. Antarctica is of particular concern, with its massive ice shelves threatening to break off and collapse into the sea.[4] Indeed, Antarctica may have passed the "point of no return" for saving its western ice shelves. Once they break off of land, they float in the sea and raise the ocean sea levels.[5]

This is a good time to clarify the difference between sea ice and land ice. "Sea ice" refers to the ice caps and glaciers that float freely in the sea. "Land ice" refers to the huge ice sheets and glaciers that are fixed to continental plates. The Arctic consists solely of sea ice; whereas the Antarctic is topped with massive amounts of land ice. The two poles provide contrasting concerns for the impacts of global warming. Arctic ice is melting at an incredibly alarming rate, eliminating the habitat for many vital Arctic species, but it does not contribute to sea level rise. Consider the Arctic as a large ice cube in a glass of water. When the ice cube melts, the level of water in the glass won't change. But Antarctica is more like a huge ice cube placed on *top* of the already full glass of water, and when it melts, the glass will overflow.

Antarctic ice is actually increasing for the time being (warmer air leads to more precipitation in the form of snow, which accumulates on the ice sheet), but global warming will eventually reverse this trend. The six key glaciers on the West Antarctic Ice Sheet are releasing ice into the sea more quickly than can be replaced with new snow. One glacier, the Thwaites Glacier, is collapsing slowly, which could destabilize more ice. This means the massive amount of what is currently land ice in the Antarctic will one day become sea ice, contributing to sea level rise. These six Antarctic glaciers alone—Thwaites, Pine Island, Haynes, Pope, Smith, and Kohler—will be responsible for an extra four feet of sea level rise over the next two hundred years. It will be a slow-moving crisis, but a crisis nonetheless.

The other factor in the sea level rise is ocean expansion. Much of the world's warming is being absorbed by the oceans, which is causing them to expand. It's a simple act of physics: as water gets warmer, its molecules move around more quickly and are a bit farther apart, and the volume increases.

Most of the global warming in the past couple of decades has been trapped in the oceans. When you hear some people talk about a recent "slowdown" in global warming (usually people trying to cast doubt on climate change), they're referring to surface air temperatures, not the temperature of the planet as a whole. Ninety percent of the heat generated by burning greenhouse gases is absorbed into the oceans, which have a far greater heat storage capacity than the atmosphere.[6]

The oceans are, in fact, warming at an unprecedented rate—fifteen times faster over the past ten thousand years, according to a study led

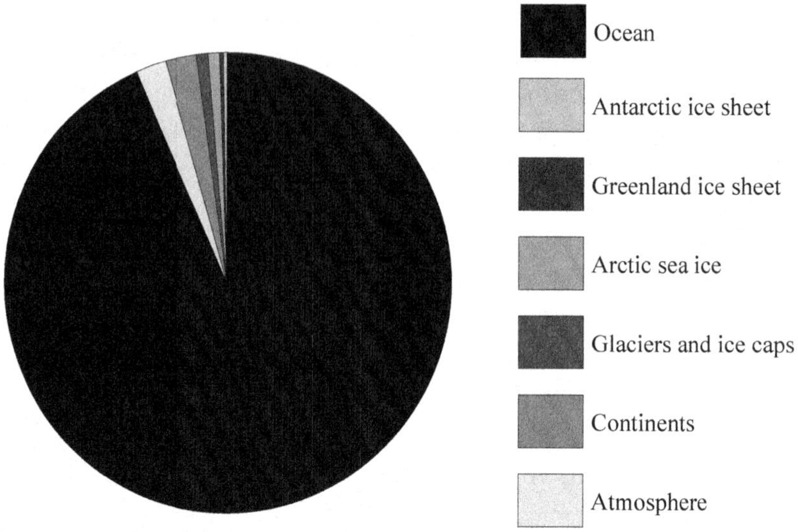

Figure 3.1: Global warming is mostly absorbed by the oceans. Global warming for the period 1993 to 2003 calculated from IPCC AR4 5.2.2.3.

by researchers at Rutgers University. The study authors explained that oceans are acting as a "storehouse" for heat and energy. This storage potential may have had a hand in slowing down the rate of global air temperature warming. However, this storehouse is limited; at the very least: "It may buy us some time . . . to come to terms with climate change," according to the study's lead author, Yair Rosenthal. "But it's not going to *stop* climate change."[7]

When the warming of the oceans combines with the melting of the glaciers and ice sheets, the reality of sea level rise is very alarming indeed. With the most conservative estimates at one to four feet, and more recent estimates much higher, it is almost certain that low-lying islands will be completely submerged. But even before they become completely submerged in the ocean, low-lying islands will still face extreme damage from the rising sea levels. Every storm surge or high tide slowly washes away bits of their land. Though ephemeral, the surges and tides can erode beaches—which often contain food sources and houses—far before the beaches are overtaken by sea level rise.[8]

CYCLONES: THE RIPPING THREAT

While the sea levels are rising slowly, extraordinary cyclones rip through the Pacific Ocean, passing over the Pacific Islands easily. There is not yet strong consensus as to whether global warming will cause cyclones to happen more frequently, but it is certain that they will become more extreme as sea levels continue to rise. Higher seas cause greater storm surges and resulting flooding, inundating villages on the islands and damaging communities beyond repair.

In March 2015, Cyclone Pam ravaged a number of Pacific islands in the Melanesia region northeast of Australia with wind speeds up to 200 miles per hour. It first tore through Tuvalu, causing a state of emergency and displacing about 4,000 people—nearly half of its population.[9] Days later, it struck the island nation Vanuatu, directly west of Fiji, a broadly scattered volcanic archipelago comprising thirteen large islands and over seventy small ones. Vanuatu is home to only about 260,000 people, and Cyclone Pam displaced 3,300 from their homes.[10]

When a category 5 cyclone like Pam blasts through, it is as if all the threats that the Pacific Islands face from global warming combine forces and hit at once. Powerful winds and rains tear the roofs from homes and flatten buildings. Even cement buildings are ripped apart. In Vanuatu's capital city, 90 percent of the buildings and houses were destroyed. The storm surges inundated entire beaches and villages for days, providing a snapshot of future sea level rise. Vanuatu's president, Baldwin Lonsdale, attributed the devastating cyclone to climate change: "We see the level of sea rise.... The cyclone seasons, the warm, the rain, all this is affected. ... This year we have more than in any year. Yes, climate change is contributing to this."[11]

Indeed, there is a direct link between sea level rise and the impacts of cyclones. Higher seas cause the storm surges to break more ground and reach farther inland. And as the atmosphere and the oceans continue to warm, the cyclones are expected to become stronger. With warmer sea surface temperatures comes increased water vapor and, subsequently, more precipitation. For every one degree centigrade of warming, rainfall from cyclones can be expected to increase by 8 percent.[12]

In response to Cyclone Pam, the Vanuatu village named Takara made a bold move: it voted to move to higher ground. Village chief Benjamin Tamata told the Associated Press that he plans to resettle the village one thousand feet inland to avoid the rising seas. He noted that many villagers escaped the storm by taking shelter in a school but that a long-term solution was needed.[13]

Takara's decision is not unique; nearly a decade earlier, the Leteu settlement on the Vanuatu island of Tegua was forced to resettle inland in order to escape the rising seas. Dangerously high tides had flooded the village five times a year, regularly creating perilous, life-threatening conditions. In 2005 the village of about one hundred people moved half a kilometer inland onto higher ground in the mountainous island. The United Nations Environment Programme said the village was one of the first, "if not the first, to be formally moved out of harm's way as a result of climate change."[14]

THE MALDIVES: THE POSTER CHILD OF CLIMATE CHANGE

If Pacific islands are the poster child for the climate refugee issue, then Mohamed Nasheed, former president of the Maldives, might be the face. The Maldives have an average height of seven feet above sea level, so the immediate dangers they face from climate change are clear. Indeed, the country is well known for taking a stance on this existential threat.

The young, charismatic Nasheed elevated the plight of the Maldives to global prominence when he was president of the island nation, making impassioned speeches to global delegates at United Nations conferences. In 2009, ahead of the UN climate conference in Copenhagen, Nasheed arranged a cabinet meeting to sign a document calling on nations to slash their atmosphere-warming greenhouse gas emissions. This, by itself, is not necessarily newsworthy, but the location was unique: the cabinet held the meeting fifteen feet underwater. Eleven cabinet ministers joined Nasheed in scuba suits, where they communicated with hand signals and white boards. Surrounded by snorkeling journalists, Nasheed said, "We're now actually trying to send our message, let the world know what is happening, and what will happen to the Maldives if climate change is not checked. . . . If the Maldives cannot be saved today we do not feel that there is much of a chance for the rest of the world."[15]

Nasheed helped drive discussion of climate refugees into global media. He told the *Sydney Morning Herald* in 2012 that fourteen Maldivian islands had already been abandoned due to erosion. He and his administration took steps to plan for the very real possibility of relocating their entire nation, including setting up a sovereign savings account from tourism revenues for this purpose. The savings account was one step ahead of some other island nations that have been considering planned migration as a response to rising sea levels. Nasheed considered purchasing swaths of land in Australia, because he did not want his people "'living in tents' for years, or decades, as refugees," he told the *Herald*.[16]

Unfortunately, Nasheed is no longer president. The country faced political troubles before and after his time as president under the autocracy of Maumoon Abdul Gayoom. Nasheed stepped down from office amid public outcry surrounding the arrest of the chief judge of the nation's criminal court and then lost the presidential election to Gayoom's half-brother, Yameen Abdul Gayoom, in 2013.[17] Nasheed characterized the situation as a political coup.[18] He was later arrested under antiterrorism charges. It was a very unfortunate ending to what was for a time a positive moment in the history of the Maldives.

Because of Nasheed's actions, the Maldives was among the first well-known climate refugee nations. And it is certainly not the only one. Hundreds of low-lying island nations face the same existential threat from sea level rise, which could eventually erase them from existence. A few other islands might actually take the claim for being home to the first official climate change refugees—most notably, Kiribati.

KIRIBATI: "THE WORLD'S FIRST CLIMATE REFUGEE"

A high-profile refugee legal case between Kiribati and New Zealand had potential to break new ground in how climate change is considered in terms of refugeedom. At risk of being deported from New Zealand, Kiribati-native Ioane Teitiota has launched a bid to become the world's first climate refugee, calling on the New Zealand government to allow him to stay.

Kiribati, like many low-lying islands, is bordered by a sea wall that is several feet high to prevent the worst of the ocean waves brought by storm surges from flooding into the shoreline and eroding the land. But storm surges and ocean waves riding high tides had destroyed part of the sea wall and flooded Teitiota's family's compound twice in four years. So they decided to pack their bags and leave. In 2007 Teitiota and his wife, Angua Erika, moved to New Zealand on work visas. Four years and three kids later, his visa had expired, and he appealed to the New Zealand government to extend his status. His lawyer on the case, Michael Kidd, saw there was a larger story than a single family appealing for a visa extension. This was the case of a climate change refugee.[19]

While in New Zealand, Teitiota learned the fuller story about the constant threat his island faced. Similar cases of people fleeing from Kiribati had been tried, unsuccessfully, in New Zealand. Seeing this as a problem larger than himself, Teitiota decided to take a unique approach to his immigration case and make it about climate change. His lawyer made the case that the Teitiotas had been persecuted by industrialized nations who failed to keep greenhouse gas emissions in check.

The legal battle spanned several years. In court, Teitiota cited the poor environmental conditions that made living in Kiribati a never-ending hardship. Kidd emphasized that this was a result of indirect persecution. Their case was rejected by both New Zealand's high court and the court of appeals. But after each rejection, Kidd refiled the papers seeking refugee status for Teitiota and his family. Each time, climate change was mentioned prominently as being responsible for the Teitiota family's refugee status. If the court ruled in their favor, the case would have immense global implications. It was finally brought to New Zealand's Supreme Court, the final avenue of appeal for the Teitiotas to reside permanently in New Zealand as refugees from climate change, but was rejected in July 2015.[20] The Teitiotas, according to New Zealand's court, did not meet the technical definition for "refugee" as defined in the 1951 Convention Relating to the Status of Refugees: someone who, "owing to well-founded fear of being persecuted for reasons of race, religion, nationality, membership of a particular social group or political opinion, is outside the country of his nationality and is unable or, owing to such fear, is unwilling to avail himself of the protection of that country."[21] They, like many other Kiribatis, do not yet have a standing to be protected under refugee laws. They simply do not fit into the half-century-old definition of "refugees."

In the end, the New Zealand government deported Teitiota. He returned to Kiribati in September 2015. But less than a week later, the former president of East Timor, José-Ramos Horta, offered a home to Teitiota and his family in his country, the nearby island nation Timor-Leste. Affected by the story, Horta offered to fly the Teitiotas to his country and help Ioane find a job.[22]

The president of Kiribati, Anote Tong, is not waiting for the legal definition of "climate change refugee" to change before taking action. Kiribati has a population of about one hundred thousand and spans a mere 313 square miles.[23] In recent years the country has faced severe storms and flooding that threaten its food and water supply. In response, the president of Kiribati has purchased land in Fiji—over five thousand acres. In the short term, Fiji's land can be used to cultivate food if Kiribati's land becomes infertile from saltwater erosion. In the long term, this land may be used to resettle the Kiribati population. The Kiribatis call it "migration with dignity." Walter Kaelin, a representative of the Nansen Initiative on Disaster-Induced Cross-Border Displacement, said this is a smart move: "They want to be able to choose more or less where they go. In that sense they want to remain masters of their own destiny."[24]

President Tong provides a provocative example of how an island nation is taking initiative to act on climate change. In addition to planning for the worst-case scenario, he is asking nations to work harder to mitigate climate change as well. Tong called for a worldwide moratorium against new coal mines, which would make great progress in reducing future carbon emissions. Ahead of the United Nations Framework Convention on Climate Change (UNFCCC) in Paris in December 2015, Tong wrote a letter to world leaders, asking: "Let us join together as a global community and take action now. . . . I urge you to support this call for a moratorium on new coal mines and coal mine expansions."[25] The nation-states achieved a landmark international agreement for climate change action at the conference, but in order to prevent the worst-case scenario for sea level rise, the world will need to ramp up efforts to address climate change in the years to come.

TUVALU: ANOTHER REFUGEE CASE MAKES WAVES

Yet another high-profile refugee court case has been driving conversation in the media. In this case, Sigeo Alesana and his family fled their imperiled island nation, Tuvalu, and were granted residency in New Zealand. However, there is a key difference between this case and that of the Teitiotas. Teitiota and his lawyer made climate change the centerpiece of their appeal, while the Alesanas used additional means to build support for their case. This has led experts to question whether the Alesanas can really be called "climate change refugees."

Tuvalu, located between Australia and Hawaii, averages about two meters above sea level. Experts predict it could disappear somewhere between thirty and fifty years from now.[26] Alesana and his family fled the country in 2007 for New Zealand and lost legal status in 2009. Unable to obtain work visas, they applied for refugee status in 2012, claiming to be threatened by climate change in Tuvalu. After their case was initially dismissed, it was ultimately approved in 2014, when New Zealand's Immigration and Protection Tribunal granted them permanent residency. The tribunal explicitly mentioned climate change in its decision, writing that Alesana's children in particular were "vulnerable to natural disasters and the adverse impact of climate change."[27]

However, the tribunal took additional factors into account, most importantly, familial ties. It "avoided a clear decision on whether climate change can or cannot be reason enough for refugees to be granted residency," reported the *Washington Post*.[28]

There is dispute over whether or not climate change itself played a role in the Alesanas' residency decision. Some experts argued that the case will not affect the status of future potential climate change refugees. Vernon Rive, a senior lecturer in law at Auckland University of Technology Law School, said, "I don't see it as delivering any kind of 'verdict' on climate change as such." He added, "What this decision will not do is open the gates to all people from places such as Kiribati, Tuvalu and Bangladesh who may suffer hardship because of the impacts of climate change."[29] Still, the fact that climate change was mentioned in the court's decision did not go unnoticed. The case was closely followed by immigration and environmental experts. The *Washington Post* called it "a landmark refugee ruling that could mark the beginning of a wave of similar cases" in Tuvalu and elsewhere.[30]

MARSHALL ISLANDS: DESTINED TO MIGRATE

"The Marshall Islands likely won't exist if we warm the planet 2 degrees," reported CNN's John Sutter. "It's one of the clearest injustices of climate change."[31]

Near the equator and slightly over the international date line, the Marshall Islands consist of a string of twenty-four low-lying atolls. Nearly seventy thousand people live on the numerous islands and islets. The islands average little more than three and a half feet above sea level and are ranked as the most endangered by climate change. "Out here in the middle of the Pacific Ocean climate change has arrived," argues Marshall Island president Christopher Loeak. Unless the Western developed nations create a carbon-free world by 2050, "no seawall will be high enough to save my country."[32]

These islands were the subject of a high-profile, long-term 2015 CNN investigation called "Two Degrees." In it, Sutter examined what our world could look like if it were warmed by two degrees centigrade, "the agreed-upon threshold for dangerous climate change."[33] The two-degrees series topics were submitted, and voted upon, by CNN's audience. The first story chosen: Pacific Island climate change refugees. This alone—the fact that a mainstream media audience voted on climate change refugees as one of the most important topics of our time—signifies a change in how people are reacting to the issue of climate change refugees and how they want to learn more. It is unlikely that CNN's audience was even aware of this issue ten years ago.

Sutter's climate change refugee report began by examining a family who woke up in the middle of the night to salt water flooding through their home; it went on to detail how their communities are threatened by high tides and rising seas. Sutter reported that many families are already deciding to move away, unable to manage the constant flooding. In his report, Sutter was surprised by the nonchalance in governmental and scientific discussion regarding the islands' inevitable fate, such as that in the Marshall Islands.[34]

Meanwhile, the country itself is taking the issue very seriously, in stark contrast with the ponderous international talks and scientific reports about the issue, deliberating the climate policies, possible choices, and subsequent impacts at stake. Currently, a bizarre migration event is taking place from the Marshall Islands to Springdale, Arkansas. Of the Marshallese population of sixty-eight thousand, 15 percent currently live in Springdale, the largest population outside of the Marshalls Islands themselves. It is about the farthest away they could possibly get from life in the Marshalls, a place "as landlocked as they come."[35] The Marshalls has a consul office set up there. Some Marshall natives work in the poultry industry; Springdale is home to the worldwide headquarters of Tyson Foods. A community of Marshallese has blossomed there; once extant, it becomes an attractive destination for others to move into as well.

The Marshall Islands and the United States have a unique relationship that allows the Marshallese to live and work freely in the country without a visa. After the American victory in the Pacific in World War II, the Marshalls became a Pacific Trust Territory under the supervision of the United States. The Marshalls achieved full sovereignty as an independent nation under the protection of the United States after 1979. The United States still maintains a military base on one of the Marshall atolls, and due to the Compact of Free Association the Marshallese are allowed to enter the United States for study or work. But their right of permanent residency remains unclear.

Many Marshallese residents have not yet resigned to leaving their country forever. The president's daughter, Milan Loeak, told Sutter, "I don't want to entertain that question. I think people should be saying, 'What can we do to help?' instead of saying, 'When will you go?'"[36]

In 2014 poet and Marshall Island resident Kathy Jetnil-Kijiner read a poem before the United Nations, bringing the hundreds of delegates to tears. The poem was written to her seven-month-old daughter, promising to protect her from the dangers of global warming. Here is an excerpt:

dear matafele peinam,
i want to tell you about that lagoon
that lucid, sleepy lagoon lounging against the sunrise

men say that one day
that lagoon will devour you
they say it will gnaw at the shoreline
chew at the roots of your breadfruit trees
gulp down rows of your seawalls
and crunch your island's shattered bones

they say you, your daughter
and your granddaughter, too
will wander rootless
with only a passport to call home
dear matafele peinam,

don't cry

mommy promises you

no one
will come and devour you
no greedy whale of a company sharking through political seas
no backwater bullying of businesses with broken morals
no blindfolded bureaucracies gonna push
this mother ocean over
the edge

no one's drowning, baby
no one's moving
no one's losing
their homeland
no one's gonna become
a climate change refugee

or should i say
no one else

to the carteret islanders of papua new guinea
and to the taro islanders of the solomon islands
i take this moment
to apologize to you
we are drawing the line here
because baby we are going to fight
your mommy daddy
bubu jimma your country and president too
we will all fight[37]

Like the other island communities, the Marshallese are not waiting for the rest of the world to act. In its submission to the United Nations climate negotiations, the country pledged to cut its emissions by one-third by 2025. It is the first developing nation to pledge carbon reductions.[38] And it is urging Australia to do the same.[39]

Island nations are already dealing with the existential threat posed by climate change. In the Carteret Islands, Papua New Guinea islands in the southwest Pacific Ocean, entire communities have already moved to higher ground on the mainland.[40] High tides have already inundated the islands, "destroying crops, wells, and homes," *Business Insider* reported. The Torres Strait Islands are located between Australia and New Guinea and are made up of 274 islands with a population over 8,000. The 100 people living on the island of Tegua were declared the world's "first climate change refugees" by the United Nations in 2005. A one-meter rise of sea levels could make the Federated States of Micronesia completely uninhabitable. One man was seen standing shin-deep in water, where a cemetery used to be. Micronesia's ambassador to the UN told ABC News, "Even the dead are no longer safe in my country."[41]

MIGRATION WITH DIGNITY

The Pacific islands will need to adapt to the impacts of climate change. Even the most aggressive fossil fuel reductions—though important—will only slow the rise of the oceans. In turn, communities in the Pacific are talking about "migration with dignity." Rather than succumbing to the inevitable fate of their homes being destroyed, they are taking charge of their own destiny. This could involve several things, as explained in the *Guardian*: "It could involve planned relocation, where entire communities move together. Cultural practices, family connections and customs are maintained and the community is reestablished in a safer location. Or it can mean migration bit by bit and integration into new communities. Many people from Pacific island nations are already working and studying abroad. Some see the continuation of this trend as the solution."[42] The small island nation of Vanuatu, for one, is planning to migrate its population farther inland. But this option is not viable for the countries comprised of atolls and sandbars that do not have a "farther inland."

The Carteret Islands also have plans to "migrate with dignity," much like Kiribati. They call it "Tulele Peisa," which in their native language means "sailing the waves on our own."[43] The program provides training and education so that the community members can make informed decisions about their own future. It also researches sustainable living practices for those who choose to stay as long as they are able. Ursula Rakova, an environmental advocate from the Carteret Islands said, "Our plan is one in which we remain as independent and self-sufficient as possible. We wish to maintain our cultural identity and live sustainably wherever we are."[44] The solution for preserving a single community's identity and culture—such as Rakova's—is not found in drawn-out international negotiations. The community's residents need to take their fates into their own hands.

SMALL ISLAND DEVELOPING STATES MAKE GLOBAL APPEAL

As island nations plan to relocate their population to escape the effects of global warming, other questions arise: When will they need to do this? And what can the developed countries do to give them more time?

These nations are urging the rest of the globe to reduce their fossil fuel emissions. A group of island nations in the Pacific, the Caribbean, and other seas—called the Small Island Developing States (SIDS)—joined together in 2015 at the UN Security Council to ask for help in combating climate change. This council, reported Agence France Presse (AFP), typically hosts debates on threats of war and political conflict concerning countries like Syria and Ukraine. Climate change is usually reserved for a different agency within the UN, the Framework Convention on Climate Change (UNFCCC).[45] Yet because of the environmental security crisis that island nations are exposed to, the Security Council is becoming an ever more appropriate arena for discussing climate change.

The small islands, SIDS, pleaded for "financial and technical assistance to help them avoid becoming washed away in the rising tides and powerful storms caused by global warming." Tong said the plight of his country has been overlooked by the United Nations for too long and he hoped the appeal would change that, AFP reported. Tong stated: "Can we as leaders return today to our people and be confident enough to say . . . that no matter how high the sea rises, no matter how severe the storms get, there are credible technical solutions to raise your islands and your homes and the necessary resources are available to ensure that all will be in place before it is too late?"[46]

How long it will take to find solutions for the Pacific island climate refugees is uncertain. It rests partially upon how long it takes to reach strong international action on climate change. Now the appeal to industrialized nations has been made. Time will tell if they listen.

NOTES

https://unfccc.int/files/meetings/lima_dec_2014/statements/application/pdf/cop20_hls_tuvalu.pdf.

1. C. H. Carling, E. Morrow, R. E. Kopp, and J. X. Mitrovica, "Probabilistic Reanalysis of Twentieth-Century Sea-Level Rise," *Nature*, January 22, 2015.

2. National Oceanic and Atmospheric Administration, "Is Sea Level Rising?" http://oceanservice.noaa.gov/facts/sealevel.html

3. Brandon Miller, "Expert: We're 'locked in' to 3-Foot Sea Level Rise," CNN, September 4, 2015, http://www.cnn.com/2015/08/27/us/nasa-rising-sea-levels/.

4. Andrea Thompson, "Melt of Key Antarctic Glaciers 'Unstoppable,' Studies Find," ClimateCentral.org, May 12, 2014, http://www.climatecentral.org/news/melt-of-key-antarctic-glaciers-unstoppable-studies-find-17426.

5. Leslie Baehr and Jennifer Walsh, "NASA: The Collapse Of The West Antarctic Ice Sheet Is 'Unstoppable,'" *Business Insider*, May 12, 2014, http://www.businessinsider.com/nasa-west-antarctic-ice-sheet-results-2014–5.

6. "NOAA Satellites Observe Warming Oceans Profile: Q&A with Sydney Levitus," NOAA Satellite and Information Service, last modified November 29, 2014, http://www.nesdis.noaa.gov/news_archives/SydLevitus_WarmingOceans.html.

7. Ken Branson, "Global Warming as Viewed from the Deep Ocean," *Rutgers Today*, October 31, 2015, http://news.rutgers.edu/research-news/global-warming-viewed-deep-ocean/20131031#.WBIRoclcj5M.

8. Erika Spanger-Siegfried, Melanie Fitzpatrick, and Kristina Dahl, *Encroaching Tides: How Sea Level Rise and Tidal Flooding Threaten US East and Gulf Coast Communities over the Next 30 Years* (Cambridge, MA: Union of Concerned Scientists, 2014).

9. "45 percent of Tuvalu Population Displaced—PM," Radio New Zealand, March 15, 2015, http://www.radionz.co.nz/international/pacific-news/268686/45-percent-of-tuvalu-population-displaced-pm.

10. Sam Rkaina, "Cyclone Pam: Vanuatu Death Toll Hits 24 as 3,300 People Displaced by 'Monster' Storm," *Mirror*, last updated March 17, 2015, http://www.mirror.co.uk/news/world-news/cyclone-pam-vanuatu-death-toll-5347338.

11. Karl Mathiesen, "Climate Change Aggravating Cyclone Damage, Scientists Say," *Guardian*, March 16, 2015, https://www.theguardian.com/environment/2015/mar/16/climate-change-aggravating-cyclone-damage-scientists-say.

12. "Hurricanes, Typhoons, Cyclones: Background on the Science, People, and Issues Involved in Hurricane Research: 'Is Global Warming Affecting Hurricanes?,'" National Center for Atmospheric Research, University Corporation for Atmospheric Research, last updated May 2013, https://www2.ucar.edu/news/backgrounders/hurricanes-typhoons-cyclones#8.

13. Nick Perry, "Wary of Climate Change, Vanuatu Villagers Seek Higher Ground," Associated Press, July 12, 2015, http://www.deseretnews.com/article/765677274/Wary-of-climate-change-Vanuatu-villagers-seek-higher-ground.html.

14. "Pacific Island Villagers First Climate Change 'Refugees,'" United Nations Environment Programme, December 6, 2005, http://www.unep.org/Documents.Multilingual/Default.asp?DocumentID=459&ArticleID=5066&1 =en.

15. "Maldives Cabinet Makes a Splash," BBC News, October 17, 2009, http://news.bbc.co.uk/2/hi/8311838.stm.

16. Ben Doherty, "Climate Change Castaways Consider Move to Australia," *Sydney Morning Herald*, January 7, 2012, http://www.smh.com.au/environment/climate-change/climate-change-castaways-consider-move-to-australia-20120106–1pobf.html.

17. Associated Press, "Ex-President Mohamed Nasheed Is Arrested in Maldives," NYTimes.com, February 22, 2015, http://www.nytimes.com/2015/02/23/world/asia/ex-president-mohamed-nasheed-is-arrested-in-maldives.html?_r=0.

18. Andrew Buncombe, "'They came to power in a coup, They will not leave': There May Never Be an Election, Claims Former Leader of Maldives," *Independent*, October 21, 2013, http://www.independent.co.uk/news/world/asia/they-came-to-power-in-a-coup-they-will-not-leave-there-may-never-be-an-election-claims-former-leader-8895102.html.

19. Kenneth R. Weiss, "The Making of a Climate Refugee," *Foreign Policy*, January 28, 2015, http://foreignpolicy.com/2015/01/28/the-making-of-a-climate-refugee-kiribati-tarawa-teitiota/.

20. "Kiribati Man Faces Deportation after New Zealand Court Rejects His Bid to Be First Climate Change Refugee," Agence France Presse, July 21, 2015, http://www.abc.net.au/news/2015–07–21/kiribati-mans-bid-to-be-first-climate-refugee-rejected/6637114.

21. United Nations High Commissioner for Refugees, "The 1951 Convention Relating to the Status of Refugees," Convention and Protocol Relating to the Status of Refugees, December 2010. Quote is from Article 1(A)(2) on p. 14.

22. "I'll Give Climate Refugee Family a Home," RadioNZ, September 27, 2015, http://www.radionz.co.nz/news/world/285388/'i'll-give-climate-refugee-family-a-home'.

23. "Kiribati," Encyclopaedia Britannica, last updated May 13, 2016, https://www.britannica.com/place/Kiribati.

24. John D. Sutter, "You're Making This Island Disappear," CNN, June 2015, http://www.cnn.com/interactive/2015/06/opinions/sutter-two-degrees-marshall-islands/.

25. Alister Doyle, "Pacific Island Nation Calls for Moratorium on New Coal Mines," Reuters, August 13, 2015, http://uk.reuters.com/article/climatechange-summit-coal-idUKL5N1001WK20150813.

26. "Tuvalu about to Disappear into the Ocean," Reuters, September 13, 2007, http://uk.reuters.com/article/environment-tuvalu-dc-idUKSE011194920070913.

27. Rick Noack, "Has the Era of the 'Climate Change Refugee' Begun?" *Washington Post*, August 7, 2014.

28. Ibid.
29. Ibid.
30. Ibid.
31. Sutter, "You're Making This Island Disappear."
32. Christopher Jorebon Loeak, "A Clarion Call from the Climate Change Frontline" Huffington Post Blog, September 18, 2014, updated November 18, 2014, http://www.huffingtonpost.com/christopher-jorebon-loeak/a-clarion-call-from-the-c_b_5833180.html?
33. John D. Sutter, "2 Degrees: The Most Important Number You've Never Heard Of," CNN.com, last updated November 24, 2015, http://www.cnn.com/2015/04/21/opinions/sutter-climate-two-degrees/.
34. Sutter, "You're Making This Island Disappear."
35. Ibid.
36. Ibid.
37. Kathy Jetnil-Kijiner, "A Poem to My Daughter," September 24, 2014, https://kathyjetnilkijiner.com/2014/09/24/united-nations-climate-summit-opening-ceremony-my-poem-to-my-daughter.
38. "Periled by Climate Change, Marshall Islands Makes Carbon Pledge," Agence France-Presse, July 20, 2015, http://www.rappler.com/world/regions/asia-pacific/99898-marshall-islands-makes-carbon-pledge.
39. "Marshall Islands Foreign Minister Tony de Brum Slams Australia's Proposed 2039 Carbon Emissions Targets," ABC.net, updated August 11, 2015, http://www.abc.net.au/news/2015–08–11/marshall-islands-slams-australia's-carbon-emissions-targets/6688974.
40. "Evacuated Carteret islanders hope to send back food," Radio New Zealand, July 8, 2015, http://www.radionz.co.nz/international/pacific-news/278263/evacuated-carteret-islanders-hope-to-send-back-food.
41. Randy Astaiza, "11 Islands That Will Vanish When Sea Levels Rise," *Business Insider*, October 12, 2012, http://www.businessinsider.com/islands-threatened-by-climate-change-2012–10/#micronesia-7.
42. Alex Randall, "Don't Call Them 'Refugees': Why Climate-Change Victims Need a Different Label," *Guardian*, September 18, 2014, https://www.theguardian.com/vital-signs/2014/sep/18/refugee-camps-climate-change-victims-migration-pacific-islands.
43. "Carteret Islands—The Challenge of Relocating Entire Islands," https://sinkingislands.com/2014/10/12/carteret-islands-the-challenge-of-relocating-entire-islands/.
44. Randall, "Don't Call Them 'Refugees.'"
45. "Island Nations Seek UN Security Council Help in Fighting Climate Change," Agence France Presse, July 31, 2015.
46. André Viollaz, "Island Nations Seek UN Help to Combat Climate Change," Agence France-Presse, July 31, 2015, http://interaksyon.com/article/115211/island-nations-seek-un-help-to-combat-climate-change.

4

The Crisis Hits Home

CLIMATE REFUGEES IN THE UNITED STATES

> Close your eyes and picture your best memory with your family and friends. If you're like me, that memory is filled with the warmth and comfort of a familiar home. I hope that, unlike me, you are never asked to put a price on that home because of the effects of climate change.
>
> *Esau Sinnok, Arctic Youth Ambassador to the United Nations**

Who will be the first climate change refugees in the United States? The answer depends on where you get your news. Multiple broadcast networks reported that an Alaskan town on a barrier island that will soon be swallowed by sea level rise may be the source of the country's first climate change refugees. Other news outlets have pointed to communities in Louisiana, where an area of land the size of a football field is disappearing each hour due to fossil fuel activities, land degradation, and sea level rise. Some point to Hurricane Katrina, which displaced thousands from New Orleans, and Superstorm Sandy, which displaced hundreds from New York City. Others point to the droughts that could send many Californians from their home state. One could also claim that the first climate refugees were displaced decades ago, when drought and poor land management practices created the Dust Bowl, prompting hundreds of thousands of farmers to move from the Great Plains to the West. The question will not be who are the "first" climate refugees but what are we going to do about the inevitable climate-induced migration to come.

PAST MIGRATION IN AMERICA: THE DUST BOWL, THE GREAT DROUGHT

It was the greatest migration event in modern American history, inspiring folk songs and novels. The Dust Bowl occurred in the United States in the 1930s when overaggressive agriculture practices and prolonged drought turned the western Great Plains into the infamous prolonged dust storm that made life in the heartland unbearable. In sum, 2.5 million people were forced to leave the region.

There is a "before" and "after" to every migration story, and as illustrated in *The Grapes of Wrath*, the "after" story for Dust Bowl refugees who fled to California was often filled with difficulties. The Dust Bowl migrants moved to many areas that were already experiencing water and resource shortages, thus stressing local tensions. The absorption of these migrants in California created more than its share of conflict. "Okies" from the plains faced slurs, discrimination, and beatings. Their shacks were burned, and police were called on to guard the California border and block new migrants from entering the state.

Alarmingly, in recent years the Great Plains area of the American Midwest has suffered from a drought similar to the one that created the famous Dust Bowl. Farmers are liquidating their stock, people are moving out, many settlements are becoming near ghost towns. Changes in environment and technology—the farmers of today have new tools and techniques, leading to larger farms and fewer workers—are emptying out the heartland. Life on the plains in the age of cell phones and technological innovations such as dry farming means the situation may not be as bad as it was during the Dust Bowl. But keeping one's fingers crossed in an age of La Niña winters that suck the region dry is the operative behavior.

Severe droughts in the US often have reverberating effects on agriculture elsewhere in the country and around the world. One western state, California, with a population of thirty-four million, can easily destabilize much of the nation in its thirst for water. With the multiyear drought have come soaring food prices in excess of 13 percent. California's need for water for its urban and agricultural areas is so great that many in the state's business community talk of building pipelines to the Pacific

Northwest and the Great Lakes to access water. The latter vision makes Canadians wary, as they have joint ownership of the Great Lakes and are in no mood to share their "Blue Gold." Michael Klare, a Hampshire College professor of peace and security studies, notes that high food prices from California's drought could "add to the discontent already evident in depressed and high-unemployment areas, perhaps prompting an intensified backlash against incumbent politicians and other forms of dissent and unrest." He adds that "it is in the international arena, however, that [severe drought in the Great Plains] is likely to have its most devastating effects. Because so many nations depend on grain imports from the United States to supplement their own harvests, and because intense droughts and floods are damaging crops elsewhere as well, food supplies are expected to shrink and prices to rise. . . . The Great Drought of 2012 is not a one-off event in a single heartland nation, but rather an unavoidable consequence of global warming," which is only going to intensify with growing international repercussions. In the coming decades, Klare argues, "millions pressed by drought and hunger will try to migrate to other countries, provoking even greater hostility."[1]

ALASKAN COMMUNITIES IN THE ARCTIC SEA

The notion of climate refugees is beginning to be taken seriously in the United States. Yet when it is discussed, it is almost exclusively in the context of foreign countries—as is immigration in general. Immigrants are often seen as alien, an idea especially trumpeted in the aftermath of Hurricane Katrina, when Rev. Jesse Jackson claimed it was "racist" to call American citizens who survived and were displaced by Katrina "refugees." Jackson claimed that "to see them as refugees is to see them as other than Americans."[2] Regardless, the term "refugee" was commonly used to describe Katrina survivors and is becoming common parlance again among major media outlets to refer to many people living in coastal communities in Alaska who will soon be forced to move.

Native tribal communities have lived on Alaska's coasts for thousands of years, living off the area's fish and wildlife and utilizing its ports for commerce. The Alaskan coastal communities now face dual threats from climate change: sea level rise and permafrost melt. As the ocean en-

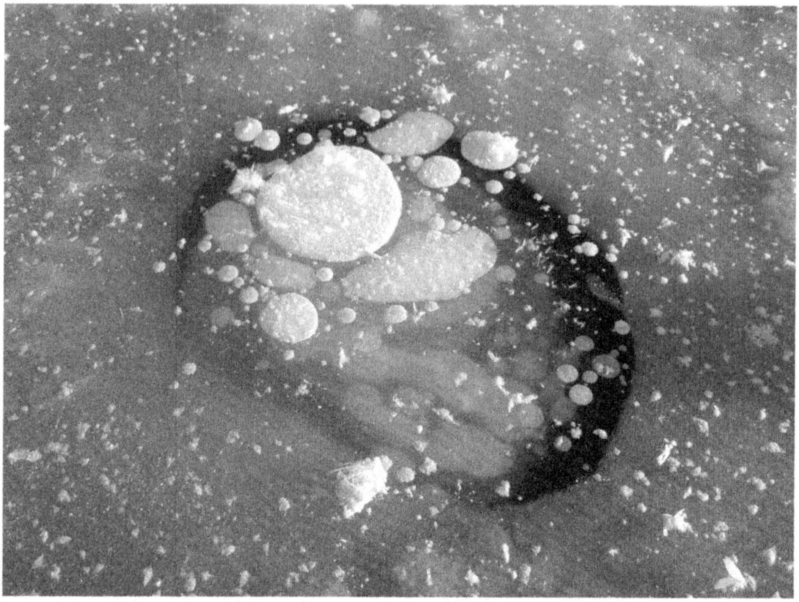

Figure 4.1: Frozen methane bubbles. Photo from US Geological Survey via Flickr.

croaches on Alaskan shores, valuable coastal lands are slowly eroding. At the same time, the foundation, the very dirt underneath the houses, is on shaky ground: Alaska's permafrost—soil that is frozen all year round—is warming up and melting.

Temperatures in Alaska and in the Arctic as a whole are heating up twice as fast as they are in the rest of the world.[3] The warmer Arctic air temperatures have drastic effects on global climate patterns. But their local effects are significant. Permafrost is vital for literally holding these communities afloat. It is comprised of a mix of ice and soil, and when it melts, the ice turns to water and flows away, and the surface turns spongy and sinks. Because of the variations in the soil and ice composition, the ground sinks unevenly, creating divots and troughs. Houses and roads that sit upon such permafrost are becoming severely damaged. Highways have cracked, houses collapsed, as the ground beneath their foundations sinks. Permafrost melt is one of the many self-reinforcing cycles of climate change: as warmer temperatures melt the permafrost, bubbles of greenhouse gases will be released from the previously frozen soil, which in turn will accelerate global warming and melt permafrost more quickly. There are immense amounts of methane and carbon dioxide currently trapped in the Arctic permafrost.

Scientist Vladimir Romanovsky, who runs the University of Alaska's Permafrost Laboratory in Fairbanks, has predicted that one-third of the permafrost in Alaska will melt by 2050, and the remaining two-thirds will do so by 2100.[4] Other organizations have different projections. According to the National Snow and Ice Data Center, 60 percent of the Northern Hemisphere's permafrost will be melted by 2200, releasing nearly two hundred billion tons of carbon into the atmosphere,[5] or the equivalent of more than forty billion cars driving in one year.[6] The United Nations IPCC estimates that 20–35 percent of the permafrost in the Northern Hemisphere will be gone by 2050, and the United Nations Environmental Programme estimates thawing will increase by up to 50 percent by 2080.[7] One thing all the models and scientists agree upon, however, is that the permafrost is melting, and it is because of climate change—previously, drastic changes to permafrost took place over thousands of years—and it is going to get much worse as the planet heats up. "Once the emissions start, they can't be turned off," Ken Schaefer of the National Snow and Ice Data Center told *USA Today*.[8] "You can see and hear the ice melting," said permafrost expert Ted Schuur.[9]

These communities face other threats as well. The ice caps that floated near the ocean shores protected these communities from storms; now that they are melted, the coasts are much more vulnerable. Tundra lakes, the region's primary source of clean drinking water, have been drying up. But while the melting permafrost, the severe storms, and the drying sources of drinking water are all problems that Alaskan communities face, there are adaptations and protections and solutions to all of them. They do not face the existential threat that coastal communities face with regard to sea level rise. No matter what happens, they need to move, and they know this, and the federal government knows it as well. The US Government Accountability Office (GAO) documented in 2003 that over two hundred Alaskan communities are threatened by sea level rise and shoreline erosion.[10] Since then, thirty-one communities have been identified as facing "imminent" threats. Twelve of those have voted to relocate, but as of 2016 none have officially made the move.[11] It takes planning and government services and, most importantly, funds, which are in short supply.

RELOCATION

The Federal Emergency Management Agency (FEMA), for one, does not make funds available until a state of emergency is declared—and, typically, slowly coming disasters such as sea level rise aren't classified as such. In fact, many of the communities that face these threats do not qualify for the federal assistance they need. In some cases, federal agencies have invested in infrastructure in towns without knowing that the town officials planned to relocate. The GAO pointed out that the Denali Commission and the Department of Housing and Urban Development (HUD) "were unaware of Newtok's relocation plans when they decided to jointly fund a new health clinic in the village for $1.1 million."[12]

The Denali Commission was set up in 1998 by Congress to research and provide economic development to Alaska's remotest communities, but the organization struggled greatly, with its own inspector general recommending in 2013 that the commission be shut down, calling it a "a congressional experiment that hasn't worked out in practice."[13] In 2015 the Denali Commission was given new life when President Obama tapped it to address the region's climate change threats. A White House initiative to improve climate change resilience stated that the commission would "assist communities in developing and implementing both short- and long-term solutions to address the impacts of climate change" and "serve as a one-stop-shop for matters relating to coastal resilience in Alaska." Its present duties include conducting "voluntary relocation or other managed retreat efforts." It was awarded $2 million for this specific task.[14]

Only in recent years have serious steps for relocating these communities begun, and for many they are currently under way. Thus, they are the sources of what many have called "America's first climate refugees." The small village of Newtok, with a population of about 350 people, ethnically Yupik Eskimos, receives that specific honor, according to Suzanne Goldberg, environmental reporter for the *Guardian*.[15] Perched on the west coast of Alaska near the Bering Sea, on the shore of the rapidly rising

Ninglick River, the town of Newtok made the decision in 2003 to relocate. They chose an area of land nine miles south, across the Baird Inlet, and, most importantly, on higher ground. The land was owned by the US Fish and Wildlife Service, the exchange approved by Congress.[16] But over a decade later, relocation has yet to take place, and Newtok's residents remain on its battered coasts, facing severe flooding and erosion.

The *Atlantic's* Alana Semuels reports the move has been slowed by legal and financial complications. It has been awarded grants in bits and pieces: $4 million in 2010, $2.5 million in 2011. After a raging storm in 2013, disastrous floods allowed Newtok to request $4 million from FEMA for relocation, through its Hazard Mitigation Grant Program. But that move in particular is problematic—how many disastrous storms will it take for relocation efforts to get the funding they need? The *Atlantic* contrasted the two decades that Newtok has been struggling to move with the experience of New Pattonsburg, Missouri, which was destroyed by the Great Flood of 1993 and reestablished on higher ground just one year later. As Semuels wrote, "All it took was a disaster."[17]

Regardless, Newtok hopes to begin moving homes in 2018 at the earliest.[18] But many residents are worried that date will already be too late. One home is placed one hundred feet from the water, but land is being washed and melted away at a rate of fifty to seventy-five feet per year. Goldberg told National Public Radio, "Every year during the storm season, that river can take away 20, 30, up to 300 feet a year. . . . It just rips it off the land, away from the village in these terrifying storms." The US Army Corps of Engineers predicts that "the town's highest point—a school—could be underwater by 2017." The full costs of moving the entire village could be upward of $130 million, predicts the GAO, and very little of that has been awarded.[19]

Yet the fact that Newtok has plans under way for relocation makes it more fortunate than the dozens of other Alaskan communities that face existential climate change threats. A town called Shishmaref was one of two highlighted on NBC's *Nightly News* in September 2015, the first time a broadcast news network mentioned even the idea of climate refugees in nearly ten years. Shishmaref—a bit larger than Newtok, with 600 residents to Newtok's 350, and a few degrees latitude closer to the North Pole—faces a similar plight. The community voted in 2002 in favor of relocating, one year before Newtok made a similar vote. Yet no new location has been agreed upon. Clifford Weyiouanna, one of the elders, explained, "You can't build nothing on tundra that's got two feet of ice. The minute you put something on it, it's going to melt and houses are going to sink."[20]

Therefore the town remains in limbo. In the meantime, the US Army Corps of Engineers built a $19 million rock wall as a temporary measure to protect the community from sea level rise. The town itself cannot afford to make the move without further government aid. Weyiouanna, former chair of Shishmaref's relocation coalition, complained about the lack of federal assistance: "You almost have to be half the way dead to get help."[21] The government estimates that if they do find a suitable relocation site, it will cost $300,000 to move each villager, for a total price tag of $180 million.[22]

Many people who are familiar with the situation in Shishmaref are frustrated at the lack of federal assistance. In 2014, Alaska Senator Lisa Murkowski urged Secretary of State John Kerry to "put America first" and help "the Alaskans who deal with this reality on a daily basis." She wrote: "As the United States prepares to assume the Chairmanship of the Arctic Council, it is essential we are prepared to address adaptation issues in our own Arctic communities."[23] Shishmaref residents have tried appealing to Congress, which has many members who deny the science of global warming. Former mayor Stanley Tocktoo said their airstrip could be wiped out after a few more storms, cutting residents off from emergency flights. The group brought with them a plastic tub full of slowly melting permafrost to symbolize the slow change happening in their homes.[24]

The other town highlighted on NBC's *Nightly News* was an Alaskan village called Kotzebue, which President Obama visited on a historic trip to the Arctic—the first time a US president has ever traveled above the Arctic Circle. Kotzebue is bigger than Shishmaref and is home to about three thousand people. It will not relocate, hoping that a $34 million rock wall built to keep out sea level rise will keep it safe.[25] Following his visit to Kotzebue, Obama visited a town called Kivalina, located on the tip of a barrier reef island. Kivalina faces similar existential threats to the other communities; some experts predict it will be inundated by sea level rise to the point of being uninhabitable by 2025.[26] It will cost Kivalina $102 million to relocate all of its four hundred residents, according to the US Army Corps of Engineers.[27] The town voted in 1992 to relocate,[28] but it has nowhere near the funds necessary to make this move yet—nor a plan for where to go.

Where will it get the money? Kivalina stands out among the other towns, as it has attempted a unique strategy for receiving the funds they need to relocate. In 2008 the village sued twenty-four of the world's biggest fossil fuel companies, including ExxonMobil, BP, Chevron, Shell Oil, and more.[29] They filed a "public nuisance" claim, accusing fossil fuel companies of inflicting "unreasonable harm" to the village for contributing the most to climate change. The residents intended for funds won in the court case to pay for the village's relocation. Unfortunately, the case faced many roadblocks and was ultimately dropped in 2013.[30] The US district court turned it down on the grounds that greenhouse gas emissions need to be regulated by Congress, not the courts.[31] The city tried to appeal to the Supreme Court, but the Court refused to hear it in 2013.[32] Environmental activist and author Bill McKibben commented on the failed case: "This story is a tragedy, and not just because of what's happening to the people of Kivalina. It's a tragedy because it's unnecessary, the product, as the author shows, of calculation, deception, manipulation, and greed in some of the biggest and richest companies on earth."[33]

But Christine Shearer, who wrote a book about Kivalina's lawsuit called *Kivalina: A Climate Change Story,* is hopeful that there will be more lawsuits in the future. She said in an interview with Public Radio International: "More communities, more cities, more states, more tribes are going to have to deal with trying to help people who are being affected by climate change. . . . I think more lawsuits will be filed, and I think it might get to a point where fossil fuel companies might find it's less costly to settle than to keep fighting these lawsuits."[34]

While these communities await relocation, they are suffering. With less sea ice to hold down waves, storm surges are constantly eating away at the land and homes. Clean water and sanitation systems are at risk in vulnerable villages like Shishmaref. Health systems are deteriorating and evacuation paths compromised. Airstrips—vital for providing access to mainland, especially to evacuate—are washing away. Investors see little reason to support a community that is planning to move. As Stanley Tocktoo put it, "The decision to move has been very costly for us."[35]

In September 2015 Kivalina received a $500,000 grant from an arts organization to study relocation, but its residents have a long way to go,[36] as do the Alaskan communities as a whole. The GAO estimates it will cost a total of $34 billion to relocate the 192 Alaskan communities that are currently at risk.[37]

LOUISIANA'S DISAPPEARING WETLANDS

Since the 1930s, Louisiana has lost nearly two thousand square miles of land, approximately the size of Delaware.[38] Every hour, an area the size of a football field vanishes into open water.[39] The entire three million acres of Louisiana bayou wetlands took seven thousand years to evolve but could largely disappear within the next fifty if nothing is done to save them.

Wetland landmarks—bays and bayous, islands and streams—are already starting to disappear into the Gulf of Mexico. This is no hyperbole: NOAA is literally removing these landmarks from its maps. In 2013 NOAA removed forty bays and features from its charts. Some of these were named in the 1700s, by the first French pioneers to explore the region; most existed in the recent memories of the residents who grew up in southern Louisiana. The agency updates its maps quite often, but such a huge number of removals in one location is unprecedented, according to NOAA geographer Meredith Westington. "It's a little disturbing. . . . It's sad to see so many names go," she said to *USA Today*. "I don't know that anyone has seen these kinds of mass changes before."[40] The places disappearing are not mere points on a map; they provide sustenance and homes to thousands of people. The region of the map removals is called Plaquemines Parish, home to nearly twenty-five thousand people, and without action, over half of the parish will be underwater by 2100.[41]

As with the river deltas in Asia, there are many factors causing Louisiana's wetlands—the mouth of the Mississippi River spilling into the Gulf of Mexico, comprised of channels, swamps, and marshes—to sink into the sea. Levees built to protect highly populated areas from flood-

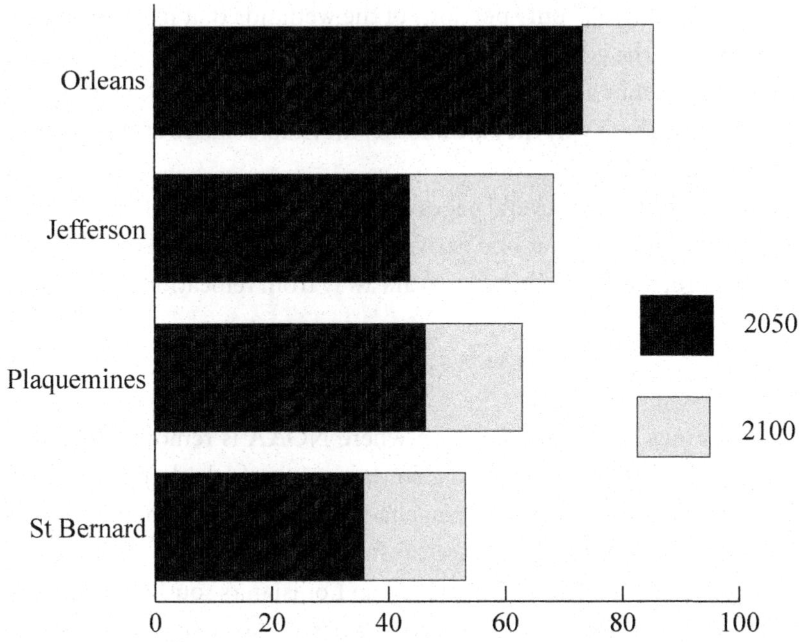

Figure 4.2: Louisiana land loss: parishes with the most to lose. Source: NASA.

ing prevent sediment, constantly brought downstream by the rivers, inlets, and channels, from washing down and replenishing the wetlands. Drought has also played a role; high tides and floods are vital for carrying sediments downstream and depositing them into the wetlands, and with less precipitation there is less water flow.[42]

Sea level rise is happening in the gulf at a greater pace than the worldwide average, and recently NOAA determined that it is happening faster even than the experts expected. The Louisiana wetlands average about three feet above sea level; NOAA now predicts that the Gulf of Mexico will rise over four feet by 2100, which would inundate everything outside of the levees with water.

Oil and gas operations are much to blame—and that is not including the global warming–driving carbon emissions that result from burning fossil fuels. For over a hundred years, oil and gas companies have dug an extensive array of canals—up to ten thousand miles in total length—to access the thousands of oil and gas rigs peppered throughout the region. Ironically, the only portions of the wetlands that may survive sea level rise are the edges of the canals dug out by the fossil fuel industry.[43] There's no doubt about it: Louisiana's wetlands are at risk of perishing completely. That's why they are another inevitable source of climate refugees in America.

Yes, we just spent several pages detailing another potential source for the "first" refugees. But one native Louisiana tribe has taken its plight one step further and is just two years away from relocation.

LOUISIANA'S TRIBAL REFUGEES

Plaquemines Parish is the region where NOAA is removing so many landmarks from its maps. It is also the region of Isle de Jean Charles, home to a tribe of Biloxi-Chitimacha-Choctaw Indians that news website Mashable has dubbed "America's first climate refugees."[44] The Isle de Jean Charles is a narrow strip of land on Louisiana's southern edge, surrounded by the waters of the Louisiana bayou. Sixty years ago the land was eleven miles long and five miles wide; now it is just two miles long and one-quarter mile wide.[45] It will soon completely disappear into the Gulf of Mexico, and the tribe that has been living there since the 1800s will be forced to move.

In early 2016 the tribe won a $48 million grant from the National Disaster Resilience Competition, a project from HUD in collaboration with the Rockefeller Foundation.[46] Tribe chief Albert White Buffalo Naquin had been advocating for relocating his tribe for thirteen years.[47] "A way of life did disappear," he said.[48] He told the Institute for Southern Studies, "This award will allow our Tribe to design and develop a new, culturally appropriate and resilient site for our community, safely located further inland."[49] The Isle de Jean Charles tribe is the first community to receive relocation funding from HUD specifically because of climate change. One can only hope it will be a model for future community resettlements as climate change continues.[50]

Not everyone in Isle de Jean Charles is happy about the move, however; some residents are unwilling to uproot and leave their history, heritage, and way of life behind. Many in the community are planning to try to stay. "This is home," said resident Edison Dardar to WDSU News, having lived there all of his life, as has his wife. "No money, no offer."[51]

The community has to begin moving in two years, but no one is being pressured to move, said Chief Naquin: "At least they will have a place to go in the event something should happen. Now it's a matter of finding a place where we could settle and where it's big enough for us to put at least 100 homes and have room for growth for the future."[52]

SUING FOSSIL FUELS TO SAVE THE WETLANDS

Beyond the Isle de Jean Charles, Louisiana's wetlands are in big trouble. The state has planned a huge, long-shot effort to save them that will take fifty years and cost at least $50 billion.[53] It will take an extraordinary amount of innovation; experts are treating the plan as more of a scientific experiment but one that is taking place in real time and affecting thousands of people's lives.

There is a great risk that it will not work, especially with the increased rates of sea level rise. "To make the project work, scientists and engineers will have to figure out on the fly how to create a manmade system that replicates the delta's natural land-building process," reported the nonprofit news corporation ProPublica.[54] Further, NOAA scientist Tim Osborn noted that the new data on sea level rise is greater than the worst-case scenario laid out in the wetland restoration plan. Garret Graves, head of the state Coastal Planning and Protection Authority, notes that the plan is structured to adapt and change every five years, so it may adapt to the new information in time. And the Mississippi River contains a massive amount of the sediment needed to rebuild, so Osborn said hope is not lost.[55]

ProPublica notes that the cost for this project is greater than that of World War II's Manhattan Project. But the costs of letting Louisiana's wetlands disappear is even greater. The wetlands serve the country's largest port, and without action to save them, extreme weather could cause shutdowns that would cost the US economy $300 million each day. So it would take less than half a year—167 days—of those ports being shut down for the costs of *not* acting to outweigh the $50 billion price tag to protect the wetlands. If they disappear completely, the costs would be astronomical.[56]

But where will the $50 billion come from? BP is expected to pay for part of the project due to penalties from the 2010 oil spill in the Gulf of Mexico. It is unclear how much of that will be allocated for wetland restoration, but even all of it would not be enough to meet the $50 billion price tag. After the funds from BP's negligence run out, then where will Louisiana turn to protect its wetlands?[57]

As it turns out, the answer may be found again in lawsuits against the fossil fuel industry.[58] In this regard, Plaquemines Parish has taken a similar tack as the Alaskan community suing for the funds to move and is home to some of the most innovative lawsuits ever aiming at environmental restoration.

The oil and gas industry is responsible for a significant portion of Louisiana wetland degradation. The ten thousand miles of land that were turned into open water via canals have disrupted the wetlands' sediment deposition processes, allowed saltwater from the gulf to breach the wetlands and destroy plant life, and removed valuable protections against storms, thus increasing the size of storm surges, which in turn speeds up erosion. In fact, the industry has admitted responsibility for 36 percent of wetland loss, although government estimates put it as high as 59 percent.[59] This fact has not gone unnoticed by the people of Louisiana who want to make the industry pay for ruining their homes.

In 2013 the South Louisiana Flood Protection Authority–East filed suit against ninety-seven oil and gas companies in what the *New York Times* called "the most ambitious environmental lawsuit ever."[60] The lawsuit argued that the fossil fuel companies were supposed to fill in the canals after they were finished using them and that they broke their permits by not doing so and now need to take responsibility for the damages.[61] But the lawsuit faced fierce opposition by local and state politicians who are interested in protecting the oil and gas industry, a major source of economic activity. In fact, Louisiana is among the top oil- and gas-producing states in the country.

E&E News said that the lawsuit's "biggest hurdle" was "not its merits, but the staunch opposition of the Jindal administration and the Legislature."[62] Former governor Bobby Jindal is a staunch defender of industry and denounced the lawsuit, blaming the case lawyers for "taking this action at the expense of our coast and thousands of hardworking Louisianians who help fuel America by working in the energy industry." The state legislature crafted bill after bill to try to block the lawsuit.[63] One bill was thrown out by a state judge as unconstitutional.[64] In the end, in February 2015 the state judge ruled against the flood authority's lawsuit. The reasons cited for throwing it out, however, had everything to do with the party filing the suit—the levee authority—not the merits of the case.[65]

Meanwhile, the council of Plaquemines Parish was pushing through its own attempt at suing the oil and gas industry for wetland damages. It filed twenty-one lawsuits, and the neighboring Jefferson Parish council filed seven, against many of the ninety-seven companies named in the levee authority's suit.[66] But the council saw fierce opposition to these suits from the oil and gas industry, which had donated heavily to the campaigns of council members in the 2014 elections. By November 2015, many of the original council members who filed the original motion to begin lawsuits were no longer in office, and the council voted 5–1 to drop the lawsuits.[67] According to the Associated Press, Sierra Club member Darryl Malek-Wiley alleged that the council members were "wooed by oil and gas companies into voting against the suits." Malek-Wiley commented, "Once again it shows the power of the oil and gas industry over the interest of our coastal wetlands."[68]

Despite the lawsuits in Plaquemine Parish having so far failed, they signify a shift in how Americans are reacting in the face of environmental degradation. The fossil fuel industry receives millions in royalties and tax breaks from the federal government, and people are increasingly turning to these funds as a possible way to pay for the environmental havoc these industries created. *E&E News* reporter Annie Snider, for one, suggested raising taxes on oil and gas production if those companies had chosen to settle in the levee authority lawsuit. But she also noted that "as long as lawmakers stand prepared to intervene and the Jindal administration maintains its opposition to the lawsuit, a deal like that is seen as a long shot."[69]

Former President Barack Obama has also repeatedly attempted to divert oil and gas royalties toward climate adaptation in Louisiana, including protecting the coasts from hurricanes. It was one of the promises he made while campaigning in 2008. And while he has tried to eliminate oil and gas royalties altogether, lawmakers have repeatedly overturned such proposals.[70] In his latest budget proposal for Alaska, where he requested raising $400 million for coastal communities, Obama laid out that the funding would come through the Department of the Interior, by abolishing current royalties for offshore oil and gas drilling.[71]

It makes perfect sense—fossil fuel emissions are driving global warming, putting the coastal communities in the path of sea level rise, so a logical conclusion for helping these communities is to also disincentivize the burning of fossils—and in a perfect world this proposed budget change would be a no-brainer. But it is not a perfect world, and Obama's budget had scant chance of passing, especially with such a large portion of the two houses of Congress accepting heavy donations from oil and gas companies. Obama's budget proposal, the last of his presidency, was dead on arrival.[72]

HURRICANE KATRINA: AMERICA'S DIASPORA

It is impossible to discuss forced migration in Louisiana without mentioning Hurricane Katrina. Because of Katrina's power and extensive destruction, Louisiana became the location of the country's greatest internal migration event since the Dust Bowl—if not ever. In fact, the degradation of Louisiana's wetlands is directly tied to Hurricane Katrina's devastation. The wetlands act as a storm barrier, slowing the intensity of hurricanes as they pass through, weakening them before they hit the heavily populated New Orleans region. They also work to absorb the storms' rains to lessen the height of storm surges, which usually turn out to be the deadliest aspect of hurricanes. Most of the wetland restoration efforts are centered on protecting New Orleans.[73] But the rebuilding efforts won't change what happened, and the devastation of Hurricane Katrina offers an instructive warning for what the future could have in store for climate refugees in America.

Katrina struck the Gulf Coast on August 23, 2005, killing more than one thousand people and displacing over one million. While most of the forced displacement was temporary, hundreds of thousands of people would remain without a home for many months to follow. Hurricane evacuee shelters held 273,000 people at their peak.[74] The disaster resulted in a diaspora, with evacuees scattered throughout the country, to Georgia, Florida, Texas, South Carolina, New York, Mississippi, Colorado, and other states.[75] The return to New Orleans was slow-going, and for some it never happened.

The ensuing recovery efforts exposed harsh realities about racism in the United States. One year after the storm, less than half the black people evacuated from New Orleans had returned (67 percent of non-black people had).[76] Five years after, one hundred thousand people—disproportionately black—still hadn't returned.[77] The racial disparities had roots before the storm. Black neighborhoods were more likely to reside in areas more vulnerable to the storm and subsequently experienced the greatest levels of flooding. The academic journal *Southern Spaces* noted that before the storm the Gulf Coast states had high levels of racial inequality and "the worst quality-of-life indicators in the nation for their poor, people of color, and women," historical leftovers of the plantations and slavery. People hoped that hurricane response would lessen inequalities, but the response only served to exacerbate them.[78]

The aftermath of Hurricane Katrina invalidates arguments that disaster relocation in America will always be temporary. Five years after the storm, entire neighborhoods were still abandoned, and the city's four major public housing complexes were destroyed or condemned. Tens of thousands of people remained displaced and homeless.

The evacuees had to resettle across the country, but many were not well received. In the weeks after Katrina, South Carolina became home to an emergency relief center for evacuees, and many eventually settled in that state's Midlands region. Columbia itself accepted up to fifteen thousand people, but that city had a paucity of adequate infrastructure and social services, having among the least available levels of affordable housing and public transportation in the country and the most restrictive social welfare policies. A deeply conservative region, it also had a political environment that was hostile to the newcomers.[79]

Houston took in the most evacuees, accepting 250,000 in the storm's aftermath—and 150,000 were still living there one year later.[80] Many were sent to live in FEMA-funded apartments in neighborhoods riddled with crime and poverty.[81] The media falsely connected the influx of evacuees to a supposed crime wave, fueling residents' deep-seated antipathy toward the newcomers.[82]

The long-term consequences of government disinvestment in social services and infrastructure were laid bare in the aftermath of Katrina and the hardships of its survivors. These systems are now vulnerable to the point where another major disaster could upend the social systems that people rely on. With every extreme weather event, those who are underprivileged are hit the worst. With every event, adaptation only serves to widen preexisting inequalities. As Vox's David Roberts has put it, climate change adaptation is "tied directly to one's wealth. Rich countries will be able to do more of it than poor countries; within rich countries, wealthier cities will be able to do more of it than poorer cities and rural areas; and even within wealthy cities, it will be the affluent residents who have access to these mechanisms and the poor who are left behind."[83]

Indeed, the Kaiser Family Foundation found deep racial divides in how New Orleans residents viewed the city's recovery even ten years after the storm. White residents were far more likely to believe that the city had mostly recovered and that their needs were being met.[84]

HURRICANE SANDY: HARBINGER OF THINGS TO COME

For the residents of New York City, thousands of miles away from Louisiana, the tragedy of Hurricane Katrina seemed largely a foreign one—that is, until Superstorm Sandy. In September 2012 Hurricane Sandy took a highly unusual path. After traveling northward up the Atlantic coast, it took a sharp left turn to barrel straight west into New Jersey and New York. It was the most expensive storm in America after Katrina, caused 147 deaths, and destroyed thousands of homes.[85] Windstorms ranging a thousand miles wide ripped apart New Jersey's famous boardwalk, and a nearly ten-foot-high storm surge breached the Manhattan seawall and flooded the city's tunnels and subways.

Superstorm Sandy displaced fewer people than Hurricane Katrina but continued to expose flaws in the government response to survivors. Thirty thousand people remained displaced from New York and New Jersey one year after the storm. Fifty-five thousand homes were destroyed or seriously damaged. Less than half of the people who requested FEMA assistance received it within one year.[86] Two and a half years later, fifteen thousand families were still displaced from the storm, and only 328 homes had been rebuilt.[87]

The storm recovery programs failed the Latino and African American communities in particular, according to the Latino Action Network and the NAACP New Jersey State Conference. Funds were directed to communities that faced less damage than those hardest hit, such as Monmouth and Ocean Counties, they argued, and the state offered less funding to low-income renters.[88]

As with Hurricane Katrina, the severe impacts of Superstorm Sandy can be directly connected to climate change—particularly, sea level rise. The storm tide in Manhattan blasted previous records, reaching fourteen feet—four feet above the previous record set in December 1992.[89] This was a combination of evening high tide and storm surge, which was exacerbated by high sea levels. The sea level off the coast of Manhattan has risen by about one and a half feet since the preindustrial era and is expected to rise another four feet by the end of the century.[90] Sea levels are rising on the East Coast about four times faster than the national average.[91]

It is, in fact, the extensive flooding from storm surges that caused the most damage in New York City and New Jersey. Floodwaters filled the tunnels and damaged electrical equipment. Power outages lasted days, or weeks in some areas. Climate scientist Kevin Trenberth said that the city's subways and tunnels may not have been "flooded without the warming-induced increases in sea level and in storm intensity and size, putting the potential price tag of human climate change on this storm in the tens of billions of dollars."[92] One study from Portland State University researchers suggests that New York City could experience storm surges that breach the Manhattan seawall once every four to five years, compared to once every one hundred to four hundred years in the nineteenth century.[93] And a study from the American Meteorological Society found that by 2050, the Jersey shore could see storm surges at the scale of Superstorm Sandy every year.[94]

More than sea level rise, climate change may have had a hand in the storm's highly unusual path. Abnormally high sea surface temperatures allowed the storm to travel farther northward and retain its strength longer than common in late October. A warmer atmosphere also causes more water to evaporate, thereby creating more precipitation.[95] All of the signs point to the possibility of future events like Hurricane Sandy, a risk that is always increasing.[96]

SOLUTIONS AND SAFE HAVENS

But while sea level threats in high profile cities such as New York City and New Orleans may have gained the most press, it is important to consider the hundreds of other US cities and regions facing similar risks. More than four hundred cities are past their "lock-in date" for sea level rise, according to a study led by Climate Central climate scientist Benjamin Strauss and published in the *Proceedings of the National Academy of Sciences* in 2015: it's guaranteed that more than half of each of those cities will be underwater no matter what actions are taken to mitigate climate change. For New Orleans, "it's really just a question of building suitable defenses or eventually abandoning the city," said Strauss to the Huffington Post.[97] But Hurricane Katrina showed that building levees is not a fail-safe plan either; the bigger the levees, the more catastrophic the results if the levees fail.

Victoria Herrmann, director of the Arctic Institute, has laid out a key first step for addressing the refugee crisis. She believes that panels of local, state, and federal experts should be convened in order to come up with a framework for relocating all climate refugees within the United States.[98] This framework does not exist; indeed, the thought of "climate refugees" in America is hard to grasp.

The other side of the equation is how to prevent future climate refugees. States and local communities need to be better prepared to adapt to future impacts of climate change—particularly, extreme weather events. And indeed, some argue that calling Alaskans the "first" potential refugees discounts the millions of Americans who have already been displaced—albeit temporarily in many instances—due to the effects of hurricanes. But those are just two aspects of the climate change crisis: one of them slow, long-term, and predictable; the other less predictable but far more immediately devastating. To not adapt to the future impacts of extreme weather like hurricanes is to take a giant risk, but that risk is

Table 4.1. US Cities with the Greatest Populations Affected by Sea Level Rise

City	Pop. Affected
New York, NY	1,870,000
Virginia Beach, VA	407,000
Miami, FL	399,000
New Orleans, LA	343,000
Jacksonville, FL	290,000
Sacramento, CA	286,000
Norfolk, VA	242,000
Stockton, CA	241,000
Hialeah, FL	225,000
Boston, MA	220,000

taken by those who have no other choice. Particularly in poor communities, residents often do not have the funds or knowledge to adequately protect themselves.

The Federal Emergency Management Agency is finally starting to help states prepare for climate change, updating its state plans to incorporate climate change for the first time ever. It is a groundbreaking development for the notoriously reactionary agency. FEMA now requires that state plans for receiving resilience-focused aid include "consideration of changing environmental or climate conditions that may affect and influence the long-term vulnerability from hazards in the state."[99] It is worth noting that the policy does *not* affect FEMA funds for disaster relief; in the event of a hurricane or extreme flood, the agency would still provide aid in the aftermath.

Disaster preparedness funds are extremely valuable in places like the Midlands, South Carolina, which in 2016 initiated plans to carry out a dozen flood prevention projects and relies on FEMA's disaster preparedness funding to do so.[100] The region saw deadly floods in October 2015, which killed at least seventeen people.[101] Other disaster preparedness plans vary by state, from earthquake-proof shelters to flood prevention levees to wind-resistant structures in hurricane-prone regions. Each is tailored to the unique threats that the regions face.

Each region also faces unique threats from climate change. The National Climate Assessment, a report from the US Global Change Research Program compiled by more than three hundred climate scientists and experts over a four-year period, lays out which impacts of climate change we can expect to see in different regions of the United States.[102] The future risks that states will face due to climate change is well known, yet many states have not taken the steps to prepare themselves. For instance, Houston, Texas, is woefully underprepared to face an intense hurricane, according to a joint investigation by ProPublica and the *Texas Tribune*, yet such a hurricane is in store.[103]

Appallingly, many Republican governors in charge of coastal states attacked FEMA on this change for the simple reason that it would require them to admit that climate change is real. Jindal said in a statement that the White House should not use the FEMA preparedness plans "for political leverage to force acquiescence to their left-wing ideology." He has previously called climate change "simply a Trojan horse" for more government regulation, saying, "It's an excuse for the government to come in and try to tell us what kind of homes we live in, what kind of cars we drive, what kind of lifestyles we can enjoy."[104]

Florida governor Rick Scott's office also suggested it would not comply with the new FEMA rule. A spokesperson told the *Washington Times* that Florida changes their mitigation plans only once every five years and that "Florida's current [plan] became effective on August 24, 2013, and is approved for use through August 23, 2018."[105] The Scott administration is notorious for climate denial; in fact, according to interviews with former officials at the Florida Department of Environmental Protection (DEP) conducted by the Florida Center for Investigative Reporting (FCIR), Scott's administration did not allow staff to utter the words "climate change." Multiple former officials at the DEP told FCIR that they were ordered not to use the terms "climate change" or "global warming" in "any official communications, emails, or reports." FCIR reported: "But four former DEP employees from offices around the state say the order was well known and distributed verbally statewide."[106]

Multiple other Republican politicians attacked the plan. Several House members signed a letter blasting it. Sent to FEMA administrator W. Craig Fugate, the letter said that climate change is still being debated, citing "gaps in the scientific understanding around climate change."[107]

California has been in a years-long drought, the worst experienced in the region in five hundred years. Even if the drought ends, another one may be in store for the state, climatologists say. With thirty-four million inhabitants, drought is no passing inconvenience. The state's dwindling water supply is putting both agriculture and urban development at risk. If the situation continues, California's fruit and vegetable farmers will move northward toward water resources. California wineries are already buying vineyards in the Willamette Valley, located in Oregon. As the mercury rises in California and other parts of the drought-stricken Southwest, people will look to the Pacific Northwest as a safe haven.

Currently the Pacific Northwest is one of the safest areas of the country in which to live as far as climate change is concerned. Dr. Cliff Mass, an atmospheric science professor at the University of Washington, predicts the Pacific Northwest will come to be "one of the best places to live as the earth warms" from global warming. He foresees a mass exodus of climate change refugees from other regions of the country settling there.[108] It is likely that the Pacific Northwest will continue to be one of the best places to live in terms of water resources and climate, but there may be a downside to that upside. It is likely that human migration patterns will shift and global warming will unleash a deluge of newcomers that will greatly strain resources and human relations in civic communities. In a blog entry Professor Mass joked about keeping Californians out with a barbed wire–topped steel fence.[109]

The Pacific Northwest has seen climate refugees before. Knute Berger of Crosscut.com recalls the Big Burn, a massive three-million-acre firestorm that swept across Idaho, Washington, and Montana in 1910, and thousands were forced off the land and converged into Missoula, Spokane, and other communities. During the Dust Bowl crisis of the 1930s, more than 2.5 million people fled the parched Great Plains for friendlier climates. Thousands of migrant farmworkers converged on the Yakima Valley looking for employment and shelter. The Pacific Northwest historically has been built by migration. Berger predicts that "with or without climate change, people are coming.... The question is whether some tipping point will send a surge of 'environmental asylum seekers'" or whether climate change will merely boost some population increases that are manageable.[110] If refugees materialize in significant numbers, will they receive sanctuary? Past history of this subject is not comforting.

In his celebrated novel *Ecotopia,* Ernest Callenbach envisions Washington, Oregon, and Northern California seceding from the United States and walling off an environmental utopia.[111] It raises the fundamental question in discussing water and climate refugees: In a warming world do we pull up the gangplanks or put out the welcome mat? Further, the long drought in the Pacific Northwest has recently become the subject of a novel by Paolo Bacigalupi. In *The Water Knife,* Bacigalupi describes a water war between Las Vegas and Phoenix that sets the scene for an important realization: most people do not think about disaster, even when it is crashing down upon them.[112] It is hard to comprehend a potential future such as that described in novels. But when disaster strikes, people move, often behaving erratically and irrationally. Bacigalupi's novel depicts a future where many climate refugees are on the road in search of water and environmental security. In America as drought continues, Bacigalupi describes a world where states become muscular about their rights, saying, "No, no, this is our territory. We don't want to share it with the state next to us." What *The Water Knife* represents is a time when there has been a lack of oversight, planning, and organization. Says Bacigalupi, "This world is built on the assumption that people don't plan, don't think, and don't cooperate—which makes for a pretty bad future."[113]

NOTES

Epigraph is from Esau Sinnok, "My World Interrupted," US Department of the Interior, December 8, 2015.

1. Michael Klare, "The Hunger Wars in Our Future," *Environment,* August 8, 2012, http://www.tomdispatch.com/blog/175579/.
2. Justin Fenton, "Use of 'Refugee' Is Called Biased," *Baltimore Sun,* September 5, 2005.
3. Michael Casey, "Temperatures in the Arctic Rising Twice as Fast as Rest of the World," CBS News, December 17, 2014.
4. Wendy Koch, "Alaska Sinks as Climate Change Thaws Permafrost," *USA Today,* December 16, 2013.
5. "Permafrost In a Warming World," Weather Underground, accessed 10–28–2016, https://www.wunderground.com/resources/climate/melting_permafrost.asp.
6. "Greenhouse Gas Emissions from a Typical Passenger Vehicle: Questions and Answers," EPA.gov, May 2014, https://www.epa.gov/greenvehicles/greenhouse-gas-emissions-typical-passenger-vehicle

7. "Permafrost In a Warming World," Weather Underground.

8. Koch, "Alaska Sinks."

9. Ibid.

10. "Alaska Native Villages: Most Are Affected by Flooding and Erosion, but Few Qualify for Federal Assistance," US General Accounting Office Report to Congressional Committees, (Washington, DC: USGAO, December 12, 2003).

11. "Alaska Native Villages: Limited Progress Has Been Made on Relocating Villages Threatened by Flooding and Erosion," US Government Accountability Office Report to Congressional Requesters (Washington, DC: USGAO, June 3, 2009), newtok's.

12. "Alaska Native Villages: Most Are Affected," USGAO.

13. Mike Marsh quoted in David A. Fahrenthold, "Federal Employee Mike Marsh's Mission: Getting Himself Fired, and His Agency Closed," *Washington Post*, September 26, 2013.

14. White House initiative quotes from "Fact Sheet: President Obama Announces New Investments to Combat Climate Change and Assist Remote Alaskan Communities," Whitehouse.gov, September 2, 2015, https://www.whitehouse.gov/the-press-office/2015/09/02/fact-sheet-president-obama-announces-new-investments-combat-climate.

15. Suzanne Goldberg, "America's First Climate Refugees," The Guardian, accessed October 28, 2016, https://www.theguardian.com/environment/interactive/2013/may/13/newtok-alaska-climate-change-refugees.

16. Lisa Demer, "The Creep of Climate Change," *Alaska Dispatch News*, August 29, 2015, https://www.adn.com/rural-alaska/article/threatened-newtok-not-waiting-disintegrating-village-stages-move-new-site/2015/08/30/.

17. Alana Semuels, "The Village That Will Be Swept Away," *Atlantic*, August 30, 2015.

18. Charles Enoch, "Newtok Feeling Nervous about Relocation Timeline," Alaska Public Media, September 21, 2015.

19. "Impossible Choice Faces America's First 'Climate Refugees,'" National Public Radio, *All Things Considered*, May 18, 2013.

20. Cynthia McFadden, Jake Whitman, and Tracy Connor, "Washed Away: Obama's Arctic Visit Buoys Climate Refugees," *NBC Nightly News*, September 1, 2015, http://www.nbcnews.com/storyline/fight-for-the-arctic/obamas-arctic-trip-buoys-climate-refugees-n413726.

21. Charles P. Pierce, "Shishmaref, Alaska Is Still Falling into the Sea," *Esquire*, December 10, 2014, http://www.esquire.com/news-politics/politics/a32091/the-lessons-from-a-dying-village/.

22. McFadden, Whitman, and Connor, "Washed Away."

23. Alex DeMarban, "Eroding Alaska Village Urges Congress to Address Climate Change," *Alaska Dispatch News*, January 16, 2014, https://www.adn.com/environment/article/eroding-alaska-village-urges-congress-address-climate-change/2014/01/17/.

24. Ibid.

25. McFadden, Whitman, and Connor, "Washed Away."

26. Stephen Sackur, "The Alaskan Village Set to Disappear Under Water in a Decade," BBC News, July 30, 2013, http://www.bbc.com/news/magazine-23346370.

27. "Shishmaref Residents Vote to Move Village," Associated Press, July 21, 2002, http://peninsulaclarion.com/stories/072102/ala_072102alapm0020001.shtml#.WBek-slcj5M.

28. Adam Wernick, "Will These Alaska Villagers Be America's First Climate Change Refugees?" Public Radio International, August 9, 2015, http://www.pri.org/stories/2015-08-09/will-residents-kivalina-alaska-be-first-climate-change-refugees-us.

29. "Kivalina lawsuit (re: global warming)," Business & Human Rights Resource Center, June 26, 2013, http://business-humanrights.org/en/kivalina-lawsuit-re-global-warming.

30. Wernick, "Will These Alaska Villagers?"

31. "Kivalina lawsuit (re: global warming)," Business & Human Rights Resource Center.

32. Lawrence Hurley, "U.S. Supreme Court Declines to Hear Alaska Climate Change Case," Reuters, May 20, 2013, http://www.reuters.com/article/usa-court-climate-idUSL2N0DW2B020130520.

33. Bill McKibben quote is a book endorsement on Amazon.com for Christine Shearer's, "Kivalina: A Climate Change Story," Haymarket book reviews, July 2011.

34. Wernick, "Will These Alaska Villagers?"

35. Pierce, "Shishmaref, Alaska."

36. Jillian Rogers, "Arts Organization to Give Kivalina $500,000 Grant for Relocation," *Alaska Dispatch News*, July 26, 2015, https://www.adn.com/rural-alaska/article/arts-organization-give-kivalina-500000-grant-relocation/2015/07/26/.

37. Don Callaway, "The Long-Term Threats from Climate Change to Rural Alaskan Communities," *Alaska Park Science* 12, no. 2: Climate Change in Alaska's National Parks, http://www.nps.gov/articles/aps-v12-i2-c15.htm.

38. Andrew Freedman, "This Louisiana Tribe Is Now America's First Official Climate Refugees," Mashable, February 18, 2016, http://mashable.com/2016/02/18/america-first-climate-refugees/#BdWnBWOIHiqL.

39. Shirley Laska et al., "Layering of Natural and Human-Caused Disasters in the Context of Sea Level Rise: Coastal Louisiana on the Edge," in Michelle Companion, ed., *Disaster's Impact on Livelihood and Cultural Survival: Losses, Opportunities, and Mitigation* (CRC Press, 2015), 227.

40. Rick Jervis, "Louisiana Bays and Bayous Vanish from Nautical Maps," *USA Today*, February 12, 2014.

41. Bob Marshall, "New Research: Louisiana Coast Faces Highest Rate of Sea-Level Rise Worldwide," The Lens, February 21, 2013.

42. Bob Marshall, Brian Jacobs, and Al Shaw, "Losing Ground," ProPublica and The Lens, August 28, 2014, http://projects.propublica.org/louisiana/.

43. Ibid.

44. Freedman, "This Louisiana Tribe."

45. Terri Hansen, "Biloxi-Chitimacha-Choctaw Get $48 Million to Move Off of Disappearing Louisiana Island," Indian Country Today, February 5, 2016.

46. Sue Sturgis, "Losing Its Land to the Gulf, Louisiana Tribe Will Resettle with Disaster Resilience Competition Award Money," *Facing South* (February 9, 2016) https://www.facingsouth.org/2016/02/losing-its-land-to-the-gulf-louisiana-tribe-will-r.html.

47. Freedman, "This Louisiana Tribe."

48. Heath Allen, "Vanishing Tribe: Coastal Erosion Threatens Survival of Biloxi-Chitimacha-Choctaw," WDSU, February 22, 2016, http://www.wdsu.com/article/vanishing-tribe-coastal-erosion-threatens-survival-of-biloxi-chitimacha-choctaw/3384770.

49. Sue Sturgis, "Losing Its Land to the Gulf, Louisiana Tribe Will Resettle with Disaster Resilience Competition Award Money," Institute for Southern Studies, February 9, 2016.

50. Freedman, "This Louisiana Tribe."

51. Allen, "Vanishing Tribe."

52. Ibid.

53. Bob Marshall, Al Shaw, and Brian Jacobs, "Louisiana's Moon Shot," ProPublica and The Lens, December 8, 2014, http://projects.propublica.org/larestoration.

54. Ibid.

55. Bob Marshall, "New Research."

56. Marshall, Shaw, and Jacobs, "Louisiana's Moon Shot."

57. Robert McLean and Irene Chapple, "BP Settles Final Gulf Oil Spill Claims for $20 Billion," CNN Money, October 16, 2015, http://money.cnn.com/2015/10/06/news/companies/deepwater-horizon-bp-settlement/.

58. Jervis, "Louisiana Bays and Bayous."

59. Nathaniel Rich, "The Most Ambitious Environmental Lawsuit Ever," *New York Times*, October 2, 2014, http://www.nytimes.com/interactive/2014/10/02/magazine/mag-oil-lawsuit.html?_r=0.

60. Ibid.

61. "As Louisiana's Coastline Shrinks, a Political Fight over Responsibility Grows," *PBS Newshour*, May 27, 2014.

62. Annie Snider, "Levee Board Picks Fight with Oil and Gas Industry, Roiling La.," *E&E News*, August 28, 2013.

63. "As Louisiana's Coastline Shrinks."

64. "Judge Rejects Suit over Louisiana Drilling," Associated Press, February 13, 2015, http://www.nytimes.com/2015/02/14/us/judge-rejects-suit-over-louisiana-drilling.html.

65. Mark Schleifstein, "Federal Judge Dismisses Levee Authority's Wetlands Damage Lawsuit against Oil, Gas Companies," *Times-Picayune*, February 13, 2015, http://www.nola.com/environment/index.ssf/2015/02/federal_judge_dismisses_east_b.html.

66. Mark Schleifstein, "Jefferson, Plaquemines Parishes File Wetland Damage Lawsuits against Dozens of Oil, Gas, Pipeline Companies," *Times-Picayune*, November 12, 2013, last updated March 15, 2016, http://www.nola.com/environment/index.ssf/2013/11/jefferson_plaquemines_parishes.html.

67. Cain Burdeau, "Louisiana Parish Drops Suits against Oil and Gas Companies," Associated Press, November 12, 2015, http://www.bigstory.ap.org/article/9c4fa662ee4c4a5585e12495fb39adcd/louisiana-parish-drops-suits-against-oil-and-gas-companies.

68. Burdeau, "Louisiana Parish Drops Suits." http://www.bigstory.ap.org/article/9c4fa662ee4c4a5585e12495fb39adcd/louisiana-parish-drops-suits-against-oil-and-gas-companies.

69. Snider, "Levee Board Picks Fight."

70. Linda Qiu, "Direct Revenues from Offshore Oil and Gas Drilling to Increased Coastal Hurricane Protection," Politifact, August 20, 2015.

71. "President Proposes $13.2 Billion Budget for Interior Department," Office of the Secretary of Interior, February 2, 2015 https://www.doi.gov/news/pressreleases/president-proposes-13-2-billion-budget-for-interior-department.

72. Kelsey Snell, "Republicans Reject Obama Budget, Facing Spending Fights of Their Own," *Washington Post*, February 9, 2016, https://www.washingtonpost.com/news/powerpost/wp/2016/02/06/republicans-ready-to-reject-obama-budget-facing-spending-fights-of-their-own/.

73. Marshall, Shaw, and Jacobs, "Louisiana's Moon Shot."

74. Allison Plyer, "Facts for Features: Katrina Impact," The Data Center, August 28, 2015.

75. "Mapping Migration Patterns post-Katrina," *Times-Picayune*, http://www.nola.com/katrina/index.ssf/page/mapping_migration.html.

76. Laura Bliss, "10 Years Later, There's So Much We Don't Know about Where Katrina Survivors Ended Up," City Lab, August 25, 2015, http://www.citylab.com/politics/2015/08/10-years-later-theres-still-a-lot-we-dont-know-about-where-katrina-survivors-ended-up/401216/.

77. Jonathan Tilove, "Five Years after Hurricane Katrina, 100,000 New Orleanians Have Yet to Return," *Times-Picayune*, August 24, 2010, http://www.nola.com/katrina/index.ssf/2010/08/five_years_after_hurricane_kat.html.

78. Lynn Weber, "No Place to Be Displaced: Katrina Response and the Deep South's Political Economy," *Institute for Southern Spaces*, August 17, 2012, https://southernspaces.org/2012/no-place-be-displaced-katrina-response-and-deep-souths-political-economy.

79. Ibid.

80. Bliss, "10 Years Later."

81. Kristin Carlisle, "It's Like You're Walking but Your Feet Ain't Going Nowhere," National Housing Institute, Fall 2006, http://www.shelterforce.org/article/729/its_like_youre_walking_but_your_feet_aint_going_nowhere/.

82. Daniel J. Hopkins, "Flooded Communities: Explaining Local Reactions to the Post-Katrina Migrants," *Political Research Quarterly* 20, no. 10 (2011): 1–17; Ryan Holeywell, "No, Katrina Evacuees Didn't Cause a Houston Crime Wave," *Houston Chronicle*, August 26, 2015.

83. David Roberts, "Hurricane Katrina Showed What 'Adapting to Climate Change' Looks Like," Vox, August 24, 2015, http://www.vox.com/2015/8/24/9194707/katrina-climate-adaptation.

84. "New Orleans Ten Years after the Storm: African Americans and Whites Live Differing Realities," Henry J. Kaiser Family Foundation, August 10, 2015, http://kff.org/infographic/new-orleans-ten-years-after-the-storm-african-americans-and-whites-live-differing-realities/.

85. "Hurricane Sandy Fast Facts," CNN Library, CNN.com, November 2, 2016 http://www.cnn.com/2013/07/13/world/americas/hurricane-sandy-fast-facts/.

86. Patrick McGeehan and Griff Palmer, "Displaced by Hurricane Sandy and Living in Limbo," *New York Times*, December 6, 2013, http://www.nytimes.com/2013/12/07/nyregion/displaced-by-hurricane-sandy-and-living-in-limbo-instead-of-at-home.html.

87. Russ Zimmer, "Report: Thousands of Sandy Families Waiting on State," *Asbury Park Press*, February 4, 2015, http://www.app.com/story/news/local/2015/02/04/sandy-recovery-report/22885571/; "The State of Sandy Recovery Two and a Half Years Later, Over 15,000 Families Still Waiting to Rebuild," Fair Share Housing Center Second Annual Report, February 2015.

88. "The State of Sandy Recovery Fixing What Went Wrong with New Jersey's Sandy Programs to Build a Fair and Transparent Recovery for Everyone," Fair Share Housing

Center, Housing and Community Development Network of New Jersey, Latino Action Network, and NAACP New Jersey State Conference, January 2014.

89. Andrea Thompson, "Storm Surge Could Flood NYC 1 in Every 4 Years," Climate Central, April 25, 2014, http://www.climatecentral.org/news/storm-surge-could-flood-nyc-1-in-every-4-years-17344.

90. Ibid.

91. "Sea Level Rise Accelerating in U.S. Atlantic Coast," USGS.gov, June 24, 2012, https://www.usgs.gov/news/sea-level-rise-accelerating-us-atlantic-coast.

92. Kevin E. Trenberth, John T. Fasullo, and Theodore G. Shepherd, "Attribution of climate extreme events," *Nature Climate Change* 5, June 22, 2015.

93. Thompson, "Storm Surge."

94. "Explaining Extreme Events of 2012 from a Climate Perspective," Special Supplement to the *Bulletin of the American Meteorological Society* 94, no. 9 (September 2013).

95. Joe Romm, "Superstorm Sandy's Link to Climate Change: 'The Case Has Strengthened' Says Researcher," ThinkProgress, October 28, 2013, https://thinkprogress.org/superstorm-sandys-link-to-climate-change-the-case-has-strengthened-says-researcher-f80927c1d033#.3b7smjjow.

96. "Risks of Hurricane Sandy–like Surge Events Rising," Climate Central, January 24, 2013, http://www.climatecentral.org/news/hurricane-sandy-unprecedented-in-historical-record-study-says-15505.

97. Lydia O'Connor, "More Than 400 U.S. Cities May Be 'Past the Point of No Return' with Sea Level Threats," Huffington Post, October 13, 2015, last updated October 14, 2015, http://www.huffingtonpost.com/entry/us-cities-sea-level-threats_us_561d338fe4b0c5a1ce60a45c.

98. Victoria Herrmann, "America's Climate Refugee Crisis Has Already Begun," *Los Angeles Times*, January 25, 2016, http://www.latimes.com/opinion/op-ed/la-oe-0125-herrmann-climate-refugees-20160125-story.html.

99. "State Mitigation Plan Review Guide," Federal Emergency Management Agency, March 2015.

100. Avery G. Wilks, "Columbia Has Extensive Flood Recovery Wish List," *The State*, March 1, 2016.

101. Rich McKay, "At Least 17 Dead as Flooding Threat Persists in South Carolina," Reuters, October 7, 2015.

102. 2014 National Climate Assessment, US Global Change Research Program.

103. Neena Satija, Kiah Collier, Al Shaw, and Jeff Larson, "Hell and High Water," *Texas Tribune* and ProPublica, March 3, 2016.

104. Dave Boyer, "Bobby Jindal Blasts New FEMA Rule on Climate Change," *Washington Times*, March 24, 2015, http://www.washingtontimes.com/news/2015/mar/24/bobby-jindal-blasts-new-fema-rule-climate-change/.

105. Ibid.

106. Tristram Korten, "In Florida, Officials Ban Term 'Climate Change,'" Florida Center for Investigative Reporting, March 8, 2015, http://fcir.org/2015/03/08/in-florida-officials-ban-term-climate-change/.

107. Lydia Wheeler, "Feds to Require Climate Change Plans for States Seeking Disaster Relief," *The Hill*, May 5, 2015, http://thehill.com/regulation/241050-gop-lawmakers-ask-fema-to-explain-new-disaster-grant-requirement.

108. "Scientist Predicts Mass Exodus of Climate Refugees to Pacific Northwest," *Global News*, January 2, 2015, http://globalnews.ca/news/1750950/scientist-predicts-mass-exodus-of-climate-change-refugees-to-pacific-northwest/.

109. Cliff Mass, "Will the Pacific Northwest Be a Climate Refuge under Global Warming?" Cliff Mass Weather Blog, July 28, 2014, http://cliffmass.blogspot.ca/2014/07/will-pacific-northwest-be-climate.html.

110. Knute Berger, "Climate Refugees Are Coming to the Pacific Northwest," September 16, 2014, Crosscut.com, http://crosscut.com/2014/09/climate-refugees-pacific-nw-knute-berger/.

111. Ernest Callnbach, *Ecotopia: The Notebooks and Reports of William Weston* (Berkely, CA: Banan Tree Books, 1975).

112. Paolo Bacigalupi, *The Water Knife* (New York: Vintage Books, 2016).

113. "What If the Drought Doesn't End? 'The Water Knife" Is One Possibility," NPR.org, May 23, 2015, http://www.npr.org/2015/05/23/408756002/what-if-the-drought-doesnt-end-the-water-knife-is-one-possibility

5

Latin America

LAND OF RAIN, LAND OF THIRST

> Rains recently have been very intense. Very intense. Without comparison, like nothing seen before. . . . We don't want to leave our land. Here are our past, our memories, our ancestors. We don't want to move to other parts. We don't know what to do there. We will turn into delinquents. We'd enter into a cycle of poverty which happens in the cities.
>
> *Octavio Rodriguez, Las Caracuchas, Sucre, Colombia*

Immigration crises are already at our doorstep and have been for years. Women and children are fleeing Central America by the tens of thousands, overwhelming border security. Many children are alone. Many are forced to turn back. Others stay, only to face racism and hostility, yet remain in the United States because it is better than the alternative.

The challenges of securing the border and providing care and social services to immigrants and refugees from our southern Americas are extensive enough to fill books themselves. This book discusses the broad-ranging environmental factors that are pushing people to flee and forcing migration and that will inevitably exacerbate the refugee crisis. Immigration is largely discussed in the public arena in the context of border security, but soon the conversation surrounding Latin American refugees may have to turn to climate change.

CLIMATE CHANGE: WHO IS MOST VULNERABLE?

The land and people in Latin America and the Caribbean are among the world's most vulnerable to the impacts of climate change and severe

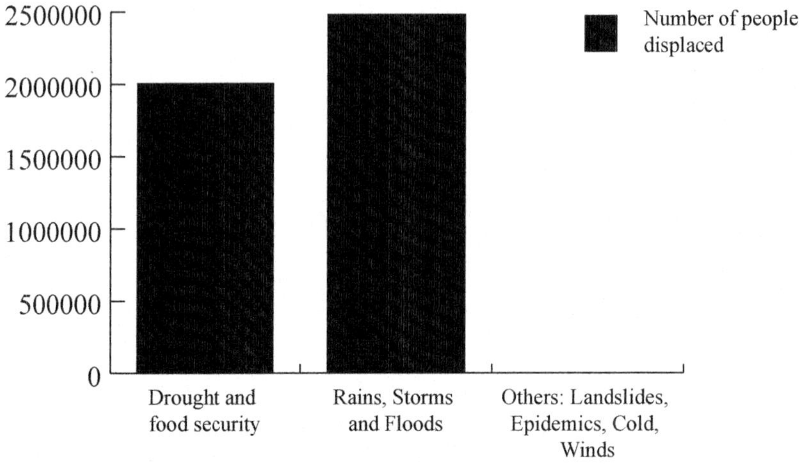

Figure 5.1: Drivers of displacement in Latin America. Source: United Nations Office for the Coordination of Humanitarian Affairs, "Humanitarian Bulletin: Latin America and Caribbean," vol. 21 (January–April 2015).

weather. Every region faces its own unique threat and harsh environment; many face more than one. In Central America, drought reigns supreme, leading to water shortages and food crises. In the same region, the short-lived rainy seasons bring a great amount of destruction. Water shortages and food crises are as common as flash floods and landslides. In the nearby coastal countries and Caribbean islands, hurricanes rip through on a consistent basis. In South America, clear-cutting of the Amazon rain forest is resulting in parched lands and fewer rains. Harsh conditions are driving people from agricultural communities into the cities, where, combined with the continent's drought, they face severe water shortages.

In the first three months of 2015 alone, four and a half million people in Latin America and the Caribbean were impacted by environmental disasters—mostly from floods and storms but a near equivalent amount from drought and food insecurity (see fig. 5.1). In an attempt to respond, the governments have been placing massive restrictions on water usage, handing out seed packets, and calling for foreign aid. However, these are short-term Band-Aids, not long-term solutions.

Meanwhile, the region faces one of the world's highest rates of violence, forcing parents to send their children to flee on solo journeys to escape potential injury or even death.[1] As more land turns unlivable and climate change accelerates, even more people will flee the region, turning Latin America into one of the world's greatest sources of environmental refugees.

DROUGHT: UNQUESTIONABLE AND GETTING WORSE

Drought in Latin America is unquestionably worsening as the planet warms. Extreme drought runs rampant even in the tropical region of Central America, a place that often conjures images of lush, wet rain forests. But while patches of tropical cloud forests are scattered throughout Central America, an arid region stretches throughout the land, known as the "Dry Corridor," or "*Corredor Seco.*" Panama, Honduras, Nicaragua, El Salvador, and the Dominican Republic all have land in this region, which has been bearing the brunt of severe drought in recent years. The Dry Corridor is cut off from ocean humidity by mountain ranges in the Caribbean, which create a rain shadow. The region experiences dry seasons that last longer than those in surrounding areas and is vulnerable to drought when its already short rainy season is reduced by El Niño—or by climate change.[2]

In 2014 Guatemala's government declared a state of emergency, prompting drastic water restrictions and increased funding for aid. In August 2015 both Panama and Honduras followed suit, declaring states of emergency.[3] The Dry Corridor is at a unique risk of drought, and therefore food insecurity and hunger, which has triggered migration away from the region and through Mexico to the United States. Many of the immigrants who arrive in the States are running from hunger or from violent conflicts that arise from such resource scarcity.

Throughout 2014 and 2015, long-lasting drought ran through the Dry Corridor, killing a huge amount of crops and affecting millions of people in the region. In total, 3.5 million people were affected, according to the United Nations' Office for the Coordination of Humanitarian Affairs (OCHA). As of October 2015, two million were in dire need of food,

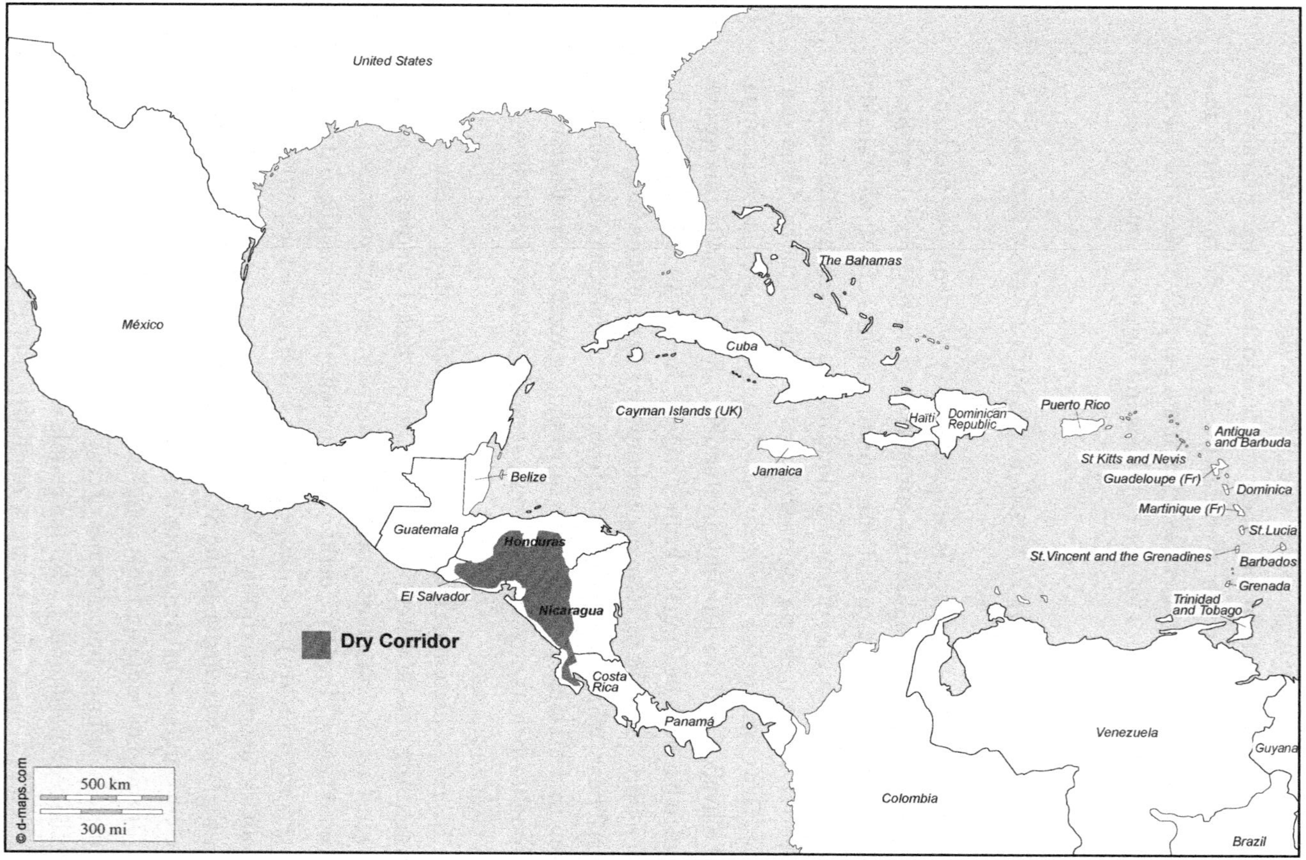

Map 5.1: The Dry Corridor

health care, and other assistance.[4] Without enough resources, many were at risk of dengue and malnutrition, especially children under five years old. A Salvadoran coffee picker by the name of Esperanza said, "We've seen severe changes in the children here. Children are malnourished. Some severely. We have also seen the elderly growing more tired because of the lack of food."[5]

The crisis highlighted the extreme vulnerability of the region's residents: subsistence farmers, laborers, and low-income families who live in the Dry Corridor rely on consistent rains to keep their way of life. When rainfall patterns change sharply in either direction, this leads to crop failures and harms food supplies, threatening the livelihoods of these farming communities. And the drought of 2014–2015 was costly: nearly $100 million in crops were destroyed in El Salvador alone, affecting over one hundred thousand farmers. The country's Ministry of Agriculture and Livestock had to step in and distribute hundreds of thousands of seed packets so that farmers could replant their corn and bean crops, which are staples for Salvadorans.[6]

Droughts, and correspondingly hunger crises, are not uncommon in the Dry Corridor. But in recent decades they have worsened. The United Nations reported that nearly half of Guatemalan children under five years old "suffer from stunting as a result of chronic under-nutrition."[7] As recently as 2009, drought and high food prices led to a severe hunger crisis in Guatemala, prompting a state of emergency. The executive director of the United Nations' World Food Programme said of the situation, "Women and children have been caught in the vortex of this hunger crisis and are in a desperate struggle for survival."[8]

Yet the 2014 drought was even worse. That year, the Dry Corridor saw its most prolonged drought in four decades. The severity highlighted the region's unique vulnerability to drought and rainfall: the land is largely unirrigated, relying solely on rainfall instead.[9] The area also has the highest levels of food insecurity in Central America, according to the European Commission Humanitarian Aid Office.

The region's dry period has historically lasted between January and April, but recently it has stretched until June or July. And in El Niño years, which occur every two to seven years, the dry period often lasts even longer. During the years of extreme drought, the dry season lasted until even October.[10] The total land area of the Dry Corridor may also be expanding. In Honduras, José Antonio Velásquez, director of international cooperation for Honduras's emergency relief agency, told Fusion.net his country's Dry Corridor has nearly tripled in size over the past three decades. "The dry corridor now covers almost 45 percent of national territory," he said, when it used to be "limited to the extreme south of the country, near the Nicaraguan border."[11] As the globe warms, the Dry Corridor's climate will become harsher and life more difficult.

FLOODS IN A DRY PLACE LEAD TO CROP LOSS, LANDSLIDES

The rainy season isn't always a saving grace, even in the Dry Corridor. Floods and storms can be just as devastating—or worse—to the region as droughts. All told, OCHA determined that floods and storms were the greatest threat to Latin Americans in the first three months of 2015, affecting two and a half million people.[12]

The Dry Corridor is extremely dependent on its rainy seasons to replenish the land. But when the dry season lasts longer than it is supposed to, and the earth gets sucked dry, the rains can prove to be a curse rather than a blessing. The rain comes in torrents, leading to flash floods, washing away the arable land. Tropical storms—and superstorms and hurricanes—destroy more than they heal.

As a case in point, 2009 saw extreme drought in the Dry Corridor, followed by a tropical storm that left thousands of victims. Guatemala, El Salvador, and Nicaragua all experienced great losses in food production during a drought and were subsequently hammered by Tropical Storm Ida. The storm affected forty thousand people in Nicaragua, leaving thirteen thousand homeless.[13]

In 2010, tropical rains battered Central America, with total precipitation well above the yearly average.[14] The heavy rains resulted in flooding and landslides and deteriorated agricultural production, which is vital for the region's food supply. One storm, Tropical Storm Agatha, destroyed thirty-five hundred houses and killed ninety-nine people, including thirteen from one landslide in Guatemala.[15]

Elsewhere in Central America in 2009, Tropical Storm Ida led to record rains in El Salvador—up to seventeen inches of rain were dumped within two days—and prompted landslides that destroyed scores of homes. At least 190 people were killed and ten thousand were displaced, forced into shelters.[16]

In 2011, landslides in Central America killed at least eighty people in El Salvador, Guatemala, Honduras, and Nicaragua. The BBC reported: "International highways have been washed out, villages isolated and thousands of families have lost homes and crops."[17]

In October 2014, landslides killed more than thirty people in Nicaragua and surrounding countries.[18] Eight hundred and ninety Nicaraguan homes were flooded and twenty-four were destroyed in the landslides.[19]

Flood-induced landslides are a result of extreme rainfall on parched land. Both of those factors are expected to get worse with climate change—some predict they already have. Since 1970, global temperatures have increased nearly two-tenths of a degree centigrade each decade.[20] Meanwhile, while the average amount of precipitation has not increased, "rainfall events are intensifying and the contribution of wet and very wet days are growing," according to a study from the agriculture research organization Consultative Group on International Agricultural Research.[21]

HOW "EL NIÑO" COMES INTO PLAY

Of course, there are natural factors at hand in Central America's climatic variations. If you do an Internet search for the phrase "What caused Central American drought?" the answer you will most certainly get is "El Niño," a natural phenomenon that has been going on for thousands of years. However, there is evidence to show that climate change has a hand in making El Niño conditions worse.

El Niño Southern Oscillation, or ENSO, is a term for a meteorological phenomenon that occurs in the Pacific Ocean once every several years and affects weather in many regions of the planet. The worst dry seasons, thereby the worst droughts, happen during ENSO years. The phenomenon was named in the 1800s by Peruvian fishermen who noticed a warm current appearing around Christmastime every few years.

Here's how ENSO works. Normally, trade winds blow from east to west over the Pacific Ocean, from the western coast of South America to the eastern coast of Asia. The winds bring warm ocean waters heated by the sun to Southeast Asia that then sink down to the bottom of the ocean and are transported back along the ocean floor to South America, due to the lack of pressure in ocean water there. The water cools down as it is transported back, and when it reaches South America, it rises up, bringing nutrients from the ocean floor and cooling the atmosphere. During ENSO years this pattern is disrupted. Westerly winds push back on the eastern trade winds, and the warm waters come back to South America's eastern shores. The result is twofold: on the Pacific coast, Central America experiences warmer temperatures, leading to hotter days and prolonged drought in the dry season; conversely, on the Caribbean coast, South and Central America experience heavier rain and flooding, as the warmer atmosphere holds more moisture.

The United Nations' Food and Agriculture Organization has previously attributed Latin America's major crop losses to ENSO.[22] In 2015 the Central American Agricultural Council, which is headed by agriculture ministers in the region, declared a state of alert after "hundreds of thousands of subsistence farmers have suffered the partial or total loss of their crops planted for the main grain season that runs from May to September," according to the FAO. But FAO economist Felix Baquedano noted that 2015's ENSO conditions were worse than they had been in the past, due in part to the "intensifying dry weather" experienced in the two previous years. As a result, Baquedano said, "It's critical that we support farmers to recuperate some of their losses by helping them achieve stronger yields in the second season."[23]

Multiple studies show that climate change could lead to more frequent "extreme" or "super" El Niños—like El Niño, but on steroids.[24] These super El Niños are particularly strong, leading to hotter, drier conditions and more storm-filled weather patterns in Central America (as noted above, whether a location will be drier or will experience more severe storms with El Niño depends on the particular region). Previous super El Niños that have occurred led to landslides in Peru, wildfires in Indonesia, and decimation of South America's anchovy fishery. They have cost up to $45 billion in damage and twenty-three thousand deaths worldwide.[25]

As climate change intensifies, such super El Niños may happen twice as often as they do now, according to climate researchers at Australia's Commonwealth Scientific and Industrial Research Organisation.[26] Extreme El Niño events have historically occurred once every twenty years; with climate change the likelihood increases to once every ten years. Other studies predict a smaller increase in extreme ENSO events.[27] But 2015, the warmest year on record, experienced the strongest El Niño in recorded history.[28] The El Niño that took place in the final months of 2015 and beginning of 2016 *was* a monster, in no less accurate terms. NASA scientist William Patzert said it could become a "Godzilla" El Niño.[29] In addition to the drought in Central America, Chile and northern Brazil face drought-worsening conditions with El Niño.[30]

DROUGHT, FOOD SECURITY HAVE BEEN SPECIFICALLY LINKED TO MIGRATION

In Central America, no stranger to drought-induced states of emergency, residents and experts have pointed to the droughts as a reason for migration from the region northward to Mexico and the United States. In the wake of a 2014 drought, Guatemalan agricultural engineer Bayron Medina of the Inter-American Institute of Agricultural Cooperation predicted: "If the drought is not over in two months, there will be famine and people will leave for the U.S. Eventually, the drought did end. But Medina vocalized a common train of thought in such a region. He added that droughts in Guatemala had been "intensifying and accelerating" over the previous decade.[31] Migration as a form of adaptation is becoming commonplace.

There are conflicting sentiments as to how poverty comes into play concerning drought-induced migration. To some, migration is considered a luxury, a privilege given to those who can afford it. "The poor can't migrate," said Manuel Orozco of the think tank Inter-American Dialogue; "that's not how migration works." Orozco said the drought could increase immigration, but "people who migrate are those who can afford to get out."[32] Others attribute migration directly to poverty, like Leoncio Vasquez, executive director of the Binational Center for the Development of Oaxacan Indigenous Communities. When asked about the 120,000 people who have moved from Mexico to the United States in recent years because of drought, Vasquez responded, "Really, it's 100 percent because of poverty." But, he added, "A lot of that poverty is coming because of the drought. If you can't farm you can't eat, and people start doing other things like cutting down trees for wood to sell. And then that starts a downward spiral where things just keep getting worse. . . . All these people—people like me—all we want to do is to make a living for ourselves, but it gets to the point that it's impossible and you have to pick up and leave."[33]

The connection between drought and migration is still being examined. Several studies find a direct link between drought and forced migration, such as in some regions of Mexico and sub-Saharan Africa. Others find no such link, suggesting that drought-induced migration is dependent on the context.[34] But it is becoming increasingly accepted that severe drought can result in migration and has already done so. As droughts worsen, migration will become ever more visible.

While the link between drought and migration may be up for dispute, the connection between food security and migration is stronger. The International Organization for Migration (IOM) and the United Nations' World Food Programme (WFP) teamed together to review the research on this very topic. A 2015 report of their findings details how migration induced by food insecurity plays out in three Central American countries: El Salvador, Guatemala, and Honduras.[35] In those countries they found that hunger, violence, and migration are intertwined, especially when the region is "suffering the effects of prolonged dry spells or droughts for the second consecutive year." The report definitely found what had been commonly assumed: food insecurity leads to migration.[36]

Despite the fact that the connection between food insecurity and migration is clear—when one takes the time to look into it—this connection is rarely discussed. The WFP/IOM report found that food security is "generally absent from the current debate on migration and development," while the issue itself "is primarily seen as an issue affecting the rural poor, who are in no way representative of the whole range of migrants."[37]

Perhaps discussing the two issues together is necessary for the public to understand the connection between climate change and refugees. After all, the link between climate change and food security is understood and is thoroughly documented by several international organizations.[38] The ramifications of food insecurity reach far and wide. The 2014 Central American drought led to a food crisis that left nearly three million people struggling to feed themselves, according to the WFP.[39] In Guatemala, 70 percent of the land was impacted by the drought, resulting in the suffering of half of its population. Chronic malnutrition among children became rampant.[40] To make matters worse, global warming will hamper efforts to fight hunger. The charitable organization Oxfam has detailed how a changed climate can set back efforts to eradicate hunger by decades.[41] Several efforts are needed to protect food systems.

So global warming wipes out food supplies and increases food insecurity while also hampering efforts to address food security and hunger—yet another vicious cycle of climate change that will inevitably result in forced migration. There may be one or two steps to take to get from global warming to refugees, but the connection is very real.

HOW SEA LEVEL RISE HARMS THE CARIBBEAN

With one meter of sea level rise expected by the end of the century, many Caribbean islands will experience catastrophic consequences.[42] As discussed in chapter 3, however, many studies indicate sea level rise will be much greater than that. In the Caribbean region, at least, the literature shows sea levels experiencing a rise of anywhere from one to two meters over the twenty-first century. Even the low end of that estimate will have severe ramifications on countries in the Caribbean community (CARICOM). A report from the United Nations detailed what that seemingly insignificant rise will mean for CARICOM. Just one meter—the low end of the spectrum—will "permanently inundate" 1 percent of the total land area, but this 1 percent is a significant portion, representing some of the region's most valuable land. The Bahamas will be particularly vulnerable, with 5 percent of its land permanently flooded, and Antigua and Barbuda with 2 percent. Subsequently, 5 and 3 percent of their respective populations will be displaced.[43]

This is the number of people who live in areas that will be permanently submerged into the ocean, but far more will be affected by persistent flooding and storm surge. In the Bahamas, for instance, 22 percent of the population is at risk of flooding due to sea level rise and storm surge. Such events will cost the country up to $2 billion a year before century's end. All told, at least 110,000 people will be displaced from their homes in the Caribbean states. This flooding is also expected to cost the area's economy billions of dollars each year, but they will have only limited resources to help their population adapt.[44] These are just the consequences of climate change that have already been locked in, as a one-meter sea level rise is all but inevitable.[45] It will be even worse if sea levels rise two meters, with double the number of displaced people.[46]

Yet even as sea levels rise, the Caribbean countries face extreme drought, bringing to mind the phrase "Water, water, everywhere, but not a drop to drink." In the summer of 2015, the worst drought in five years spread through the region.[47] In Haiti 50 percent of crops were lost, and the Dominican Republic was expected to lose 30 percent of its crops. The drought particularly impacted Puerto Rico, where over half the country was in severe drought.[48] Under imposed water restrictions, tens of thousands of residents received water only one every three days.[49] This level of severe water rationing, in some areas, leads to civilian unrest. Between the drought, the sea level rise, and intensified hurricanes, the Caribbean has, in the words of Florida reporter Tim Padgett, "begun to feel like a climate-change doormat."[50]

The interplay between sea level rise and drought is also present in Central America, which, as discussed previously, is vulnerable to drought. United Nations climate reports have highlighted the region's vulnerability to sea level rise, particularly that of the "isthmus countries"—Nicaragua, Costa Rica, and Panama. The regions rely on flat coastal plains for agriculture and economic activities. Sea level rise will exacerbate coastal erosion in the region, stressing countries that are already stressed by agricultural problems. Furthermore, as a result of sea level rise, ocean saltwater will infiltrate coastal aquifers, further threatening the region's water supply.[51]

ABOVE THE AMAZON: THE HURRICANE BELT

Hurricanes, bringing winds that blow at multiple hundreds of miles per hour and surging waves, leveling houses, flooding streets, are much more frightening, and immediate, than the long-standing issues of drought, soil erosion, and sea level rise. They are the final battering ram of global warming that hits islands that are already vulnerable to climate change. In the past, migration that has resulted from hurricanes has been temporary and has resulted in only internal migration. But as the impacts of global warming worsen, if a community is ravaged by drought and food scarcity, having a home destroyed by a hurricane may be the final straw that forces residents to leave the country.[52]

Hurricanes have a history of displacing Central American people by the thousands, even millions. One historical hurricane exemplified this. In 1998 Hurricane Mitch ravaged the region. With wind speeds of 180 miles per hour and ten-foot storm surges, the strongest storm of the season killed as many as 18,000—the highest death toll since 1780.[53] The storm displaced millions of people from Nicaragua, Honduras, and El Salvador, many of them permanently. In Honduras international emigration rates increased by 300 percent.[54]

The Council on Hemispheric Affairs has characterized this situation as a warning for the rest of the world, calling it "an illustration of the normally low capacity of response present in areas of Latin America."[55] The organization notes that disaster prevention and relief responses, as they are, currently leave hundreds of thousands of people homeless during the hurricane season.

In 2004 Hurricane Ivan wreaked the Caribbean Basin; 2005 saw a record hurricane season; and in 2010 Tropical Storm Matthew damaged Venezuela. Of great concern is that hurricanes are expected to get stronger in coming decades, because as much of the global warming is being absorbed by the oceans, warmer ocean waters fuel stronger storms.[56]

In Central America the multipronged ramifications of climate change are clear. Being vulnerable to severe weather events from all sides, it is no wonder why the region is one of the world's most vulnerable to climate change. Migration between Central America and South America, and between South America and the United States via Central America, will be an important issue in the years to come.

URBANIZATION: HOTSPOTS FOR STRESS AND CONFLICT

Climate change–induced displacement doesn't always require someone registering as a refugee or even leaving their own country. Rather, climate change effects can lead people to migrate away from rural areas—where their pastoral, agricultural lifestyles are vulnerable to intense droughts or floods—into cities.

The urbanization trend is massive and predicted to increase across the globe. Yet Latin America is on the forefront of this trend, in recent decades becoming the most urbanized continent. In 1950 just 40 percent of the Latin American population was living in cities. In 1990 that proportion was 70 percent. And currently about 80 percent of Latin Americans are city dwellers.[57] This proportion is far greater than that of any other continent.[58] But the rest of the world is evolving in a similar fashion; by 2050, 70 percent of the global population will be living in cities.[59] The problems Latin America faces as a result of rapid urbanization can be warning signs—or lessons—for other regions. Policies responding to urbanization can provide equitable governance and long-term economic solutions, or they can fail to prevent shocks to the economic system, placing stresses on resources such as food, water, and medical services, and in some cases, as seen in Brazil, erupt in violence.

For those facing extreme drought and crop failure in the countryside, migration into the cities may seem like a promising alternative. But urban populations also face unique risks when it comes to climate change. For one thing, urban dwellers are the most vulnerable to the extreme heat events that will happen with increased frequency as the globe warms. This is partially due to the urban "heat island effect." By clearing away forests and the natural environment and replacing it with concrete sidewalks and tall dark buildings, the built environment in cities absorb

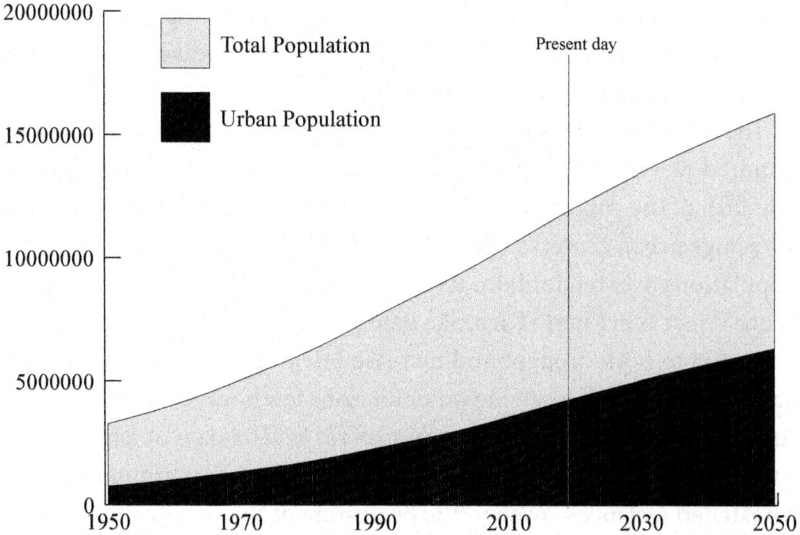

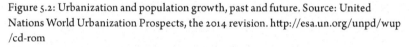

Figure 5.2: Urbanization and population growth, past and future. Source: United Nations World Urbanization Prospects, the 2014 revision. http://esa.un.org/unpd/wup/cd-rom

and amplify hot temperatures. The heat island effect can be deadly; in cities in northern Mexico, heat waves have resulted in increased mortality rates,[60] and in Buenos Aires, 10 percent of deaths in the summer are due to heat stress.[61] Despite the risks, the city remains a mecca for impoverished farmers, and the rate of urbanization will continue to increase in Latin America, as well as around the world. By 2050, 90 percent of the Latin American population will be living in cities.[62] To see how this results in serious problems—water scarcity, paucity of infrastructure, poverty, and strife—one may look to Brazil.

BRAZIL: SPIKES IN URBAN MIGRATION FOLLOWED YEARS OF DROUGHT

In Brazil drought in the agricultural rural regions have spurred migration into its rapidly growing coastal cities. Agriculture has particularly suffered in northeastern Brazil, so farmers have left for the cities on the coast and in the south.[63] The increase in urbanization is mostly coming from surrounding agricultural areas that previously supported a huge portion of the country's labor.[64] As temperatures increase, Brazil's rural areas are expected to continue to depopulate.

The living standards for these new migrants are less than ideal. One hundred eleven million Latin Americans live in shanty towns (nearly one-fifth of the population of the continent) that sprawl from the country's huge urban centers.[65] Brazil is now host of three "megacities" with populations over ten million: Rio de Janeiro, São Paulo, and Belo Horizonte.[66] Just as in Puerto Rico, São Paulo has faced extreme water restrictions due to both drought and increased demand. The city's residents have struggled with receiving water for just a few hours each day. Several thousands have had their water shut off for several days at a time. This has led to apartment building managers seeing vicious arguments and threatened violence—even in the beginning of the water crisis, in February 2015.[67]

It worsened later that year. In March the drastic water shortages led to public uprisings. Hundreds of citizens protested in the streets of São Paulo, chanting, "Water is a resource that must be preserved."[68] Igor Silva, who led the chants, said they were "demanding equitable distribution of water in all the cities in São Paulo state." The Brazilian government wasn't admitting it was rationing water, according to Silva.[69]

Unable to deal with the drought and water shortages, many people have actually started moving *away* from São Paulo, unable to deal with the drought. An unidentified manager drilling for water reserves told NPR he moved his family to the countryside after his building went under water rationing; he called himself a "water refugee."[70]

In response to the civil unrest, Brazilian officials considered turning to military intervention to keep the peace. At a conference between government officials, academics, and military employees, some predicted the city would run out of water. Others predicted that water would be shut off for five days at a time.[71]

Paolo Massato, engineer at the state's water company working to bring water to São Paulo, told Telesur a worst-case scenario would be "terrible. No [*sic*] would be no food, no [*sic*] would be no electricity. . . . It would be a scene from the end of the world. There [would be] thousands of people, and it could cause social chaos. It would not only be a problem of water shortage, it would be much more than that."[72] Brazil has not (as of 2016) turned to police intervention, but the mere fact that such actions have even been discussed does not bode well.

Moreover, this threat is not limited to São Paulo. One year before, the city of Itu—one hundred kilometers away from São Paulo—water shutoffs led to fighting in water queues, looting, and theft from water trucks.[73] One can only imagine that water shutoffs in other megacities will lead to similar cases of unrest, sparking violence and creating a bad situation that will force others to leave.

THE AMAZON RAINFOREST BEING REMOVED BY THE MINUTE

The Amazon rainforest is not only full of ecological treasures, beauty, and culture; it is also an important environmental safeguard for both South America and the world as a whole. It is the lifeblood for much of the continent. And not only is it getting cleared away by the minute, but it is also expected to decrease in size even further because of climate change.

The clear-cutting of the Amazon rain forest has had huge ramifications for the rest of the continent's economy, culture, and climate. In the short term it has had a hand in amplifying the region's ongoing drought.[74] Antonio Nobre, one of Brazil's leading scientists, has warned that the degradation of the Amazon has reduced moisture in the atmosphere and lengthened dry seasons, contributing to the drought that led to such unrest in São Paulo.[75]

Conversely, deforestation is contributing to massive *flooding* in the lower region. Deforestation leads to increased erosion and water runoff, so the land is much less resistant to protecting itself from floods. At the same time that São Paulo was facing severe drought, the Bolivian Amazon region experienced floods that displaced thousands of people.[76] In February 2015 more than four thousand people were forced from their homes in a northern Bolivian town called Cobija.[77] However, this was minor compared to the impacts of the 2014 floods and resulting landslides, which killed at least fifty-six people and affected over fifty thousand families.[78] Bolivia has long had a problem with people displaced from floods, but the floods of 2014 were the worst in twenty-five-years, with up to four hundred thousand people affected.[79] Bolivian officials are adamant that the floods have gotten worse in recent years, citing climate change.[80] This was affirmed in 2007 by the United Nations' Intergovernmental Panel on Climate Change, which stated that there was an 80 percent probability that global warming had worsened Bolivian flooding.[81]

The Amazon River is essential for regulating the region's water and climate. An amazing phenomenon that comes from the Amazon is its "rivers in the sky" or "flying rivers." The rain forest trees essentially act as one giant water pump, absorbing moisture from the soil and pumping it out as water vapor, a process called transpiration. This process produces a vast amount of moisture, so much so that there is more vapor discharged into the sky than the Amazon discharges into the ocean. In one day, while the Amazon River discharges seventeen million tons of water into the Atlantic Ocean, the Amazon rain forest evaporates twenty billion tons of vapor.[82] This process is hugely important for bringing water to nearby countries. The clouds move across Latin America and fall as rain, nourishing agricultural economies. More than two-thirds of the rain in southeastern Brazil comes from these sky rivers.[83]

The hydrological system of the Amazon is at a dangerous tipping point. In the past two decades, an area twice the size of Germany has been removed. The destruction of the Amazon will lead to more extreme drought and other severe weather events, according to Nobre's review of the scientific literature on the topic. He warns that the "vegetation-climate equilibrium is teetering on the brink of the abyss."[84]

Nobre and many others concerned about the state of the Amazon are calling for a halt in deforestation practices and for replanting projects. Brazil's current president, Dilma Rousseff, has loosened efforts to protect the Amazon.[85] In the past two years the deforestation rate has *increased*.[86] This is due in large part to illegal logging, but some activists blame the government for poor oversight on illegal operations. If the current rate of deforestation keeps up, according to senior researcher Rita Mesquita, with Brazil's National Institute for Research in the Amazon, the rainforest "could be gone in 30 or 40 years."[87]

While illegal logging is contributing to climate change, climate change in turn is contributing to the destruction of the Amazon. Global warming is going to cause extreme damage to the forests. Higher temperatures will reduce rainfall in the region and subsequently less "homegrown" rainfall provided by the forests, drying out the land.[88] The rain forest tree species are not meant to grow in dry soil; their roots collapse and the trees fall.

Currently the Amazon rain forest's dry season is three weeks longer than it was thirty years ago. The IPCC predicts it will continue to increase up to ten days longer by 2100. The dry season is the "most important climate condition controlling the rain forest," according to University of Texas climate scientist Rong Fu.[89]

The UK's national weather service, the Met Office, predicted in 2009 that global warming could result in dieback rates up to 40 percent.[90] It has since figured that this would be the worst-case scenario, yet it is a scenario to prepare for nevertheless.[91]

The destruction of the Amazon forest is one of the processes that provides "positive feedback" to global warming; it will increase the rate of global warming, thus speeding up the process of rain forest degradation and so on. As one of the world's major carbon sinks, the Amazon rain forest could be invaluable for fighting global warming. Replanting will be of utmost necessity. Yet currently deforestation rates have more than compensated for any positive efforts taken to protect the region.[92]

Meanwhile, tree die-off in the Amazon is yet another major source of greenhouse gas emissions. During the 2005 and 2010 droughts, the Amazon rain forest unleashed huge quantities of emissions; in 2005 it released more than the annual emissions of Europe and Japan combined, and though the quantity of emissions released during the 2010 drought was not calculated, its effects were even more severe.[93] As if that's not enough, there is one more addition to the deforestation/emission/climate-change cycle: the greater amount of carbon dioxide in the air can actually speed up the trees' life cycles, making them die sooner.[94] Thus the cycle repeats—tree die-off fuels drought, and the emissions from the dying trees raise temperatures, killing more trees—it builds on itself, and repeats again.

Latin America is a land of much beauty and history. It also faces multiple threats from global warming in nearly every region, threatening the way of life for people who have lived there for thousands of years. While extreme weather events have created massive migration movements, these movements have largely been contained within the continent, though they are no less life-threatening. However, it is only a matter of time before the climate migrants fleeing this continent have global ramifications, through immigration to the United States and elsewhere. Efforts to make the land more resilient in the face of climate change have been initiated, but at a certain point, reality must be faced and a solution made for the inevitable migration to come.

NOTES

Alex Randall, "Moving Stories: Latin America," January 28, 2014, *Climate and Migration Coalition*, http://climatemigration.org.uk/moving-stories-latin-america/1. "Violence Is Causing Children to Flee Central America," Center for American Progress, August 12, 2014.

2. Hugo G. Hidalgo, "Hydroclimatological Processes in the 'Central America Dry Corridor,'" http://envsci.rutgers.edu/~lintner/eftswg/Hidalgo_CorredorSeco.pdf.
3. "Central America; Drought—2014–2015," ReliefWeb, accessed October 27, 2015, http://reliefweb.int/disaster/dr-2014–000132-hnd.
4. Ibid.
5. "Worst Drought in 40 Years Puts More Than 2 Million People in Central America at Risk," European Commission Humanitarian Aid Office," October 11, 2014, http://updates4696.rssing.com/chan-13436333/all_p513.html.
6. "Drought Causes $100 Million in Crop Losses in El Salvador," Phys.org, August 10, 2015, http://phys.org/news/2015–08-drought-million-crop-losses-el.html#nRlv.
7. "Worst Drought in Guatemala in Decades Affecting 2.5 Million People, UN Reports," UN News Centre, September 18, 2009, http://www.un.org/apps/news/story.asp?NewsID=32109#.WBo_kMlcj5M.
8. "Hunger Crisis in Guatemala Draws Mounting Concern from UN Food Agency," United Nations News Centre, September 11, 2009, https://desertification.wordpress.com/2009/09/12/guatemala-hunger-crisis-unnews/.
9. "Worst Drought in 40 Years."
10. Jan-Albert Hootsen, "As Climate Changes, Central America Lags on Improving Food Security," World Politics Review, October 30, 2014, http://www.worldpoliticsreview.com/articles/14313/as-climate-changes-central-america-lags-on-improving-food-security.
11. Tim Rogers, "Will Climate Change Hasten Central American Migration to US?" Fusion, August 14, 2014, http://fusion.net/story/6288/will-climate-change-hasten-central-american-migration-to-us/.

12. United Nations Office for the Coordination of Humanitarian Affairs, "Humanitarian Bulletin: Latin America and Caribbean," vol. 21, (January–April 2015).

13. "Hurricane 'Ida' Leaves at Least 40,000 Victims in Nicaragua," Agence France-Presse, November 6, 2009; "Nicaragua: Storm 'Ida' Gains Hurricane Status," Agence France-Presse, November 8, 2009.

14. "State of the Climate: Global Analysis For 2010," NOAA National Centers for Environmental Information, published online January 2011, retrieved on November 10, 2016 from http://www.ncdc.noaa.gov/sotc/global/201013.

15. Juan Carlos Llorca, "First Tropical Storm of 2010 Kills 99 in Central America," Associated Press, May 30, 2010, http://www.seattletimes.com/nation-world/first-tropical-storm-of-2010-kills-99-in-central-america/.

16. "Global Hazards—November 2009," National Oceanic and Atmospheric Administration, https://www.ncdc.noaa.gov/sotc/hazards/200911#flooding.

17. "Central America Floods and Landslides 'Leave 80 Dead,'" BBC News, October 18, 2011.

18. Adonai, "Days of Heavy Rain, Floods, and Deadly Landslides across Central America," The Watchers, October 20, 2014, http://thewatchers.adorraeli.com/2014/10/20/days-of-heavy-rain-floods-and-deadly-landslides-across-central-america.

19. "Record Rains Flood Homes, Touch off Landslides in Nicaragua," Associated Press, October 10, 2014, http://globalnes.ca/news/1608751/record-rains-flood-homes-touch-off-landslides-in-nicaragua/.

20. LuAnn Dahlman, "Climate Change: Global Temperature," National Climatic Data Center, January 1, 2015, accessed at http://www.climate.gov/news-features/understanding-climate/climate-change-global-temperature.

21. Marengo JA, Chou SC, Torres RR, Giarolla A, Alves LM, Lyra A. 2014. Climate change in Central and South America: Recent trends, future projections, and impacts on regional agriculture. CCAFS Working Paper no. 73, https://cgspace.cgiar.org/rest/bitstreams/33625/retrieve.

22. "Central America Faces Major Crop Losses Due to El Niño, Warns UN Agency," http://www.un.org/sustainabledevelopment/blog/2015/09/central-america-faces-major-crop-losses-due-to-el-nino-warns-un-agency/.

23. "Major Crop Losses in Central America due to El Niño," Food and Agriculture Organization, September 14, 2015, http://www.fao.org/news/story/en/item/328614/icode/.

24. "Global Warming-El Niño Link Stronger but Still Not Proven," Climate Central, January 3, 2013, http://www.climatecentral.org/news/global-warming-el-nino-link-stronger-but-still-not-proven-15427; Jeff Tollefson, "Frequency of Extreme El Niños to Double as Globe Warms," *Nature*, January 19, 2014, http://www.nature.com/news/frequency-of-extreme-el-ni%C3%B1os-to-double-as-globe-warms-1.14546, doi:10.1038/nature.2014.14546.

25. Brian Kahn, "Climate Change Could Double Likelihood of Super El Niños," Climate Central, January 19, 2014.

26. Wenju Cai, Simon Borlace, Matthieu Lengaigne et al., "Increasing Frequency of Extreme El Niño Events Due to Greenhouse Warming," *Nature Climate Change*, January 19, 2014, http://www.nature.com/nclimate/journal/v4/n2/full/nclimate2100.html.

27. "Global Warming–El Niño Link Stronger but Still Not Proven," Climate Central, January 3, 2013.

28. Hunter Cutting, "El Niño + Climate Change = Godzilla?" Huffington Post, November 17, 2015, http://www.huffingtonpost.com/hunter-cutting/el-nino-climate-change-go_b_8578956.html

29. Rong-Gong Lin II, "Latest Forecast Suggests 'Godzilla El Niño' May Be Coming to California," *Los Angeles Times*, August 13, 2015.

30. Eric Leister, "South America Summer Forecast: El Niño to Bring Flooding Rain to Argentina, Uruguay, and Southeast Brazil," Accuweather, October 31, 2015.

31. Tim Rogers, "Will Climate Change Hasten Central American Migration to US?" Fusion, August 14, 2014, http://fusion.net/story/6288/will-climate-change-hasten-central-american-migration-to-us/.

32. Ibid.

33. Daniel Rivero, "UN Summit to Address a New Category of Refugees: People Fleeing the Effects of Climate Change," Fusion, December 11, 2014, http://fusion.net/story/33163/un-summit-to-address-a-new-category-of-refugees-people-fleeing-the-effects-of-climate-change/.

34. Étienne Piguet and Antoine Pécoud, "Migration and Climate Change: An Overview," *Refugee Survey Quarterly* 30, no. 3 (2011): 8.

35. "Hunger without Borders: The Hidden Links between Food Insecurity, Violence, and Migration in the Northern Triangle of Central America," United Nations World Food Programme and the International Organization for Migration, 2016, http://reliefweb.int/sites/reliefweb.int/files/resources/wfp277544.pdf.

36. "New Study Highlights Food Insecurity as Driver of Migration in Central America," World Food Programme, September 17, 2015, https://www.wfp.org/news/news-release/new-study-highlights-food-insecurity-driver-migration-central-america.

37. "Hunger without Borders," 9.

38. "Climate Change and Food Security: A Framework Document," Food and Agriculture Organization of the United Nations Rome, 2008; Gerald C. Nelson, Mark W. Rosegrant, Amanda Palazzo et al., "Food Security, Farming, and Climate Change to 2050; Scenarios, Results, Policy Options," International Food Policy Research Institute, 2010.

39. Gustavo Palencia, "Drought Leaves up to 2.81 Million Hungry in Central America: U.N.," Reuters, September 4, 2014.

40. Cynthia Flores Mora, "Record Drought in Central America: Four Countries, 40 Days without Rain, Two Million Facing Hunger," World Bank, September 10, 2014.

41. "How Will Climate Change Affect What We Eat?" Oxfam America, March 24, 2014.

42. Andrew Freedman, "Zeroing In on IPCC's Sea Level Rise & Warming 'Hiatus,'" Climate Central, September 27, 2013, http://www.climatecentral.org/news/zeroing-in-on-ipccs-sea-level-rise-warming-hiatus-16532.

43. "Quantification and Magnitude of Losses and Damages Resulting from the Impacts of Climate Change: Modelling the Transformational Impacts and Costs of Sea Level Rise in the Caribbean," United Nations Development Programme (UNDP), 2010, http://ckan.c-read.net:8000/dataset/quantification-and-magnitude-of-losses-and-damages-resulting-from-the-impacts-of-climate-changefobb9.

44. Ibid.

45. "Warning for Caribbean Countries as Sea Level Continues to Rise," *Jamaica Observer*, July 14, 2014.

46. "Quantification and Magnitude of Losses."

47. "Puerto Rico Expands Water Rationing Measures amid Drought," Associated Press, June 25, 2015, https://www.yahoo.com/news/puerto-rico-expands-water-rationing-measures-amid-drought-171018832.html?ref=gs.

48. Danica Coto, "Caribbean Braces for Worsening Drought as Dry Season Approaches," Associated Press, September 22, 2015, https://www.yahoo.com/news/caribbean-braces-worsening-drought-dry-season-nears-190402750.html?ref=gs.

49. "Puerto Rico Expands Water Rationing."

50. Tim Padgett, "Danny and the Drought: How El Niño Left the Caribbean Parched," WLRN, August 25, 2015, http://wlrn.org/post/danny-and-drought-how-el-ni-o-left-caribbean-parched.

51. Grant Ferguson and Tom Gleeson, "Vulnerability of Coastal Aquifers to Groundwater Use and Climate Change," *Nature Climate Change*, February 19, 2012; "The Regional Impacts of Climate Change."

52. ECLAC, "International Migration and Development in the Americas," Symposium on International Migration in the Americas, United Nations Economic Commission for Latin America and the Caribbean (ECLAC), San Jose, Costa Rica, 2001.

53. "Hurricane Mitch, Facts & Summary," History.com, http://www.history.com/topics/hurricane-mitch.

54. M. Glantz and D. Jamieson (2000). "Societal Response to Hurricane Mitch and the Intra- versus Intergenerational Equity Issues: Whose Norms Should Apply?" *Risk Analysis* 20, no. 6 (2000): 869–82, http://environment.as.nyu.edu/docs/IO/1192/societalresponses.pdf; R. McLeman and L. Hunter, "Migration in the Context of Vulnerability and Adaptation to Climate Change: Insights from Analogues," *Wiley Interdisciplinary Reviews: Climate Change* 1, no. 3 (2011): 450–61 https://www.ncbi.nlm.nih.gov/pmc/articles/PMC3183747/; "Turn Down the Heat: Confronting the New Climate Normal," World Bank, 2014, http://documents.worldbank.org/curated/en/317301468242098870/pdf/927040v20WP00000u110Report000English.pdf.

55. "Climate Migration in Latin America: A Future 'Flood of Refugees' to the North?" Council on Hemispheric Affairs, February 22, 2010, .

56. Ker Than, "Warmer Seas Creating Stronger Hurricanes, Study Confirms," Live Science, March 16, 2006, http://www.livescience.com/642-warmer-seas-creating-stronger-hurricanes-study-confirms.html.

57. "Urbanization in Latin America," Atlantic Council, February 5, 2014, http://www.atlanticcouncil.org/publications/articles/urbanization-in-latin-america.

58. "Urbanization in Latin America and the Caribbean: Trends and Challenges," USAID, April 13, 2010.

59. "Urbanization in Latin America," Atlantic Council.

60. L. J. Mata and C. Nobre, "Impacts, Vulnerability, and Adaptation to Climate Change in Latin America," background paper, UNFCCC, Lima (2006), https://unfccc.int/files/adaptation/adverse_effects_and_response_measures_art_48/application/pdf/200609_background_latin_american_wkshp.pdf.

61. A. De Garin and R. Bejaran, R., "Mortality Rate and Relative Strain Index in Buenos Aires City," *International Journal of Biometeorology* 48 (2003): 31–36.

62. "Urbanization in Latin America," Atlantic Council.

63. J. J. Bogardi, "Impact of Gradual Environmental Change on Migration: A Global Perspective," Expert Seminar: Migration and Environment, International Organization for Migration, 2008.

64. S.A.F. Barbieri, E. Domingues, B. L. Queiroz et al., "Climate Change and Population Migration in Brazil's Northeast: Scenarios for 2025–2050." *Population and Environment* 31, no. 5 (2010): 344–70.

65. Paulo A. Paranagua, "Latin America Struggles to Cope with Record Urban Growth," *Guardian*, September 11, 2012, https://www.theguardian.com/world/2012/sep/11/latin-america-urbanisation-city-growth.

66. Elizabeth Warn and Susan B. Adamo, "The Impact of Climate Change: Migration and Cities in South America," *World Meteorological Organization Bulletin* 63, no. 2 (2014), http://public.wmo.int/en/resources/bulletin/impact-of-climate-change-migration-and-cities-south-america.

67. Claire Rigby, "São Paulo—Anatomy of a Failing Megacity: Residents Struggle as Water Taps Run Dry," *Guardian*, February 25, 2015, https://www.theguardian.com/cities/2015/feb/25/sao-paulo-brazil-failing-megacity-water-crisis-rationing.

68. Lourdes Garcia-Navarro, "Sao Paulo's Drought Pits Water Prospectors against Wildcatters," NPR, *Morning Edition*, March 10, 2015, http://www.npr.org/2015/03/10/392014833/sao-paulo-s-drought-pits-legitimate-prospectors-against-wildcatters.

69. Catherine Olson, "São Paulo Residents Demand Their City Take a New Attitude about Water," Public Radio International, *The World*, March 13, 2015, http://www.pri.org/stories/2015–03–13/s-o-paulo-residents-demand-their-city-take-new-attitude-about-water.

70. Lourdes Garcia-Navarro, "São Paulo's Drought"

71. "Military Could Step in Over Brazil Drought Chaos," teleSUR, May 6, 2015, http://www.telesurtv.net/english/news/Military-Could-Step-in-Over-Brazil-Drought-Chaos-20150506–0040.html

72. "Military Could Step In."

73. Rigby, "São Paulo."

74. Jonathan Watts, "Amazon Rainforest Losing Ability to Regulate Climate, Scientist Warns," *Guardian*, October 31, 2014.

75. Ibid.

76. Sandra Postel, "Lessons from São Paulo's Water Shortage," *National Geographic*, March 13, 2015, http://voices.nationalgeographic.com/2015/03/13/lessons-from-sao-paulos-water-shortage/.

77. "Bolivia Flooding Displaces Thousands in Pando Province," BBC News, February 25, 2015, http://www.bbc.com/news/world-latin-america-31620668

78. Richard Davids, "Thousands Displaced by Floods in Northern Bolivia," Floodlist, February 26, 2015, http://floodlist.com/america/thousands-displaced-by-floods-in-northern-bolivia.

79. Sabine Dolan, "Bolivia's Worst Floods in Decades Displace Families and Disrupt Children's Lives," UNICEF, March 12, 2007, http://www.unicef.org/emergencies/bolivia_39044.html.

80. Sam Jones, "Bolivia after the Floods: 'The Climate Is Changing; We Are Living That Change,'" *Guardian*, December 8, 2014, https://www.theguardian.com/global-development/2014/dec/08/bolivia-floods-climate-change-indigenous-people; Eduardo Garcia, "Bolivia Blames Rich World Pollution for Floods," Reuters, March 2, 2007, http://www.reuters.com/article/dcbrights-bolivia-floods-dc-idUSN0245951820070304.

81. Sasha Chavkin, "Cash for Thunder: Bolivia Demands 'Climate Reparations,'" *Mother Jones*, November–December 2009, http://www.motherjones.com/environment/2009/11/bolivia-paying-rain.

82. Jan Rocha, "Drought Takes Hold as Amazon's 'Flying Rivers' Dry Up," Climate Central, September 28, 2014.

83. "Tree-Cutting Impairs Amazon's Rain-Giving 'Sky Rivers': Study," Associated Press, December 4, 2014, http://www.nbcnews.com/science/environment/tree-cutting-impairs-amazons-rain-giving-sky-rivers-study-n261686.

84. Watts, "Amazon Rainforest Losing Ability."

85. Ibid.

86. Richard Schiffman, "Brazil's Deforestation Rates Are on the Rise Again," *Newsweek*, March 22, 2015, http://www.newsweek.com/2015/04/03/brazils-deforestation-rates-are-rise-again-315648.html.

87. Ibid.

88. Roheeni Saxena, "Climate Change Will Make the Amazon Rainforest Less Rainy," Ars Technica, June 10, 2015, http://arstechnica.com/science/2015/06/climate-change-will-make-the-amazon-rainforest-less-rainy/.

89. Becky Oskin, "Global Warming Forecast for Amazon Rain Forest: Dry and Dying," Live Science, October 21, 2013, http://www.livescience.com/40573-amazon-rainforest-drying-out.html.

90. David Adam, "Amazon Could Shrink By 85% Due to Climate Change, Scientists Say," *Guardian*, March 11, 2009, https://www.theguardian.com/environment/2009/mar/11/amazon-global-warming-trees.

91. Met Office, "Understanding Climate Change Impacts on the Amazon Rainforest," January 2013, http://www.metoffice.gov.uk/research/news/amazon-dieback.

92. Jonathan Watts, "Amazon Deforestation Report Is Major Setback for Brazil ahead of Climate Talks," *Guardian*, November 27, 2015, https://www.theguardian.com/world/2015/nov/27/amazon-deforestation-report-brazil-paris-climate-talks.

93. Chelsea Harvey, "Climate Change Could Triple Amazon Drought, Study Finds," *Washington Post*, October 12, 2015, https://www.washingtonpost.com/news/energy-environment/wp/2015/10/12/climate-change-could-triple-amazon-drought-study-finds/.

94. R.J.W. Brienen, O. L. Phillips, T. R. Feldpausch et al., "Long-Term Decline of the Amazon Carbon Sink," *Nature* 519, 344–48, March 19, 2015.

6

Africa

ENVIRONMENTAL CONFLICTS IN A WAR-TORN LAND

> I cannot believe that people in developed countries, when informed about the issues, would support rescuing bankers and oppose partial compensation for poor countries and regions. I cannot believe that they will let such an injustice occur. If they are not expressing their outrage over the injustice of it all, it can only be because they are inadequately informed.
>
> *Meles Zenawi, former prime minister of Ethiopia*

Africa is no stranger to refugees. It is home to some of the largest refugee camps in the world, with some camps hosting hundreds of thousands of people. A continent where conflict, poverty, and displacement are frequent tragedies throughout, Africa is also a land where climate science or change and refugees clearly intersect. But the connections between these migration drivers and climate change are rarely discussed. It is easy to conjure a refugee fleeing violence and war, but what about the millions who have fled homes destroyed by flash floods? And what about the ways that drought and famine have led to violent uprisings, thereby creating a source of more refugees? The link between climate change and African refugees fleeing violent countries is not an obvious one, but it is an important one. In decades to come, the number of refugees will grow as the planet warms, so it is worth examining the many factors that come into play, as well as the possible solutions at hand.[1]

"No continent will be struck as severely by the impacts of climate change as Africa," according to the United Nations Environment Programme effects of climate change.[2] A 2008 study estimated that there are over twenty-six thousand observable changes in "natural systems" which are attributable to warming worldwide, and Africa will experience many of them.[3] The IPCC predicted that 75–250 million Africans will be exposed to stressed water sources by the 2020s, and 350–600 million will be vulnerable by the 2050s.[4] Of the countries ranked on the Notre Dame Global Adaptation Index, which ranks those most vulnerable to climate change and least able to adapt to its impacts, almost the entire continent of Africa has an ND-GAIN score below 50 (on a 0–100 scale).[5]

Africa's economy is largely dependent on agriculture. Thus a large majority of the population is dependent on rainfall for their livelihood; even those who don't work directly in the agricultural sector depend on it. Food security, which will be largely threatened by climate change, could become the greatest challenge faced by the continent—if it is not already. A study commissioned by the World Bank and carried out by University of Potsdam researchers found that if the world's temperature increases one and a half to two degrees centigrade above preindustrial levels in the next few decades, farmers in sub-Saharan Africa will lose 40 to 80 percent of land used for growing staple crops.[6]

Without government action and agricultural innovation, extensive land loss is all but guaranteed. The World Bank offers evidence that the world is already locked into a warming of one and a half degrees centigrade above preindustrial levels due to the burning of fossil fuels.[7] Keeping global warming under two degrees above preindustrial levels is essential, according to many scientific bodies and government officials, but it requires immediate action to cut fossil fuels. Based on the projections of hundreds of scientific reports, the World Bank predicted that we will experience warming of four degrees or greater if no action is taken to address climate change.[8] What will that mean for African agriculture? What will it mean for human life? How will it affect human displacement, who will have to leave their homes behind, and where will they go? The answers to those questions are complex and interconnected.

As Africa's climate worsens and becomes the theater for regional conflicts, there will be an exodus of migrants. The impacts of climate change will vary from place to place, a fact that rings prominently true in a continent as big as Africa. Northwest Africa is at risk of desertification while at the same time sea level rise and coastal erosion threaten many areas on the continent's border, and deforestation and loss of land quality are issues in many regions. Food security and malaria spread will also be issues of concern.[9] In all areas the average temperature is going to drastically increase, particularly if nothing is done to mitigate global warming.[10]

Between 75 and 250 million people are projected to be exposed to increased water stress due to climate change by 2020, according to data from the IPCC. The panel noted in its most recent assessment: "The area suitable for agriculture, the length of growing seasons and yield potential, particularly along the margins of semi-arid and arid areas, are expected to decrease."[11]

Overall temperature increases will lead to extreme weather stresses everywhere, be it through drought or storms. Later on this chapter will address how those stresses play out and contribute to conflict and refugees, but first it is important to look at the refugee landscape in Africa.

AFRICA REFUGEES BY THE NUMBERS

Africa is already home to some fourteen million people worldwide displaced by political turmoil and war, but experts say climate change is driving Africa's displacement crisis to new heights. An estimated ten million people worldwide have already been driven out of their homes by rising seas, rain, desertification, or other climate-driven factors.

The year 2014 saw a record number of displaced people, and a significant portion of the refugees were from Africa. A United Nations report found that 59.5 million people were forcibly displaced worldwide, the greatest increase in a single year. The report includes a frightening statistic: one in every 122 humans is either a refugee, internally displaced, or seeking asylum; the total number, if it constituted the population of a country, would be the twenty-fourth biggest population in the world. The UN reported that in 2014 the number of refugees in sub-Saharan Africa was only "marginally lower" than those from the Middle East. Sub-Saharan Africa saw 3.7 million refugees and 11.4 internally displaced people. Four and a half million of these were newly displaced during the year 2014 alone, the equivalent of a 17 percent overall increase.[12]

Many African countries comprise the world's major source countries of refugees, including Somalia, Sudan, South Sudan, and the Democratic

Republic of Congo (DRC).[13] Of course, much of this is due to violent conflict in these areas. The UN report notes that eight violent conflicts have erupted in Africa in the previous five years—in Côte d'Ivoire, the Central African Republic, Libya, Mali, northeastern Nigeria, DRC, South Sudan, and Burundi. Somalia, a country that has not seen recent uprisings but is experiencing ongoing problems of drought and food scarcity, is also the third-biggest source of refugees.

Climate change is creating hardships for farmers, and combined with population growth this is creating a large migration from rural areas to urban. At least half the African population is expected to be living in cities by 2030 solely due to population growth and migration patterns.[14] Climate change is expected to place even more stresses on agricultural life, further exacerbating the rate of urban migration.[15] So although migration is not a physical impact of climate change, it is a societal impact that will need to be considered in the frame of context and refugees.

THE LAND OF DROUGHT

When you take away all of the complex, unpredictable factors in Africa's refugee situation—the political conflict, the flash floods, the storms—there is still one pervasive issue that cannot be ignored: severe, emergency-inducing drought will not go away anytime soon, and it will undoubtedly be exacerbated by global warming.

There are two key aspects to drought: inputs (rain or other precipitation) and outputs (moisture evaporated from the ground). In Africa land temperature is the driving force for worsening drought. Hotter temperatures cause moisture to evaporate from the soil and dries out the land. Even when it rains, the land still suffers of thirst, because the rain can't be easily absorbed into rock-hard soil—and severe rains are more likely to cause floods and degrade the land.

Drought has been an overarching issue in Africa for a long time—with desert comprising a large part of the continent—but it has only gotten worse with climate change. Since 1970, intense, widespread droughts have become more frequent. In 2007 one-third of Africans lived in areas prone to drought and were vulnerable to its impacts.[16]

Map 6.1: The Horn of Africa

Countries in the Horn of Africa, the Sahel region, and southern Africa are bearing the brunt of severe droughts. And some in the Horn of Africa are directly connecting it to climate change.

Mr. Benon Twineobusingye, senior human resource manager in the Office of the President of Uganda, said his country is seeing "serious drought that has not happened before. This drought has caused famine in parts of the country. . . . It has been very hot these days. Over the years it has gotten hotter with more unpredictable weather."[17]

The Sahel region—one of the most vulnerable to drought—is actually expected to get *increased* annual rainfall, at least in the very short term. In warmer temperatures the tropical rain belt moves north to the Sahel sooner than it would otherwise, bringing with it more total rain.[18] At the same time, moisture is being evaporated at an increased rate with climate change, which more than compensate for the increased rainfall.[19]

A scientist from the study explaining this phenomenon said that warmer temperatures are "leading to a higher drought risk regardless of changes in rainfall. And that will be something that's true across most of Africa. . . . If you get more rain and it just evaporates really quickly then it's not much good for the crops, for example."[20] Drought has been plaguing Africa for decades, so there are many examples to show the havoc it can wreak. The 2011 drought in the Horn of Africa killed hundreds of thousands—estimates ranged up to 260,000 fatalities.[21] This is what connects drought to forced migration: the link between drought and famine. A season with insufficient rainfall results in reduced crop yield and drastic food shortages, leaving many no option but to leave.

Even with increased rainfall, science shows that crops in and around the Sahel will suffer. The increased total rainfall is often connected to severe weather events; heavy storms can lead to flash floods, which pose an unmistakable risk to communities and in fact erode valuable topsoil even further. With these two extreme weather events working in concert, it's no wonder drought is expected to increase in such severity as to alter the lives of hundreds of millions of Africans by 2050.[22]

Population in the Sahel increased by 30 percent between 2000 and 2010, but its food supply remained largely the same.[23] In that period, drought has forced a significant proportion of the population to leave their homes, but estimations of how many people have had to move as a result of drought are ambiguous and likely underestimate the facts. The Internal Displacement Monitoring Centre (IDMC) estimated that 12.5 million people in sub-Saharan Africa were displaced by natural disasters at the end of 2013. However, that figure does not include those displaced by droughts or other global warming impacts.[24] The IDMC includes in its natural disaster monitoring earthquakes, volcanic eruptions, rockslides, hurricanes and other storms, floods, avalanches, wildfires, cold snaps, and heat waves. A huge majority of IDPs in Africa are displaced because of weather and climate-related events, but an exact number is elusive. What is known is that severe drought is an ongoing issue that will only get worse as the planet warms. The question is not whether these long-term droughts will happen but what people can do to prepare for them.

EXPANDING DESERTS DRIVE PEOPLE TO NEW LANDS

The combination of droughts and flash floods will increase the amount of land that is simply unlivable, through desertification. Between the Sahara and the Kalahari deserts nearly half of the surface area in Africa is already "characterized as extreme desert,"[25] and with climate change, many regions surrounding these deserts are degrading into unusable, unlivable land.

At risk are the semi-arid lands surrounding Africa's expansive deserts and in other areas. Desertification is a process that is partially a result of poor land-use management and overly intensive agriculture, but it is exacerbated by a harsh climate with low rainfall. Particularly, when farmers cultivate crops in areas at high risk from drought, the soil may degrade to a point where it can't replenish itself. Nearly half of Africa's non-desert land is vulnerable to this largely irreversible process.[26]

The Sahel region shares a border with the Sahara, thereby facing particular risk of land degradation and desertification. A 2011 study found that trees throughout the region—vital for preserving soil fertility and water retention, thereby preventing desertification—are dying at an alarming rate due to rising temperatures and lower rainfall rates. The study found that at some key sites, average temperatures rose by nearly one degree centigrade and rainfall decreased by 48 percent.[27]

In recent years, rainfall in the Sahel has actually increased—as a result of an interesting, temporary impact of global warming. The equatorial rain belt normally moves northward in the summer months, bringing the Sahel region rains once a year. With warmer temperatures, the rain belt moves up even farther north and intensifies. However, that is highly unlikely to relieve the region's intense droughts. Professor Rowan

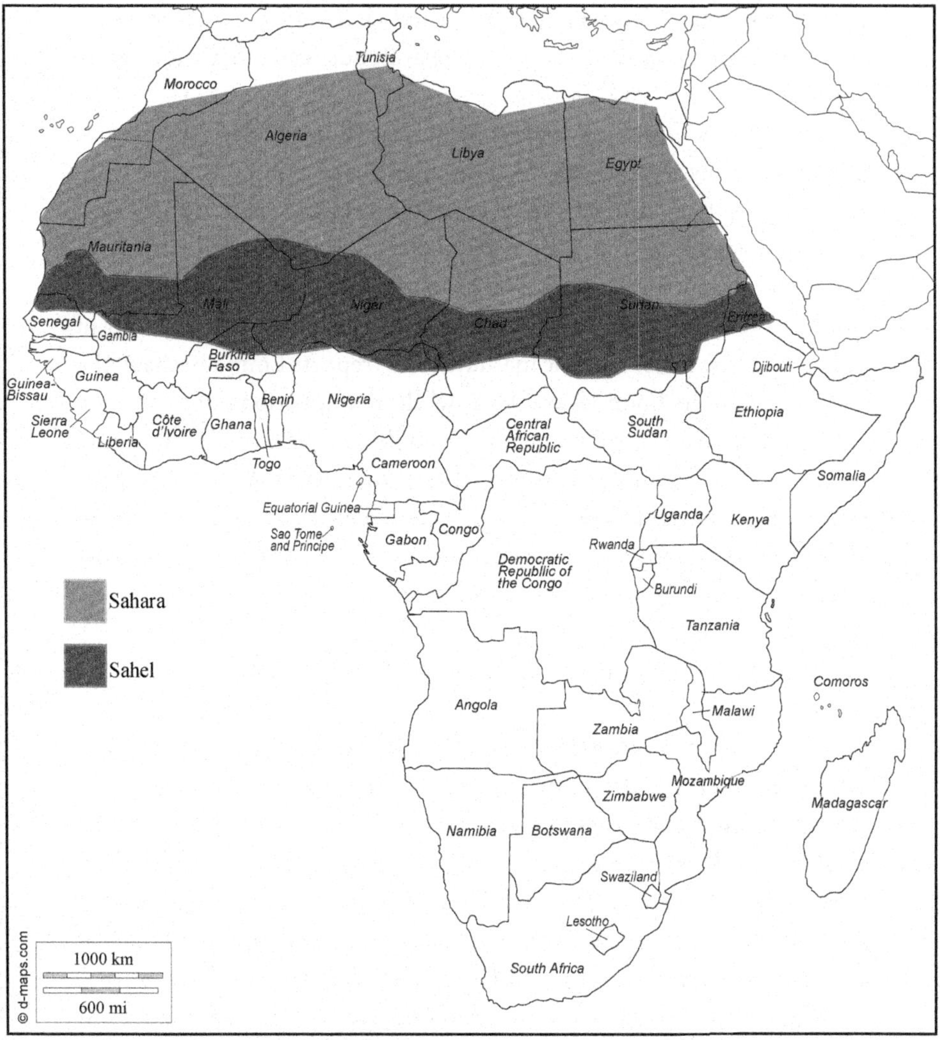

Map 6.2: The Sahel and Sahara regions of Africa

Sutton, director of climate research at England's National Center for Atmospheric Science at the University of Reading, argues that rising temperatures will lead "to a higher drought risk regardless of changes in rainfall." Warmer temperatures lead to greater evaporation rates, so "if you get more rain and it just evaporates really quickly then it's not much good for the crops," says Sutton.[28] If anything, it may lead to more flash floods, which are even worse for land vitality. The combination of years-long droughts punctuated by flash floods leads to a thoroughly degraded region.

Despite this temporary respite (incorrectly identified by some as global warming's "greening" of Africa), twenty million people were still at risk of hunger in the Sahel region in 2014 according to UN estimates—a huge leap from eleven million the year before.[29] In 2012 one million children were at risk of starvation. In a handful of countries in the Sahel—Burkina Faso, Niger, Chad, and Mali—"nearly half of young children suffer chronic malnutrition," reports Emma Batha of the Thomson Reuters Foundation. Meanwhile, malnutrition rates continue to "regularly exceed the emergency threshold of 15 percent."[30] The region is still incredibly vulnerable to desertification in the long term, and the catastrophic drought-fueled food crisis will have lasting consequences. One of these consequences—the most visceral, and the one that most often makes the US news—is violent conflict.

DROUGHT, FOOD SECURITY, AND CONFLICT

Now it is time to discuss the connections between climate change and violent conflict, which in Africa is a huge factor in forcing migration. Already malnutrition is rampant in several African countries. Drought plays a key role, as a large majority of Africa's agricultural activities and food supplies are sensitive to rainfall levels. A full "95% of [its] agriculture relies on rainfall for water."[31] An extreme, prolonged drought in the late 2000s led to a famine crisis in the Horn of Africa between 2010 and 2012, killing 260,000 people. In 2014 yet another famine raised concern in Somalia, threatening efforts to restore peace to the country.[32]

Any diminution of agricultural production in Africa can shake up the global food system. Concurrently, Africa is vulnerable to changes and insecurities in the global food system, as many African countries rely largely on importing food from Europe and Asia. Extreme weather, such as Somalia's flash floods, can harm food supplies in a way that reverberates throughout the supply chain. Extreme weather has already been responsible for production shocks and subsequent price spikes for basic crops.

The effects of climate change on food supplies are expected to get worse. A joint United Kingdom and United States task force predicts huge food supply shortages brought about by climate change. Because of extreme weather brought by climate change, says the UK-US Taskforce on Extreme Weather and Global Food Resilience, the risk of a one-in-one-hundred-year production shock will likely happen in the next few decades. The report also highlighted sub-Saharan Africa as being particularly vulnerable, as many countries in the region are highly dependent on food imports.[33] For example, 50 percent of the food consumed in Egypt is imported.[34] North Africans, as well, are dependent on importing food from other countries—over half of the food consumed there is imported.[35] When extreme weather harms food supplies in China or Russia, food prices in African countries can drastically increase as a result, leading to conflict.

Ethiopia has been affected by desertification for decades, and in this country, drought and food scarcity had a direct role in sparking violent conflict. In the 1970s and 1980s, a famine that killed tens of thousands of Ethiopians and brought millions of others to the edge of starvation helped bring Ethiopia's last emperor, Haile Selassie, to his downfall.

The Ethiopian famine was used to garner opposition to Emperor Selassie, who was "widely revered" at the time. A group of dissident soldiers used a film called *The Unknown Famine*, which had been produced to expose the extent of Ethiopia's devastating famine and mass starvation. The dissidents cut in images of Selassie "presiding at a wedding feast in the grounds of his palace" to contrast with images of starvation. Jonathan Dimbleby, who created the original film, reported that after the emperor was seized by rebels, their edited film cut with images of the emperor was "wheeled out at mass rallies all over Ethiopia to reassure the 'masses' that the new regime was indeed on the side of the angels." Dimbleby added, "Tens of thousands of young people, intoxicated by the televisual imagery of starvation and the rhetoric of revolution, signed up for Mengistu's [Haile Mariam] cause and, without a second thought, became footsoldiers for genocide." The replacement government was a dictatorship that led the "Red Terror," which took at least one hundred thousand lives and prompted residents to flee the country in large numbers.[36]

Over the years, many Ethiopians have moved to Seattle, Washington. Seattle has an East African population of about thirty-nine thousand, according to the Horn of Africa Services, including migrants from several countries in East Africa—but from none more than Ethiopia.[37]

The Arab Spring demonstrates how this process can play out for the worst. Again, one can easily make the connection between climate change and refugees fleeing from political unrest. It starts in Russia, which in 2010 experienced its worst drought in over a century, followed by catastrophic wildfires. The drought destroyed one-fifth of the country's wheat crop,[38] then sparked devastating wildfires that tore through the country, ravaging even more farmland. Between the two events, one-third of Russia's cultivable land was wiped out in a single summer.[39]

In response, Russia placed a ban on grain exports. At the same time, China—the world's largest producer of wheat—was experiencing a two-hundred-year drought, which scientists also attributed to climate change and which made a huge dent in the global wheat supply.[40] Food prices surged all over the world, particularly in North Africa and the Middle East. Egyptians, who rely on grain for one-third of their caloric intake, were particularly vulnerable to Russia's grain export ban and China's reduced output.

Several security experts have linked the subsequent high food prices in North Africa to the driving forces behind the uprisings known as the Arab Spring. Riots over food, political unrest, and poverty expanded into large-scale protests. Rami Zurayk, an agronomy professor at the American University of Beirut, said, "I think that the prices of food mobilized people." He added that the Tunisian uprising "started in the rural area," where a young man set himself on fire in protest. This man's burning was widely credited for spurring the Arab Spring.[41]

As Sarah Johnstone and Jeffrey Mazo of the International Institute for Strategic Studies concluded, "The Arab Spring would likely have come one way or another, but the context in which it did is not inconsequential. Global warming may not have caused the Arab Spring, but it may have made it come earlier."[42]

Though the Arab Spring was unique, the food crisis that may have helped catalyze it was not a one-time occurrence. Just two years later, in

2012, Russia saw another devastating drought.[43] Following this drought and others in the United States, global food prices jumped 10 percent in a single month. From June to July, maize and wheat prices each rose by 25 percent. This increase has varying influences on different countries that import the crops. Regions in the Sahel and East Africa experienced 220 percent price increases in sorghum, and sub-Saharan Africa saw a 113 percent price increase in maize.[44]

In general, lower-income countries are more sensitive to global food prices and more likely to break out in civil unrest. A report from researchers at the University of Adelaide concluded that in low-income countries, food price increases "lead to a significant deterioration of democratic institutions and a significant increase in the incidence of anti-government demonstrations, riots, and civil conflict." Food prices fluctuate on the international market and are shaped by demand in developed countries.[45] Some countries are more vulnerable than others. Meanwhile, the global population is expected to increase from seven billion to nine billion by 2050, and food demand is expected to increase 60 percent in that time, which will further strain the global food supply.[46]

Even the regions that are not resource dependent but grow their own crops are vulnerable to the impacts of climate change on food supply. The Sahel region is particularly vulnerable in this respect, according to Refugees International.[47] In many vulnerable African countries and communities, food price spikes have profound consequences that can shake the foundation of society. The link between climate change, food crises, unrest, and refugees requires several links. These links are an important part of the picture and worth considering as the impacts of climate change become worse while population increases. Addressing food security is inherent in a strategy to help Africa cope with the effects of climate change over the next decades and centuries.[48]

GOVERNMENT INSTITUTIONS RECOGNIZE CLIMATE CHANGE AS SOURCE OF CONFLICT

Climate change is considered a "threat multiplier" by the US Department of Defense (DOD), because it creates resource scarcity. The DOD's

2014 Quadrennial Defense Review stated specifically that the effects of climate change will "influence resource competition while placing additional burdens on economies, societies, and governance institutions around the world." These effects, in turn, "will aggravate stressors abroad such as poverty, environmental degradation, political instability, and social tensions—conditions that can enable terrorist activity and other forms of violence."[49] In addition, US Defense Secretary Chuck Hagel said that climate change "has the potential to exacerbate many of the challenges we already confront today—from infectious disease to armed insurgencies—and to produce new challenges in the future."[50]

In rural areas, resource scarcity is the heart of conflict. Farmers and communities have competed with each other over land and water sources for decades, particularly in the Horn of Africa. UNICEF (United Nations Children's Emergency Fund) consultant Meedan Mekonnen once wrote about this phenomenon:

> Drought is linked to conflict, as competition for the already limited natural resources in arid areas increases when drought occurs, given the low available water and crop yield. During drought, movement of pastoralists increases as they are forced to compete for the same scarce resources, causing conflicts between communities. There is a history of pastoral communities fighting for scarce resources in the Horn and, although most conflicts have been manageable, they are exacerbated and become more entrenched by drought. Drought-affected people often migrate, putting greater pressure on resources and resulting in conflict spreading to other areas. There is often conflict between farmers and cattle herders, as currently seen in several parts of the Horn.[51]

A 2014 study published in *Environmental Research Letters* found that food supplies have not been keeping up with population growth, which, combined with hotter temperatures from climate change that reduce crop output, means that many areas in Africa's Sahel region will be at greater risk of famine.[52] The study's lead author, Hakim Abdi, connected this to tensions in Sudan, saying in an interview in the *Guardian*, "Tensions in Darfur are between nomadic pastoralists and agriculturalists. . . . This tension stems partially from a lack of resources."[53] As always, there are other issues at play. The *Guardian* article noted that in addition to the violence in Darfur, "the Sahel faces Islamist insurgencies in parts of Libya, Chad and Niger, along with an uprising by ethnic Tuareg separatists in Mali."[54]

Famine also plays a role in reinforcing existing tensions. In 2014 a hunger crisis in the Sahel spurred calls for emergency funds to the tune of a hundred million dollars. The food shortages were partially due to rain shortages and also partially due to an influx of refugees. The Boko Haram insurgency in Nigeria drove more than fifty thousand refugees into Niger, which itself faces drought and hunger. Conflict in Mali drove thirty-five thousand refugees into Burkina Faso. According to the UN, "Low rainfall has worsened food security in Nigeria, Togo, Benin, Burkina Faso and Niger, while drought has prevented farmers in Senegal and Chad from planting crops." The agency has a $2 billion, three-year program intended to break the cycle of food insecurity in that region.[55]

When refugees are forced into areas with poor agricultural conditions and climate change vulnerabilities, food shortages increase and the cycle intensifies. Resource scarcity sparks conflict and catalyzes refugees, and subsequently refugees are extremely vulnerable to global warming–worsened drought and famine.

COASTAL FLOODS, TROPICAL STORMS, AND SEA LEVEL RISE

While drought devastates one region of Africa, rain and sea level rise plague another. And while the direct connection between climate change and refugees from violent conflict may be uncertain, some things *can* be quantified. This includes the predicted number of people who will be forced to leave due to sea level rise. Since the late nineteenth century, sea levels have risen about eight inches. But scientists expect them to rise much faster in the decades and centuries ahead. In 2100 sea levels could rise up to six feet.[56]

The British Royal Society has estimated that up to 187 million people currently living in coastal areas will be displaced around the world due to sea level rise, noting that Africa and parts of Asia are the most vulnerable and that coastal areas of Africa are likely to see high levels of abandonment. These areas simply don't have the resources to create necessary barriers and adaptations that other countries might—unlike the United States, where such barriers are already being planned to surround New York City, as part of a $19.5 billion climate resiliency plan.[57] Yet countries like Mozambique and Egypt, which are particularly vulnerable to sea level rise, may not have the billions of dollars necessary to protect themselves.

In addition to sea level rise, several countries in Africa will experience intensified monsoon seasons, leading to severe flooding. Tanzania, Nigeria, Niger, and Chad are all countries that have "experienced severe flooding because of an unusually active African monsoon season."[58] For example, floods during the rainy season in August 2014 displaced 159,000 Sudanese people in one single month, according to data from the Internal Displacement Monitoring Centre, which compiled numbers of people displaced by conflicts and natural hazards between 2010 and 2014.[59]

Unfortunately, many refugee camps themselves will be vulnerable to these impacts, meaning some refugees will be forced to move again. This is the case in Somalia, where refugee camps have been devastated by flash floods.[60] Refugees will have to flee refugee camps. And then where will they go?

SOMALIA AND SUDAN: VICTIMS OF THE CLIMATE REFUGEE CRISIS?

Somalia serves as a case in point on the intersection of droughts, floods, and refugees. The country has sent thousands of refugees to Kenya, fleeing from drought-induced famine, violence, and a combination of the two. Somalia experiences flash floods every year. As extreme rainfall events are expected to increase in the country due to climate change, its flash floods could get worse. But the population already faces trials and tribulations from flooding, and this situation is not expected to go away anytime soon. In less than two months during spring 2015, sixteen thousand people in Somalia were displaced due to the flash floods.[61] The flooding had also destroyed sixty-eight hundred hectares of farmland, affecting fourteen thousand Somali workers' jobs.[62]

Seventy percent of the Somali population depends on climate-sensitive agriculture and pastoralism, according to the United Nations Development Programme (UNDP). The UNDP warned that Somalia's climate and weather patterns have changed in recent years, including "increasing uncertainty for seasonal and annual rainfall levels, rising surface temperatures, sea level rise, and the loss of lives and livelihoods dependent on fragile or over-exploited ecosystems and natural resources."[63]

A large portion of the Somali population is already displaced, put up in temporary housing or refugee camps. However, that does not mean they are safe. Already displaced people are far more vulnerable to flooding than those who have a home. Many of their homes are made of no more than "twigs and branches, cardboard boxes, and plastic sheets." After their few resources were wiped out by floods, the residents of Somali camps became even less likely to return to their original lives.[64]

At the same time the Somalis try to build their resilience to drought, they deal with intense flash floods on a yearly basis. The combination of these two factors explains why the food security situation in Somalia is so dire. April and May fall in Somalia's dry season, or the *Gu* season. The rainy season takes place during October and November, or the *Deyr* season. It is when unexpected rains happen during the dry season—when the ground is parched and hard as a rock—that the most risk of flash floods is created.

There's a vicious cycle to Africa's climate refugee situation: the refugees themselves are more vulnerable to climate change simply by already being displaced. Refugee tents are far less resilient to the battering winds and flash floods of rainy season than the huts and buildings in cities and villages. The refugees don't even have to leave their own country to face these risks—IDPs often live in precarious conditions and are uniquely threatened by climate change. In fact, between January and September 2014, over 130 thousand Somalis were forced to relocate, but the majority remained in the country as IDPs.[65] By the end of 2014 there were 1.1 million Somali IDPs, nearly one-tenth of the country's population. Most of them were living in dire conditions. At one point in 2014 a camp of Somali IDPs was devastated by flash floods, which killed three children in one week.[66]

Internally displaced persons consistently face risks to their lives, safety, security, and dignity, according to the Internal Displacement Monitoring Centre. IDMC states in a report that they are "disproportionately at risk of gross abuses of human rights, especially women and unaccompanied children." The IDPs also face sexual and gender-based violence and many people from clan-based communities face intense discrimination without their clan's protection. They live in regions with little access to clean water or health facilities and where there is poor sanitation—a toxic combination, where deadly diseases can spread.[67] Babar Baloch, a spokesperson for the UNHCR, said of the IDPs: "Many people are living in sites lacking basic services in shelters made of sticks, grass and empty cardboard boxes."

It is worth noting that usually multiple factors force large populations to leave their homes. Environmental disasters and stresses are a "major" factor in Somalia's large population of displaced people, according to the IDMC, but not the only one; political conflict and violence may play a larger role in the 1.1 million displaced people statistic. Several African countries are rife with long-standing conflict. In Somalia, for instance, the jihadist group Al-Shabaab has control over large parts of southern and central Somalia, and the Somali government has launched a military offensive in response. The resulting conflict has been a major factor in uprooting communities.[68]

Climate change can act as an aggressor to already existing conflicts. It also can create the preconditions for vulnerable, impoverished communities, of which military forces can take advantage. When Somalia was in the grip of a famine exacerbated by drought, Al-Shabaab denied humanitarian assistance to people in their areas of control.

The Somali government is partnering with the UNDP to enhance climate resilience of their most vulnerable communities. It is hoped that this will lead to fewer people forced to leave their homes. Somalia released a draft national policy on internal displacement in October 2014 to provide the IDPs assistance and protection in a nondiscriminatory manner. This plan is now in the works of being approved and implemented;[69] however, the IDMC notes that implementing these policies "will remain particularly challenging due to weak state capacity and scarcity of resources."[70]

Not all refugees stay in the country, however. Eleven thousand Somalis fled to Yemen between January and September 2014, "mostly affected by drought, food insecurity and poverty," according to the United Nations News Centre. Several hundred thousand fled to Ethiopia in 2015.[71] And the world's largest refugee camp, in Kenya, is just fifty-five miles from the Somali border and home to many who have fled violence in their country, famine, and severe drought. The camp is called the Dadaab and is facing overcrowding.

The refugee camp in Dadaab, Kenya, is the largest in the world. On the eastern edge of Kenya just past its border with Somalia, the camp is home to more than 300,000 Somalis.[72] This is a huge jump from 2011, when there were 113,000 refugees living in the camp. Even at that time, Doctors Without Borders (Médecins Sans Frontières, or MSF) called the camp "completely full" and documented its overstressed state. Once new refugees arrived in the camp, MSF reported, they had to wait an average of twelve days to receive their first ration of food and thirty-four days for blankets, utensils, and other essentials. With a lack of vaccines, deadly diseases such as tuberculosis spread among children.[73]

Many of Dadaab's residents are fleeing from the harms of climate change. According to United Nations officials, as many as 10 percent of Dadaab's refugees could be considered as fleeing from drought that has made their former rural lifestyles impossible. The *Los Angeles Times* spoke with several residents, including Adam Abdi Ibrahim, who said he left his home because he was unable to survive after four years of drought, which killed off his livestock. Ibrahim joined many other herders and families who left due to drought and entered the stream of refugees. About ten million people worldwide are estimated to be environmental migrants.[74]

Ethiopia is home to many Somalis and to many from South Sudan as well. In 2014 Ethiopia became the largest refugee-hosting country in Africa and the fifth largest worldwide, according to the UNHCR.[75] As such, its resources are incredibly strained. Heavy rains make the situation worse, flooding the shelters, destroying the latrines, thus creating a serious health concern.[76] Camps are vulnerable to flash floods and subsequently bouts of malaria with the rainy season. Ethiopia lies just to the east of South Sudan, which has been facing civil conflict for decades, and therefore is home to many South Sudanese.

South Sudan's conflict—namely, in Darfur—was driven by climate change and environmental degradation, according to United Nations researchers. UN secretary-general Ban Ki-moon wrote in the *Washington Post*: "Amid the diverse social and political causes, the Darfur conflict began as an ecological crisis, arising at least in part from climate change." He explained that the violence "erupted during the drought," after the rains stopped, and "there was no longer enough food and water for all. Fighting broke out. By 2003, it evolved into the full-fledged tragedy we witness today."[77]

After twenty-two years of civil war, the Sudanese government signed a peace agreement with the Sudan People's Liberation Army in January 2005. Subsequently, the United Nations Environment Programme released a report detailing how ecological crises and climate change played a role in driving the conflict. The report found that oil and gas competition, fights over land in drier parts of the country, desertification, and land degradation were all closely correlated with the region's conflict.[78] Concurrently, Ethiopians have fled their country to arrive in Somalia—on the route to Yemen. BBC News documented the many journeys refugees take from Africa to reach a safe haven in Europe. Some cross two seas; others rely on smugglers.[79]

CLIMATE CHANGE ADAPTATION IS A NEEDED RESPONSE

With a set level of global warming essentially locked in, the word on many people's tongues is "adaptation," including such solutions as building sea walls, finding new sources of clean water, and shifting agriculture practices. Adaptation for coastal regions is possible but very expensive, and many of the countries hosting the most refugees are also the poorest.[80] This is particularly true in Africa. In fact, nine of the ten countries with the highest number of refugees per dollar per capita are in Africa, including Ethiopia and South Sudan.

Recently, the FAO called for $100 million in emergency humanitarian aid to address the Sahel region's food crisis, as discussed above. This was part of a three-year, $2.2 billion effort. This level of spending is simply not sustainable.

One course of action to combat desertification is re-afforestation with mangroves, which are coastal swamps that flood at high tide. Certain shrubs and trees can survive in these flooded conditions, and such vegetation is useful for preventing land erosion from sea level rise.[81] Other

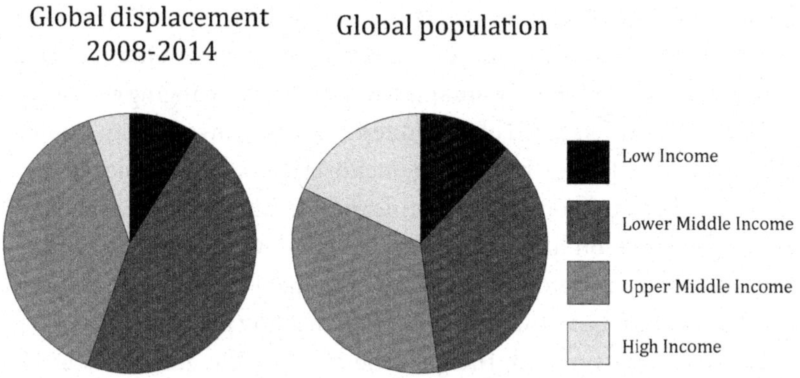

Figure 6.1: Countries with high displacement per GDP rates. Source: UNHCR Global Trends: Forced Displacement in 2014.

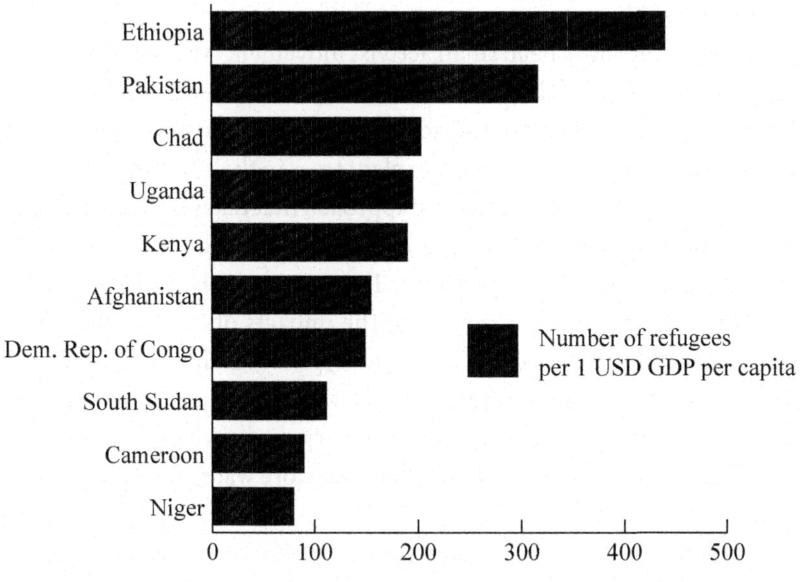

Figure 6.2: Global displacement by income level: People with low incomes are disproportionately displaced. Source: IDMC's Global Estimates 2015.

countries and communities are planting small trees to prevent land degradation. The *Guardian* reported: "Farmers in the region are already being forced to alter their techniques in response to changing climate."[82]

But Luc Gnacadja, head of the United Nations Convention to Combat Desertification, has warned that their efforts may succeed unless people "go to the fields and roll back desertification, it takes implementation."[83] Yet implementation has not come to pass in developing African countries, largely because of poor land management practices. Prevention may be more effective than rehabilitation in many places.

In Gnacadja's opinion, the good news "is at the grassroots level." "There are amazing success stories. We ought to reflect these success stories into our policies and institutions to enhance and measure them. Tanzania, Niger, Burkina Faso, and Mali have provided some success stories. Malawi, a country perceived to be unable to feed itself, broke new ground."[84]

Indeed, there have been small activist movements that have achieved some success. One of these is the Green Belt movement, established by Kenyan Wangari Maathai, the 2004 Nobel Peace Prize recipient. She organized women in rural Kenya to plant trees in their communities and restore ecosystems, using a holistic approach that takes into account underground water flows and natural watersheds, helping to preserve water in the soil and restore land quality. The movement helps to empower women, who are more vulnerable to the impacts of climate change in those communities, being the ones who typically gather water and harvest crops in their communities—in fact, the World Bank estimates that up to 80 percent of agricultural labor in Africa is provided by women.[85] The Green Belt movement has worked to restore water and land quality in several communities so far.

A combination of local and international efforts, along with immediate and long-term changes and actions, will be necessary to combat land degradation and improve resilience. Grassroots advocacy, though inspiring, is not enough. Gnacadja, in his appeal for grassroots advocacy and government land management to prevent desertification, declared that a meeting of international governments needs to result in "not with business as usual, but with a decision for business as unusual."[86] What is needed are real actions, with real plans to follow up and make sure that governments follow through.

The IDMC, in a report focusing on drought-induced displacement in the Horn of Africa, also gives suggestions for how communities can enhance resilience so as not to be forced to leave their homes. The report's authors argued that the drought-induced displacement was based in large part on "social systems and power, not by natural forces," suggesting that there are primarily social and political solutions. Among the solutions, they suggest drought-tolerant livestock herds, writing: "One way to enhance resilience to drought is by shifting herd composition away from cattle and toward more drought-tolerant animals, such as camels. An alternative strategy to enhance resilience to drought is to increase access to water points, emergency food stocks and veterinary services."[87]

All of these efforts go hand in hand with improving a landscape in Africa for preventing future refugees. A report from the UNHCR includes four strategies for preventing and protecting environmental migrants: (1) preventing environmental migration from happening in the first place (requiring measures to reduce communities' vulnerability to environmental hazards and strengthen capacities to cope with disaster); (2) managing migration as an adaptation measure (suggesting measures such as "managed regular migration schemes"); (3) creating protections for environmental migrants, including movement-related and status rights; and (4) adapting to the impacts of climate change itself. In coastal areas this means creating barriers to protect communities from sea level rise.[88]

These steps can, and should, be considered. The climate refugee crisis will impact every country and every continent. The crises in Africa have sent refugees to Europe, driven conflict in the Middle East, and are a cause for concern across the globe. The answers, in part, may be found in addressing climate change. Climate change has become intrinsically connected to mass migration in Africa and will continue to play an important role moving forward.

But unless countries in Africa begin efforts to adapt to climate change right away—and countries around the world lend a hand to help—we will have to face the consequences of catastrophic climate changes leading to more uprisings and refugees. Climate change is already leading to massive upheavals, and it is the poor who are hit the hardest. Africa's environmental refugees will reign as one of the world's greatest humanitarian challenges in decades to come.

NOTES

Meles Zanawi, "Africa at Risk," *Project Syndicate,* November 6, 2009, https://www.project-syndicate.org/commentary/africa-at-risk1. BBC News, "Horn of Africa Sees 'worst drought in 60 years,'" June 28, 2011, http://www.bbc.com/news/world-africa-13944550.

2. United Nations Environment Programme, Regional Office Africa, "Climate Change," http://web.unep.org/roa/regional-programmes/climate-change.

3. C. Rosenzweig, David Karoly, et al., "Attributing Physical and Biological Impacts to Anthropogenic Climate Change," *Nature,* May 15, 2008, http://www.nature.com/nature/journal/v453/n7193/abs/nature06937.html.

4. M. Boko, I. Niang, A. Nyong, et al., *Climate Change 2007: Impacts, Adaptation, and Vulnerability,* Contribution of Working Group II to the Fourth Assessment Report of the Intergovernmental Panel on Climate Change, M. L. Parry, O. F. Canziani, J. P. Palutikof, P. J. van der Linden, and C. E. Hanson, eds. (Cambridge, UK: Cambridge University Press, 2007), 433–67.

5. Notre Dame Global Adaptation Index (as of January 11, 2017, data for 2015), http://index.gain.org.

6. World Bank, "Turn Down the Heat: Why a 4°C Warmer World Must Be Avoided," November 1, 2012, http://documents.worldbank.org/curated/en/2012/11/17097815/turn-down-heat-4%C2%B0c-warmer-world-must-avoided.

7. World Bank, "World Is Locked into about 1.5° C Warming & Risks Are Rising, New Climate Report Finds," November 23, 2014, http://www.worldbank.org/en/news/feature/2014/11/23/climate-report-finds-temperature-rise-locked-in-risks-rising.

8. World Bank, "Turn Down the Heat: Confronting the New Climate Normal," November 23, 2014, http://documents.worldbank.org/curated/en/317301468242098870/Main-report.

9. Paul V. Desanker, World Wildlife Foundation, "Impact of Climate Change on Life in Africa," June 2002.

10. I. Niang, O. C. Ruppel, M. A. Abdrabo, A. Essel, C. Lennard, J. Padgham, and P. Urquhart, *Climate Change 2014: Impacts, Adaptation, and Vulnerability,* Part B: Regional Aspects, Contribution of Working Group II to the Fifth Assessment Report of the Intergovernmental Panel on Climate Change, V. R. Barros, C. B. Field, D. J. Dokken, M. D. Mastrandrea, K. J. Mach, T. E. Bilir, M. Chatterjee, K.L. Ebi, Y. O. Estrada, R. C. Genova, B. Girma, E. S. Kissel, A. N. Levy, S. MacCracken, P. R. Mastrandrea, and L. L. White, eds. (Cambridge, UK: Cambridge University Press, 2014), 1199–1265.

11. "Climate Change Seriously Affecting S. Africa: Minister," *Global Times,* November 30, 2015.

12. United Nations High Commissioner Agency, "2014 in Review; Trends at a Glance," Executive Summary, June 18, 2015.

13. Ibid.

14. United Nations Human Settlements Programme (UN-HABITAT), *State of the World's Cities 2006/7* (Nairobi, Kenya: United Nations Human Settlements Programme, 2006), 1–108.

15. S. B. Adamo, "Environmental Migration and Cities in the Context of Global Environmental Change," *Current Opinion in Environmental Sustainability* 2, no. 3 (2010): 161–65.

16. Boko et al., *Climate Change 2007*, 433–67.

17. Lauren Vallez and John Abraham, "East African Countries Are Dealing with the Impacts of Climate Change," *Guardian*, March 17, 2014.

18. B. Dont and R. Sutton, "Dominant Role of Greenhouse-Gas Forcing in the Recovery of Sahel Rainfall," *Nature Climate Change*, June 1, 2015.

19. Carbon Brief Staff, "Factcheck: Is Climate Change Helping Africa?" CarbonBrief.org, June 3, 2015.

20. Ibid.

21. United Nations Food and Agriculture Organization and USAID-funded Famine Early Warning Systems Network, "Somalia Famine Killed Nearly 260,000 People, Half of Them Children, Reports UN," UN News Centre, May 2, 2013.

22. Boko et al., *Climate Change 2007*, 433–67.

23. A. M. Abdi, J. Seaquist, D. E. Tenenbaum, L. Eklundh, and J. Ard, "The Supply and Demand of Net Primary Production in the Sahel," *Environmental Research Letters*, September 9, 2014; Chris Arsenault, "'Population Growth Far Outpaces Food Supply' in Conflict-Ravaged Sahel," *Guardian*, October 22, 2014.

24. Internal Displacement Monitoring Centre, "Global Estimates 2014: People Displaced by Disasters," Annex A.

25. P. F. Reich, S. T. Numbem, R. A. Almaraz, and H. Eswaran, "Land Resource Stresses and Desertification in Africa," in *Responses to Land Degradation. Proc. 2nd. International Conference on Land Degradation and Desertification, Khon Kaen, Thailand*, ed. E. M. Bridges, I. D. Hannam, L. R. Oldeman, F.W.T. Pening de Vries, S. J. Scherr, and S. Sompatpanit (New Delhi: Oxford University Press, 2001).

26. R. Lal and B. A. Stewart, *Advances in Soil Science: Soil Degradation* (New York: Springer, 1990), 154.

27. P. Gonzalez, C. J. Tucker, and H. Sy, "Tree Density and Species Decline in the African Sahel Attributable to Climate," *Journal of Arid Environments* 8 (December 2010): 55–64.

28. Carbon Brief Staff, "Factcheck: Is Climate Change Helping Africa?" June 3, 2015.

29. Jeremy Hance, "20 Million People Face Hunger in Africa's Sahel Region," Monga Bay, February 20, 2014.

30. Emma Batha, "Sahel Set to See Rise in 'Climate Refugees'—Report," Thomson Reuters Foundation, August 2, 2013.

31. Richard Munang and Jessica Andrews, "Despite Climate Change, Africa Can Feed Africa," *Africa Renewal*: Special Edition on Agriculture 2014, July 2014, 6.

32. Zlatica Hoke, "Prolonged Droughts Threaten Renewed Famine in Somalia," VOA News, September 24, 2014.

33. "Extreme Weather and Resilience of the Global Food System, 2015," Final Project Report from the UK-US Taskforce on Extreme Weather and Global Food System Resilience, Global Food Security Programme, UK.

34. Magdi Amin, Ragui Assaad, Nazar al-Baharna, Kemal Dervis, Raj M. Desai, Navtej S. Dhillon, Ahmed Galal, *After the Spring: Economic Transitions in the Arab World* (New York: Oxford University Press, 2012).

35. World Bank Sector Brief, "Agriculture & Rural Development in MENA," September 2008.

36. Jonathan Dimbleby, "Feeding on Ethiopia's Famine," *Independent*, December 8, 1998.

37. Horn of Africa Services, "East Africans in Seattle," http://www.hoas.org/east-african-community-in-seattle.

38. Food Security Portal, "Fires in Russia, Wheat Production, and Volatile Markets: Reasons to Panic?" August 9, 2010.

39. Tom Parfitt, "Vladimir Putin Bans Grain Exports as Drought and Wildfires Ravage Crops," *Guardian*, August 5, 2010.

40. Jeff Masters, "Drought in China Adds Pressure to World Food Prices," Wunderground, February 23, 2011.

41. Dalia Mortada, "Did Food Prices Spur the Arab Spring?" *PBS Newshour*, September 7, 2011.

42. Sarah Johnstone and Jeffrey Mazo, "Global Warming and the Arab Spring," *Survival* 53, no. 2 (2011): 11–17.

43. Food Security Portal, "Fires in Russia."

44. World Bank, "Severe Droughts Drive Food Prices Higher, Threatening the Poor," *Food Price Watch*, August 30, 2012.

45. R. Arezki, M. Bruckner, "Food Prices, Conflict, and Democratic Change," School of Economics Working Paper, University of Adelaide School of Economics, December 2010.

46. Nikos Alexandratos and Jelle Bruinsma, "World Agriculture towards 2030/2050: The 2012 Revision," Food and Agriculture Organization of the United Nations, June 2012.

47. Refugees International, Sahel: "Recurrent Climate Shocks Propel Migration; Resilience Efforts Face Challenges," August 1, 2013 .

48. UN Intergovernmental Panel on Climate Change, "The Regional Impacts of Climate Change," 2007.

49. Department of Defense, Quadrennial Defense Review, March 2014.

50. Zack Colman, "Hagel: Climate Change a 'threat multiplier,'" *Washington Examiner*, October 13, 2014.

51. African Ministerial Conference on the Environment, "Drought in the Horn of Africa: Challenges, Opportunities, and Responses," September 13, 2011.

52. A. M. Abdi, J. Seaquist, D. E. Tenenbaum, L. Eklundh, and J. Ardö, "The Supply and Demand of Net Primary Production in the Sahel," *Environmental Research Letters* 9, no. 9 (2014).

53. Arsenault, "Population Growth."

54. Ibid.

55. Mark Anderson, "Refugees and Patchy Rains Trigger New Sahel Hunger Crisis," *Guardian*, July 31, 2014.

56. Brandon Miller, "Expert: We're 'locked in' to 3-Foot Sea Level Rise," CNN, September 4, 2015.

57. Andrew Freedman, "New York Launches $19.5 Billion Climate Resiliency Plan," Climate Central, June 11, 2013.

58. *Turn Down the Heat: Climate Extremes, Regional Impacts, and the Case for Resilience*, Report for the World Bank by the Potsdam Institute for Climate Impact Research and Climate Analytics (Washington, DC: World Bank, 2013).

59. Internal Displacement Monitoring Centre and Norwegian Refugee Council, "Global Estimates 2015: People Displaced by Disasters," July 2015.

60. Katy Migiro, "Thousands Homeless as El Niño Floods Sweep Somalia," *African Independent*, October 28, 2015.

61. "Humanitarian Bulletin: Somalia April 2015," ReliefWeb, May 25, 2015.

62. "Agriculture > Workers per Hectare: Countries Compared," Nation Master, http://www.nationmaster.com/country-info/stats/Agriculture/Workers-per-hectare.

63. "Enhancing Climate Resilience of the Vulnerable Communities and Ecosystems in Somalia," United Nations Development Programme, November 21, 2014.

64. "Somalia: Displaced People Hit Hardest by Flooding," ReliefWeb, May 6, 2013.

65. "Forced Displacement in Somalia Shows 'no signs of easing,' UN Agency Warns," United Nations News Centre, September 16, 2014.

66. "Somalia: Kismayo Hit by Flash Floods," *Somali Current*, June 8, 2014.

67. "Somalia: Over a Million IDPs Need Support for Local Solutions," Internal Displacement Monitoring Centre, March 18, 2015.

68. Ibid.

69. "Workshop Report: Adopting and Implementing Somaliland's Draft Policy Framework on Internal Displacement," Internal Displacement Monitoring Centre, March 1–2, 2015.

70. "Somalia: Over a Million IDPs Need Support."

71. "2015 UNHCR Country Operations Profile—Ethiopia," UNHCR, http://www.unhcr.org/ethiopia.html, accessed March 30, 2016.

72. "Refugees in the Horn of Africa: Somali Displacement Crisis," UNHCR, http://data.unhcr.org/horn-of-africa/regional.php, accessed October 21, 2015.

73. Médecins Sans Frontières, "Dadaab: The Biggest Refugee Camp in the World Is Full," June 16, 2011.

74. Edmund Sanders, "Fleeing Drought in the Horn of Africa," *Los Angeles Times*, October 25, 2009.

75. United Nations High Commissioner Agency, "2014 in Review; Trends at a Glance," June 18, 2015.

76. "Ethiopia Overtakes Kenya as Africa's Biggest Refugee-Hosting Country," UNHCR, August 19, 2014

77. Ban Ki-moon, "A Climate Culprit in Darfur," *Washington Post*, June 16, 2007.

78. United Nations Environment Programme, "Sudan: Post-Conflict Environmental Assessment," June 2007.

79. Paul Adams, "Migration: Are More People on the Move Than Ever Before?" BBC News, May 28, 2015.

80. Elliott Negin, "Think Today's Refugee Crisis Is Bad? Climate Change Will Make It a Lot Worse," Huffington Post, June 30, 2015.

81. G. O. Ouma and L. A.Ogallo, "Desertification in Africa," *Promotion of Science and Technology* 13, no.1 (2007): 22–25.

82. Busani Bafana, "Climate Change Killing Trees across the Sahel, Says Study," *Guardian*, December 20, 2011.

83. Africa Renewal, "Desertification a Threat to Africa's Development," Africa Renewal Online.

84. Ibid.

85. Amparo Palacios-Lopez, Luc Christiaensen, and Talip Kilic, "How Much of the Labor in African Agriculture Is Provided by Women ?" Policy Research working paper no. WPS 7282, World Bank Group, June 2, 2015.

86. Africa Renewal, "Desertification a Threat to Africa's Development," Africa Renewal Online.

87. Norwegian Refugee Council and Internal Displacement Monitoring Centre, "Assessing Drought Displacement Risk for Kenyan, Ethiopian, and Somali Pastoralists," April 26, 2014.

88. Walter Kalin and Nina Schrepfer, "Protecting People Crossing Borders in the Context of Climate Change: Normative Gaps and Possible Approaches," University of Bern, Switzerland, for the United Nations High Commissioner for Refugees, February 2012.

7

Middle East

THE BOILING POINT OF CLIMATE CHANGE AND NATIONAL SECURITY

> Climatologists say Syria is a grim preview of what could be in store for the larger Middle East, the Mediterranean, and other parts of the world.
>
> *John Wendle,* Scientific American, *December 2015*

In the region of the world where the refugee crisis is at its peak and most prevalent, there's no need to hammer that environmental migration is a serious issue. But it has some roots in climate change. And the science shows that global warming may make future refugee crises more likely to happen. The key insight from all of this is that climate change made the world's biggest ever refugee crisis more likely to happen. In the future, climatic stresses will continue to contribute to political unrest and be influential in creating even more refugees.

THE SYRIAN REFUGEE BOY SEEN AROUND THE WORLD

A photo of a drowned three-year-old Syrian boy washed up on a beach captured the world's attention. His name was Aylan Kurdi. He drowned, along with his brother and mother, when a boat of migrants capsized en route from Syria to the Greek island of Kos. His father, Abdullah, survived the journey. Twelve refugees, including Aylan, did not.[1]

The image, which came into prominence in early September 2015, propelled the Middle East's refugee crisis into the forefront of international debate. Of course, the crisis comprised far more people than the one toddler. More than one million refugees and migrants fled for Europe in 2015—about half of those were Syrian.[2] Four million Syrians have fled their homes in the past several years due to climactic disruption and war.[3]

The refugee crisis extends far beyond Syria. Wars, social conflict, and instability across much of the Arab world have led to 16.7 million refugees being displaced worldwide. In addition to the 16.7 million refugees, 33.3 million from these regions are internally displaced—that is, displaced within their own countries.[4] This internal displacement itself has implications for security in those countries. Climate disruption combined with rapid urbanization and population growth in Syria is a toxic mix.

THE CLIMATE ROOTS OF THE SYRIA CRISIS

There have been enough discussions and articles on the political conflicts that led to the Syrian refugee crisis to fill several books, so this one will not delve too deeply. Rather, here we will take a broader look at the scope of Syria's crisis and focus on the connections between the crisis and climate change.

Syria is driving the refugee crisis, and climate change has driven the Syrian refugee crisis; it is the clearest scientifically established link yet between climate change and refugees who are fleeing political unrest. It began, as do many sources of unrest in the Middle East and North Africa, with a case of prolonged, severe drought—a drought that was three times more likely to happen because of global warming. Specifically, "Syria faced a devastating drought between 2006 and 2010, affecting its most fertile lands. The four years of drought turned almost 60 percent of the nation into a desert. It was a huge amount of land that could not support cattle herding and trading."[5]

The years-long drought had reverberating impacts for Syria's agricultural sector, causing widespread crop failures—75 to 100 percent failures in some areas—and killing up to 85 percent of the country's livestock: "Between 2 and 3 million of Syria's rural inhabitants were reduced to 'extreme poverty.'"[6] The agricultural difficulties resulted in a mass internal migration. About 1.5 million people moved from rural communities to Syria's urban centers and its surrounding areas. Those towns, already flooded with Iraqi refugees from another war, were short on food and economic opportunities. The internal migration resulted in population shock, which placed increased pressure on already strained resources. Near-urban settlements grew quickly, increasing by over 50 percent in just eight years from 2002 to 2010. Urban peripheries were filled with "illegal settlements, overcrowding, poor infrastructure, unemployment, and crime.... [These problems] were neglected by the Assad government and became the heart of developing unrest."[7] Additionally, "the [Syrian] government began awarding the rights to drill for water on a sectarian basis. So when the rains dried up, desperate people began digging illegal wells, which also became a political act."[8]

As for the tipping point of the unrest, many argue that it was the imprisonment of several teenage boys for spray-painting "Down with the regime" on a school wall in Daraa soon after the Arab Spring, where Egypt ousted its dictator.[9] Protests erupted around the country, and President Bashar al-Assad brutally cracked down on the protesters, with thousands killed and resulting in civil war.[10]

The drought itself had a "catalytic effect," according to a flagship study published in March 2015 in the *Proceedings of the National Academy of Sciences*. The study catalogued the links between global warming, the drought, and Syria's unrest, definitely concluding that global warming contributed to the region's instability.[11]

Syria is not the only country affected by the multiyear drought. According to Columbia University professor Richard Seager, quoted in the *Independent*, climate change is "steadily making the whole eastern Mediterranean and Middle East region even more arid." Seager noted that "Lebanon, Jordan, Israel, Iraq and Iran" are drying out as well and that "however the various social, religious and ethnic wars play out, in the coming years and decades the region will feel the stress of declining water resources."[12]

SYRIA CRISIS LED TO MILLIONS OF REFUGEES, WITH STAGGERING IMPLICATIONS

As the Syrian civil war progressed, by November 2015 there were over four million Syrian refugees and six and half million IDPs.[13] No government or international agency would give Syrians the status of "environmental refugee" or "climate refugee." They are already "refugees" as the term is currently defined by the Geneva Convention, fleeing from war and conflict. The connection between these refugees and climate change is complex, as discussed above. Certainly the region's politics had a large hand in the civil unrest; climate change was merely the spark under a preexisting tinderbox of turmoil.

Significantly, this crisis shows what happens when there are far too many refugees than the current system is able to handle. There has been an extraordinary increase in refugees since 2011, and Syria's crisis is the primary reason for this increase. Each day in 2014 an average of 42,500 people became refugees, asylum seekers, or IDPs. The UN called Syria's war the "world's single-largest driver of displacement."[14] The surge in Syrian refugees happened at an unprecedented rate: in 2015 the number of refugees "far surpassed" sixty million in 2015, according to the UNHCR, the highest since 1992.[15]

ARAB SPRING: INSPIRATION FOR SYRIAN UPRISINGS AND SUBSEQUENT WAR

According to most news reports, the Arab Spring began in Tunisia when peaceful protests led to the resignation of President Zine El Abidine Ben Ali and spread to uprisings in Egypt, Libya, and across the Middle East.[16] But the momentum from the Middle Eastern democracy movement may have actually had its roots in Asia, with years-long droughts.

A severe, prolonged drought in China and the Arab Spring uprisings that led to the oustings of multiple dictators—these two events seem to be unrelated, but in fact they are inherently connected. During the winters preceding the Arab Spring, China and Russia experienced a once-in-a-century drought. The climate patterns had changed; the wheat supplies in both regions were devastated. This caused global wheat prices to skyrocket, and because Egypt and other countries in that region are highly dependent on wheat imports, they were particularly affected. The drought resulted from lack of rain the preceding fall, along with subsequently less snow and less moisture in the ground. The 2009–2010 drought caused water shortages for over four million people and harmed nearly twenty-five million acres of wheat croplands.[17]

But this chapter is about the Middle East, not China. China's drought exemplifies how "a localized hazard [becomes] globalized," in the words of Oxford University research fellow Troy Sternberg.[18] One drought induced by climate change can have ramifications in far places, even on the other side of the world.

Though a Tunisian protester may have kicked off protests in the Arab world, Egypt is the country that set things into motion. In addition, Egypt was most harshly affected by the wheat price spikes caused by the Asian droughts. In Egypt food prices more than doubled from 2010 to 2011.[19] The government then cut down on food subsidies to its residents. Food prices were one of the major grievances in the protests. Waving loaves of bread as a symbol of protest, the activists chanted, "Bread, Human Dignity."[20] Egypt, ousting its dictator, triggered conflict in the region. Subsequently, several other Arab countries rose up in an attempt to follow suit.

Libya's dictator Moammar Gadhafi was ousted during the Arab Spring, but this led to civil war and exacerbated the refugee crisis. Previously, Libya had been seen as a stopgap between refugees in the Middle East and Europe—under horrible circumstances, to be sure: Gadhafi dealt with migrants by throwing them into prison, where rape and torture were prevalent.[21] But without Gadhafi, a huge flow of migrants surged into Europe. In the chaotic, unregulated state, previously closed refugee routes were reopened, allowing refugees to travel west apace.

The disruptions in Syria were reflected in other Middle Eastern nations. The Arab world became a cockpit for war and death after the Arab Spring. It is no wonder that so many have tried to flee since that time. And they tried to flee farther than they had ever been: outside the Arab world, into Western Europe. To do so, they had to cross the Mediterranean Sea.

THE PERILS OF CROSSING THE MEDITERRANEAN

For refugees fleeing their homes, the dangers of crossing the Mediterranean increased. In 2014 the European Union cut down on its boat rescue missions, hoping to discourage refugees from crossing the Mediterranean, despite warnings that reducing the number of rescues would greatly increase the death toll of refugees capsizing in the sea.[22] For the refugees, however, there was no other choice. Hundreds of thousands of refugees continued to cross the Mediterranean and still continue to do so. In 2014 more than 219,000 refugees and migrants crossed the Mediterranean Sea, three times the previous high of 70,000, which happened during the Arab Spring. That number continued to increase in 2015: in the first eight months, 300,000 made the trek.[23] The smuggling of refugees by boat across the Mediterranean has become a major industry. Indeed, the trade in climate change and war has become quite profitable in certain sectors of the Middle East, with profits projected to be as high as $1 billion for the year 2015.[24]

In 2013, 700 migrants and refugees attempting to cross the Mediterranean Sea into Europe were reported as dead or missing. In 2014 that number rose to 3,166, and in 2015 it was 3,601.[25] A huge portion of these migrants—nearly half—came from Syria. In April a ship holding over 800 refugees capsized, killing almost everyone on board. There were just 27 survivors.[26] That month, 1,308 refugees and migrants drowned or went missing.[27] The shipwrecks spurred the European Union into developing a more effective response to save distressed and sinking vessels.[28] The results were "immediate," according to the UNHCR. While there were over a thousand missing or drowned migrants in April, that number fell to 68 in May and 12 in June. Though as UNHCR notes, "even one death at sea is one death too many."[29] The perils of crossing the Mediterranean continue, with a number of routes.

DIRE STATE OF REFUGEE CAMPS AND TRAVELS

For those lucky enough to survive the trek, their destination is, first and foremost, a refugee camp. But the ever increasing number of refugees is making it nearly impossible for the camps to house all of those in need, and the camps themselves are overcrowded and unsafe.

The Syrians alone are greatly in need. At the end of 2014 the United Nations said it would need $8.4 billion to help the Syrian people, with a major share of that for neighboring countries to host the refugees.[30] Less than half of that amount has been pledged so far by countries around the

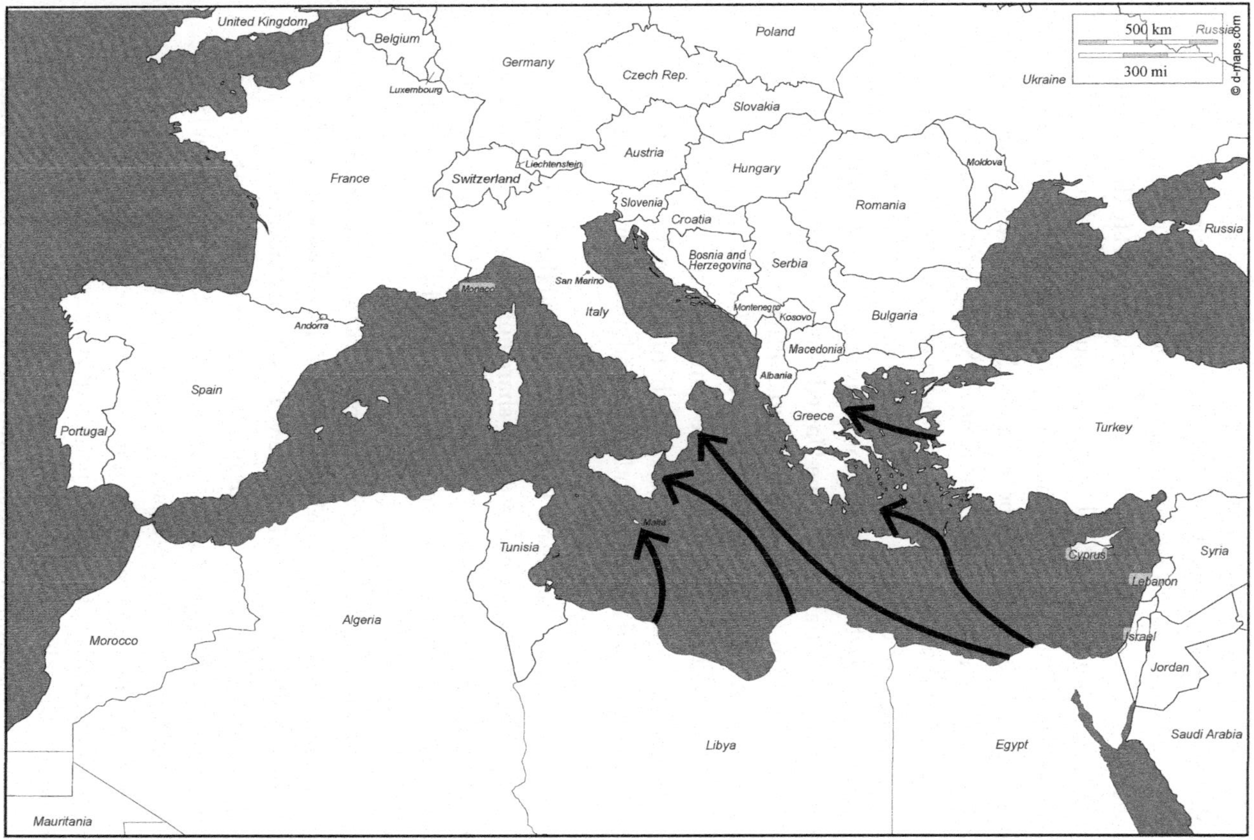

Map 7.1: Mediterranean Crossings. Source: "The Sea Route to Europe: The Mediterranean Passage in the Age of Refugees," UN High Commissioner for Refugees, July 1, 2015

world.[31] Host countries are "at breaking point," according to UN High Commissioner for Refugees António Guterres. The crisis has spurred international institutions to reconsider how to best aid the refugees, what Guterres calls a new "aid architecture" that "links support to the refugees with what is being done to stabilize the communities who host them."[32]

The UN's call for aid is to improve services in health, education, water, and sewage, along with policy and administrative support. The need for documentation is a serious issue for Syrian refugees in Turkey, where many of those without proper documentation are sent back to Syria.[33] Because of backlogs and lack of resources, refugee camps can keep families stuck there, in limbo, for many years.[34] In December 2015, one year after its initial request, the United Nations' Regional Refugee and Resilience Plan (3RP) was published. In that time the number of registered Syrian refugees increased by over a million, and the plan was only halfway funded. Furthermore, the communities surrounding the refugee camps have experienced economic hardships in the form of wage depression, worsened working conditions, and underemployment, due to an excess of refugees and lack of jobs.[35]

Lebanon, Jordan, Egypt, and Turkey have hosted the largest number of Syrian refugees, if only because they share borders with Syria or are close by. Each of these countries is dealing with specific problems, and refugees are trying to move farther away from the Middle East—farther from instability—into Europe.

Jordan is home to the largest Syrian refugee camp in the world: Zaatari. Located six miles east of Mafraq, Zaatari formed in 2012 and was set up in just nine days.[36] In the three years since its inception, Zaatari has grown to host eighty-one thousand refugees. It is the largest refugee camp in the Middle East, and its "population" makes it the ninth largest "city" in Jordan.[37] Furthermore, more than half of the Syrians in the camp are children, and many do not receive any education. Without education or training, the young people in the camp never learn sufficient skills to make a living.[38] This makes life in the real world much more difficult for them upon release and may encourage people to stay in the camps.

Once out of the camps, life is not always better. Most of the Syrians living in Jordan earn less than ninety-five dollars a month. Finding life

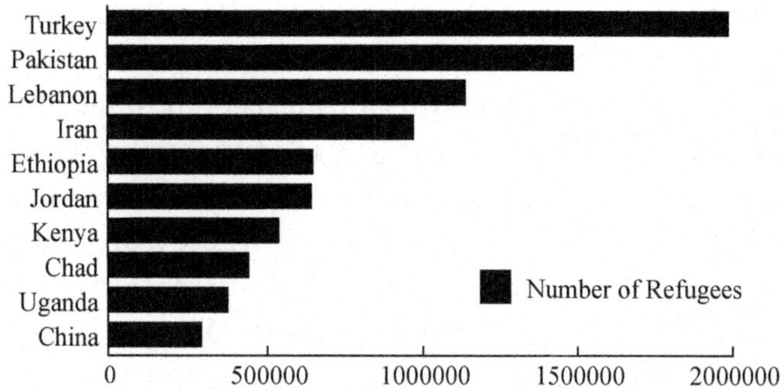

Figure 7.1: Countries hosting the largest numbers of refugees. Source: https://www.amnesty.org/en/latest/news/2015/10/global-refugee-crisis-by-the-numbers

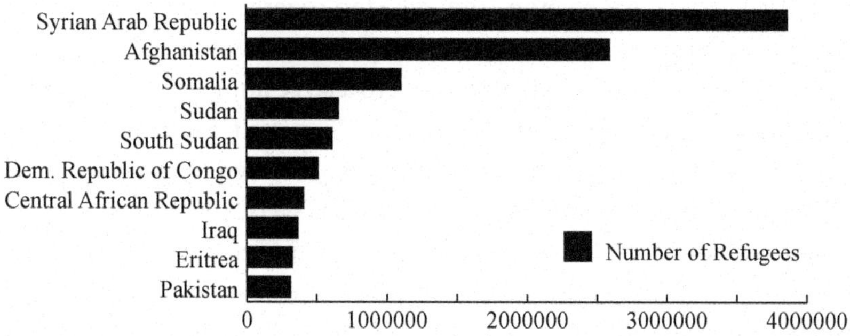

Figure 7.2: Source countries for largest numbers of refugees. Source: http://data.worldbank.org/indicator/SM.POP.REFG.OR?order=wbapi_data_value_2014+wbapi_data_value+wbapi_data_value-last&sort=asc

in Jordan too difficult, many refugees have turned back to Syria.[39] Jordan was home to over 650,000 refugees at the end of 2014, mostly from Syria. But although it is so heavily affected by Syria's refugee crisis, Jordan is still only the sixth largest refugee-hosting country in the world.[40]

The largest Syrian refugee population is in Turkey, which shares the longest border with Syria. The country shelters nearly half of the world's registered Syrian refugees: nearly 2.3 million at the end of 2015.[41] Of those, more than half are younger than seventeen years old, and 14 percent are currently living in refugee camps.[42] One million refugees were registered in Turkey over the course of 2014 alone. Most live in cities throughout the country.[43] In December 2015 the United States called on Turkey to seal its border, citing fears of the militant Sunni jihadist group ISIS (Islamic State in Iraq and Syria) transporting fighters and weapons.[44] While that may be the case, it will certainly have an impact on the refugees trying to leave as well. Already, over ten thousand Syrians are held up at crossing points on the border with Turkey.[45]

Lebanon is the host country for the third-largest number of refugees, almost half of whom are Syrian.[46] The country was host to 1.17 million refugees at the end of 2014, what the United Nations said stretched "the country's socio-economic absorption capacity to its limit."[47] Before the outbreak of Syria's civil war in 2011, it hosted only 8,000 refugees. The number of refugees living in Lebanon increased 14,500 percent in just four years. Turkey, Lebanon, and Pakistan together host 30 percent of all refugees (including non-Syrians).[48]

Strangely enough, Iraq is also a host to a large number of Syrian refugees. This may come as a surprise because Iraq itself is a major source of refugees. But indeed, it is host to around 250,000 Syrian refugees.

These host countries all share borders with Syria. The difficulties they face have been long known and are often considered apathetically by Western civilization—it is easy enough to consider the Middle East a problematic, unsolvable situation in and of itself, as long as it doesn't affect the rest of us.

But as the number of refugees has increased, camps are no longer able to hold the numbers, and integration in the new countries is becoming impossible, the refugees are heading for more distant destinations: across the Mediterranean Sea, farther north into Europe, and even across oceans. Through perilous and deadly routes, the refugee crisis finally received the media attention it deserved—but at what cost?

EXTREME HEAT WAVES MAKING AREAS "UNLIVABLE," AND IRAQ'S INSTABILITY

While refugees in the Middle East have become an unfortunately reality of today, it is also exceedingly important to consider how climate change events could influence refugee crises in the future. We begin by considering plainly what rising temperatures will mean for the Middle East: unendurable heat.

As it happens, global warming will not increase temperatures uniformly around the world; some areas will get less hot than others, some will even see decreases in temperatures, at least temporarily. But the Middle East region is going to be disproportionately affected by warming, warming at a rate twice as high as the global average. This will place scarce water resources under increased pressure, which—as seen in Syria—can lead to massive agricultural die-offs. Yet as residents move to the cities, as is common in these situations, the cities themselves will experience more extreme heat waves. Global warming will be concentrated in large cities due to the urban heat island effect.[49]

Such extreme heat can shut down an entire city, as has already happened in Iraq. In summer 2015 a large part of the Middle East experienced a raging heat wave, with temperatures exceeding 120 degrees Fahrenheit (50–52 centigrade) and high humidity levels creating a heat index reaching 159 degrees Fahrenheit in Iraq and over 160 in nearby Iran.[50] The government of Iraq instigated a four-day lifesaving holiday in response.

This is what it looks like for a city to be "unlivable," a term that scientists started using in 2015 when a study found that parts of the Middle East would become "unlivable" in the near future. Prolonged heat waves will be ten to twenty times more common than before. Dr. Karsten Haustein of the Environmental Change Institute in Oxford told the organization Responding to Climate Change (RTCC): "What used to be a 1 in 50–100 year event is a 1 in 5 year event now."[51]

Iraq has been highlighted for its potential for such heat waves to break out in unrest. There are already currently nearly three hundred thousand refugees and one and a half million internally displaced Iraqis.[52] Those already displaced have little or no shelter to protect them from the unbearable heat.

The heat wave of 2015 was the subject of protests in Iraq that summer. It was hot enough to melt traffic cones.[53] Citizens protested power outages: "All of the people we spoke to here say they want to see an end to rampant corruption, they want the return of basic services, they want electricity, they want to have air conditioning at a time when Iraq is experiencing a blazingly hot record heatwave and they want to have clean water," reported the Middle East news organization Al Jazeera.[54] Thousands of residents took to the streets to protest the power outages and government corruption. One man protesting the power outages was killed. Iraqi prime minister Haider al-Abadi referred to the protests as an "early warning" about "an error that we must solve immediately," adding, "The people will resort to revolutionary sentiments if this situation continues."[55]

Pakistan was also hit exceptionally hard by the heat wave, with over 1,250 deaths, including 1,000 deaths in the southern city of Karachi alone. Heat strokes, dehydration, heart attacks, and other heat-related ailments were rampant. Mortuaries were overfilled. Power outages across the city made things worse.[56]

It is a sad irony that this region that is one of the biggest sources of global warming—the heart of the oil industry—is one that is becoming too hot to handle. Prolonged, impossible heat waves, where being outside is not an option, are expected to become far more common by 2050. Areas will become virtually uninhabitable, according to a study from MIT scientists Jeremy S. Pal and Elfatih A. B. Eltahir, who found that several cities in the Persian Gulf will experience heat waves so extreme it will be impossible to survive outdoors, forcing residents into air-conditioned buildings for safety.[57] Yet this creates a new source of unrest if the government should shut off electricity, as they've done in Iraq, for hours or days at a time.[58]

In a world that is two degrees centigrade above preindustrial levels (the level of global warming to which the United Nations is striving to limit), major cities in the Middle East will experience many more "exceptionally hot" days such as those experienced in the summer 2015 heat wave: up to 62 days in Amman, Jordan; up to 90 days in Baghdad, Iraq; and up to 132 days in Riyadh, Saudi Arabia, among others. If the world fails to limit global warming to two degrees centigrade, the number of unbearably hot days in those cities will be much higher: over 115 days per year in all these cities.[59]

As we have seen in Iraq and Pakistan, many of the places most likely to experience extreme heat also experience frequent power outages, so there is nowhere to escape to for relief. Middle Easterners will either need to eventually move away from the hardships of the city or face the perils of living in an overcrowded, overheated land.

DROUGHT

In a land of sand and desert, it comes as no surprise that drought and water scarcity are frequent hazards in the Middle East. Yet it is too easy to dismiss these concerns as something the region has always experienced. The fact is that droughts are going to get worse and severe droughts more frequent. There will be less rain falling in the summer months, and increased temperatures will evaporate moisture from the soil—what little moisture is left.[60] Irrigation systems will falter and the agricultural economy will collapse. The constant hardship of water scarcity will be exacerbated to a tipping point.

The telltale signs of climate change can be found in Syria's multiyear drought that led to civil uprising, but drought is by no means limited to Syria. Over the past four decades, about thirty-eight million people in the Middle East have been affected by drought.[61] In coming decades, Middle Eastern countries will be among the most water stressed in the world. The World Resources Institute has ranked the countries that will be most water stressed in 2040, projecting that fourteen of the thirty-three countries that will face "severe water stress" are Middle Eastern, with Bahrain, Kuwait, and Qatar projected to fare the worst. The reason for many of these countries: climate change. More extreme precipitation (droughts punctuated by flash floods) will deplete surface water sources. The US National Intelligence Council acknowledged that as droughts become more frequent, water stresses in the Middle East "will increase the risk of instability and state failure" and "exacerbate regional tensions."[62]

The droughts have long-standing economic impacts. In Syria, after the third consecutive year of drought, in 2010, nearly one million people lost their entire livelihoods.[63] Countries are already starting to import water or, rather, importing "virtual water" by importing the water-intensive crops that they can no longer grow. The capital city of Yemen, for one, is on track to be the first without access to a viable supply of water. While many oil-rich countries in the Middle East have the economic leverage to import water, balanced by exporting oil, poorer countries like Yemen do not have this option. Currently, every Yemeni has access to just 140 cubic meters of water per year.[64] Their reserves of freshwater are drying up, depleting faster than they are being replenished. Its groundwater levels, which come from the mountain regions in the countryside, have plummeted by six meters a year. "Ten future generations' worth of Yemen's water is being used up now," according to the World Bank.[65] As water resources continue to decline, who knows what they will do? Importing "virtual water" is not a solution for the farmers, whose livelihoods depend on a steady source of water. More farmers are demanding basic rights to water, inspired in part by the Arab Spring.[66]

WATER WARS

We will increasingly see water resources used as a weapon of war. ISIS, for one, has taken over dams with that very intent. By restricting water to nearby villages, ISIS increases its power.[67] Control over scarce water resources is a huge asset for those like ISIS to use in opposing the government and exacerbating tensions. ISIS has taken over multiple dams along the Euphrates River as a strategic move, providing electricity to communities that previously saw only an hour a day in order to gain more support. Water supplies that were previously allocated to nearby communities were dammed up under ISIS's control.[68]

The World Bank has noted that droughts, which advance slowly and are not as noticeable as floods or earthquakes, nonetheless contribute to a "disaster situation" when "combined with pre-existing conflict." Water scarcity in the Middle East is a case in point; it is "increasingly becoming a cause of conflict, leading communities to fight over water-irrigated pastures and forcing people to leave their homes looking for safe access to water."[69]

HOW WATER SCARCITY LEADS TO CONFLICT

Climate change and water scarcity are interrelated concerns. IPCC Chair Rajendra Pachauri has said that "Unfortunately, the world has not really woken up to the reality of what we are going to face in terms of the crises as far as water is concerned . . . there are going to be profound changes in the water cycle due to climate change."[70] When it comes to water and the satisfaction of the planet's monumental thirst, calamities seem to be coming to our water resources that border on the biblical. We seem ill prepared for disasters whether they are hurricanes, drought, or the poisoning of our aquifers—or a catastrophic rise in sea levels, for that matter. We bemoan the disasters that befall our society as acts of nature, but we do not seem inclined to engage in long-term planning to prepare for them. We can't seem to get upset about a collapse or catastrophe that seems so abstract, as it may be years down the road. But sometimes we receive a grim reminder when a tsunami displaces thousands of people or when the water begins to disappear in Middle Eastern countries.

Some 783 million people lacked access to clean drinking water as of 2013.[71] Two billion die each year from unhealthy water conditions. According to United Nations reports, two-thirds of the global population will suffer intermittent water shortages by 2025. Oil may have been the defining resource of the twentieth century, but we are in a new century now, which many consider to be the century of water. Suffice it to say that water scarcity is an issue that is driving societies toward a tipping point in history. That point is one of growing conflict and instability in the future among water-resource-deprived nations.

The Center for Strategic and International Studies argues that "On one hand, global water challenges are the result of too many people demanding too much water."[72] On the other hand, these challenges are brought about when changes in climate combine with dysfunctional infrastructures and poor government frameworks that are unable to manage water supplies for countries and their populations. Sometimes historically settled populations can be turned into refugees because of bad decisions that lead to conflict.

Today Jordan, one of the world's driest countries, is dumping much of its water into the sand. Aging infrastructure is to blame. As an Atlantic Council report put it, "Of all the water that Jordan pumps, billions of liters never reach a family's tap. Instead it gushes out of broken pipes. The amount of water lost nationwide could satisfy the needs of 2.6 million people: more than one-third of Jordan's current population."[73] Meanwhile, as refugees from the neighboring Syrian civil war stream into Jordan's urban areas, they further strain a water system that may collapse of age and ill repair. Jordan's case is classic insofar as it demonstrates how bad decisions about infrastructure can have a ruinous impact on national populations. Furthermore, a warmer world is ripe for conflict and danger.

Most of the Middle East is in water crisis mode, and the region is approaching dangerous water shortages and contamination. As Joyce Starr has observed, as early as the 1980s the US government intelligence services estimated that there were at least ten places in the world where war could break out over dwindling shared water—Jordan, Israel, Cyprus, Malta, and the six countries of the Arabian Peninsula.[74] What are the implications for water and societies in terms of climate change? Already social scientists at the International Peace Institute have observed that climate change–induced migration appears in many climate-change-to-violence scenarios.

Today environmental problems play a role in migration. Some migrations occur when there is either too much water, as in rising seas, tsunamis, and floods, or not enough water. In these countries people depend on the environment for their livelihood. For example, land degradation and scarcity have been growing in Bangladesh. Frequent storms and floods are destroying the Bangladeshian landscape. Largely due to this, twelve to seventeen million Bangladeshis moved to India and a half million moved internally in the 1990s.[75] A similar tragedy occurred in the United States in the 1930s when aggressive agriculture and prolonged drought turned the western plains into the infamous Dust Bowl that forced two and a half million people to leave the region.

"Water conflict," strictly defined, is a term used for describing a conflict between countries, states, or groups over access to water resources. Water wars or conflicts have been a recurring theme over five thousand years, according to a historical study by the Pacific Institute.[76] These conflicts occur over both freshwater and saltwater, both between and within nations. Freshwater, however, is vital for community survival. Its availability is certainly a matter of life or death. Recent humanitarian catastrophes such as the Rwandan genocide or the war in Sudanese Darfur have been linked to water conflicts of long standing. Current disputes in the Middle East have been water-based and have been the catalyst for an outflowing of climate refugees. These disputes include conflict stemming from the Tigris and Euphrates rivers among Turkey, Syria, and Iraq; the Jordan River conflict among Israel, Jordan, Lebanon, and Palestine; and Nile River conflicts between Egypt, Sudan, and Ethiopia. As Shane Harris wrote in *Foreign Policy,* the strains of growing populations, coupled with the effects of pollution and climate change, have taxed many of the water systems that feed the world's people and are vital for agriculture. More than half the world's wetlands have disappeared, and climate change around the world has altered weather patterns and led to water shortages.[77] Such developments may unleash conflict and major out-migrations in developed countries as well.

In both Africa and the Middle East, future wars are more likely to be fought over water than over oil. Water hegemony and climate refugees are two sides of the same coin of climate change. Those who dominate the hydropolitics of their state or region ultimately decide the fate of the great mass of people who are dependent on this vital resource. Syria is an excellent example of how hydropolitics mixed with severe drought can produce one of the largest tsunamis of climate and political refugees in this century.

FLOODS: DRIVERS OF DISPLACEMENT

As we observed in chapter 1, drought and floods are not mutually exclusive. In fact, the two work together to degrade agricultural land and create food and resource scarcity. Worldwide, floods are the most frequent disasters recorded, and this is also the case in the Middle East.[78] While other climate events are slow-going crises, floods have a heavier hand in immediately forcing displacement. In nearly every country in the Middle East, floods are the most frequent natural disaster (with the exception of Iran, where earthquakes overtake them).[79]

In 2014 severe floods in the Balkan region were the single most responsible event for disaster-induced displacement in Europe.[80] In May 2014 heavy rains in Bosnia and Herzegovina flooded the rivers and destroyed water banks, resulting in severe floods and landslides. Forty-five thousand homes were destroyed and ninety thousand people were displaced. As a result, over forty thousand people sought refuge. In a region where most people already struggle to find decent housing, the flooding and landslides wrought devastation.[81]

Yemen has also experienced strong floods, year after year, forcing tens of thousands of Yemenis to leave their homes.[82] Yemenis in refugee camps themselves are vulnerable to flooding. In a case in 2013, torrential floods wiped out half of the tents at three refugee camps. Eight thousand camp residents were affected.[83]

The UNHCR said it would do its part to "continue its efforts to help those Yemenis affected by this natural disaster."[84] But it is not in their legal mandate to do so, so the displaced people are largely dependent on the mobilization from other UN agencies and the kindness of donors and other forms of foreign aid.

PAKISTAN'S TRAVAIL

As with heat waves, floods have seemed to disproportionately target Pakistan in recent years.[85] In 2010 heavy monsoon rains flooded the Indus River basin. About one-fifth of the country was underwater, and two thousand died. More than ten million people were displaced and relocated in drastically underfunded refugee camps. Much of the agricultural economy was wiped out, meaning the refugees had no livelihood once the floodwaters subsided and they could move back to their homes.[86] An estimated $43 billion was wiped out of the economy.[87]

Life for the displaced was hard. Pakistanis were forced to live in camps with scarce clean water. The dramatic loss of livestock killed in the floods resulted in severe food shortages. With inadequate water sanitation, there were concerns of typhoid, hepatitis, and cholera outbreaks.[88] The camp residents were at risk of "a second wave of deaths induced by the floods in the shape of water-borne diseases," according to Jacques de Maio, head of operations for South Asia at the International Committee of the Red Cross.[89]

But 2010 was not the end of Pakistan's flood hardships. A year later, in 2011, flooding destroyed 1.7 million homes and displaced 18 million people.[90] In 2014 monsoon rains and floods killed 367 and affected over 2 million people.[91] In 2015 more than 1 million people were evacuated at risk of floods, and 835 new relief camps were established to accommodate them.[92]

Pakistani scientists argue there was "strong evidence" that climate change was responsible for the devastating 2010 floods.[93] Indeed, the United Nations' science assessment has found that the severity of monsoon rains is proportional to increased atmospheric temperatures. Worsened monsoon rains are in line with a warming world and expected to get worse as global temperatures continue to increase.[94] The 2010 floods—the worst of them yet—ravaged southern Pakistan, but northern Pakistan is also expected to get more floods and landslides in the future.[95]

Still, Pakistan stands out from many of the other countries that experience such frequent devastating floods as a model of resilience. In Punjab, a region in eastern Pakistan that stretches into India, the Pakistani government has been building model villages to replace the ones that were washed away, and these replacements will be far more resilient to floods and climate change. Mud huts washed away by the monsoon rains are replaced with resilient brick homes, built to withstand both earthquakes and floods. New schools and health infrastructure replace what was lost. Solar and biogas plants are replacing old, emissions-intensive fossil fuel plants. These actions, along with promoting economic development in the region, constitute a "triple win" for adaptation: low emissions, disaster-resilient, economy-boosting communities.[96]

This model may become a necessity for other Middle Eastern communities. Even without climate change, the sheer pace of urbanization means every time a disaster strikes there is more damage, more lives lost. Flood mortality, while on a global decline, has continued to increase in the Middle East partially because of urbanization (and also because of climate change), and the percentage of gross domestic product (GDP) endangered by floods has tripled over the past four decades.[97]

It is worth noting that building climate-resilient communities, like in Pakistan's Punjab, is far from inexpensive. Each community costs about US$20 million.[98] But the dollar amount of economic assets lost in the floods far outpaces that figure; in 2008, floods in Yemen districts Hadramout and Al-Mahara cost US$1.6 billion.[99]

Another key piece of the flood problem is urbanization. About 60 million people live in coastal regions in the Middle East—about 17 percent of its population. It is one of the world's most rapidly expanding populations. By 2030, the Middle East's urban population will increase by 45 percent, with more than 106 million additional people.[100] As urban development continues in those areas, so too will the risks of surging tides. Furthermore, expanding urban settlements tend to lack proper infrastructure to respond to floods. Housing infrastructure to receive the new migrants is constructed quickly and poorly. Adequate drainage systems, catchment systems, warning systems, and emergency plans are scarcely found in many Middle Eastern urban settlements.[101]

As climate change worsens conditions in the rural areas and people continue to migrate from the countryside to the cities, urban infrastructure that is resilient to sea level rise and floods will become an increasingly important requirement.

CYCLONES IN THE ARABIAN SEA

Cyclones making landfall off the Arabian Sea used to be uncommon, but now some fear this may become the new norm. The environment of the Arabian Sea has everything against allowing cyclones to form. Cyclones and hurricanes require wide-open spaces to form and warm waters to gather strength, and while the Arabian Sea is warm, it is too small for cyclones to develop. Instead, cyclones spin out of the Indian Ocean and steer through the cramped Arabian Peninsula.

In fall 2015 two cyclones formed in the Arabian Sea and made landfall in Yemen in one single week.[102] The first, Cyclone Chapala, which was the worst, struck Yemen with devastating consequences. The region where the cyclone hit was home to one hundred thousand IDPs and twenty-seven thousand refugees, and they bore brunt of the cyclone.[103] While the death toll is unknown (Mukala, the region hardest hit, had been governed only by tribal councils and al-Qaeda for months), dozens of people were left missing and six thousand fled for higher ground.[104]

Yemen barely had time to reel in shock before a second cyclone made landfall, Cyclone Megh. It was less powerful than Cyclone Chapala but no less deadly, killing six on Yemen's island of Socotra. On the mainland, where it lessened to a tropical depression, Megh flooded a hospital holding those displaced from Chapala and ruined the houses of three thousand others.[105] Mercy Corps, an Oregon-based humanitarian organization, estimated that up to forty thousand Yemenis were displaced from the intense floods following the storm.[106]

Before that fateful week, there had not been a single *year* with two cyclones making landfall in Yemen. By all accounts the cyclone was unusual. Only one or two cyclones form in the Arabian Sea each year, and they rarely gain enough strength to be classified as severe. But Cyclone Chapala formed over record-warm sea temperatures. It was the second strongest and the longest-lived cyclone in the Arabian Sea on record; those two factors added together meant the cyclone generated the most energy of any on record in the area.[107]

Many scientists do not expect cyclones to become more frequent with global warming, but they will become more intense. So while only one or two cyclones may continue to form each year on average over the Arabian Peninsula, the likelihood of their being strong enough to make land and wreak damage is substantially higher.[108]

A LOOK AT AFGHANISTAN

Afghanistan is the second largest source of refugees, after Syria. In 2013, before Syria's uprising, it was ranked number one. In fact, for the past several decades, Afghanistan has been ranked the number-one refugee source country between 1981 and 2013; it is only recently, with Syria's uprising, that it was demoted to number two.[109] So while its crisis is nothing new, its refugees face unique vulnerabilities to climate change.

Afghanistan's refugee crisis has escalated in recent years. The refugee crises are often interconnected; Syria's refugee crisis has impacts in Afghanistan and other nearby countries. Most Afghan refugees have ended up in neighboring Pakistan. It has often been the world's largest refugee-hosting country, falling to second place behind Turkey for the first time in 2014, when it hosted one and a half million refugees, the majority of whom were Afghan.[110] But relations between the two countries are fragile. Many Afghani officials and residents blame Pakistan for attacks carried out by the Taliban in Kabul in August 2014.[111] Nevertheless, the Afghani and Pakistani governments are trying to work together to discern how to handle what is the largest protracted refugee population

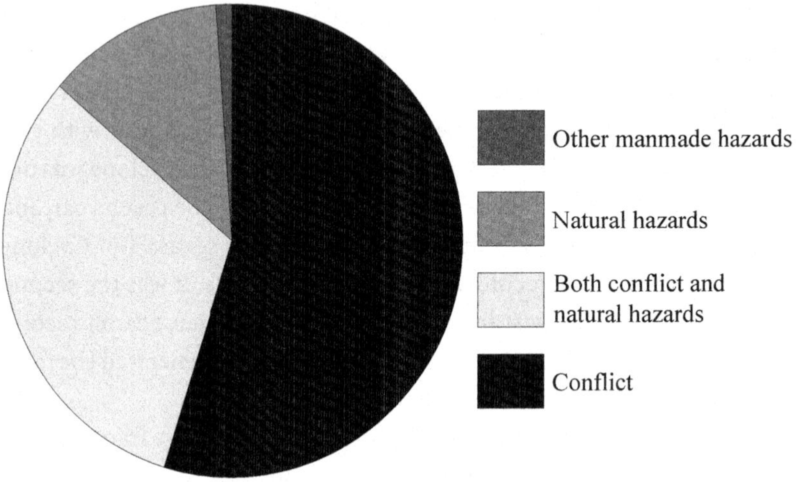

Figure 7.3: Drivers of displacement in Herat and Helmad (Pakistan). Source: IOW/ Samuel Hall Consulting, 2014. Data: IOM DTM, December 2013.

in a single country, working to extend Proof of Registration cards for Afghan refugees in the country.

Afghanistan is ranked 169th of 180 countries on the Notre Dame Global Adaptation Index, which ranks countries according to their risk given climate change[112]—to heat waves, drought, and floods—as well as least capable of coping with its impacts.[113] Decades of armed conflict and .environmental degradation have weakened the country's ability to invest in disaster risk management and climate adaptation.[114] And while the military presence and political conflict is cited as the primary driver of displacement in Afghanistan, the Internal Displacement Monitoring Centre notes that climate drivers are making it worse.

Natural hazards aggravate local tensions surrounding scarce resources and land disputes (see fig. 7.3).[115] Yet despite the overlap between natural disasters and conflict as drivers of displacement, the two phenomena are tracked and assisted separately, by different organizations and with different forms of response. The two organizations—UNHCR and the Afghanistan National Disaster Management Authority—will need to work together to form a comprehensive response and better their assistance to those in need.

As it happens currently, those who cite political conflict as the reason for their displacement receive better long-term assistance. As a result, displaced people are more likely to cite political insecurity as the reason for their migration rather than natural disasters or climate change.[116] However, Afghanistan's national policy on IDPs, adopted in November 2013, applies to people forced to flee from political conflict *and* those displaced by natural disasters. It remains to be seen how this policy plays out in practice.[117]

ADAPTATION

As a region that is not only the largest current source of refugees but also has historically dealt with a harsh climate and environment, the Middle East exemplifies the worst-case scenarios interacting. Its experience thus provides important lessons that can be adopted there and elsewhere. First and foremost, this region will need to adapt to a world with less water. Water scarcity is already a driver of conflict, and as water sources continue to deplete, there will be even more competition over what's left. If not, water will become the region's main geopolitical resource, and "water wars" may become the main source of strife.

Desalination, a process that removes the salt and impurities from water taken from salty oceans and seas, is seen by many as a last resort to address water shortages, but for some Arabian countries it is a major source of potable water. Currently, more than 70 percent of the world's desalination plants take water from the Arabian Gulf and Mediterranean Sea to serve the region.[118] But after the process, the salt brine is returned to the seas and can harm the region's environment. Some regions of the gulf have salt levels eight times higher than they should be, affecting the region's fishing industry. As time goes on and salty waste keeps getting dumped back into increasingly saline seas, the desalination process will become increasingly inefficient and in turn will harm the region's ecology and wildlife.

Until it becomes unviable, however, the desalination industry is booming, particularly in oil-rich countries, which makes sense given that it is such an energy-intensive process.[119] Yet the availability of this process is often an excuse for waste. The reliance on such a fossil fuel–

intensive means to deliver clean water will become increasingly out of step as these countries work to reduce greenhouse gas emissions—as they should, to prevent even *further* future cases of drought and water depletion. Some countries are experimenting with powering desalination plants with solar power instead.[120]

Even so, the process remains expensive and difficult for poor countries like Yemen. It should only be seen as a last resort and not as an excuse to waste water, as has been done in the past. Golf courses and parks are watered with valuable drinking water.[121] The tourism industry has also resulted in water waste, with demand for longer and more frequent baths and showers, swimming pools, and green lawns.

Drastic changes to agriculture are needed. For too long the region has grown crops that are not suitable for the region: cotton, rice, wheat. A shift to crops that use less water will be necessary. Purchasing "virtual water" via crops is another option, as discussed above. But the idea of completely replacing an entire industry with imports is simply not economically feasible.

Saving water through wastewater recycling will be key, especially in urban settings. Recycled water—the water that is flushed, showered, or rinsed down the drain—can be used to irrigate farms, to water landscapes, and to fill toilets. Fortunately, wastewater recycling technology is making rapid advancements.[122] Yet it has its risks, especially as wastewater is used in agricultural settings; it could increase exposure to chemicals and diseases for both farmers and communities. This will be an issue to monitor as recycling technology is employed more thoroughly. It is currently done with little government monitoring; this will need to change.[123]

Already some smaller cities have completely run out of water, the *Guardian*'s environment editor, John Vidal, reported in 2015. Many others have water supplies restricted to just a few hours a day. Water aquifers are the major source of water in many parts of the region, and they are being depleted at alarming rates, an irreversible process.[124] Cut-off water supplies may become the norm if nothing is done.

Policies that have worked out well could become a model for other regions. Jordan, for instance, is aiming to "maximize the use of available water through water conservation . . . and substitution of freshwater with reclaimed water for agriculture," according to Jordanian officials.[125] Morocco is working with the World Bank to "make irrigation in the basin more sustainable, more profitable, and more resilient to climate change" by providing a fixed amount of water and subsidizing efficient irrigation equipment.[126]

Some cities are coming around to the fact that drastic water-saving measures are needed. A couple of cities in the United Arab Emirates are on the forefront of such efforts. Abu Dhabi is currently building a futuristic city called Masdar, which will be run on renewable energy and employ extreme water-saving measures: concrete instead of grass shoulders on the road, and water-saving devices in all buildings. Schools and mosques within Abu Dhabi itself are also working to save water, notes Vidal, by building two thousand mosques in Abu Dhabi fitted with devices that save the water people wash in before prayer and initiating school competitions to reduce water usage.[127]

The European Union assembled a set of policy orientations in 2007, including recommendations to put the right price tag on water, allocate water-related funding more efficiently, and finance water efficiency and land-use planning, and improve drought risk management and monitoring systems.[128] There needs to be a shift in water-saving culture as well. In addition, the depleted aquifers need to be restored, be it through rainwater collection or treated wastewater.

One thing is certain: though regional and local solutions will be needed, international collaboration will also be necessary to prevent a catastrophic worldwide water crisis. Many water sources cross international lines, like the Tigris and Euphrates rivers and the seas. Water in the Tigris and Euphrates rivers, which are points of contention and control, is depleting faster than nearly every place on earth, except in northern India.[129] Professor Ralf Ludwig, who coordinated the EU-funded CLIMB ("Climate Induced Changes on the Hydrology of Mediterranean Basins") project, has said: "International collaboration is often a stronger, and obviously a preferable mechanism to sustainably manage scarce water resources than conflict. When you start to collaborate you may be able to find enduring solutions for the benefit of all those involved. In any case, adaptive and preferably collaborative action is needed to reduce the likelihood of conflict and increase water security."[130]

Talib al-Shehhi, director of preaching at the United Arab Emirates,' ministry of Islamic affairs has said, "Allah does not like those who waste. . . . Safeguarding resources and water especially is central to religion. The Qu'ran says water is a pillar of life and consequently orders us to save [it], and Muhammad instructs us to do so." Regardless of belief, opposing parties will have no choice but to cooperate or face ruinous conflict. In fact, some experts point to the water crisis as an opportunity for a new form of peace.[131]

In addition to water control, adaptation to other impacts of climate change will be necessary. As people flock to the coastal cities—Kuwait City, Doha, Abu Dhabi, and Dubai—barricades to prevent flooding from sea level rise will be necessary. The official systems for responding to natural disasters and to refugees will need to work increasingly together. Helping this region become resilient to the impacts of climate change—*without* requiring such a heavy use of oil, which exacerbates climate change—will be key for preserving its political security and preventing conflict that leads to further refugee crises.

The Middle East, long roiled in conflict and strife, will be a stage for conflict in the decades to come. With much of the region's economy dependent on oil, it will have to become a major player in the global effort to reduce fossil fuels and combat climate change. The world is left with two options. We can let things lie, allowing political conflict to increase and oil-addicted governments to do nothing to help the Middle Eastern refugees, continuing to spiral the refugee crisis to new heights. Or we can work with the region to fight climate change and to protect people from its catastrophic harms.

NOTES

John Wendle, "The Ominous Story of Stria's Climate Refugees," *Scientific American,* December 17, 2015, https://www.scientificamerican.com/article/ominous-story-of-syria-climate-refugees/.

1. John Withnall, "Aylan Kurdi's Story: How a Small Strian Child Came to Be Washed up on a Beach in Turkey," *The Independent,* September 3, 2015, http://www.independent.co.uk/news/world/europe/aylan-kurdi-s-story-how-a-small-syrian-child-came-to-be-washed-up-on-a-beach-in-turkey-10484588.html.

2. Jonathan Clayton and Hereward Holland, "Over One Million Sea Arrivals Reach Europe in 2015," UNHCR, December 30, 2015, http://www.unhcr.org/en-us/news/latest/2015/12/5683d0b56/million-sea-arrivals-reach-europe-2015.html.

3. Mosin Ali and Yarno Ritzen, "Syrian Refugee Crisis in Numbers," Al Jazeera America, December 9, 2015, http://www.aljazeera.com/indepth/interactive/2015/12/151209100759278.html.

4. Patrick Kingsley, "Arab Spring Prompts Biggest Migrant Wave Since Second World War," *Guardian*, January 3, 2015. http://www.theguardian.com/world/commentisfree/2015/jan/03/arab-spring-migrant-wave-instability-war.

5. "How Could A Drought Spark A Civil War?," September 8, 2013, NPR, http://www.npr.org/2013/09/08/220438728/how-could-a-drought-spark-a-civil-war.

6. William R. Polk, "Your Labor Day Syria Reader, Part 2," *Atlantic*, September 2, 2013, http://www.theatlantic.com/international/archive/2013/09/your-labor-day-syria-reader-part-2-william-polk/279255/.

7. Data and quotes from Colin P. Kelley et al., "Climate Change in the Fertile Crescent and Implications of the Recent Syrian Drought," *Proceedings of the National Academy of Sciences* 112, no. 11 (2015), http://www.pnas.org/content/112/11/3241.full.pdf.

8. "Water Security," Sustainability.org, September 12, 2013, http://www.sustainability.org.il/home/news-updates/Water-Security-Drought-Called-a-Factor-in-Syrias-Uprising-0913.

9. Clarissa Ward, "How Teens Started Syria's Uprising 1 Year Ago," CBS News, March 16, 2012, http://www.cbsnews.com/news/how-teens-started-syrias-uprising-1-year-ago/

10. Audrey Kurth Cronin, "ISIS Is Not a Terrorist Group," *Foreign Affairs* (March/April 2015), https://www.foreignaffairs.com/articles/middle-east/isis-not-terrorist-group.

11. Kelley et al., "Climate Change in the Fertile Crescent."

12. Tom Bawden, "Refugee Crisis: Is Climate Change Affecting Mass Migration?," *Independent*, September 7, 2015, http://www.independent.co.uk/news/world/refugee-crisis-is-climate-change-affecting-mass-migration-10490434.html.

13. "Syrian Arab Republic: Humanitarian Snapshot," Office for the Coordination of Humanitarian Affairs, November 30, 2015, http://reliefweb.int/report/syrian-arab-republic/syrian-arab-republic-humanitarian-snapshot-30-november-2015-enar.

14. "A World at War: Worldwide Displacement Hits All-Time High as War and Persecution Increase," UNHCR, June 18, 2015, http://www.unhcr.org/en-us/news/latest/2015/6/558193896/worldwide-displacement-hits-all-time-high-war-persecution-increase.html.

15. "World at War: UNHCR Global Trends, Forced Displacement 2014," UNHCR, June 18, 2015, http://www.unhcr.org/en-us/statistics/country/556725e69/unhcr-global-trends-2014.html; Stephanie Nebehay, "World's Refugees and Displaced Exceed Record 60 Million: U.N.," Reuters, December 18, 2015.

16. Boris Kelly, "Egypt Rises," *Overland*, February 14, 2011, https://overland.org.au/2011/02/egypt-rises/.

17. Austin Ramzy, "China Suffering Worst Drought since 1951," *Time*, February 6, 2009, http://content.time.com/time/world/article/0,8599,1877552,00.html.

18. "The Arab Spring and Climate Change: A Climate and Security Correlations Series," Center for American Progress, ed. Caitlin E. Werrell and Francesco Femia, February 2013.

19. Fatima Bishtawi, "What Ignited the Arab Spring?" *Yale News*, August 5, 2015, http://archive.epi.yale.edu/the-metric/what-ignited-arab-spring.

20. Ibid.

21. Matthew Carr, "How Libya Kept Migrants out of EU—At Any Cost," *The Week*, August 5, 2011.

22. Lizzie Davies, Arthur Nelson, "Italy: End of Ongoing Sea Rescue Mission 'puts thousands at risk,'" *Guardian*, October 31, 2014.

23. Melissa Fleming, "Crossings of Mediterranean Sea Exceed 300,000, Including 200,000 to Greece," UNHCR, August 28, 2015.

24. Tom Miles, "Europe Gets One Million Migrants in 2015, Smugglers Seen Making $1 Billion," Reuters, December 22, 2015.

25. "Mediterranean Sea Data of Missing Migrants," International Organization for Migration, http://missingmigrants.iom.int/mediterranean.

26. Alessandra Bonomolo, "UN Says 800 Migrants Dead in Boat Disaster as Italy Launches Rescue of Two More Vessels," *Guardian*, April 20, 2015.

27. UNHCR, "Mediterranean Crisis 2015 at six months: refugee and migrant numbers highest on record," July 1, 2015, http://www.unhcr.org/uk/news/press/2015/7/5592b9b36/mediterranean-crisis-2015-six-months-refugee-migrant-numbers-highest-record.html.

28. "The Sea Route to Europe: The Mediterranean Passage in the Age of Refugees," UNHCR, July 1, 2015.

29. Ibid.

30. "UN and Partners Seek US$8.4 Billion for New Syria Programme in 2015," UNHCR, December 18, 2014.

31. "Donors Pledge $3.8 Billion in Aid to People Affected by Syria Crisis at UN-Backed Conference," UN News Centre, March 31, 2015.

32. "UN and Partners Seek US$8.4 Billion."

33. Tania Karas, "Not Syrian, Not Turkish: Refugees Fleeing War Lack Documentation," Al Jazeera America, September 24, 2015.

34. Max Fischer and Amanda Taub, "The Refugee Crisis: 9 Questions You Were Too Embarrassed to Ask," Vox, September 9, 2015.

35. "3RP Regional Refugee & Resilience Plan, 2016–2017, Regional Strategic Overview," http://www.3rpsyriacrisis.org.

36. Christopher Jones-Cruise, "Refugee Camp in Jordan Is Biggest in Middle East," VOA News, August 9, 2015.

37. "Inside the Largest Syrian Refugee Camp—Zaatari Camp Three Years On," *Telegraph*, August 7, 2015. http://www.telegraph.co.uk/news/worldnews/middleeast/jordan/11782854/Inside-the-largest-Syrian-refugee-camp-Zaatari-camp-three-years-on.html.

38. Jones-Cruise, "Refugee Camp in Jordan."

39. Ibid.

40. "World at War: UNHCR Global Trends, Forced Displacement 2014," UNHCR, June 2015, http://www.unhcr.org/en-us/statistics/country/556725e69/unhcr-global-trends-2014.html.

41. Michael Martinez, "Syrian Refugees: Which Countries Welcome Them, Which Ones Don't," CNN.com, September 10, 2015; "Syria: Conflict without Borders: Number and Locations of Refugees and IDPs," UNHCR, https://hiu.state.gov/Products/Syria_ConflictWithoutBorders_Displacement_2015Aug27_HIU_U1283.pdf.

42. "Syria: Conflict without Borders."

43. "World at War: UNHCR Global Trends."

44. Geoff Dyer, "US Urges Turkey to Seal Border with Syria," *Financial Times*, December 1, 2015, https://www.ft.com/content/94001904-9851-11e5-9228-87e603d47bdc.

45. "Not-So-Open Borders for Syrian Refugees?" IRIN News, December 24, 2012.

46. "World at War: UNHCR Global Trends."

47. "UNHCR Launches 'Voices for Refugees' Aimed at Mobilising Support for Displaced Civilians and Refugees," *Ammon*, June 29, 2015, http://en.ammonnews.net/article.aspx?articleno=29346#.WImCjLYrKRs.

48. Ibid.

49. "Hot and Getting Hotter: Heat Islands Cooking U.S. Cities," Climate Central, August 20, 2014, http://www.climatecentral.org/news/urban-heat-islands-threaten-us-health-17919.

50. Nick Wiltgen, "Feels-Like Temp Reaches 164 Degrees in Iran, 159 in Iraq; Days Off Ordered as Mideast Broils in Extreme Heat Wave," Weather.com, August 5, 2015.

51. Freya Palmer, "Extreme Weather Events of 2015: Is Climate Change to Blame?" Climate Home, August 21, 2015, http://www.climatechangenews.com/2015/08/21/extreme-weather-events-of-2015-is-climate-change-to-blame/.

52. "2015 UNHCR Country Operations Profile—Iraq," UNHCR, http://www.unhcr.org/pages/49e486426.html.

53. Kareem Shaheen and Saeed Kamali Dehghan, "Middle East Swelters in Heatwave as Temperatures Top 50C," *Guardian*, August 4, 2015.

54. "Iraq Cabinet Backs PM Abbadi's Sweeping Reforms," Al Jazeera, August 9, 2015.

55. Anne Barnard, "120 Degrees and No Relief? ISIS Takes Back Seat for Iraqis," *New York Times*, August 1, 2015, https://www.nytimes.com/2015/08/02/world/middleeast/iraqis-protest-electricity-shortage-during-heat-wave.html?_r=0.

56. "Pakistan Heatwave Death Toll Climbs Past 1,200," Al Jazeera, June 27, 2015; Saba Imtiaz and Zia ur-Rehmanjune, "Death Toll from Heat Wave in Karachi, Pakistan, Hits 1,000" *New York Times*, June 25, 2015.

57. Jeremy S. Pal and Elfatih A. B. Eltahir, "Future Temperature in Southwest Asia Projected to Exceed a Threshold for Human Adaptability," http://eltahir.mit.edu/wp-content/uploads/2015/08/Paper.pdf.

58. "Iraqis Protest over Baghdad Heatwave Power Cuts," BBC News, August 1, 2015.

59. Maria Sarraf, "Two Scenarios for a Hotter and Drier Arab World—and What We Can Do about It," World Bank, November 24, 2014, http://blogs.worldbank.org/arabvoices/two-scenarios-hotter-and-drier-arab-world-and-what-we-can-do-about-it.

60. *Climate Change 2007: Working Group II: Impacts, Adaptation and Vulnerability; Floods, and Droughts*, IPCC Fourth Assessment Report: Climate Change 2007.

61. World Bank, "Natural Disasters in the Middle East and North Africa: A Regional Overview," January 2014, http://documents.worldbank.org/curated/en/211811468106752534/pdf/816580WP0REPLA0140same0box00PUBLIC0.pdf.

62. "Intelligence Community Assessment on Global Water Security," US National Intelligence Council, http://www.state.gov/e/oes/water/ica.

63. World Bank, "Natural Disasters in the Middle East and North Africa."

64. John James, "Export Oil, Import Water: The Middle East's Risky Economics," IRIN News, March 5, 2013.

65. Foad Al Hazari, "Future Impact of Climate Change Visible Now in Yemen," World Bank, November 24, 2014.

66. James, "Export Oil, Import Water."

67. Walaa Hussein, "How IS Uses Water as Weapon of War," AL Monitor, http://www.al-monitor.com/pulse/originals/2015/05/arab-world-water-conflict-isis-control-war.html.

68. Danya Chudakoff, "'Water War' Threatens Syria Lifeline," Al Jazeera, July 7, 2014.

69. World Bank, "Natural Disasters in the Middle East and North Africa."

70. Nita Bhalla, "World Has Not Woken Up to Water Crisis Caused by Climate Change," *Scientific American,* https://www.scientificamerican.com/article/world-has-not-woken-up-to-water-crisis-caused-by-climate-change/.

71. "World Water Day 2013—Year of International Cooperation," UN Water, http://www.unwater.org/water-cooperation-2013/water-cooperation/facts-and-figures/en/.

72. Erik R. Peterson, "Addressing Our Global Water Future," Center for Strategic and International Studies (CSIS) Sandia National Laboratories, September 30, 2005, p. 21, https://csis-prod.s3.amazonaws.com/s3fs-public/legacy_files/files/media/csis/pubs/csis-snl_ogwf_sept_28_2005.pdf.

73. Keith Proctor, Refugee Crisis Draining Jordan's Water Resources," Atlantic Council, March 21, 2014, http://www.atlanticcouncil.org/blogs/menasource/refugee-crisis-draining-jordan-s-water-resources.

74. Joyce Starr, "Water Wars" *Foreign Policy* 82 (Spring), 17–36, available at http://dlc.dlib.indiana.edu/dlc/bitstream/handle/10535/3267/Reproduced.pdf?sequence=1.

75. Rafael Reuveny, "Climate change-induced migration and violent conflict," *Political Geography* 26 (2007) 656–673, available at http://n.ereserve.fiu.edu/010030490–1.pdf

76. Peter H. Gleick and Matthew Heberger, "Water Conflict Chronology," Pacific Institute, December 10, 2009, available at http://worldwater.org/wp-content/uploads/2013/07/ww8-red-water-conflict-chronology-2014.pdf.

77. Shane Harris, "Water Wars," *Foreign Policy,* September 18, 2014, http://foreignpolicy.com/2014/09/18/water-wars/.

78. World Bank, "Natural Disasters in the Middle East and North Africa."

79. Ibid.

80. "Global Estimates 2015: People Displaced by Disasters," Internal Displacement Monitoring Centre and Norwegian Refugee Council, July 2015.

81. Ibid.

82. "Yemen: Over 10,000 Displaced by Floods," UNHCR, October 27, 2008.

83. "Yemen Flash Floods Destroy Camps for Displaced People," *Guardian,* August 29, 2013.

84. "Yemen: Over 10,000 Displaced by Floods."

85. While Pakistan is technically an Asian country, it aligns more closely with the Middle East both in culture and in climate/environment, so discussion of such is included in this chapter.

86. Asian Development Bank, *Addressing Climate Change and Migration in Asia and the Pacific,* 1st ed. (Mandaluyong City, Philippines: Asian Development Bank, 2012), p. 5, box 3, available at http://www2.warwick.ac.uk/fac/soc/pais/research/researchcentres/csgr/green/foresight/demography/2012_adb_addressing_climate_change_and_migration_in_asia_pacific.pdf

87. Hasan Mansoor, "Pakistan Evacuates Thousands in Flooded South," Agence France-Presse, August 22, 2010.
88. Ibid.
89. "UN Chief: Pakistan Needs More Aid," Al Jazeera, August 15, 2010, http://www.aljazeera.com/news/asia/2010/08/201081552627441712.html
90. Office for the Coordination of Humanitarian Affairs, "Pakistan Media Factsheet," 2011, http://bit.ly/151MVsY
91. "Pakistan: Floods—Sep 2014," Relief Web, http://reliefweb.int/disaster/fl-2014-000122-pak.
92. Ibid.
93. "'Strong Evidence' Climate Change Caused Devastating Pakistan Floods," *Scotsman*, October 13, 2010, http://www.scotsman.com/news/strong-evidence-climate-change-caused-devastating-pakistan-floods-1-824487.
94. M. L. Parry, O. F. Canziani, J. P. Palutikof, P. J. van der Linden, and C. E. Hanson, eds., *Climate Change 2007: Impacts, Adaptation, and Vulnerability* (Cambridge, UK: Cambridge University Press, 2007).
95. Asian Development Bank, *Addressing Climate Change and Migration* (Mandaluyong City, Philippines: Asian Development Bank, 2012).
96. "News: Pakistan's Punjab Builds Model Villages to Withstand Disasters," Climate and Development Knowledge Center, December 17, 2013.
97. World Bank, "Natural Disasters in the Middle East."
98. "News: Pakistan's Punjab."
99. UN-HABITAT, "The State of Arab Cities 2012: Challenges of Urban Transition, 2012," downloadable at http://unhabitat.org/books/the-state-of-arab-cities-2012-challenges-of-urban-transition/.
100. Ibid.
101. "Natural Disasters in the Middle East."
102. Yamiche Alcindor, "Unprecedented Back-to-Back Cyclones Hit Arabian Sea," *USA Today*, November 7, 2015.
103. "Deadly Cyclone Triggers Heavy Flooding in Yemen," Al Jazeera, November 3, 2015.
104. Angela Fritz, "Historic Cyclone Chapala Ravages Coastal Yemen with Catastrophic Flash Flooding," *Washington Post*, November 3, 2015.
105. "Tropical Cyclone Megh—Nov 2015," Relief Web, http://reliefweb.int/disaster/tc-2015–000152-yem.
106. Kelly Montgomery, "Helping Displaced Families after Cyclone Chapala Flooding," Mercy Corps, November 5, 2015.
107. Bob Henson, "Chapala Slams Yemen: First Hurricane-Strength Cyclone on Record," Wunderground, November 3, 2015.
108. James Renwick, "IPCC Special: Future Climate Phenomena and Regional Climate Change," Climatica, January 7, 2014.
109. "World at War: UNHCR Global Trends."
110. Ibid.
111. Khalid Aziz, "Pak-Afghan Relations: Hanging by a Thread," *Dawn*, September 12, 2015.
112. Lonnie Shekhtman, "How to Help the Countries Most Vulnerable to Climate Change. (Energy/Environment)," Christian Science Monitor, April 5, 2016, http://www

.csmonitor.com/Environment/2016/0405/How-to-help-the-countries-most-vulnerable-to-climate-change.

113. Notre Dame Global Adaptation Index, http://index.gain.org/ranking.

114. "Global Estimates 2015: People Displaced by Disasters."

115. Ibid.

116. Ibid.

117. Government of the Islamic Republic of Afghanistan, Ministry of Refugees and Repatriation, "National Policy on Internally Displaced Persons," November 25, 2013, http://morr.gov.af/Content/files/National%20IDP%20Policy%20-%20FINAL%20-%20English(1).pdf, 14.

118. Alexandra Barton, "Water in Crisis—Middle East," The Water Project, https://thewaterproject.org/water-in-crisis-middle-east.

119. John Vidal, "What Does the Arab World Do When Its Water Runs Out?" *Guardian*, February 19, 2011, https://www.theguardian.com/environment/2011/feb/20/arab-nations-water-running-out.

120. James, "Export Oil, Import Water."

121. Vidal, "What Does the Arab World Do?"

122. Julia Devlin, "Is Water Scarcity Dampening Growth Prospects in the Middle East and North Africa?" Brookings Institution, June 24, 2014, https://www.brookings.edu/opinions/is-water-scarcity-dampening-growth-prospects-in-the-middle-east-and-north-africa/.

123. "Climate Change Adaptation to Protect Human Health: Jordan Project Profile," World Health Organization, http://www.who.int/globalchange/projects/adaptation/en/index5.html.

124. John Vidal, "Middle East Faces Water Shortages for the Next 25 Years, Study Says," *Guardian*, August 27, 2015, https://www.theguardian.com/environment/2015/aug/27/middle-east-faces-water-shortages-for-the-next-25-years-study-says.

125. Jennifer Hattam, "Adapting to Climate Change in the Arid Middle East," Treehugger, November 15, 2009, http://www.treehugger.com/corporate-responsibility/adapting-to-climate-change-in-the-arid-middle-east.html.

126. "Adaptation to Climate Change in the Middle East and North Africa Region," World Bank, http://web.worldbank.org/archive/website01418/WEB/0__C-152.HTM.

127. Vidal, "What Does the Arab World Do?"

128. Commission of the European Communities, 2007, "Addressing the Challenge of Water Scarcity and Droughts in the European Union," http://ec.europa.eu/environment/water/quantity/pdf/comm_droughts/impact_assessment.pdf.

129. Devlin, "Is Water Scarcity Dampening Growth Prospects?"

130. Zaria Gorvett, "Mediterranean States Must Work Together to Adapt to Water Scarcity—Prof. Ralf Ludwig," *Horizon*, April 27, 2015.

131. Vidal, "What Does the Arab World Do?"

8

Asia

THE LOOMING CRISIS

> We cannot sit and stay helpless staring at this international climate stalemate. It is now time to take action. We need an emergency climate pathway.
>
> I speak for my delegation. But more than that, I speak for the countless people who will no longer be able to speak for themselves after perishing from the storm. I also speak for those who have been orphaned by this tragedy. I also speak for the people now racing against time to save survivors and alleviate the suffering of the people affected by the disaster.
>
> *Yeb Sano, Philippines delegate to the United Nations Climate Change Conference, Warsaw, 2013*

A rickety boat of refugees is turned away from port after port in country after country until after months of searching for safe haven the ship crew gives up and abandons its passengers, leaving them adrift in the Andaman Sea with no food or water and only scant hope of rescue. Meanwhile, the capital of Bangladesh sees thousands of new people migrating in from their homes in the countryside, which is slowly being overtaken by rising seas. Elsewhere, Asia's teeming urban centers and sprawling slums are dangerously close to oceans, and a single flood can devastate town after town. In Asia, multiple refugee crises are currently underway, but they are all too easily forgotten by the media.

Asia is vast beyond comprehension, and with its immense size comes great and varied vulnerabilities to climate change. The continent with the greatest population in the world, it is also unfortunately home to the greatest number of people who will be affected by climate change—most notably, sea level rise.

Table 8.1. Countries with the Greatest Populations Affected by Sea Level Rise

Country	Pop. affected (millions)
China	85
Vietnam	32
India	28
Indonesia	23
Bangladesh	22
Japan	21
United States	17
Egypt	12
Brazil	11
Netherlands	10

Climate Central, the nonprofit news organization that reports on climate science, analyzed sea level rise data under a number of different scenarios, depending on how quickly the world moves to stem fossil fuel emissions. Alarmingly, all Asian countries take top positions in the data. The six countries that will have the greatest population affected by sea level rise are China, Vietnam, India, Indonesia, Bangladesh, and Japan. These countries contain much coastal, low-lying land. Over two hundred million people in those countries live on land that will be affected.[1]

Much like in the drowning Pacific Islands, the connection between climate change and displacement in Asia is impossible to deny. Sea level rise is unstoppable; the only questions are how much we can reduce the rate and what countries can do to adapt.

Adaptation to sea level rise—creating sea walls and barriers, moving cities inward—is unquestionably expensive. Low-lying developing countries like Bangladesh and Vietnam particularly vulnerable, projected to lose a far greater proportion of their GDP than other Asian countries. But for Asian residents of every socioeconomic status, measures taken to protect coasts from sea level rise will be less expensive in the long run than the economic damage that would happen otherwise.[2]

It is not just sea level rise that makes Asia the most vulnerable to global warming; tropical cyclones, drought, intense rain and hail, and more also come into play. Many Asian countries rank among the most vulnerable on the Notre Dame Global Adaptation Index, which ranks countries by their vulnerability to climate change and least able to adapt to its impacts.[3]

Indeed, the impacts of sea level rise will be far-reaching and multi-pronged. Low-lying coasts will be slowly inundated. River deltas will flood, coastal wetlands will be destroyed, agricultural areas will be rendered ungrowable. Floods in cities will damage infrastructure; floods in lowlands will ruin crops. Already the beaches are being slowly chipped away. Coastal communities will have much to face, and they already are, as can be seen in Myanmar and Bangladesh in alarming ways. Residents of the communities on the coast of Bengal Bay, off the Indian Ocean, are already being forced to abandon their homes to face the dangers at sea.

MIGRANTS ADRIFT IN BENGAL BAY

In spring and summer 2015, boats carrying thousands of refugees from Myanmar drifted in the middle of the Bengal Sea with nowhere to go. They were fleeing ethnic persecution in their home country and subsequently were turned away from Indonesia and then Malaysia. Thailand would not allow any Myanmar refugees during this period of mass exodus. They were Muslims, turned away from their country, where they were recognized as citizens. They would cry out for food and water to the Thai officials who passed by. On one boat ten passengers died during the months they were adrift after the boat's captain and crew had abandoned them.

Just as Syria has the image of the washed-up toddler boy, Asia has its own poster child for climate change—hundreds of them, stranded on boats, banished from their destinations and consigned to life on the perilous seas, often referred to in the media as "boat people." Oftentimes, boats of hundreds or thousands of refugees are at sea for months, unable to find port. Many have been abandoned by the ship crews without food or water, still more have capsized.[4] It is an exceedingly dangerous journey, but the refugees who have been forced to leave Myanmar and Bangladesh have nowhere else to go.

Many of the people fleeing are being persecuted for their religious views—particularly, the Rohingya, the Muslim minority that resides in Myanmar and Bangladesh. They are a stateless people; the government of Myanmar has denied their citizenship since the Burmese nationality law in 1982. Only in recent years, the government has cracked down on persecuting them, placing them into camps or throwing them into jail if they do not call themselves Bengali. Across the border in Bangladesh, they face even more persecution, as they are usually considered illegal migrants,[5] or the government lets them sit in refugee camps for years and years without a plan for an eventual home.[6]

And they are being turned away from Malaysia, Indonesia, and Thailand and left to float in the sea, with minimal supplies of water and food. Malaysia and Indonesia have announced they would turn away boats of refugees. Thailand has stopped several refugee boats from making port; refugees instead have to be smuggled in and are at great risk of being arrested. After Thailand cracked down on human smugglers, boat crews abandoned refugees in the middle of the sea. It was a "potential humanitarian disaster," Jeffrey Savage, a senior protection officer with the Office of the United Nations High Commissioner for Refugees, told the *New York Times*.[7] Human Rights Watch has called it a dangerous and deadly game of "human ping pong."[8]

Yet it took such a deadly game and subsequent public outcry to make any progress on protecting the refugees at sea. At the behest of the United Nations, countries in Southeast Asia, including Indonesia, Thailand, and Malaysia, gathered to discuss the crisis in early 2015. These three countries had turned away an estimated eight thousand refugees from making land in their country. Turning away the boats full of migrants, with no food or water, would transform the ships into what the United Nations secretary-general Farhan Haq called "floating coffins."[9] The governments of Indonesia and Malaysia agreed to allow some of the migrants to come ashore. The United Nations called it an "important initial step."[10] But a temporary Band-Aid will not heal the long-term problem.

There is another aspect to the plight of the Rohingya. The majority of the Rohingya reside on the quickly degrading coast of the Bay of Bengal, where sea level rise is a daily reality. Many refugees are the destruction of their communities.

When migrants aren't risking the illegal, deadly trip at sea, they are moving inland. As has been seen in Syria and in Africa, farmers who can no longer make a living in the degraded coastal plains in the countryside have been forced to move to urban centers. However, the cities are packed, so migrants are forced into the slums. As a result, Dhaka—the capital of Bangladesh—has faced a population explosion, and its infrastructure is struggling to keep up.[11] One slum, Korail, is home to seventy thousand people. Families there live in one-room shanty huts that are poorly held together. The sewage system is nonexistent in most of the city, which is worrisome beyond just living in a smelly hut. When the rains pour during monsoon season, the water overflows the sewage system, allowing diseases to run rampant with common outbreaks of malaria and cholera.

This is no ordinary hardship. Life has not always been like this for Dhaka's newest slum-dwelling climate refugees. Dhaka, including its surrounding areas, is one of the fastest-growing megacities in the world.[12] An estimated three and a half million people—40 percent of Dhaka's population—lives in slums. A full 70 percent of the slum dwellers moved there after experiencing environmental difficulties in the countryside, according to the International Organization for Migration.[13]

It has long been common for rural dwellers of Bangladesh to move to Dhaka slums temporarily as a way to earn money, but as the impacts of global warming worsen, it is becoming harder for those residents to move back. Coastal flooding ruins rice paddies and destroys crops. Saline water damages the water supplies. Storms have demolished homes and communities. Climate change is forcing people to move to Dhaka and stay there.[14]

Life is perilous in the crowded cities. Those who are lucky enough to get a job work under horrible conditions. The garment industry—the source of clothes for the likes of Tommy Hilfiger and the Gap—is prominent; sweatshops are widespread. In April 2013 the Savar building in the Rana Plaza collapsed, killing 1,134 people inside and injuring thousands of others.[15] It was the worst industrial accident ever to happen in the garment industry. It caused public outcry around the world, leading to political charges for the garment industry for the first time; in the past, there would be no charges for smaller accidents. The building owner and government officials faced murder charges.[16] Yet years later, working conditions in Bangladesh's garment factories are not much better.[17] And even under safe working conditions, workers are often paid less than two dollars a day. They start at minimum wage, which is the equivalent of thirty-seven dollars a month.[18] Clean water is hard to find; without flowing taps, slum villagers have to purchase it from middlemen at fifty times its usual price. They live in houses made of bamboo stilts in the most flood-prone areas. In the case of a storm or cyclone, they are the most at risk.

Unable to find refuge in Indonesia and Malaysia, the Rohingya and others then head for Australia. The trip to Australia is expensive and dangerous. After Australia loosened its refugee restrictions in 2008, the number of trips—and the number of deaths—multiplied. About nine hundred people died at sea in the following five years.[19] Many get lost; Australians have urged their government to expand its search and rescue operations.[20] But Australia's policies on asylum seekers are particularly harsh. Labor leader Bill Shorten announced in July 2015 that it would turn back refugee boats.[21] This follows years of that party's harsh attitude toward refugees: in 1992 Labor prime minister Paul Keating wanted there to be mandatory detention for unauthorized arrivals.[22] One last potential refuge for the boat people has proven to a pipe dream.

THE ROLE OF THE RISING SEAS

Over one-quarter of Myanmar's borders consist of coastline.[23] The country borders the Bay of Bengal, which extends northward from the Indian Ocean. Nearby countries bordering the bay and the ocean include India, Bangladesh, Thailand, Malaysia, and Indonesia. Millions of people living in these countries will be affected by coastal flooding and sea level rise–related land loss. Anywhere from thirteen to ninety-four million people will be living in coastal populations that will experience floods. One meter of sea level rise, which is a conservative estimate, will put 4.1 million people at risk. In Bangladesh's Ganges-Brahmaputra-Meghna river delta alone, more than one million people will be directly affected by sea level rise by 2050, well before the one-meter rise is predicted.[24] In a possible worst-case scenario, Bangladesh will lose one-quarter of its land area, displacing thirteen million people by 2100.[25]

Huge river deltas and surrounding areas in Bangladesh, India, Myanmar, Thailand, Cambodia, and Vietnam are at risk of decay. The deltas are being slowly degraded as sea levels rise and storms batter the beaches, flooded by both overflowing rivers and the rising ocean during extreme precipitation events. Cyclones cause acute damage as well. The deltas, which contain deposits of sediment brought from water sources upstream, are normally replete with nutrients, thus they act as an important agricultural resource. But saline water brought in from storm surges and coastal flooding can render them infertile.

Two-thirds of Bangladesh is "basically a vast river plain," according to the United Nations' Nansen Initiative. That area is less than five meters above current sea level and is expected to experience frequent flooding as sea levels rise.[26] Two hundred fifty million poor rural farmers live in the surrounding low-lying plains, whose livelihoods depend on fertile, productive soil.[27]

Two large rivers cut through Bangladesh: the Ganges (called the Padma in local language) from the Indian border and the Brahmaputra from Tibet. It is the largest delta in the world. It is also fed by the huge network of smaller rivers that feed into the basin, dubbed "100 Mouths of the Ganges." Every year during monsoon season, the region degrades; rivers flood with force, entire riverbanks collapse, fields and homes are washed away. River erosion has erased and displaced entire villages that sit on the low-lying plains. The rivers are known to carve out new paths or grow deeper into their current paths. The "old Ganga," or "Buriganga," is a river that was once connected to the Ganges River but today lies forty miles away.[28] This process of eroding river plains has historically been accompanied by rebuilding; one riverbank turns into a river, and the silt carried by that river forms a new island elsewhere. But the "rebuilding" process happens at a lesser scale each year. The region is unable to react to the erosion in time due to greater levels of water runoff and because of the area's hydropowered dams, which trap the silt and sediment that would otherwise move down the river. There is a scientific consensus that the greater levels of water runoff are more to blame than the hydropower dams.[29]

In its fourth assessment on the state of climate change, the United Nations' Intergovernmental Panel on Climate Change (IPCC) noted that there is strong agreement that sea level rise will accelerate the degradation of the deltas.[30] Huge swaths of land will disappear by 2050, particularly surrounding river deltas in Asia. In Bangladesh, more than three million people around the Ganges-Brahmaputra-Meghna delta may become displaced. In Vietnam, up to seven million of the eighteen million people living along the Mekong delta may be forced to leave by 2050.[31] In Thailand, the delta surrounding the Chao Phraya River has sunk in parts to 1.5 meters below sea level already; it is possibly the worst delta affected by ground loss in the world.[32]

FOR CLIMATE-INDUCED DISPLACEMENT, ASIA WILL FARE THE WORST

Multiple reports throughout the years have predicted the number of people who will be displaced due to the consequences of climate change.[33] They may come to slightly different conclusions, taking different variables and projections into account, yet they all seem to agree on one thing: of all the continents, Asia will have far and away the most people displaced by climate change.

For the past several years, natural disasters have displaced more people in Asia than any other continent. Asia is home to 60 percent of the global population, but between 2008 and 2013, 80 percent of the global population of displaced persons were from Asia; in 2013 that number jumped to 87 percent.[34] Disaster risks are most highly concentrated in Asia and will only become more so. As Jan Egeland, secretary-general of the Norwegian Refugee Council, said: "This increasing trend will continue as more and more people live and work in hazard-prone areas. It is expected to be aggravated in the future by the impacts of climate change."[35]

Sea level rise is often cited as the greatest risk to Asia, and for good reason. If China, for example, does not adapt to sea level rise, an estimated half million people will be forced to leave their homes and communities. The good news is that adaptation is not only feasible but also economically viable in China, and if carried out, it will prevent a large percentage of the vulnerable population from having to move.[36] There are multiple ways to adapt to sea level rise, including building dikes to prevent submergence and rebuilding beaches to prevent erosion. Port cities will also have to be upgraded, their infrastructures and buildings lifted.

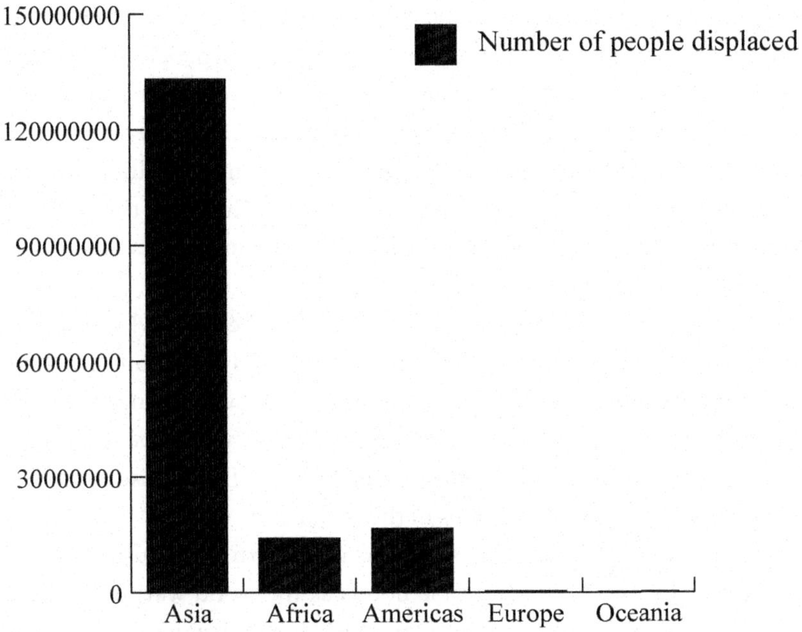

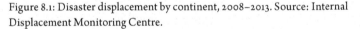

Figure 8.1: Disaster displacement by continent, 2008–2013. Source: Internal Displacement Monitoring Centre.

Adaptation makes economic sense as well; it will reduce the financial damages that will incur from sea level rise and cyclones dramatically. These regions will need every bit of finance they can get to adapt and prevent the worst of climate change, so every dollar invested will come back in multiples.[37] Infrastructure adaptation is a good way for protecting people who would otherwise migrate in climate change scenarios. Before going further into adaptation, it is worth taking a look at the multitude of risks that Asia will face.

EAST ASIA: COASTAL CITIES AND ISLANDS AT RISK

Huge coastal cities are the norm in East Asia. Famous for its towering skyscrapers and packed streets, where when a city runs out of room it accommodates by simply extending its already existing buildings up and up, East Asia is full of teeming urban metropolises. Most of them are extremely vulnerable to sea level rise—Singapore and Hong Kong are excellent examples.[38] The condensation of packed people and packed economic value means that when sea levels rise, people in these areas will face proportionately greater damages. In East Asia there are twenty-three cities on the coast that are home to more than one million people. Fourteen are in China, six in Japan, and three in Korea. In those cities, twelve million people and $864 billion in economic assets are at risk when it comes to sea level rise.[39]

In Japan, residents fled heavy floods in September 2015, when the city of Joso was hit by unprecedented rain that displaced at least one hundred thousand people from their homes. After storm surges burst through riverbanks and flood barriers, a tsunami-like wall of water swept through the town, tearing houses from their foundations.[40] The intense rains also led to more than sixty landslides in the region.[41]

Japan, along with other coastal areas in Eastern and Southern Asia, can generally expect to see worse floods as the world warms.[42] Flood damages are expected to increase greatly. Already Japan spends an average of $240 million to repair coastal damage from typhoon-related flooding and winds.[43] About one and a third million Japanese people will be at risk of coastal flooding.[44]

Warmer air holds more moisture, and in Japan's case a large block of stationary humid air led to the record-breaking precipitation that prompted the evacuation of thousands. In just days, the region saw more rainfall (twenty inches) than double the amount that normally occurs in the entire month of September.[45] There will be fifteen fewer rainy days per year but greater total precipitation, meaning more drought punctuated by heavy storms.[46]

While most Asian countries do not face the same existential threat as many Pacific Islands, sea level rise will slowly—or, by some estimates, not so slowly—chip away at the coastlines, degrading them and destroying them and swallowing up the land. Every inch of sea level rise erodes many times as much land; in some areas in Asia, thirty centimeters of sea level rise will erode forty-five meters of coastal land. In Boreal Asia—northern China, Japan, and the Koreas—the coasts are expected to recede about six meters per year.[47] Sea level rise assaults on the coastlines are palpable, very visible, and very damaging.

SEA LEVEL RISE AND AGRICULTURE

Rice has long been intertwined in the culture of Asia. For millennia it has been grown, consumed, and mythologized. It has inspired art throughout the ages and is discussed in Asia's oldest scriptures. As one Chinese tale has it, several great floods wiped out the land and destroyed its plants, leaving little too eat. After the floods had drained, a dog came through with rice seeds hanging from his tail, which were planted, and food was restored to the land. Thus there is a Chinese adage that says, "The precious things are not pearls and jade but the five grains," where rice comes foremost.

Rice is abundant in Asia because of the region's ideal growing conditions, scattered with river deltas and monsoon-fed paddies. Most rice needs to be grown in paddy fields, parcels of arable land that remain mostly flooded in two-foot-deep water for at least a month. The river deltas and monsoon-fed grass of Asian flatlands help to sustain these ideal growing conditions. Outside the river deltas, farmers have carved grassy steppes, or terraces, into the Himalayan mountainsides, where glacial runoff provides the area's main source of freshwater.

Rice is the lifeblood of Asia's agricultural economy. Millions of farmers and others in the industry rely on it to make a living. It supports the highest level of agricultural population. In addition, Asians have historically relied on rice for the majority of their calories. One could easily argue that it is a food that has fed the most people in the history of agriculture.

Therefore it is troubling that Asia's rice economy, which produces and consumes nearly the vast majority of the world's rice, could be threatened by sea level rise.[48] While rice thrives in wet conditions, and even requires land to be partially submerged for at least a month, it cannot survive if flooded too much for too long.

Nearly 88 percent of the world's rice supply is produced in the low-lying deltas in South and Southeast Asia.[49] These deltas are especially vulnerable to climate change. Vietnam grows nearly half of its rice in the Mekong River delta alone; the *entire delta area* would be impacted by sea level rise. Vietnam's Mekong River delta provides 40 percent of the country's agricultural production and 50 percent of its agricultural exports.[50] Within the Mekong delta lands, 80 percent of the population lives in rural areas and 76 percent are engaged in agriculture.[51] In Indonesia, flooding has reduced agricultural output by 1.3 million tons, a loss of about US$353 million per year.[52]

The International Food Policy Research Institute (IFPRI) predicts that by 2050, rice production levels will decrease by up to 15 percent worldwide and prices will increase by up to 37 percent. The impacts of sea level rise will entail more than simply flooding arable lands. The frequent flooding of river deltas irreversibly changes the region's hydrology, and major flooding events are expected to increase in rice-growing areas.[53]

Rice agriculture is also sensitive to heat and could suffer under warmer global temperatures. High temperatures reduce rice growth productivity; already, higher temperatures have stagnated rice production levels in Southeast Asia. Every degree centigrade increase in global temperature results in a 10 percent drop in rice yield in some areas; in the Philippines this statistic is 15 percent.[54]

China is home to 10 percent of the world's wetlands. But these wetlands are disappearing at an alarming rate, nearing what American Association for the Advancement of Science writer Christina Larson called the "critical red line."[55] The wetlands are not only home to valuable fisheries, but they are also an important source of fresh, clean water. In addition, they work as vital flood control mechanisms, helping to mitigate lands and cities further inland.

Yet over half of China's wetlands have disappeared due to economic development and coastal reclamation. And over the past forty years, 13 percent of China's lakes have disappeared. As a result, half of its cities do not have a good source of clean drinking water.[56] It took decades of wetland destruction before the government decided to do anything about this problem, but today the Chinese government is working to restore valuable wetlands and preserve what few remain. The National Wetland Conservation Action Plan designated fourteen new wetlands sites, with environmental groups aiming to increase this number to fifty. Doing so will benefit ecosystems of China's giant rivers, including the Yellow, the Yangtze, and the Yarlung Tsangpo, which turns into the Brahmaputra in Vietnam.[57]

Given the ravages of climate change, some wetlands in China and Japan are considered un-savable. There is no easy way to protect them from the impending sea level rise as there is with dry lands via sea walls and infrastructure. Wetlands are dependent on a certain amount of moisture and precipitation,[58] yet too much permanent submergence will kill vital plants and habitats. The Asian Development Bank's wetland adaptation analysis estimates tat Japan will lose about 28% of its coastal wetlands by 2050 while the losses in the PRC and the Republic of Korea will be 19%–22% by 2050, independent of adaptation choices.[59]

FRESHWATER SCARCITY

While many agricultural fields will be threatened by rising seas and extreme precipitation, others will be parched for water. As mentioned in previous chapters, China faced terrible droughts that accelerated the world's grain prices and helped catalyze the Arab Spring uprisings and led to civil unrest spreading across the Middle East. But of course droughts have an impact on the country's residents themselves and the surrounding region.

China is the world's largest wheat producer and consumer.[60] Its historical drought in 2010 led the government to purchase wheat on the international market, for fear of crop losses. This in turn is what led to global wheat price spikes in other markets, including Egypt, infamous for its bread riots. In addition to increasing global food prices, the Chinese drought severely affected the local economy. The Chinese government attempted to ameliorate the situation by providing $2 billion in aid to farmers, pledging upward of $15 billion, but aid does not cause the rain to fall.[61] Farmers were forced to move if they were not too old and had the resources to do so.

India has also faced long hardships with widespread climate change–induced drought. India's junior finance minister, Jayant Sinha, called climate change "the number one risk we face," particularly regarding how it will affect monsoons and drought. India's agricultural sector comprises nearly $370 billion and hundreds of millions of jobs and is heavily dependent on the monsoons during the rainy season to replenish the region with water.[62] Three-quarters of the rain in India falls during monsoon summer months. Now monsoon rain patterns have become more erratic and unpredictable. In 2012 the Punjab region saw rain levels nearly 70 percent below average. The government was forced to import many food staples in response to low food production. Yet that solution only serves to drive up food prices to unaffordable rates and hurt the farmers who have no crops to sell.

For many Indian farmers, life has become truly unbearable, so they have turned to what may seem to be the only way out: suicide. Suicide among farmers is common in central India. The suicide rate among Indian farmers is 47 percent higher than the national average.[63] Extreme weather—both drought and downpours of rain and hail—leads to crop failures, which leads to debt, which leads to a cycle of crippling poverty with no end in sight, to many farmers, except death. The number of farmer suicides tends to increase after extreme weather events.[64] Environmental activists, most prominently environmental activist Vandana Shiva, have blamed the suicides on the system of genetically modified (GMO) crops. Monsanto requires farmers to purchase new seeds each year and has raised the price 8,000 percent since their GMO crops were introduced. Shiva has been working to provide non-GMO seeds to farmers so they can stay out of debt traps and be less dependent on Monsanto.[65]

Farmers take out loans against their land to borrow enough from local money lenders to pay for Monsanto's seeds, but if they aren't able to cultivate the crops they need to, they wind up in a debt trap. They rely on praying for a good season to grow the crops they need in order to pay off their loans. But with extreme weather and flash floods happening more often, the likelihood of such a season is becoming all the more rare.

As with floods, droughts are starting to damage Asia's rice economy. Water scarcity harms more than twenty-three million hectares of rice in South and Southeast Asia. Droughts are expected to recur more often and extend further into irrigated lands.[66]

Many rice farmers are more concerned about droughts than floods. Scientific researchers and food organizations have been developing varieties of rice that can survive in drier conditions. While normally dependent on flooded fields, new forms of rice can survive even in dry months. The Asian Development Bank, which is carrying out much of this research in conjunction with International Rice Research Institute, notes that rice is the staple food for a huge portion of the people living in Asia and plays a "key role" in ensuring food security there.[67] As an example, it points to farmers in Bangladesh, where drought is one of the biggest threats farmers face.[68] Will this keep possible climate refugees at home?

MEGACITIES

With climate change expected to drive people into Asia's urban centers, it's worth looking at the risks they will face once they arrive. As in Bangladesh, this can lead to troubling patterns—migrants forced into slums, working in sweatshops under dangerous conditions. But Bangladesh is not alone. Most of the world's largest megacities—cities with a population of multiple millions, some say ten million or more—reside in Asia.

The global population is rapidly urbanizing and cities are struggling to keep up. Yet climate change's impacts on cities are no laughing matter. Cities are more vulnerable to food insecurity and poverty traps. Many Asian megacities are in high-risk locations: on the coasts. It makes sense why they would form there, because coastal cities have long been meccas of economic activity and sea-wide trading, the economic hubs of cross-country trading. But they will face hardships as the seas continue to rise.[69]

The Organization for Economic Co-operation and Development (OECD) predicted the cities that would be most at risk of flooding in terms of exposed population by 2070. Of the top ten, just one city is *not* in Asia: Miami (which is ranked ninth). The others, in order: India's Kolkata and Mumbai take the top two ranks, Bangladesh's Dhaka, then China's Guangzhou, Vietnam's Ho Chi Minh City, China's Shanghai and Bangkok, Myanmar's Yangon, and Vietnam's Haiphong.[70] In a different study conducted in conjunction with the World Bank, the OECD also ranked cities most vulnerable measured as a percentage of GDP, and once again Asian cities take top rank: (1) Guangzhou; (2) New Orleans; (3) Guayaquil, Ecuador; (4) Ho Chi Minh City; (5) Abidjan; (6) Zhan-

Table 8.2. Global Cities with the Greatest Populations Exposed to Sea Level Rise

City	Pop. exposed in 2070 (millions)
Kolkata	14
Mumbai	11.4
Dhaka	11.1
Guangzhou	10.3
Ho Chi Minh City	9.2
Shanghai	5.5
Bangkok	5.1
Rangoon Myanmar	5
Miami	4.8
Hai Phong	4.7

jing; (7) Mumbai; (8) Khulna, Bangladesh; (9) Palembang, Indonesia; and (10)[71] Shenzen.

Many lists of cities most vulnerable are ranked in terms of predicted economic damage. But in terms of people, Asian coastal cities are far and away most at risk. When considering population movements and migrations, sea level rise is the more important factor to discuss here.

Twelve million people dwell in Mumbai, India, which sits on a set of islands and has a drainage system that is more than 150 years old.[73] Floods during the monsoon summer months are already near the level of the subway.[74] The city is surrounded by a set of gates that close during high tides to prevent flooding, but during periods of intense rains, floods have nowhere to go. The East-West Center, a nonprofit established by Congress in 1960, described the situation there as "near panic" in such cases. One meter of sea level rise will cost Mumbai an estimated $71 billion.[75]

Ho Chi Minh City is home to eight million people, and that figure is projected to grow to upward of twenty-two million by 2050. Accounting for 40 percent of Vietnam's GDP, the city is already vulnerable to floods; in 1997 half of its population was affected by floods. In 2050, thirty-year-flood events are expected to impact millions, even "create 2 million 'climate refugees,'" according to the East-West Center.[76]

Hundreds of thousands of people were forced to evacuate from Manila, in the Philippines, in 2009 after rains brought by Typhoon Ketsena inundated 80 percent of the city.[77] The East-West Center notes that many officials in Asian coastal cities are simply not aware of the risks of flooding or how much these risks are going to compound over coming years as population growth and urbanization increase and sea levels rise. This must be overcome before we can expect cities to implement life-saving flood-protection measures that will become increasingly important.

These cities will require significant investment in basic amenities and living infrastructure. More than half the population of many of these cities are crowded in slums that lack basic protections from floods. Without investing in basic amenities and infrastructure, climate change will worsen vulnerabilities.[78]

Adaptation is becoming common among discussion at global governance levels. The World Bank, for instance, has released their recommendations for city-specific solutions to climate change risks, noting that "cities need to make a proactive effort to consider climate-related risks as an integral part of urban planning and to do so now."[79] City-specific solutions including "infrastructure investments, zoning, and ecosystem-based strategies" are all necessary. Each city has distinct climatic, hydrological, and socioeconomic features, but in each city the poor are most at risk and thus will require the most investment.[80]

In addition to adaptation within cities, coastal protections, which include construction of sea dikes and port upgrades, along with beach nourishment and dike maintenance, are needed. The Asian Development Bank (ADB) has explained how it will be economically beneficial to "climate-proof" the infrastructure in cities.[81] Either way it will be costly—up to $44 billion per year through 2050 in China, for instance. Yet much of the infrastructure in China and Mongolia, the ADB found, is not worth saving—from an economic standpoint, at least. In Japan and Korea it is economically justified to "climate-proof" *most* types of infrastructure. But in China it is only justified for water systems, sewers, and roads, not for housing or buildings or educational services. In countries other than Japan and Korea, the ADB notes, countries may have to adapt a "partial" adaptation strategy rather than "full adaptation"—in other words, parts of their country will simply be left to be swallowed by the sea.[82] In China, on the other hand, the benefits of adaptation will outweigh the costs by a longshot: costs will be less than 10 percent of expected losses.[83]

DEADLY TYPHOONS AND A PLEA FOR AID

Typhoons are one of the deadliest weather events in the world, with both winds strong enough to lift trees and floods that overtake homes. Alarmingly, both of those aspects of typhoons are expected to get worse with global warming. While scientists don't necessarily predict *more* typhoons to form as a result of climate change, it is common knowledge that those that do form will be far worse. Warmer ocean waters drive stronger storms with faster winds. Sea level rise makes every storm surge worse, flooding areas that previously had not been flooded.

It's not always a matter of temporary evacuation when a typhoon is slated to come; typhoons can have lasting impact on land degradation, as well. Many people may be evacuated before a storm and not have a home to which they can return afterward. This pertains particularly to river deltas, and in Asia there are many.[84]

Typhoons will have an increasingly great impact on the river deltas of Asia. Indeed, the IPCC points to countries in South, Southeast, and East Asia as being particularly vulnerable to sea level rise in general, adding that these countries are therefore more vulnerable to typhoons. In Asia more people and economic assets are at risk of sea level rise than any other continent. By 2050, 350 million people will be exposed to one-in-one-hundred-year coastal floods.[85] In Asia this has largely to do with urbanization and socioeconomic trends: the population keeps growing, and everyone keeps moving to cities on the sea coasts. With such rapid urbanization, cities and governments often don't have time or capacity to accommodate everyone, thus the emergence and expansion of slums. These slums are even more vulnerable to the impacts of extreme weather and sea level rise.

Here is how many people in Asia typhoons displaced in 2014 alone: in China, 1.17 million people; in Japan, 570,000 people; and in the Philippines, 4.81 million people. This was the result of two typhoons: Typhoon Rammasun and Typhoon Hagupit.[86] These two typhoons prompted evacuations in the Philippines that ultimately ended up the greatest displacement event in world history. This is partially because the Philippines is more vulnerable to typhoons, less capable of dealing with their impacts, than other countries—even though its population is not growing as quickly as those of wealthier countries that are more resilient to typhoons.

Therein lies the problem: lower-income countries are more vulnerable, and exposure to typhoons will only increase, particularly in Asia.[87] These countries do not have the effective early warning systems and disaster response policies in place that many high-income countries do. And indeed, the Philippines is continually battered by impacts of climate change, despite being among the countries that contribute the least to it. One year before, in 2013, Typhoon Haiyan rampaged through the country with deadly and devastating effects. It was one of the strongest storms to hit land ever recorded, with wind speeds nearing 200 miles per hour and gusts up to 235 mph. It is estimated that 6,300 people were killed and 4.1 million people were displaced.[88] It was the largest displacement event of the year, displacing one million more people than those forced to flee their homes in Africa, the Americas, Europe, and Oceania combined.[89]

After the storm, the Philippines' lead negotiator Naderev "Yeb" Sano made a tearful appeal at the UN climate summit for international aid to adapt and protect his country from the impacts of climate change.[90] He announced he was fasting "in solidarity with my countrymen who are now struggling for food back home" until there were "concrete pledges" to the Green Climate Fund, which helps developing countries cope with climate change and reduce their own emissions.[91]

The Philippines is the thirteenth most vulnerable country to the effects of climate change, despite contributing far less greenhouse gas emissions than the United States or Australia.[92] And the country barely pulled itself together before being battered by typhoons the following year.

The United Nations noted that of the 4.1 million people originally displaced by Typhoon Haiyan, most either made it home or were resettled, but in truth 20,000 people were still displaced one year later.[93] Still, over the year, the impact of the money raised to aid the millions of survivors was invaluable. The United Nations brought relief, including blankets, tents, hygiene kits, solar lanterns, and kitchen sets, to more than 700,000 of the most vulnerable survivors.

Of those still displaced, the UN noted that land and property issues stood in the way of finding a permanent home. Some people were told they would have to stay in temporary shelters for at least two years as the government searched for permanent relocation.[94] Indeed, the Internal Displacement Monitoring Centre noted that lack of access to land is one of the most frequently cited obstacles to solutions. Without access to land—being either unable to return to their own homes or unable to be resettled—those displaced after a disaster may become "informal settlers" who move into urban slum areas. As International Organization for Migration Philippines program director Conrad Navidad said, those settlers "would likely tell you 'we are victims of typhoons or natural disasters, and we couldn't wait for solutions from the government.'"[95]

The UN also highlighted "the urgent need for the Philippines to adopt legislation to protect the rights of internally displaced people—in what is one of the world's most natural disaster-prone countries."[96] It will be necessary to do so before many citizens can return home or relocate somewhere new.

The fact that such legislation is not yet in place is just one cause for concern. The Brookings Institution highlighted other issues with the relocation process after Typhoon Haiyan in a case study. It found that one and a half years after the typhoon, less than 18 percent of the population felt life had returned to "normal." Only 32 percent of households were able to meet their basic needs (that figure was 83 percent before the typhoon).[97]

Improving the response system to typhoons such as Haiyan will take work at all levels, from foreign institutions and NGOs to local councils. Institutions need to coordinate better with on-the-ground efforts, and localities need to improve their capacity to respond to such events. The Brookings report made the following recommendations to the Philippine government and international supporters:

> 1. Recognize durable solutions to displacement as a multisectoral concern, including both humanitarian and development inputs, and extending beyond the housing sector.
>
> 2. Redouble investment in the strengthening of evacuation centers, safer construction techniques and other disaster risk reduction programs.
>
> 3. Establish an interactive, rights-based monitoring system for relocation plans, policies and projects, linking local and national levels.

4. Develop and implement enhanced, culturally sensitive livelihood strategies for the affected areas, based on IDPs' [internally displaced persons] active participation.[98]

Such plans as detailed by the Brookings Institution and the United Nations require a significant amount of aid. It took a massive amount of aid and efforts to serve the needs of those displaced by Typhoon Haiyan. The United Nations released $25 million in emergency funds immediately and appealed for $300 million more.[99] Yet international money flooding in after the fact is not always helpful, as explained by Brookings; preparation is key. A country can only do so much with the limited finances and government response mechanisms they have. Thus, the reason for Yeb Sano's tearful appeal.

An excerpt from his speech follows:

> The picture in the aftermath is ever so slowly coming into clearer focus. The devastation is colossal. And as if this is not enough, another storm is brewing again in the warm waters of the western Pacific. I shudder at the thought of another typhoon hitting the same places where people have not yet even managed to begin standing up.
>
> What my country is going through as a result of this extreme climate event is madness. The climate crisis is madness.
>
> We can stop this madness.[100]

It can take years to recover from a cyclone. In Bangladesh the Internal Displacement Monitoring Centre found that many people were still displaced by the impacts of Cyclone Aila six years after the event.[101] It hit the country in 2009, inundating villages and displacing 842,000 people. Around 200,000 people were still displaced after six months, as the recovery systems and agencies did not have the capacity to handle so many displaced. Those who were displaced lived in makeshift shelters near the coasts, "surrounded by unruly water at high tide and at low tide by thousands of hectares of muddy land."[102] In the following years, additional environmental disasters displaced more than 4.7 million more Bangladeshis.

Many of those who were hit by Cyclone Aila in 2009 were still left without a permanent solution years later. Those who tried to go back to their homes found the land degraded beyond repair. Their lifestyles are constantly disrupted by repeated coastal flooding and storms. Yet without aid the process of relocating is simply unaffordable for most who live in Bangladesh and other poor Asian communities. The move is estimated to cost around $1,000 per household, according to the IOM, while the average annual income in Bangladesh is just $1,190.[103]

Typhoons are but one climate threat that Asian countries face, but arguably the most devastating. They bring immediate destruction that puts the plight of Asian people into the national media spotlight. And as Yeb Sano has tearfully exemplified, they may be used to make the prescient case that Asian countries need help preparing for and adapting to climate change if they want to avoid the death and displacement of events past.

ASIAN COUNTRIES WANT ACTION

It is clear to those living in Asia that climate change is a very real threat that will harm them personally, if it has not already. A Pew Research Center poll found that climate change is considered the top threat in many Asian countries, including India, China, Indonesia, the Philippines, and others.[104] According to a YouGov survey released in June 2015, people from China favor action on climate change more than every other country in the world. Only 2 percent of Malaysians, 3 percent of Indonesians, and 4 percent of Chinese consider climate change "not a very serious problem" or "not a serious problem at all." Even in Thailand, the *most* skeptical country, only 6 percent consider climate change not a serious problem.[105]

These countries wanted their country to "play a leadership role" at the United Nations climate conference in December 2015, according to the survey, urging them to set "ambitious targets to address climate change as quickly as possible."[106]

CLIMATE AID, READINESS ASSISTANCE

It appears that Bangladesh's climate change plight, at the least, has not gone unnoticed. Bangladesh is one of the targets for a White House climate readiness initiative announced in 2015, along with Colombia and Ethiopia. The public-private partnership will provide $34 million to these countries to help them prepare for climate change from the US government, the American Red Cross, Asian Development Bank, Esri, Google, Inter-American Development Bank, the Skoll Global Threats Fund, and the UK government.[107]

The program will include "scalable, replicable, comprehensive, and integrative climate services" in Bangladesh, which was chosen to represent the entire subregion of South Asia and Southeast Asia[108]. With its combination of sea level rise, floods, and droughts, Bangladesh indeed seems a good representative candidate for the rest of Asia. The Bangladesh program will focus on "collaboration between the partners and local stakeholders to ensure long-term ownership and sustainability of the partnership's impact in focus countries."[109] This sounds well and good, in contrast to how the Brookings Institution saw last-minute foreign aid play out in the aftermath of Typhoon Haiyan.

Time will tell how this plan—and other proposals to help Asian countries respond to climate change—actually plays out. We are at a crossroads. Will we live in a world where a huge majority of the Asian population will have to migrate, or will we act?

NOTES

"'It's Time to Stop This Madness'—Philippines Plea at UN Climate Talks," *Climate Home*, http://www.climatechangenews.com/2013/11/11/its-time-to-stop-this-madness-philippines-plea-at-un-climate-talks/

1. "Surging Seas: Sea Level Rise Analysis by Climate Central," Climate Central, http://sealevel.climatecentral.org
2. IPCC Working Group II, "Coastal Systems and Low-Lying Areas," *Climate Change 2014 Impacts, Adaptation, and Vulnerability*, United Nations, March 2014.
3. Notre Dame Global Adaptation Index, http://index.gain.org
4. Caroline Davies, "Migrants on Boat Rescued off Indonesia Recall Horrific Scenes," *Guardian*, May 15, 2015, https://www.theguardian.com/world/2015/may/15/asian-migrant-crisis-grows-as-700-more-boat-people-rescued-off-indonesia.
5. "Rohingya Refugees Face More Restrictions," IRIN News, October 12, 2012.
6. "Bangladesh Plans to Move Rohingya Refugees to Island in the South," Agence France-Presse, May 27, 2015.
7. Thomas Fuller and Joe Cochrane, "Rohingya Migrants from Myanmar, Shunned by Malaysia, Are Spotted Adrift in Andaman Sea," *New York Times*, May 14, 2015, https://www.nytimes.com/2015/05/15/world/asia/burmese-rohingya-bangladeshi-migrants-andaman-sea.html.
8. Davies, "Migrants on Boat Rescued."
9. "Thousands of Refugees Stranded on 'floating coffins' in Southeast Asia," Associated Press, May 15, 2015.

10. Jonathan Kaiman and Shashank Bengali, "Indonesia, Malaysia to Take in Migrants Stranded at Sea, Reversing Stance," *Los Angeles Times*, May 20, 2015, http://www.latimes.com/world/asia/la-fg-ff-indonesia-malaysia-migrants-20150520-story.html.

11. Raveena Aulakh, "Climate Change Forcing Thousands in Bangladesh into Slums of Dhaka," *Toronto Star*, February 16, 2013.

12. Joe Myers, "These Are the World's 10 Fastest Growing Megacities," *World Economic Forum*, November 1, 2016, https://www.weforum.org/agenda/2016/11/the-10-fastest-growing-megacities-in-the-world/.

13. "Climate Migration Drives Slum Growth in Dhaka," Cities Alliance, http://www.citiesalliance.org/node/420.

14. Ibid.

15. Tansy Hoskins, "Reliving the Rana Plaza Factory Collapse: A History of Cities in 50 Buildings, Day 22," *Guardian*, April 23, 2015, https://www.theguardian.com/cities/2015/apr/23/rana-plaza-factory-collapse-history-cities-50-buildings.

16. "Bangladesh Murder Trial over Rana Plaza Factory Collapse," BBC News, June 1, 2015.

17. Marc Bain, "Years after the Rana Plaza Tragedy, Too Many of Bangladesh's Factories Are Still 'Death Traps,'" Quartz, October 25, 2015, https://qz.com/530308/more-than-two-years-after-the-rana-plaza-tragedy-too-many-of-bangladeshs-factories-are-still-death-traps/.

18. George Black, "Your Clothes Were Made by a Bangladeshi Climate Refugee," *Mother Jones*, July 30, 2013.

19. Sarah Davies and Alex Reilly, "FactCheck: Have More Than 1000 Asylum Seekers Died at Sea under Labor?," Conversation, July 22, 2013.

20. Amie Hamling, "Rohingya People: The Most Persecuted Refugees in the World," Amnesty International, October 7, 2015.

21. "Turning Back Boats 'Has to Be on Table' as Labor Policy, Says Bill Shorten," Australian Broadcast Corporation, July 22, 2015.

22. Alex Lee, "The Harsh Treatment of Asylum Seekers Is One Thing Labor and the Liberals Can Agree On," Buzzfeed, July 23, 2015.

23. "Basic Facts about Myanmar," Myanmar Embassy, http://www.myanmar-embassy-tokyo.net/about.htm.

24. *Climate Change 2007: Impacts, Adaptation, and Vulnerability*, United Nations Intergovernmental Panel on Climate Change, 2007, chapter 6, box 6.3, p. 327, https://www.ipcc.ch/pdf/assessment-report/ar4/wg2/ar4_wg2_full_report.pdf.

25. Union of Concerned Scientists, "Ganges-Brahmaputra Delta, Bangladesh," http://www.climatehotmap.org/global-warming-locations/ganges-brahmaputra-delta-bangladesh.html.

26. Justin Ginetti and Chris Lavell, "The Risk of Disaster-Induced Displacement in South Asia," Internal Displacement Monitoring Center, April 2015, 32, http://www.internal-displacement.org/assets/publications/images/2015/201504-ap-south-asia-disaster-induced-displacement-risk-en.pdf.

27. Kourtnii S. Brown, "Top 3 Ways Sea Level Rise Threatens Asia-Pacific Region," The Asia Foundation, June 4, 2014; *Climate Change 2007: Impacts, Adaptation, and Vulnerability*, http://asiafoundation.org/2014/06/04/top-3-ways-sea-level-rise-threatens-asia-pacific-region/.

28. George Black, "Your Clothes Were Made by a Bangladeshi Climate Refugee," *Mother Jones*, July 30, 2013, http://www.motherjones.com/environment/2013/07/bangladesh-garment-workers-climate-change.

29. Joydeep Gupta, "Villages Swallowed as River Erosion Accelerates in Bangladesh," The Third Pole, May 28, 2013.

30. Intergovernmental Panel on Climate Change, *IPCC Fourth Assessment Report: Climate Change 2007*, 6.4.1.2, box 6.3, https://www.ipcc.ch/publications_and_data/ar4/wg2/en/ch6s6-4-1-2.html#box-6-3.

31. Brown, "Top 3 Ways."

32. Ben Block, "Deltas Sink Worldwide, Increasing Flood Risk," Eye on Earth (Worldwatch Institute's online news service), http://www.worldwatch.org/node/6267.

33. E.g., Brown, "Top 3 Ways."

34. Internal Displacement Monitoring Centre and Norwegian Refugee Council, "Global Estimates 2014: People Displaced by Disasters," September 2014, p. 25, section 3.1, http://www.internal-displacement.org/assets/publications/2014/201409-global-estimates2.pdf.

35. Norwegian Refugee Council, "22 Million People Displaced by Disasters in 2013," September 17, 2014, http://news.trust.org//item/20140917071049-k6xeo/.

36. Michael Westphal, Gordon Hughes, and Jörn Brömmelhörster, eds., *Economics of Climate Change in East Asia* (Mandaluyong City, Philippines: Asian Development Bank, 2013), p. 30, box "Key Findings," https://www.adb.org/sites/default/files/publication/30434/economics-climate-change-east-asia.pdf.

37. Ibid.

38. Kevin Brown, "Hong Kong and Singapore Warned over Global Warming," *Financial Times*, November 12, 2009, http://www.ft.com/cms/s/0/52b4f25e-cf2a-11de-8a4b-00144feabdc0.html?ft_site=falcon&desktop=true#axzz4XAWAX18M.

39. Westphal et al., *Economics of Climate Change*, p. 61.

40. Johnlee Varghese, "Japan Floods: Thousands Flee Homes as Tsunami-like Waves Hit City Near Tokyo [video]," *International Business Times*, September 10, 2015; "More Than 100,000 Flee Floods after Heavy Rains in Japan," Reuters, September 10, 2015.

41. "Tropical Storm Leads to Floods in Japan," Earth Observatory, http://earthobservatory.nasa.gov/NaturalHazards/view.php?id=86584&src=eorss-nh.

42. Brown, "Top 3 Ways."

43. "Climate Hot Map Global Warming Effects around the World," Union of Concerned Scientists, http://www.climatehotmap.org/global-warming-locations/osaka-japan.html.

44. Alva Lim and Brendan F. D. Barrett, "Japan to Suffer Huge Climate Costs," Our World, June 30, 2009.

45. "Tropical Storm Leads to Floods."

46. Ram Manohar, Shrestha Mahfuz, Ahmed Suphachol, and Suphachalasai Rodel Lasco, *Economics of Reducing Greenhouse Gas Emissions in South Asia Options and Costs*, (Mandaluyong City, Philippines: Asian Development Bank, 2013).

47. *Climate Change 2007: Impacts, Adaptation, and Vulnerability.*

48. M. K. Papademetriou, "Rice Production in the Asia-Pacific Region: Issues and Perspectives," Food and Agriculture Organization Corporate Document Repository, http://www.fao.org/docrep/003/x6905e/x6905e04.htm.

49. Brown, "Top 3 Ways."

50. Toru Konishi, *Climate Change on the Vietnam, Mekong Delta: Expected Inpacts and Adaptations,* World Bank East Asia Infrastructure, http://www.fao.org/fileadmin/templates/rome2007initiative/FAO_WB_TCIO_CC_Meeting_May_2011/TORUKO_1.PDF.

51. Ibid.

52. Suzanne K. Redfern, Nadine Azzu, and Jessie S. Binamira, "Rice in Southeast Asia: Facing Risks and Vulnerabilities to Respond to Climate Change," Plant Production and Protection Division, FAO, Rome, April 24, 2012.

53. "Rice and Climate Change," International Rice Research Institute, http://irri.org/news/hot-topics/rice-and-climate-change.

54. Redfern, Azzu, and Binamira, "Rice in Southeast Asia."

55. Christina Larson, "China's Vanishing Coastal Wetlands Are Nearing Critical Red Line," American Association for the Advancement of Science, October 23, 2015.

56. "Wetland Conservation and Restoration," World Wildlife Fund China, http://en.wwfchina.org/en/what_we_do/freshwater/wetland_conservation.

57. Ibid.

58. Westphal et al. *Economics of Climate Change.*

59. Ibid., p. 60, box "Key Messages."

60. Casey Chumrau, "Crop Shifts in China Could Influence World Wheat Market, *Southwest Farm Press,* October 5, 2012, http://www.southwestfarmpress.com/grains/crop-shifts-china-could-influence-world-wheat-market.

61. Boris Cambreleng, "Drought Rattles Farmers in Eastern China," Phys.org, February 25, 2011; "China Drought Threatens Wheat Crops," BBC News, February 17, 2011.

62. Maria Gallucci, "India Drought 2015: Climate Change Is Biggest Threat to India's Economy, Modi Finance Aide Says," *International Business Times,* November 2, 2015.

63. Baba Umar, "India's Shocking Farmer Suicide Epidemic," Al Jazeera, May 18, 2015, http://www.aljazeera.com/indepth/features/2015/05/india-shocking-farmer-suicide-epidemic-150513121717412.html.

64. Zigor Aldama and Miguel Candela, "India's Deadliest Epidemic," *Diplomat,* October 20, 2015.

65. Vandana Shiva, "Seeds of Suicide and Slavery versus Seeds of Life and Freedom," Al Jazeera, March 30, 2013.

66. "Rice and Climate Change," "Water Scarcity."

67. Asian Development Bank, "Rice in Asia: Climate Change and Resilient Crops," September 25, 2013, https://www.adb.org/fr/node/40902.

68. Ibid.

69. Robin McKie, "Global Warming to Hit Asia Hardest, Warns New Report on Climate Change," *Guardian,* March 22, 2014.

70. R. J. Nicholls et al., "Ranking of the World's Cities Most Exposed to Coastal Flooding Today and in the Future," Organization for Economic Cooperation and Development, December 4, 2007, https://www.oecd.org/env/cc/39721444.pdf (executive summary).

71. Tran Viet Duc, "Which Coastal Cities Are at Highest Risk of Damaging Floods? New Study Crunches the Numbers," http://www.worldbank.org/en/news/feature/2013/08/19/coastal-cities-at-highest-risk-floods

72. Roland J. Fuchs, "Cities at Risk: Asia's Coastal Cities in an Age of Climate Change," Asia Pacific Issues, no. 96, July 2010, http://www.eastwestcenter.org/system/tdf/private/api096.pdf?file=1&type=node&id=32434.

73. Fuchs, "Cities at Risk," p. 4.

74. Ibid.

75. Ibid.

76. Ibid: 4.

77. Ibid.

78. "Addressing Climate Change and Migration in Asia and the Pacific," Asian Development Bank, 2012, p. 14, para. 59, https://www.adb.org/sites/default/files/publication/29662/addressing-climate-change-migration.pdf.

79. "Climate Risks and Adaptation in Asian Coastal Megacities," World Bank: xvi, http://siteresources.worldbank.org/EASTASIAPACIFICEXT/Resources/226300-1287600424406/coastal_megacities_fullreport.pdf.

80. Ibid.

81. Westphal, Hughes, and Brömmelhörster, *Economics of Climate Change.*

82. Ibid.

83. Ibid.

84. P. P. Wong et al., "Coastal systems and low-lying areas," in *Climate Change 2014: Impacts,Adaptation, and Vulnerability. Part A: Global and Sectoral Aspects,* March 2014, https://www.ipcc.ch/pdf/assessment-report/ar5/wg2/WGIIAR5-Chap5_FINAL.pdf.

85. Ibid.

86. "Global Estimates 2015: People Displaced by Disasters."

87. Ibid.

88. UNHCR, "1-Year on from Typhoon Haiyan, Thousands of People Still Rebuilding Lives," November 7, 2014, http://www.unhcr.org/uk/news/briefing/2014/11/545c9cda6/1-year-typhoon-haiyan-thousands-people-still-rebuilding-lives.html.

89. Internal Displacement Monitoring Centre and Norwegian Refugee Council, "Global Estimates 2014," p. 8.

90. "'It's Time to Stop This Madness'—Philippines Plea at UN Climate Talks," *Climate Home,* http://www.climatechangenews.com/2013/11/11/its-time-to-stop-this-madness-philippines-plea-at-un-climate-talks/.

91. Green Climate Fund, "What Is GCF?" https://www.greenclimate.fund/home.

92. Pia Ranada, "Philippines Drops in 2016 List of Countries Vulnerable to Climate Change, *The Rappler,* November 17, 2015, http://www.rappler.com/science-nature/environment/113064-philippines-2016-climate-change-vulnerability-index.

93. "1-Year on from Typhoon Haiyan."

94. Ibid.

95. "Global Estimates 2015: People Displaced by Disasters."

96. "1-Year on from Typhoon Haiyan."

97. Angela Sherwood et al., "Resolving Post-Disaster Displacement: Insights from the Philippines after Typhoon Haiyan (Yolanda)," Brookings Institution, June 15, 2015, https://www.brookings.edu/wp-content/uploads/2016/06/Resolving-PostDisaster-DisplacementInsights-from-the-Philippines-after-Typhoon-Haiyan-June-2015.pdf.

98. Ibid.

99. "Typhoon Haiyan: Aid in Numbers," BBC News, November 14, 2013.

100. "'It's Time to Stop This Madness.'"
101. "Global Estimates 2015: People Displaced by Disasters."
102. Ibid.
103. Ibid.
104. Jill Carle, "Climate Change Seen as Top Global Threat," Pew Research Center, July 14, 2015.
105. "Global Survey: Chinese Most in Favor of Action on Climate Change," YouGov Survey, June 4, 2015.
106. Andrew Griffin, "UK and US Main Barriers to Addressing Climate Change, Survey Finds," *Independent*, June 7, 2015, http://www.independent.co.uk/life-style/gadgets-and-tech/news/uk-and-us-main-barriers-to-addressing-climate-change-survey-finds-10303279.html.
107. "Fact Sheet: Launching a Public-Private Partnership to Empower Climate-Resilient Developing Nations," White House Office of the Press Secretary, June 9, 2015, http://reliefweb.int/report/world/fact-sheet-launching-public-private-partnership-empower-climate-resilient-developing.
108. Ibid.
109. Ibid.

PART THREE
Policy Implications and Conclusions

9

Current Affairs and Climate Refugees

> Current refugee laws are unwelcoming to environmental refugees, but the severity of their plight deserves attention, especially in light of its predicted increase in the coming decades.
>
> *Amanda Doran,* Villanova Environmental Law Journal

As actors on the world stage, refugees are hardly the helpless victims described by NGOs. Rather, they are diasporic communities that evolve and change the cultures they find themselves in, sharpen nationalistic perceptions, and make significant cultural contributions to art, poetry, and theater. Despite the cant of "right of return" or repatriation by international agencies, transfers of environmental refugees involving either repatriation or resettlement in a new country defy political reality and bump hard against economic fear and sectarian prejudice.

When people flee to escape conflicts or natural disasters, they suffer some of the most traumatic of human experiences. But flight in many cases outweighs the suffering and abuse of returning. Small wonder that thousands of IDPs cross borders, sea barriers, and dangerous landscapes in search of a better life. Those who remain behind "exist" in squalid, overcrowded camps. In Iraq, for example, some 1.9 million people have been displaced, uprooted by wars, the creation of dams and mines, and drought. An additional two million have fled Iraq to neighboring countries. As representatives for the International Migration Organization point out, "There is a fundamental interdependency between migration and the environment."[1] Yet without water or food as a result of drought or flooding, what other options are available?

CLIMATE REFUGEES IN THE UNITED STATES

In August 2005 Hurricane Katrina struck New Orleans and the Gulf Coast with a twenty-eight-foot storm surge that left only a few structures along the coast standing. New Orleans survived the initial hit but was heavily flooded. As levees were breached, the swirling waters flooded neighborhoods, leaving people stranded on rooftops. All told, during the course of the storm, over one million people were evacuated from New Orleans and small towns in rural and resort coastal areas.

After the storm subsided, it was widely assumed in the media and among government agencies that people who left New Orleans and other towns along the coast would return to reclaim their homes and rebuild their flood-stricken lives. Several hundred thousand did not. They had neither job nor home to return to. Thus hundreds of thousands of Americans had transitioned from the role of evacuees to that of climate refugees.

This was not the first time that Americans had been overwhelmed by their environment and had to seek refuge elsewhere. The Dust Bowl of the 1930s in the American Midwest disrupted the lives of over two million people and propelled more than 250,000 Americans in search of a better life in California and in the Pacific Northwest.

Katrina's refugees settled mostly in Texas, a new and unfamiliar environment. Given that these climate refugees were poor, African American, or aged, they were not exactly welcomed enthusiastically in Texas. The state was already in the grip of a nativist-localist mentality because of large numbers of legal and illegal immigrants from Mexico and Latin America generally in their midst. Houston absorbed most of the refugees and at times suffered from compassion fatigue. But a 2007 survey of 765 Houston-area residents by Rice University sociologist Stephen Klineberg found that three-fourths believed that helping the refugees put a "considerable strain" on the community, and two-thirds blamed evacuees for a surge in violent crime. Half thought Houston would be worse off if evacuees stayed, while one-fourth thought the city would be better off.[2]

Houston police reported an increase of 32 percent over the previous year in the murder rate in the first year after the Katrina refugees' arrival. According to Houston Police Chief Harold Hurtt, refugees were involved—as victims or suspects—in 35 of the 212 murders in that time period. In January 2006, Houston police arrested eight members of rival New Orleans gangs in the murders of eleven fellow refugees. In March, half of the eighteen people arrested in an auto theft sweep were evacuees.[3] Hurtt said some of the crime wave was attributable to Katrina refugees, but added, "I don't mean to send the message that all Katrina evacuees are involved in drug dealing, gangs and violent offenses."[4] Klineberg observed, that the arrival of 150,000 refugees, 90 percent of whom were black, did contribute to "a palpable rise in racial tensions."[5]

Significantly, fifteen thousand of the refugees in Houston were of Vietnamese descent and were easily absorbed by the large Houston Vietnamese community of sixty thousand families. According to sociologist Klineberg, the city of Houston ultimately adjusted to the refugee influx but only with a high degree of social tension and compassion fatigue. Also, he found that many Houstonians, white and black, had helped Katrina victims at the height of the crisis. After a passage of ten years, Klineberg noted a moderation of feelings toward the refugees who still remained in Houston.[6]

It is a mistake to assume that climate change will not be a problem for affluent countries like the United States. Houston itself is a "sitting duck" for the next great hurricane on the level of Hurricane Katrina, notes a joint investigation from the *Texas Tribune* and ProPublica.[7] With global warming the United States will face ferocious storm patterns, extensive droughts, and tidal incursions that will engulf large areas of coastal land. Loss of vital wetland regions may bring about the collapse of ocean fisheries. In turn, populations from coastal areas will be on the move, and the United States will face a new phenomenon: the internally displaced climate refugee. The United States may have to struggle to resettle millions of its own citizens who have been displaced by high water in the Gulf of Mexico, South Florida, and much of the Atlantic coast reaching toward New England.

TEMPORARY PROTECTION IS NO SOLUTION

Haiti experienced a devastating 7.0 magnitude earthquake in January 2010. Leaving a death toll of some 250,000 and a billion dollars in damage, the earthquake was the strongest Haiti had experienced in two centuries. The US Department of Homeland Security granted "temporary protective status," or TPS, to 100,000 Haitians who were residing illegally in the States.[8] It did not admit Haitians as "refugees" or provide protection for those crossing the border illegally. ("Environmentally-forced migrants," notes Villanova legal scholar Amanda Doran, "do not fit the traditional refugee definition, and consequently, many countries refuse to grant them asylum.") But TPS is no solution, and like other situations and events, these "special cases" are a way of getting around the American animus toward accepting refugees. Haiti had previously requested—and been denied—several requests for TPS after tropical storms and hurricanes killed hundreds, decimated Haiti's food crops, and caused a billion dollars in damage. Nevertheless, the Haitian earthquake did place the dilemma of the climate refugee in the world's forefront, concludes Doran, "making it impossible to ignore and begging the international community for a solution."[9]

THE UNCHARTED TERRITORY OF CLIMATE MIGRATION

In the summer of 2015 Europe was flooded with migrants and refugees, most of whom were fleeing Syria's bloody civil war. While either terrified or suspicious populations greeted many of these refugees, afraid that their economies could not support a massive poor influx of migrants, Germany was a notable exception. In its actions it has shown one alternative that may be used in dealing with climate refugees. Germany decided to take in nearly one million migrants. Instead of causing physical chaos in the country, leaders believed that the migrants would uplift the country. Germany's birth rate is the lowest in the world and its workforce is rapidly aging. Many of the Syrian refugees had money, education, and training, according to Sigmar Gabriel, Germany's vice chancellor.[10] Resettling and assimilating these migrants is costly; over time, Germany expected to spend $7 billion.

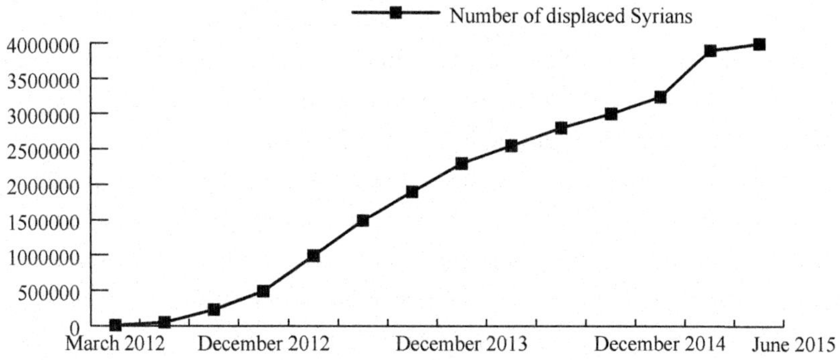

Figure 9.1: Syrian refugee crisis reaches new heights. Source: UNHCR.

A large and growing body of evidence, according to *Fortune* magazine, suggests "accepting refugees is often economically savvy."[11] Immigrants start businesses more often than native citizens, and they don't usually linger to collect unemployment. Also, they have a powerful motivation in getting a second chance on life. Refugee success in a new land often takes time. For the first five years, immigrants struggle even to maintain the lifestyle and economic position of the old country. But after ten years in the new land, refugees are often more prosperous than they had ever been prior to migrating.

Not all climate refugees will fare as well as those who manage to make it to Germany. Millions will be washed up in new and strange surroundings like flotsam and jetsam. The new host environment, either within a new region of the native land or in a new country, may cast the refugee into a life of hardship. Especially if climate refugees come from the countryside into the city, they will be cast into an alien environment. Many will have difficulty surviving if they lack decent housing and access to services. There is a high risk, reports Christian Aid, that "they will fall into chronic poverty, passed on from one generation to another."[12] The situation is particularly dire in countries like Columbia, Myanmar, and Mali, where political corruption, paramilitary activity, and climate change work together as a perfect storm for the displacement of thousands of people. Many are driven off their farms with the simple deadly admonition, "If you don't sell to us, we will negotiate with your widow."[13]

The right to return to their homes after an environmental or military calamity is supposed to be a fundamental right of all internally displaced people. But the reality is that once your land is stolen, you can expect only impoverishment with no help from the state.

A similar reality awaits refugees at the Mae Ra Luang camp on the Thai-Myanmar border. At least thirty-five hundred refugees have come to this camp and more are coming. Myanmar is one of the poorest countries in the world, but nearly half of its government's budget is spent on the military.[14] Over 10 percent of Myanmar's children die before their fifth birthday from disease and malnutrition. Land that could be used for much-needed food production has been turned into palm oil plantations. Meanwhile, Myanmar maintains one of the largest armies in Asia even though it has no neighbors who pose a threat.

The change in rainfall patterns in Mali, Africa, is creating a new wave of migrants who are being driven from their homes in search of water.[15] As refugees leave their native villages, they must sever close family ties and a strong sense of community that helped to sustain[16] them while they eked out a living. In recent years droughts have diminished harvests. Every year more people leave for good. There is just not enough food to survive the dry season. At one time the farmers of Mali could predict the rains and plant accordingly. Now the rains disappear in the middle of the growing season with disastrous results. Thus a twin development occurs as the land is lost and with it subsequent generations that gave the region culture and subsistence.

The most striking thing about today's migration crisis is that it is expected to get bigger. Even if Western nations are able to absorb the millions of migrants from Syria and the Middle East, millions will be coming from Eritrea, Libya, and North Africa generally. A recent poll of Nigerians found that 40 percent of all Nigerians would migrate if they could. Borders in the Middle East and Africa that were drawn by colonial powers years ago are breaking down as climate change roils societies. In a recent article on the global migration crisis by *New York Times* international correspondent Rod Norland, Sonja Licht of the International Center for Democratic Transition observed, "The global north must be prepared that the global south is on the move, the entire global south. This is just not a problems for Europe but for the whole world."[17]

It is difficult to create transborder temporary refugee sanctuaries. Host nations are sometimes suspicious of them, and xenophobes point out that "temporary" easily morphs into "permanent" camps as experiences in Palestine and Jordan and South Pacific post-atomic islands suggest. It is difficult to inculcate an idea that refuge is in itself "temporary" especially if that camp is in an affluent host country. Also with "temporary refuges" come issues of freedom of movement of climate refugees and others in host countries. Freedom of movement for climate refugees or others can deteriorate from a humanitarian concern to one of national and regional security.

The consequence of large numbers of climate refugees will most likely be among "the most significant of all upheavals entrained by global warming," argues environment scholar Norman Myers.[18] Refugees arrive with a host of different religious and cultural practices. Resettlement, Myers says, is difficult, and "full assimilation is rare."[19] Economic and political upheavals will likely proliferate. Ethnic problems will multiply. "The political fallout would be extensive."[20] Whatever form it takes, resettlement will be expensive, costing developing nations over $20 billion to accommodate climate refugees. Plus significant financial outlays will be needed to combat pandemic diseases as well as problems with allocating food and water.

Even under the best of conditions, resettlement is not an easy process. It is costly, and refugees seldom have the skill sets required for a new life in a new country. It was found that even during the period of postwar sympathy for displaced persons, states were disinclined to accept groups so large as to resist absorption. As Jane McAdam notes in a recent article, "The political and practical obstacles that stood in the way of relocation in the past still remain today." Modern scholarship on resettlement shows that it is "a fraught and complex undertaking, and rarely considered successful by those who move."[21] Looking back on history it is easy to say, "This time it's different." But one wonders whether or not we will keep repeating the mistakes of the past regarding refugees.

The media is filled with news of the desperate exodus of thousands of Syrian refugees into Europe. While chaos will no doubt prevail in the short run, eventually European countries like Austria and Germany will sort out the problem of housing, feeding, and employing a very large displaced population. Europe accommodated nearly nine hundred thousand refugees from Kosovo and other areas of the Balkans during a multiyear civil war in what once was Yugoslavia. These refugees all fall under the purview of the Geneva Convention as political refugees from war and will receive aid and eventual placement from UN and other relief agencies. Climate refugees currently receive no such help. However, the plight of both kinds of refugees threatens to morph from a humanitarian crisis to a geopolitical one. Today many are seeking asylum in the West, and not all will receive it, because Europeans fear their culture will be overwhelmed by a foreign tide.

CULTURAL BACKLASH

Once the refugees arrive safely in their final destinations—increasingly, these destinations are Italy, the United Kingdom, Germany, and Sweden—new problems arise. Syrian refugees have been facing cultural backlash in European countries and, after the ISIS terrorism attacks in Paris, around the world. But in fact the rise of ISIS was dependent on Syria's unrest. The Islamic State, a militant Sunni jihadist group that derived from al-Qaeda, then took advantage of the unrest and opposition to the Shiite Assad government, established ground forces in Syria and rebranded itself as the Islamic State of Iraq and Syria. After the Paris terrorism attacks, hostility toward Syrian refugees—and other Middle Eastern refugees—kicked into overdrive.

Of the European Union, Germany had one of the most open policies for accepting refugees, handling 70 percent of asylum seekers—it received approximately one million refugees in 2015. Subsequently, Chancellor Angela Merkel faced backlash from the Germans for the open policy, and anti-immigrant sentiment swelled. In the late summer of 2015, attacks on refugee centers and refugees themselves increased. An apartment building renovated by the government and planned to house dozens of refugees was burned to the ground. The nearby residents blamed the building owner, not the arsonists, for turning the building into a shelter. In Germany latent racism was brought to the surface, particularly when refugees moved into the white, post-neo-Nazi neighborhoods of East Germany.

Sweden has seen similar acts of violence. The Nordic country received the second most Syrian asylum applications in the European Union, and it was one of the more tolerant and open countries to refugees. But as the number of refugees living in Sweden has increased over recent years, a hostile backlash has been brewing. The Sweden Democrats party, which takes an anti-immigration position, rose considerably in the polls to become the most popular party by the end of 2015. Xenophobic acts of violence were seen across the country; buildings that were supposed to become refugee asylums were burned to the ground—one building already housing refugees burned down, forcing fourteen asylum seekers to escape through the window. Other European countries have recently elected parliaments that are further to the right than previously, promoting anti-immigration policies. Poland and Denmark have joined Sweden in increasing anti-immigrant sentiment.

The xenophobia is by no means limited to the European Union. In Egypt, Syrian refugees were at first welcomed by the Islamist president Mohamed Morsi—up until the summer of 2013, when Morsi was ousted. After that the government wrongly tied the rebel Free Syrian Army—with which many Syrian refugees share common ground—to violence in Syria, and Syrians faced harassment by police and on the streets, were increasingly mugged and robbed, faced discrimination, and were clamped down on by the government. At the time, one of the only countries friendly to the Syrian refugees was Yemen, which was fraught with instability, still recovering from its own uprising.

In the United States President Donald Trump's call to ban all Muslims entering the United States revealed uncomfortable truths about xenophobia in the country. A large segment of Republicans supported Trump, and during the presidential campaign, state governors across the country announced they would not accept Syrian refugees, although the United States had only allowed an embarrassingly small number of Syrian refugees in the country—fewer than than three thousand since 2011. The State Department planned to increase its intake to about ten thousand Syrians for 2016, but the backlash was palpable as anti-Muslim sentiment in the States increased.

American xenophobia is as old as the United States. Even during the colonial period Benjamin Franklin warned that a tide of German immigrants threatened to overwhelm colonial British American society. Franklin feared that Americans would eventually speak German. Americans have always been uncomfortable with immigrants in their midst, even though they themselves are part of the immigrant mix.[22] While Americans agree on humanitarian ideas in principle, they are reluctant to put them into practice. Historically, Americans have been suspicious of Catholics, especially Irish ones; Jews; and immigrants generally of darker skin color. Ideology too has played its xenophobic part. The Cold War after 1950 spurred a rampant fear of communism in the United States and of all socialist ideologies. Refugees from national uprisings like that of Hungary in the 1950s were admitted because the American government invoked emergency powers rather than welcome them as refugees. After the Vietnam War, Americans were reluctant to admit Vietnamese refugees partly out of a fear of oriental peoples that went back to America's Chinese Exclusion Acts of the nineteenth century.

If we adopt a long historical view, the xenophobia of our current crop of political leaders is rooted in American culture. Among our presidents, Barack Obama and Jimmy Carter have been the only national leaders to extend a welcoming hand to refugees in the modern age. President Carter, when he signed the Refugee Act of 1980, referred to the United States' " long tradition as a haven for people uprooted by persecution and political turmoil."[23] Given the present nativist mood in the United States, however, this policy is not completely accurate.

The Syrian refugee crisis is having global ramifications, and its disastrously high numbers are fueled by climate change. While pundits may continue to bicker over whether or not these refugees can rightfully be called "climate refugees," there is no doubt that the process of global warming is not only contributing to a deep unraveling in political stability in the Middle East but also has the possibility to do more so, in Africa and Asia and elsewhere. It is a force to be reckoned with and considered in the context of climate change in the decades ahead.

While Syria's refugee crisis is palpable and the effects are clear, it is just one result of a crisis worsened by climate change. Many regions in the Middle East face threats from global warming—similar and unique—that could create another refugee crisis. If the world can barely handle

Syria's crisis, what will happen when this becomes even more widespread? The implications are not good.

Climate change, notes Yale historian Timothy Snyder, raises grave social dangers. A country like China with over a billion people could easily fall into an "ecological panic" and take drastic steps to protect its people and its standard of living.[24] China is already buying up vast tracts of land in Africa and in the United States to guarantee food security for its people. China owns or leases a tenth of Ukraine's arable soil and buys up food when global supplies tighten, says Snyder.[25] However, nations in need of food and land could easily resort to a Hitlerian "*lebensraum*" policy and begin to grab farmlands and expel local native populations during times of drought or other food crises. Writes Snyder: "Nations in need of land would likely begin with tactfully negotiated leases or purchases; but under conditions of stress or acute need such agrarian export zones could become fortified colonies, requiring or attracting violence."[26]

THROUGH A GLASS DARKLY

After nearly a century of effort and experience in dealing with the international movement of peoples, the old problems of hostility toward migrants remain. At this moment Europe appears to be fracturing as the migration crisis in Europe worsens. Despite all the intelligent calls for human rights conventions for migrants, the only mutually agreeable strategy for EU nations to come up with is to pay Turkey to care for the millions of migrants in its territory and keep them there. The Balkan approach has been to build border fences across Hungary, Slovenia, Croatia, and Macedonia. Meanwhile, Germany, a generous country that has admitted a million migrants, suffers a nativist backlash that could unseat Chancellor Angela Merkel and pull out the immigration welcome mat.

Humanitarian agencies argue that planned or managed relocation is increasingly being seen as a logical and legitimate climate change adaptation strategy.[27] Critics fear the creation of refugee "gulags" in their countries while proponents of the idea see managed relocation as a means of acculturation, adaptation, and rehabilitation from the onslaught of environmental hazards. It is important to raise worldwide knowledge-based public awareness of the issue and its social and economic dimensions. People need to realize that climate refugees are first people who have faced real hardships. They have not come to a new country to "steal" people's livelihoods.[28] This is the kind of awareness that needs to be generated by heads of states and humanitarian agencies. One of the fundamental problems that we see today is that while migration from an environmentally ruined area to a more prosperous one is often championed as a "human right," currently the right of a country to protect and secure its borders is enshrined in international law. Whether people can be admitted to another state in a disaster context and seek assistance and stay for an undetermined period is a key question.

In Wiesbaden, Germany, today you can see the remnants of the great fortified wall that was built by centurions in the declining days of the Roman Empire to keep the barbarians out. Over the course of time the wall was notoriously unsuccessful in its mission. Goths, Visigoths, and other tribes poured into Rome's dominions and the empire collapsed. Today a specter is haunting Europe, a specter of a proud, optimistic, and moral Europe falling victim to climate change and demographics. In Paris, Rome, Brussels, Stockholm, and Berlin, the question uttered by people on the street is pretty much the same: "Can Europe protect its citizens? Can Europe protect its borders?"

Climate refugees come from a variety of classes and cultures. The specter of wholesale relocation of diverse populations raises fundamental questions about citizenship and nationality. Once land has been lost, will a residual nationality be able to persist? In the event of a wholesale evacuation, as in the case of island nations, what happens to an abandoned country's exclusive economic zone, its territorial waters and nationhood? It is not easy to carve out new space for a nation. The experiences of Israel, Palestine, the Ukraine, Pakistan, and Bangladesh attest to this.

A recent Brookings Institution report states that Pacific Island countries are regarded as "a barometer of the impacts of climate change."[29] For the people of these islands, climate change means an assault on their homes and livelihoods. The residents of the Cook Islands in the South Pacific, for example, do not want to leave their homes because of rising sea levels. They fear that if they leave their islands, their entire way of life, including their language and customs, will become extinct. Small wonder that Pacific Island leaders like Anote Tong of the Republic of Kiribati have been in the forefront of demands for developed nations to reduce greenhouse gas emissions. Islanders are also exploring means of adapting to climate change through change in local infrastructure—from sea walls to new techniques to stem beach erosion, such as planting sturdy seashore grasses and rebuilding wetlands.

Cross-border migration means loss of home, and it is a sensitive issue especially in Mexico and other parts of Latin America where droughts and storms have propelled millions northward to the United States. And now, despite numerous difficulties—climatic, financial, and political—Mexicans are returning home. According to a recent Pew Research Report, more Mexicans have returned to Mexico than migrated to the States since the recession of 2008: "From 2009 to 2014 1 million Mexicans and their families (including U.S.-born children) left the United States for Mexico."[30] This exceeded those 870,000 migrants heading northward. The main reason given by Mexicans for their return was the preservation of home and family. In "el Norte" Mexicans, for example, have difficulty maintaining their culture across the generations. Mexican American youth take on the cultural attributes of the dominant American culture to the dismay of their elders. Thus Mexican immigrants share many of the same concerns as the Cook Islanders as elucidated by Jane McAdam.[31]

A 1998 report by the IPCC stated that a one-meter rise in sea levels would inundate three million hectares of land in Bangladesh, displacing fifteen to twenty million people. The Mekong Delta in Vietnam could lose two million hectares of land, ultimately displacing nearly ten million people. In West Africa nearly 70 percent of the coast would be inundated by a one-meter rise. Further, the same rise in sea level in Shanghai would displace nearly six million of the city's seventeen million people. Will there be boards of international equity for resettlement to help these people?

Other kinds of migrants in the future will be from countries that have ceased to exist—some sunk into rising seas, others succumbing to tsunamis, flooding, or desertification. Storms swell rivers; they wash away the soil and create new flood plains. Economic survival on changing environmental landscapes becomes increasingly problematic. Numerous questions arise about these migrants. Can a whole nation ever pack up and leave? Can a citizenry exist if their country is no longer on the map?

As McAdam has noted, without systematic approaches to the problems engendered by climate change, "there is a risk that regional concerns become diluted or homogenized to some abstract 'universal experience,' and with the loss of nuance comes the loss of appropriate interventions."[32]

The question is whether some tipping point will send a surge of "environmental asylum seekers" or if climate change will merely boost some population increases that are manageable. If refugees materialize in significant numbers, will they receive sanctuary? Past history of this subject is not comforting.

NOTES

Amanda A. Doran, "Where Should Haitians Go—Why Environmental Refugees are up the Creek without a Paddle," *Villanova Environmental Law Journal,* 22(11), p. 132, available at http://digitalcommons.law.villanova.edu/cgi/viewcontent.cgi?article=1015&context=elj

1. International Organization for Migration, "A Complex Nexus," http://www.iom.int/complex-nexus.

2. Associated Press, "Katrina Evacuees' Welcome Wearing Thin in Houston," March 29, 2006, http://www.foxnews.com/story/2006/03/29/katrina-evacuees-welcome-wearing-thin-in-houston.html.

3. Ibid.

4. Ibid.

5. Stephen Kleinberg, "Four Myths about Katrina's Impact on Houston," August 26, 2015, https://urbanedge.blogs.rice.edu/2015/08/26/four-myths-about-katrinas-impact-on-houston/#.WI9647YrKRs.

6. Ibid.

7. Neena Satija, Kiah Collier, Al Shaw, and Jeff Larson, "Hell and High Water," ProPublica, March 3, 2016, https://www.propublica.org/article/hell-and-high-water-text.

8. Amanda A. Doran, "Where Should Haitians Go—Why Environmental Refugees are up the Creek without a Paddle," *Villanova Environmental Law Journal,* 22(11), p. 132, available at http://digitalcommons.law.villanova.edu/cgi/viewcontent.cgi?article=1015&context=elj 132.

9. Ibid.

10. Henry Chu, "For Germany, Refugees Are a Demographic Blessing as Well as a Burden," *Los Angeles Times,* September 10, 2015.

11. Jon M. Jachimowicz, "The Link between Europe's Migrant Crisis and the Climate Change Debate," *Fortune,* November 11, 2015.

12. Roberta Cohen, "Human Tide: The Real Migration Crisis," Christian Aid Report, May 2007: 30, https://www.christianaid.org.uk/Images/human-tide.pdf.

13. Ibid: 31.

14. Ibid., p. 37.

15. Ibid., p. 40.

16. Ibid., p. 41.

17. Rod Norland, "A Mass Migration Crisis and It May Yet Get Worse," *New York Times*, October 31, 2015, https://www.nytimes.com/2015/11/01/world/europe/a-mass-migration-crisis-and-it-may-yet-get-worse.html.

18. Norman Myers, "Environmental Refugees in a Globally Warmed World," *Bioscience* 43, no. 11 (1993): 752.

19. Ibid: 759.

20. Ibid.

21. Jane McAdam, "Lessons from Planned Relocation and Resettlement in the Past," *Forced Migration Review* 49 (May 2015), http://www.fmreview.org/sites/fmr/files/FMRdownloads/en/climatechange-disasters/mcadam.pdf.

22. For good background on this, see Peter Schrag, *The Unwanted: Immigration and Nativism in America*, ImmigrationPolicy.org, September 2010, http://www.immigrationpolicy.org/perspectives/unwanted-immigration-and-nativism-america.

23. Jimmy Carter, "Refugee Act of 1980 Statement on Signing S. 643 Into Law," http://www.presidency.ucsb.edu/ws/?pid=33154.

24. Timothy Snyder, "The Next Genocide," *New York Times*, September 12, 2015, https://www.nytimes.com/2015/09/13/opinion/sunday/the-next-genocide.html.

25. Ibid.

26. Timothy Snyder, "The Next Genocide," Sunday Review, *New York Times*, September 12, 2015, https://www.nytimes.com/2015/09/13/opinion/sunday/the-next-genocide.html.

27. Brent Dobersteain and Anne Tadgell, "Guidance for 'Managed' Relocation," *Forced Migration Review* 49, p. 27, http://www.fmreview.org/sites/fmr/files/FMRdownloads/en/climatechange-disasters/doberstein-tadgell.pdf.

28. Fabrice Renaud et al., "Environmental Degradation and Migration," *Berlin-Institut für Bevölkerung und Entwicklung*, http://www.berlin-institut.org/en/online-handbookdemography/environment/environmental-migration.html.

29. Michael M. Cernea, Elizabeth Ferris, and Daniel Petz, "On the Front Line of Climate Change and Displacement: Learning from and with Pacific Island Communities," Brookings Institution Report, London School of Economics, September 20, 2011: 1, https://www.brookings.edu/wp-content/uploads/2016/06/09_idp_climate_change.pdf.

30. Ana Gonzale-Barrea, "More Mexicans Leaving Than Coming to the United States," Pew Foundation Report, November 19, 2005 (material provided by Mexican National Survey of Demographic Dynamics).

31. Jane McAdam, "Pacific Islanders Lead Nansen Initiative Consultation on Cross-Border Displacement from Natural Disasters and Climate Change," Brookings Up Front Report, May 30, 2013, https://www.brookings.edu/blog/up-front/2013/05/30/pacific-islanders-lead-nansen-initiative-consultation-on-cross-border-displacement-from-natural-disasters-and-climate-change/.

32. McAdam, "Pacific Islanders."

10

The Shape of Things to Come

> No country can seal itself off from the rest of the world. In no country or city can the rich fortify themselves for long against the poor. No frontier is impermeable.
>
> *Crispin Tickell, former British ambassador to the United Nations*

Once it becomes clear that one of the defining characteristics of our time is the swelling flow of environmental refugees across the planet, further questions arise. What kind of world do refugees find themselves in once they are displaced by destructive storms, expanding deserts, water shortages, and dangerously high levels of toxic pollutants in the local environment? And what are the nations of the world prepared to do about it?[1]

How can we gauge what has happened recently to our planet in the past few decades, and where do we stand today? According to scientific estimates, the number of those likely to relocate due to climatic reasons—sea level rise, increased water scarcity, desertification, and so on—ranges between 50 and 350 million by 2050.[2] Admittedly these are difficult numbers to absorb. But reality plods on, often defying scientific prognostication. Other estimates offer a clear-cut assessment. We know, for example, that there are already 135 million people, mostly in sub-Saharan Africa, threatened with severe desertification. In Africa and elsewhere, writes Norman Myers, we see "the phenomenon of marginal people driven into marginal environments."[3] These people in search of livelihood are moving into lands that are too dry or too steep. Others are rapidly cutting down forests with slash-and-burn techniques in order to wrest a living from soil that quickly loses its fertility.

We should recognize that the crisis of climate refugees has occurred in the context of meager spending by affluent nations, especially the United States. For example, in the fiscal year 2014–2015, about 1 percent of the American national budget was appropriated for foreign assistance. The lion's share of this aid went to Israel, Egypt, and Afghanistan.[4] The deplorable circumstances that we have described in various parts of the world are not just the result of economic and technological forces over which we have no control. They are also the result of conscious decisions made by nations preoccupied with their own self-interest. In her book *Damned Nations: Greed, Guns, Armies, and Aid,* Samantha Nutt, a Canadian public health specialist, deplores the growing militarization of foreign aid and what she terms naive "tourist" humanitarian actions like sending inappropriate Western food and supplies to distressed areas. Education, she claims, particularly the education of women in distressed areas of the developing world, alleviates poverty far better than sending shiploads of shoes, used T-shirts, and Enfamil that can't be used with dirty water.[5] As foreign aid approaches the 1 percent mark of national budgets, European and other Western nations worry about whether aid will force them to raise taxes in their respective countries, always a hot-button political issue.

If we appreciate the variability of our global climate system, it is worth remembering how easily communities and nations can be destroyed. One approach might be to have an international agency accord with a graduating scale of refugee protection based on the immediacy of environmental threats. One can hope that people who are displaced by environmental events can return to their homeland after storms and floods subside, for example, while sea level rise will be a permanent fixture. Furthermore, the notion of environmentally displaced persons is unlikely to ever be incorporated within the existing framework of the Refugee Convention, concludes New Zealand environmental lawyer Angela Williams.[6] As of now, the plight of climate refugees continues largely unrecognized and mostly devoid of support by the international community.[7] Since the Kyoto accords were signed, refugee organizations are demanding new programs of regional cooperation with respect to refugee adaptation activities. It is safe to say that the phenomenon of climate change has now created a new and independent category of refugee that needs to be recognized by the international legal system.[8] Currently the United States, New Zealand, Australia, Canada, and other nations are adopting a piecemeal approach to the problem of climate refugees. In lacking a well-articulated and programmatically defined approach to the problem, these nations are in effect absolving themselves of any responsibility to deal with the problems of climate refugees.[9]

FORECASTING AND DATABASES

At present there is only a limited knowledge base about the number of people displaced by sudden-onset disasters. Government tracking systems are inadequate, and questions remain about how many times people are displaced by environmental calamity, where they go, or if they eventually return home.[10] At what juncture does an environmental hazard become a tipping point that creates climate refugees? For example, we need to identify how and when a drought in Somalia triggered a famine in that country, which was already plagued by persistent political instability. In order to identify vulnerable populations, scientists argue for better forecasting instruments that can help to identify vulnerable populations in areas both of origin and destination, notes Susan Martin, a professor of international migration at Georgetown University.[11] Also, as Maria Waldinger and Sam Fankhauser have pointed out in their recent valuable study on climate change, "One of the most important drivers of migration patterns across the world are differences in income levels." Climate change is highly influential in increasing "income differentials," and this means that the poorest and most at-risk populations—who are already at risk—will be further harmed by climate change.[12]

Historically, efforts to aid refugees have been laced with skepticism and not a little irritation in the West. The evolving definition of the term "refugee" promulgated by governments and international agencies has been driven by political and ideological concerns very much removed from circumstances on the ground. Benjamin Glahn of the Salzburg Global Seminar notes the unfortunate consequences: "Without an official definition of what constitutes a 'climate refugee,' and lacking some form of official recognition under international law, persons forced to migrate across international borders as a result of climate change may continue to be, as the International Bar Association has said, 'almost invisible in the international system . . . unable to prove political persecution in their country of origin they fall through the cracks of asylum law.'"[13]

IMPERILED SCHENGEN RULES

The European Union's thirty-year-old Schengen Agreement is at the very heart of Europe's refugee crisis. The agreement allows a person to travel in the EU's vast area, stretching from Sweden in the north to Italy in the south, without ever having to show a passport. Prosperous countries like Sweden, the Netherlands, and France have no control over migrants through Schengen-area territories and thus no control over who enters or exits their countries. For decades, Schengen has held a kind of tranquil sway as long as movement across developed Europe consisted mostly of either European or middle-class migrants. Since 1985, travel document checks within the region have been abolished. And in 2007 travel and internal border controls were also abolished in nine—mostly eastern—EU nations.

The massive influx of migrants into Europe has put the future of the Schengen Agreement at stake. Many EU ministers have agreed to press ahead with plans to suspend the Schengen passport-free travel zone for two years and introduce new border checks at national frontiers.[14] Johanna Miki-Leitner, then Austrian interior minister, claimed that "Schengen is on the brink of collapse."[15] In a backlash against immigrants, Sweden has proposed the closing of its bridge to Denmark, and Denmark itself has recently passed a law making the transport of refugees to the Swedish border a crime of human smuggling.[16] Officials have discussed the possibility of "in effect, suspending Greece from Schengen, in a move that would force Greek citizens to go through passport control when flying to other parts of the area," according to the *Financial Times*.[17]

For the European Union's future, Schengen will have to be profoundly modified or scrapped. The current refugee crisis has made what was once unimaginable now become imaginable. The Schengen Agreement is no match for the driving forces of desperate needy people who have access

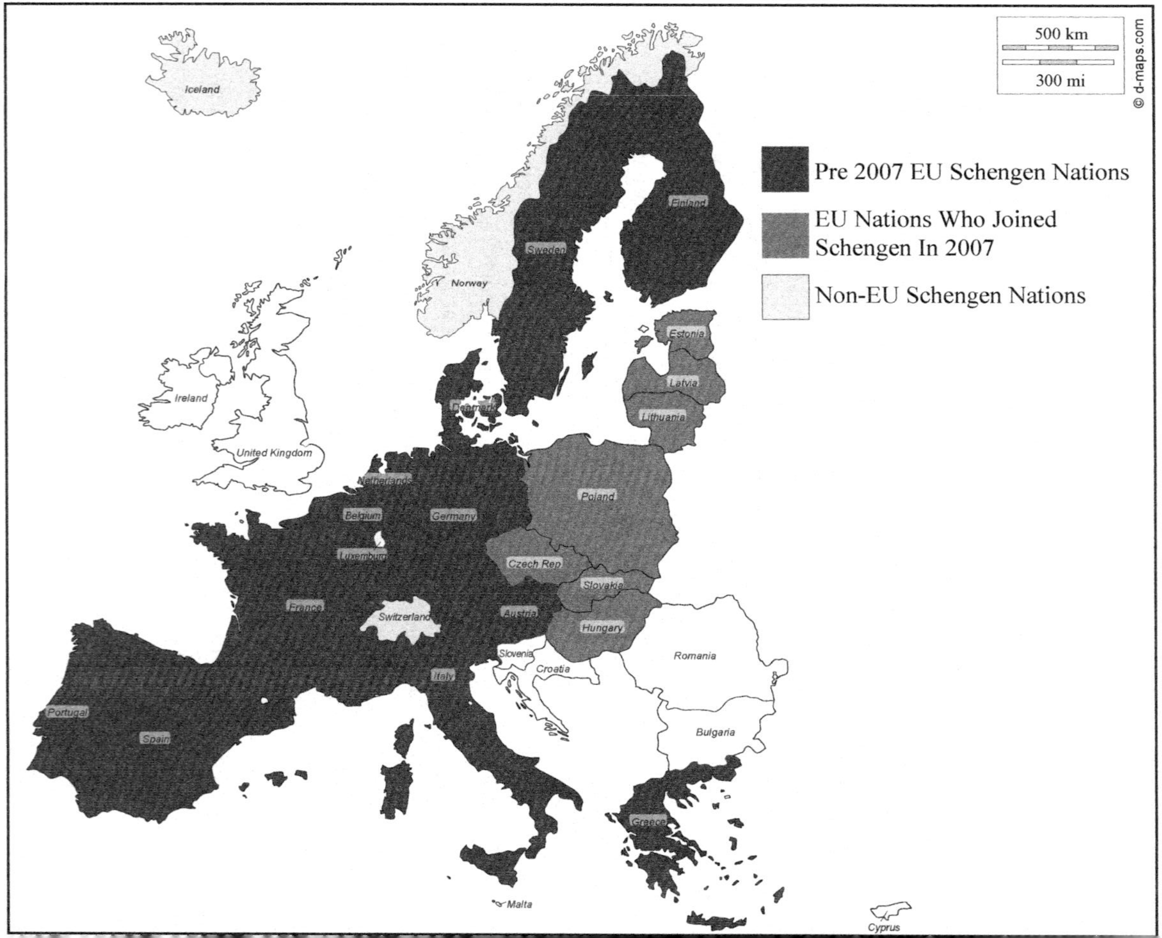

Map 10.1: Schengen Agreement Countries

to modern communication. At the moment, everything depends on the protection of the Greek-Turkish border. If current plans by the EU to pay for the warehousing of refugees in Turkey fail, EU ministers may urge the closure of national borders for two years.

Current immigration policies are not even remotely capable of dealing with the numbers involved.[18] Meanwhile, as the free flow of goods and services and money is protected by international agreements, it seems perverse to deny the same rights to people.[19] At present, however, the indications are not promising. State protection of climate refugees has its limits. To claim that they can be accommodated within their own countries ignores three facts. First, the governments in those countries have initiated dam projects involving the forced removal of thousands, uprooting countless villages and towns. The Three Gorges Dam in China, for example, displaced 1.4 million people with the government's blessing. Second, entire countries—or large parts of them—may become uninhabitable or disappear completely. Third, governments may simply lack the resources to cope. The current anarchic situation in Libya and civil war in Syria are case studies in this regard.

Molly Conisbee and Andrew Simms of the New Economics Foundation have summed up the matter succinctly: "Globalisation does not just mean rapid capital transfers and unlimited cheap travel. Nor does it mean treating the world as a playground, a museum, or a supermarket. It means that ignoring our neighbours is no longer an option."[20]

The one "refugee success story" that we know of is the case of Chandigarh, India. In the 1950s the Indian government commissioned the noted French architect Le Corbusier to design a city for sixty thousand refugees from Pakistan.[21] This well-planned city is a delight to both walk in and drive in—a refreshing antidote to India's traffic-plagued cities. Le Corbusier's heavy concrete structures today, however, serve less as testimony to the refugee than to the French architect's ego. The refugees have been long settled, and Chandigarh is now known mostly as an Indian army staging area for possible conflicts in the Punjab. Little is mentioned of the six thousand peasant families who were expelled from their ancestral lands to make way for Chandigarh.

NEW IDEAS, NEW POLICIES

First and foremost, developed nations that have huge intakes of climate refugees and others will have to develop standards, internationally agreed to, for the categorization and processing of migrants. Agencies working with climate refugees will have to determine whether an individual is a refugee or an opportunity migrant and examine the severity of the environmental process in the old homeland to determine if it is possible to return to the place of origin. Currently many agencies are considering a multifaceted policy approach to address the relationship between environmental degradation and forced migration.[22] The components of this policy are as follows: there needs to be long-term funded scientific research on the cause-effect mechanism between environmental degradation and forced migrations.[23]

As refugee populations go on the move, one of the moral questions is how organized nations can deal with human trafficking. Regional free-movement protocols among nations outside of Africa do not exist to protect mobile peoples. Borderless and people-centered regions championed by refugee advocates are a long way from being implemented. In fact, the current assault on "borderless" Western Europe by millions of refugees may make resettlement of displaced peoples more difficult than ever. As most displaced migrants live at or near the poverty level, they are disproportionately affected by changes in climate. In agrarian regions, as drought makes it harder for populations to sustain themselves, food insecurity climbs and it becomes difficult to remain. In subsistence communities the key is not to pressure people to move but to develop strategies that will allow them to remain with their culture and communities intact. Improved water installations, for example, can go a long way in keeping communities from becoming disaster zones. Other strategies such as attempts to combat soil erosion and developing centers whereby people can learn new skills to sustain themselves in their environment have recently been popularized.

The development of temporary refuges for displaced populations fleeing desertification or flooding has a strong tradition in many African countries. When a massive volcano eruption occurred on Mt. Nyiragongo in the Democratic Republic of the Congo in 2002, those fleeing the volcano were allowed to stay in Uganda until it was safe to return despite not being granted refugee status. According to the UNHCR, temporary protection is a pragmatic tool for offering sanctuary to those fleeing humanitarian crises.[24]

As many climate refugees will ultimately settle in urban areas, much of the urban infrastructure will be unable to cope with the influx and breakdown. Thus major attention needs to be paid to our world-class cities, which require having infrastructure repair programs in place. In terms of housing, sanitation, and public safety, international aid to new huddled masses in large cities in both developed and developing countries won't be worth much if climate refugees are forced to cluster in Bantu-style segregated urban slums.

A case in point is Rome. Take a trolley from the center of the city near the Coliseum and ride for a while. Fancy apartments and condominiums give way to dilapidated settlements—first come the Asian neighborhoods, then finally the stark, depressed buildings that are the homes of people from the sub-Sahara. The migrants in cities—poorly educated, bereft of friends, unfamiliar with the language and the culture—spread their meager blankets, baskets, and trinkets on urban sidewalks to sell to tourists and passers-by. Meanwhile, no fewer than nine developed countries, almost one in three, are taking steps to restrict the flow of climate refugees from developing countries. What follows are some suggested policy responses that we believe will have impact on the climate refugee problem. As Sir Nicholas Stern and others have argued, strong deliberate policy action is required.

POLICY RESPONSES TO CLIMATE REFUGEES

An examination of current literature on the subject shows possible remedies for climate refugees. First it is important to update the Geneva Convention, which has not been revised since the 1960s. The Geneva Convention needs to be updated to compensate for ecological debts that could be agreed to in terms of sustainable per capita level of fossil fuel consumption. Emissions can be cut through increased efficiency, and demand for carbon-based power can be changed by the adoption of cleaner technologies. Coal, for example, can be better regulated and controlled through pricing and taxation. This would help to clarify the overconsumption of coal by some nations that increases pollution in parts of the developing world and contributes to the refugee burden. Any policy that prevents environmental degradation, such as reforestation projects, should receive immediate action. As the *Stern Review* noted, "The loss of natural forests around the world contributes more to global emissions each year than the transport sector."[25]

In her study on climate change refugees and international law, Angela Williams, formerly of Sussex University Law School in England and now an international environmental lawyer in New Zealand, argues that there is a way nations can deal with this problem, pointing out that there are already international agreements among nations, such as the United Nations Law of the Sea Convention, which involves 140 nations and 13 regional programs. The primary purpose of the convention is to protect their shared marine environment through treaties and action plans. Williams argues that it ought to be possible for nations to work out similar approaches to the problem of climate refugees.[26]

In his highly regarded report *Environmental Refugees,* Norman Myers forcefully lays out an intelligent approach to the problem of climate exiles/refugees: "We cannot continue to ignore environmental refugees simply because there is no institutionalized mode of dealing with the problem."[27] First and foremost Myers believes that we have to look at the root causes of the problem and address them with what he calls "silver bullet options." Foreign aid should be specifically targeted to improve the underlying economic and political situations that generate environmental refugees. Today, he notes, there are ten developing countries with well over two-thirds of the world's "poorest of the poor" that receive only one-third of foreign aid.[28] The World Bank and other financial institutions need to stop treating these nations as just another credit account when it comes to foreign debt. Too much money is extracted from developing countries in the form of debt service when what is needed is debt relief. Myers suggests some form of debt relief for poor nations through "debt-for-environment swaps."[29]

Other forms of relief might be in rooting out political corruption and lowering military expenditure to 1970 levels. Simple policy initiatives like tree planting in environmentally endangered poor countries would supply timber and firewood as well as yield additional benefits by preventing soil erosion, offering windbreaks for crops, and restoring watersheds. Myers concludes by saying, "For all countries, whether developing or developed, the overriding objective must be to reduce the motivation for environmentally destitute people to migrate by supplying them with acceptable lifestyles."[30]

Writing in the journal *Global Environmental Politics,* Frank Biermann and Ingrid Boas lay out a dynamic schema for governing the climate refugee crisis.[31] While the singular events of environmental disaster cannot be predicted, the governance of climate refugees can be better organized and planned. Too much emphasis has been placed on programs of disaster response and disaster relief when it comes to climate refugees. Biermann and Boas argue for programs not of relief but of "planned and voluntary resettlement over longer periods of time."[32] In the long term, they note, most climate refugees will not be able to return to their homes. Thus an institutional framework is needed to conceive of most climate refugees as "permanent immigrants to the countries that accept them."[33]

Also, as others have already pointed out, this regime will have to focus on protecting people within their own territory. Developed countries will have to bear more of the cost of maintaining people displaced by environmental or climatic events in their own country. The only danger in establishing this new regime is that it will become just another bureaucracy that is heavy-weighted with nationalism and economic argument. However, this regime can be successful if the UN finally embraces an adaptation protocol for "climate refugees" that includes a combination of adaptation and voluntary resettlement programs. As Biermann and Boas point out, "Dealing with the resettlement of millions of climate refugees over the course of the century will require not only a new legal regime, but also one of several international agencies to deal with this task."[34]

One of the boldest prescriptions for the legal and human rights protection of climate refugees is contained in an essay by Bonnie Docherty and Tyler Giannini in the *Harvard Environmental Law Review*.[35] Because climate change is global, they contend, the international community should accept responsibility not only for mitigating climate problems but also for helping the tempest-tossed climate refugee. Docherty and Giannini argue for "an innovative, international, and interdisciplinary approach that can be implemented before the situation reaches a crisis state."[36] The existing international legal framework does not address the crisis of millions of people on the move. The best solution to this problem, they believe, is the creation of an independent and parallel convention to the UNHCR.[37] This new convention would have a commission much like the UNHCR, with both the political and fiscal power to approach climate refugee problems and search for solutions.[38] The problem is so new and substantial that climate refugees, by their very nature of being without UNHCR protection, need a new regime to handle their problems. There is an urgency to this matter, as many small island regimes, such as the Maldives and delta regions like Bangladesh, will soon disappear under rising tides.

The bottom line for these scholars is that neither current climate change law nor refugee law precisely and definitively addresses the issue of climate change refugees. In their words, "Climate change is a de facto problem currently lacking a de jure solution."[39] Currently the United Nations offers little institutional protection of climate refugees. Significantly, the UNHCR does not try to broker cross-border climate refugee problems that can lead to armed conflict and increase population flows. Docherty and Giannini argue for a new approach that covers relocation of these people that is both temporary and permanent. A new convention for climate refugees would involve a nexus between environmental disruption and human action.

Their de jure approach would involve six elements being met in order for a refugee to be considered a victim of climate change: (1) forced migration, (2) temporary or permanent relocation, (3) movement across national borders, (4) disrupted lives consistent with climate change, (5) sudden or gradual environmental disruption, and (6) a "more likely than not" standard for human contribution to the disruption.[40]

With a new international administration in place to elaborate and resolve issues in a fast and efficient manner in place, Docherty and Giannini argue, climate refugees could be helped and relocated in new and vital ways. This new convention would guarantee legal identity and assistance to climate refugees and force all nations to share in the fiscal responsibility of helping these people with "binding upfront contributions." Most assuredly, this idea of both a new international convention and a rival bureaucracy would not sit well with the UNHCR, which tends to look at climate refugees merely as displaced persons. Nevertheless this kind of scholarly inquiry shows the variety and creativity of current humane legal thought on the subject of climate refugees.

As Biermann and Boas have stated, the protection and resettlement of possibly over two hundred million climate refugees over the course of this century will require substantial funds, which will have to come largely from the developed West (which bears much of the blame for causing global warming).[41] These will be the donor countries, and the question is whether or not these countries will be ready for programs that may seriously tap into national wealth. Only by creating new legal responsibilities toward climate refugees will the international community, especially the industrialized nations, accept their obligations[42]. The people liable to be displaced by environmental change, crisis, and degradation are among the world's poorest and have the least political muscle.[43]

Because there are currently no frameworks or guidelines to help climate refugees, they risk falling through the cracks of international refugee and immigration policy.[44] Since it takes time to implement slow-onset "frameworks" and "conventions," Roger Zetter, an Oxford scholar on refugee issues, recommends stop-gap emergency procedures, or what he calls a "protection gap," in terms of specifying and protecting migrant rights before displacement, especially in the area of resettlement and rights related to return.[45] This can only be done if there is a mutually used knowledge base for intergovernmental agencies providing advocacy, capacity strengthening, and improved communication between civil society organizations. The place to begin is working with those migrants who have been internally displaced in their own countries in order to allow them to stay in their homeland. Lastly, there has to be an internationally agreed-upon apparatus for the protection of climate refugees from violence during their movements.[46]

THE NANSEN INITIATIVE

The Nansen Initiative was launched in 2012 by the governments of Norway and Switzerland in recognition of the dire fact that under existing law there was no assurance that people forced by environmental disasters to flee across borders would be admitted and receive assistance, let alone find durable solutions to their displacement.[47] As scholar Walter Kälin has commented on the subject, "Such displacement creates not only legal protection problems but also operational, institutional, and funding challenges."[48]

While the purpose of the Nansen Initiative is to build consultative arrangements among Western countries impacted by climate and political migration on an illegal and large-scale basis, it has a strong focus on disasters, especially the adverse impacts of climate change. Disaster displacement across international borders is now an unpleasant fact of life for those countries involved. And those participating in Nansen consultations have tried to develop strategies to prevent displacement when possible "and when it cannot be avoided, to protect displaced peoples and to construct durable solutions for their displacement."[49] The Nansen Initiative has also pointed out that laws and policies do not sufficiently address the problem of cross-border displacement.[50]

The one major positive development of Nansen is that it has given countries a forum for regional and subregional discussion of the problem rather than discreetly sweeping cross-border displacement under the rug. Nansen has conducted valuable studies on infrastructure and land reform in immigrant-exporting countries. It has also worked in the area of disaster-related human displacement. Thus far the work of the Nansen Initiative has taken place outside the United Nations system.[51] Advocates of the Nansen Initiative hope to put climate change and disasters squarely back on the UN agenda. What Nansen faces is the situation that all the affected nations—rich and poor—need: to develop a set of common understandings and practices for handling the problem of climate refugees. The authors of the Nansen Initiative recognized that action must be taken *now*. As climate change inflicts itself on the planet in the coming years, altruism and generosity among nations are likely to be blunted.

POSSIBLE FUTURE SCENARIOS

What follows are two scenarios, one of them pessimistic and the other somewhat optimistic. By no means are these scenarios predictive. They merely sketch out the possibilities for the future that we see here and now.

Scenario One

Most nations have chosen to collectively ignore the problem until now, when the demographic tsunami is flooding Europe with migrants from conflict-ridden Middle Eastern countries. Until the Syrian refugee crisis, there were no legal conventions or norms to provide help and succor to climate refugees in search of sanctuary. Currently the pressure of international events is helping to change public attitudes toward climate refugees. But these attitudes could easily swing from positive to negative depending on political and cultural pressures. The easiest way to deal with this problem is to abandon many of the official terminologies used for refugees. The main challenge then becomes how to develop credentials for safe passage as well as norms of treatment and settlement for these displaced persons. Further, climate refugees have "human rights" as identified in the United Nations Charter.

For everyday purposes, these rights need to be spelled out in ways that can facilitate the process of adequate care for climate refugees. As José Riera of the UNHCR has noted, "A major question is whether there is an appetite at the international level to embark on a new process to come up with new norms and protections. . . . My suspicion is that there is zero appetite for this."[52] Regardless of how nations and their governments feel about rights and protocols, the fact remains that refugees will keep migrating to developed nations as long as conditions in their old homelands remain intolerable. Certain areas of the planet are in the so-called climate hotspots—low-lying islands, coastal regions, and large river deltas that remain in danger of catastrophic environmental change.[53]

Thus far we have been talking about legal and normative frameworks or the lack thereof. But how do we develop a capacity for them? Roger Zetter notes that protecting climate refugees poses three distinctive challenges: "determining whether displacement is voluntary or forced:

(2) whether it is temporary or permanent, and how protection needs differ between internal or international displacement."[54]

Under this challenging sociopolitical umbrella is the even more important question of process. How do we process climate refugees for a new and hopefully more stable and productive life in countries where the language, politics, and culture is not theirs? Context shapes sensitivity toward displacement, and countries like Bangladesh, India, and Kenya have had to deal with a series of economic, political, and environmental traumas since their independence. In these countries only the state provides a protection apparatus, and it is one that has a large element of violence to it. Countries like Sudan and Libya may be so fragile economically that they cannot commit to developing effective economic and legal protection for their refugees. What needs to happen first in the receiving countries is the development of a national plan for dealing with climate change. Unfortunately, one term now describe how most nations deal with the problem: ad hoc.

Until now, the Western developed nations have deliberately remained ignorant of demographic realities like that of West Africa, where economic, politics, violence, and environmental degradation are so intertwined that it is difficult to tell where one trend starts and another begins. Indeed the whole of West Africa is in the middle of large-scale border upheaval that may set millions of Africans on the march. France, long one of the stabilizing forces for economy and security in West Africa, has pulled out. And oil-rich Nigeria, always a bellwether of national development, is seeing massive urbanization of rural peoples, especially in the city of Lagos, whose crime, pollution, and dysfunction make it a cliché in the developing world.[55] Sixty-six percent of the population of Lagos lives in slums, with little or no access to roads, clean water, electricity, or waste disposal. In 1970 the population of Lagos was 1.4 million; today, according to the *World Population Review,* it is the largest city in Africa, with a population of twenty-five million.[56] Population experts estimate that at its current rate of growth, in twenty-five years Nigeria will have three hundred million people, the same as the present-day United States, living in an area the size of Arizona, New Mexico, and Nevada.[57] Meanwhile, the country is rapidly depleting its resources. People can only endure so long the streets with floating garbage, mosquitoes and malaria, the random violence, and the generally debilitating quality of environmental decline before they decide to strike out for something better.

Owing to environmental decline and poverty, countries in the developing world like Sierra Leone and the Ivory Coast are becoming chaos-ridden regions where lawless private armies provide a bare minimum of stability to the region. Thus environment in developing countries becomes an important refugee issue. It also becomes a major issue of national security. Water, for example, will be in dangerously short supply in many areas of the world. War could erupt between Egypt and Ethiopia over Nile water. Even in Europe tensions have arisen between Hungary and Slovakia over the damming of the Danube—a classic case of how ethnic tensions are inflamed by environmental disputes.[58]

Thomas Homer-Dixon, a professor studying conflict and environment at the University of Toronto, believes that the planet is currently on the threshold of acute conflict because of environmental change. What Homer-Dixon calls "hard regime" countries—autocratic governments with very strong armies—will survive in the future. The survival of "softer," democratic nation-states is far less certain, he says. While a minority of the world's population will live very well in shiny, affluent, high-tech metro regions of the West where most ethnic and religious problems have been quelled by bourgeois prosperity, he writes, "An increasingly large number of people will be stuck in history, living in shantytowns where attempts to rise above poverty, cultural dysfunction, and ethnic strife will be doomed by a lack of water to drink, soil to till, and space to survive in."[59]

China, in Homer-Dixon's view, is the quintessential example of environmental degradation. China's current success masks its environmental problems, but not for long. Diminishing water supplies in China's interior will unleash large-scale population migrations to urban areas that are already under considerable environmental stress. The whole of China may become fractured by its water problems, and in the future China may look profoundly different on the geopolitical map. Looking at other cities like Delhi and Calcutta, we will see worsening air and water quality. Like Beijing, the stage is being set for a drama of surging populations, environmental degradation, and ethnic conflict. Homer-Dixon speculates that as the situation worsens in Africa, whatever the laws and barriers, refugees will find a way to crash official borders and bring their religions and passions with them. Even the United States and Europe will be weakened by the cultural disputes that arise from the tidal surge of climate refugees.

As large refugee populations begin to swarm and move north and west, the state as a governing ideal may founder as arbitrary impositions on a world map that has very little in common with the new demographic realities. In the future the map of the world with its 190 or so countries may be relegated to the status of another quaint document on the historical shelf. There is little compelling evidence that outside of a few Western industrialized countries, the nation-state as a governing ideal can be transported in our time and made to work.[60] Already Lebanon, Syria, El Salvador, Peru, and Colombia have few working parts in their nation-state schema. Suffice it to say that these "quasi nations" are plagued by violence, and local governments in these places have great difficulty protecting their citizens.

None of this even takes into consideration what climate change in this century will do to erode the capacity of existing nations to cope. Places today that call themselves countries may degenerate into a collection of cultures with highly marginalized populations. Such dismal prognostications strike at the heart of all of us who hope for rationality and peace in the global context of massive demographic shifts. The most difficult problem in the future will be public acceptance of climate as a rationale for massive population displacements. Specifically, new forms of disease such as Ebola will influence public decisions about refugees in general. With these problems in mind, we should also examine new methods of immigration and refugee absorption that spread aliens throughout new environments to prevent the development of refugee camps, slums, and ethnic ghettos of people of color in primarily Caucasian landscapes.

Many industrialized countries of North America, Europe, and Australasia are seeking to protect themselves as wealthy enclaves from what they perceive to be the singular pressure of increasing international migration movements.[61] Today the United Nations estimates that there are some forty-three million refugees at risk in various parts of the planet. Of those, some twenty-five million have been displaced by natural and human-caused disasters. Of these, eleven million are Africans, mostly from the Sudan. While many will stay behind, adrift and displaced in their own landscapes, others will take the migration route from poorer to richer countries. Some writers like Anthony H. Richmond are using the forceful analogy of apartheid to describe the strategy being developed by many Western developed nations to restrict and control these migrants. He points out that while the political structure of apartheid in South Africa has been dismantled, when it comes to movements of climate refugees, developed countries and others seem bent on constructing instruments that bear striking resemblance to those developed in South Africa in the 1950s.[62] Richmond points to the following strategies being put into place in Western nations: (1) defense of existing cultural and social institutions, (2) state security, (3) maintenance of law and order, (4) the need to protect ethnic identity, and (5) the preservation of economic privilege.[63] Thus the main response to stemming the flow of migrants has been to label them illegal or undesirable people.[64]

Resistance to the "onslaught of the refugee" takes the form of armed frontier patrols, computer data banks, fingerprinting, and various forms of travel documents.[65] The problem of the flow of climate refugees toward these wealthy enclaves is accelerated by technology and globalization, which has bred a greater number of highways of economic interdependence than ever before. Of course the glaring contradiction of globalization is that money, goods, and information flow relatively freely across borders, whereas people do not.[66]

Meanwhile, we are witnessing an era of change fraught with cultural contradictions[67]—millions of people are on the move and no effective global institutions exist to deal with the problem. All that have emerged thus far are short-term solutions of "containment" born of political nativism and hysteria whipped up by the media. Richmond and others see that it will be difficult to maintain state sovereignty in the future against the vast mix of migrants. As Richmond notes, "All boundaries are permeable and borders can no longer be defended with walls, iron curtains, armed guards or surveillance systems."[68]

Scenario Two

In his 2015 encyclical, *Laudato Si*,[69] Pope Francis framed the question of our common future on earth perhaps better than any scientist or philosopher: how can anyone claim to be building a better world without thinking of the environmental crisis and the suffering of the excluded?[70] New dialogue is needed about the future of the planet, the pope argued. With the earth "beginning to look more and more like an immense pile of filth,"[71] the throwaway culture of the West has to be constrained. By "throwaways" the pope noted that treating people and environments as if they were expendable items of mass consumerism brought about by a "numbing of conscience" negatively affects the entire planet.[72] "A true ecological approach *always* becomes a social approach, it must integrate questions of justice in debts on the environment so as to hear *both the cry of the earth and the cry of the poor.*"[73]

The pope writes that he is especially concerned that there has been a "tragic rise in the number of migrants seeking to flee from the growing poverty caused by environmental deterioration."[74] These migrants, he continues, "are not recognized by international conventions as refugees; they bear the loss of the lives they left behind, while enjoying no legal protection whatsoever."[75] Sadly, Pope Francis notes, there is widespread indifference to such suffering. He pointed out the problem of a massive world water shortage in the coming decades: "It is also conceivable that the control of water by large multinational businesses may become a major source of conflict in this century."[76] He noted that a true "ecological debt" exists between the global north and south. It is connected to the commercial imbalances with decisions of government and by disproportionate use of natural resources by certain countries over long periods of time. "The Earth is being despoiled with a cheerful recklessness," the pope lamented.[77]

Laudato Si is the Vatican's powerful pronouncement in favor of a new social and environmental paradigm for the planet that through the moral suasion of religion seeks to transcend the traditional market culture of profit and loss into the realm of community. The question remains, however, whether Western developed nations will be willing to reduce their lifestyles and current patterns of consumption to achieve the pope's vision of community. It is fitting that a spokesman for the world's largest church should confront a question of human survival that is so biblical in nature.

With *Laudato Si* in mind, we need to clarify and redefine the United Nations' legal framework that applies to people crossing borders in the wake of environmental disasters. Also, the bureaucracy of the UN is severely bloated with "empires within empires" and is in dire need of reorganization. Multilateral treaties similar to regional initiatives need to be put in place to set standards for the treatment of environmental refugees. Further, we need an asylum policy for environmental refugees that goes farther than the current UN strategy. Some countries can be subsidized by international agencies to offer temporary protective regimes for people who are uprooted by environmental change.

AN AGENDA FOR THE FUTURE

The way we live now on the planet is an affront to environmental morality. We pollute and poison the earth while the overwhelming bulk of its human population is treated as a mass of insignificant economic widgets to be used at will at the lowest possible cost. Add to this the glaring fact that countries that were once in the forefront of being civilized, democratic nations are now succumbing to authoritarian and xenophobic solutions to the problem of dealing with climate and other types of refugees.

In the United States politicians have a breathtaking ignorance of the real world and concentrate almost exclusively on overtly partisan issues. Environmental problems and the plight of climate refugees are tragically far down on the congressional action list. The belief that human-caused climate change is nothing but a scientific hoax is alive and well in our state and national legislatures.

The United States seems to be slipping its transatlantic bonds, and the nations of Europe have let a few Islamic fugitive gangsters frighten them out of their wits. The United States has not experienced the tramp of hostile invading armies on its soil since the Civil War; thus a long domestic peace has conditioned its outlook on the world. Few of us are alive today who experienced the shock of seeing displaced persons in our midst after World War II with concentration camp numbers tattooed on their arms. To understand the appalling reality of being a refugee in America we must resort to fiction like Cormac McCarthy's dystopian novel, *The Road.*

Meanwhile, as millions on the planet plan their desperate departures from drying, drowning, and decaying landscapes, what is to be done? Who will provide the leadership during a period of one of the most dramatic demographic shifts in history? As we move forward through troubled times, we owe it to our children and grandchildren to make an effort to deal creatively with issues spawned by global migration. Many of the countries that we have discussed in this book are failing or dysfunctional. If something is to be done, that "something" has to come from the developed nations. What follows are comments that can help point the way for survival in an unsettled and increasingly mobile world.

WHITHER THE UNITED NATIONS?

We end this book on a somewhat hopeful note. While we realize that hope is not a practical strategy for the future, we nonetheless base this feeling based on historical facts. First, Europe has had a long history of dealing with refugees, and although parts of that history are sordid, Europe has handled its refugee population problems in the past in a manner that approached decency. Second, on the subject of climate refugees, there is only one international organization with the experience and the grit to deal with the massive flows of people driven by the forces of climate change. We refer, specifically, to the United Nations. Yes, the UN has problems. Eric Shawn, in his book *The UN Exposed,* claims that this body is rife with humbug, professional disillusionment and bureaucratic paralysis, and the UN's critics have excoriated its leadership as nothing more than a self-serving gang, barely above the rank of hoodlums.[78]

A good bit of this criticism, perhaps racially based, stems from the fact that many of the leadership positions in the UN are held by representatives from developing nations who have the temerity to criticize the United States and the EU. Yet, despite the criticism, some of it well-deserved, the United Nations has done noble work in its refugee outreach. Who else can be found with the large-scale talent, compassion, and money to deal with the wrenching problems of poverty, migration, disease, and human loss? The United Nations has been proactive in many areas of the world in defending human rights, improving the treatment of minorities, and increasing the medical support of distressed populations. They know what refugee camps are like; they have been in the business of assisting refugees since the end of World War II.

The late historian Tony Judt pointed out the dilemma of the UN's relationship with the United States: "A petulant United States, expecting the UN to sweep up after it and generally perform international miracles but resolutely opposed to furnishing it with the means to do so and intent upon undermining its credibility at every turn, is an insuperable handicap and a leading source of the very shortcomings American commentators deplore."[79] As Judt argued, the United Nations has made many contributions to maintaining world order through its agencies (World Health Organization, UNESCO, the United Nations Relief Works, and the UNHCR). In the future the United Nations will neither collapse nor go away like the ill-fated League of Nations after World War I. The basic task ahead will be to fine-tune the organization's mission to include rescue, rehabilitation, and possibly resettlement of climate refugees in an even-handed manner.

One very hopeful development has been the Paris Climate Conference of 2015, where 188 nations signed a global accord setting a cap of two degrees centigrade on anthropogenic or greenhouse emissions. During the deliberations some six hundred thousand people took part in worldwide demonstrations in favor of reducing carbon emissions. Although many participants originally had low expectations about the conference outcome, the end result was surprising. The conference kept alive the hope that the earth's warming would be held at two degrees. The conference pledged to monitor global emissions and to revisit this international goal every five years beginning in 2023.[80]

IN HISTORY'S SHADOW

As the dramatic movements of people across the earth take place, we cannot afford to be mere bystanders. Our support for a safer, cleaner, more temperate world must be decisive. The struggle for the future is not so much poor against rich as it is between survival and non-survival of the human species. As Naomi Klein has stated, we need to build something in this age of climate change that is bigger than we ever dared to hope: "Yes there will be things that we will lose, luxuries that some of us will have to give up, whole industries that will disappear."[81] It is too late to stop climate change, but it is not too late to adapt and survive in changing circumstances.

The way forward, if there is to be a way forward, will involve the reevaluation of approaches and attitudes toward aliens crossing borders in both poorer countries and developed nations as prosperous as the United States. Ironically, the international myopia about climate refugees exists at the same time that a wealth of strategies, procedures, and policies to ameliorate this problem have been developed by scholars and humanitarian agencies.

Environmental refugees exist and suffer and should be helped instead of being allowed to wallow in decrepit camps. People forced to flee through no fault of their own deserve a decent future. If climate refugees are not recognized in terms of what changes in the natural world are doing to them, they will continue to be more than a marginalized economic drag. Out of their camps will come all the evils of tomorrow—from disease to ethnic upheaval and terrorism.

The world's climate is changing at a rate that far exceeds historical records. And one thing is certain: adaptation to climate change through migration has always been a possible human strategy. Now, however, what population experts call a "new human tsunami" is just one step away.[82] A good start in developing new approaches to our current dilemma is by looking first at where we have been in the arc of history. We like to think that "things are different now," but they really are not. We live in the long shadows of history, and whether or not we can learn from what has gone on before will determine how we deal with the onrushing crush of climate refugees in our present era. There is always hope.

NOTES

Crispin Tickell, "Risks of Conflict—Resource and Population Pressures," http://www.crispintickell.org/page13.html1. Lester R. Brown, "Environmental Refugees: The Rising Tide," chap. 6 in *World on the Edge: How to Prevent Environmental and Economic Collapse* (Earth Policy Institute, 2011), http://www.earth-policy.org/books/

2. Petra Ďurková, Anna Gromilova, Barbara Kiss, and Megi Plaku, "Climate Refugees in the 21st Century," Regional Academy of the United Nations, https://fusion dotnet.files.wordpress.com/2015/02/climate-refugees-1.pdf.

3. Norman Myers, Environmental Exodus: An Emergent Crisis in the Global Arena (Washington, DC: Climate Institute, 1995).

4. See Foreign Aid Explorer website, https://explorer.usaid.gov, USAID, July 27, 2015.

5. Samantha Nutt, *Damned Nations: Greed, Guns, Armies, and Aid* (Toronto: McClelland and Stewart, 2011).

6. Angela Williams, "Turning the Tide: Recognizing Climate Change refugees in International Law," *Law and Policy* 30:4 (October 2008), p. 523.

7. Ibid., p. 502

8. Ibid., p. 514.

9. Ibid., p. 517.

10. Susan Martin, "The State of the Evidence," *Forced Migration Review*, May 28, 2015, 82–83.

11. Ibid.

12. Maria Waldinger and Sam Fankhauser, "Climate Change and Migration in Developing Countries: Evidence and Implications for PRISE Countries," ESRC Centre for Climate Change Economics and Policy, Grantham Research Institute on Climate Change and the Environment, October 2015: 10, http://www.cccep.ac.uk/wp-content /uploads/2015/10/Climate-change-and-migration-in-developing-countries_final.pdf.

13. Benjamin Glahn, "'Climate Refugees?' Addressing the International Legal Gaps," International Bar Association, June 11, 2009, http://www.ibanet.org/Article/New Detail.aspx?ArticleUid=B51C02C1-3C27-4AE3-B4C4-7E350EB0F442.

14. Duncan Robinson and Alex Barker, "EU to Press Ahead with Plans to Suspend Schengen Rules," *Financial Times*, December 4, 2015, https://www.ft.com/content /42214a5c-9aa1-11e5-be4f-0abd1978acaa.

15. Ian Traynor and Helena Smith, "EU Border Controls: Schengen Scheme on the Brink after Amsterdam Talks," Guardian, January 26, 2016.

16. Griff White, "Denmark Turns Hostile on Refugees," Washington Post, April 12, 2016.

17. Robinson and Barker, "EU to Press Ahead."

18. Andrew Simms, Memorandum Submitted by the New Economics Foundation, Select Committee on International Development, https://www.publications.parliament .uk/pa/cm200304/cmselect/cmintdev/79/79we29.htm.

19. Ibid.

20. Molly Conisbee and Andrew Simms, *Environmental Refugees, The Case for Recognition* (London: New Economics Foundation, 2003), p. 35, https://ia600703.us.archive .org/14/items/fp_Environmental_Refugees-The_Case_for_Recognition /Environmental_Refugees-The_Case_for_Recognition.pdf.

21. Gatrell, *Making of the Modern Refugee*, pp. 165–166.

22. Renaud et al., "Environmental Degradation and Migration," p. 7.

23. Ibid.

24. UNHCR, Guidelines on Temporary Protection or Stay Arrangements, February 2014, available at http://www.refworld.org/docid/52fba2404.html.

25. The *Stern Review* presented a pioneering comprehensive analysis for understanding the world of the climate refugee. Nicholas Stern, The Stern Review: The Economics

of Climate Change (Cambridge: Cambridge University Press, 2007), ix, available at http://mudancasclimaticas.cptec.inpe.br/~rmclima/pdfs/destaques/sternreview_report_complete.pdf.

26. Williams, "Turning the Tide," p. 518.

27. Norman Myers, "Environmental Refugees," *Philosophical Transactions of the Royal Society B*, p. 612, https://www.ncbi.nlm.nih.gov/pmc/articles/PMC1692964/pdf/12028796.pdf.

28. Ibid.

29. Debt-for-environment swaps: "Arrangement in which a debtor nation trades a portion of its liabilities to fund local protection efforts. Also called debt for nature swaps." BusinessDictionary.com.

30. Myers, "Environmental Refugees."

31. Frank Biermann and Ingrid Boas, "Preparing for a Warmer World: Towards a Global Governance System to Protect Climate Refugees," *Global Environmental Politics* 10, no. 1 (2010), p. 60–88, available at https://www.researchgate.net/publication/227627225_Preparing_for_a_Warmer_World_Towards_a_Global_Governance_System_to_Protect_Climate_Refugees.

32. Ibid., p. 75.

33. Ibid.

34. Ibid., p. 79.

35. Bonnie Docherty and Tyler Giannini, "Confronting a Rising Tide: A Proposal for a Convention on Climate Change Refugees," Harvard Environmental Law Review 33 (2009): 349–450, http://www.law.harvard.edu/students/orgs/elr/vo133_2/Docherty%20Giannini.pdf.

36. Ibid., pp. 349–350.

37. Ibid., p. 350.

38. Ibid: 349–403.

39. Ibid., p. 357.

40. Ivid., p. 372.

41. Biermann and Boas, "Preparing for a Warmer World," p. 79.

42. Conisbee and Simms, *Environmental Refugees*, p. 29.

43. Ibid.

44. Glanh, "Climate Refugees"?

45. Roger Zetter, "Protecting Environmentally Displaced People: Developing the Capacity of Legal and Normative Frameworks," Oxford Department of International Development, University of Oxford, Refugee Studies Center Report, February 2011: 58.

46. Walter Kälin, "The Nansen Initiative: Building Consensus on Displacement in Disaster Contexts," *Forced Migration Review* 49 (May 2015), p. 5, available at http://www.fmreview.org/sites/fmr/files/FMRdownloads/en/climatechange-disasters/kaelin.pdf.

47. The Nansen Initiative was named after Fridtjof Nansen (1861–1930), celebrated polar explorer, scientist, and peace advocate who became high commissioner for refugees for the League of Nations in 1921 and won the Nobel Peace Prize in 1922 for his humanitarian work in dealing with displaced populations in the aftermath of World War I.

48. Kälin, "The Nansen Initiative," p. 5.

49. Ibid.

50. Ibid.

51. Ibid., p. 7.

52. Glahn, "Climate Refugees"?

53. Ibid.

54. Zetter, "Protecting Environmentally Displaced People," p. 4.

55. Robert D. Kaplan, "The Coming Anarchy," *Atlantic* (February 1994), https://www.theatlantic.com/magazine/archive/1994/02/the-coming-anarchy/304670/.

56. "Nigeria," World Population Review, http://worldpopulationreview.com/countries/nigeria-population, September 13, 2015.

57. Elisabeth Rosenthal, "Nigeria Tested by Rapid Rise in Population," *New York Times*, April 14, 2012, http://www.nytimes.com/2012/04/15/world/africa/in-nigeria-a-preview-of-an-overcrowded-planet.html?_r=0.

58. Kaplan, "The Coming Anarchy."

59. Quoted in Kaplan, ibid.

60. Kaplan, "The Coming Anarchy."

61. Kathleen Valtonen, review of Anthony H. Richmond, *Global Apartheid: Refugees, Raciosm, and the New World Order*, in *Refuge* 14:6, p. 25.

62. Ibid.

63. Ibid.

64. Ibid.

65. Ibid.

66. Ibid.

67. Ibid.

68. Anthony H. Richmond, *Global Apartheid: Refugees, Raciosm, and the New World Order* (Toronto: Oxford University Press, 1994), p. 205, quoted in ibid., p. 26.

69. Francis (pope), *Laudato Si* (Vatican City: Libreria Editrice Vaticana, 2015), http://w2.vatican.va/content/francesco/en/encyclicals/documents/papa-francesco_20150524_enciclica-laudato-si.html.

70. Ibid., para 13.

71. Ibid., para. 21.

72. Ibid., para. 22.

73. Ibid., para. 49.

74. Ibid., para. 25.

75. Ibid.

76. Ibid., para. 31.

77. Ibid., para. 59.

78. Eric Shawn, *The UN Exposed: How the United Nations Sabotages American Security and Fails the World* (New York: Sentinel, 2006).

79. Tony Judt, "Is the UN Doomed?" *When the Facts Change: Essays 1995–2010* (New York: Penguin, 2015), p. 263.

80. United Nations Framework Convention on Climate Change, Adoption of the Paris Agreement, 30 November to 11 December 2015, Paris; see section 31.

81. Naomi Klein, *This Changes Everything: Capitalism vs. the Climate* (New York: Simon and Schuster, 2014), 28.

82. Liberation Forum, September 2008, held a debate on the theme "Climate Refugees: A New Tsunami?"

JOHN R. WENNERSTEN is a successful environmental affairs writer with nine books to his credit dealing with the Chesapeake Bay, maritime fisheries, world water issues, and river pollution. His most recent book is *Global Thirst: Water and Society in the 21st Century.* This book was favorably reviewed in the media and received meritorious attention in the *Washington Independent Review of Books* and the national newspaper of India, *The Hindu.* Wennersten's books and articles have been reviewed at length in journals such as *Mother Earth News,* the *Baltimore Sun,* the *New York Times Sunday Magazine,* and the *Washington Post.*

DENISE ROBBINS is an environmental affairs journalist at Media Matters in Washington, DC. A graduate of Cornell University, Denise regularly publishes articles dealing with all aspects of global and national environmental change with a special interest in climate refugee problems in South Asia and Africa. She is a member of the Society of Environmental Journalists.

CPSIA information can be obtained
at www.ICGtesting.com
Printed in the USA
LVOW13s2157151117
556395LV00019B/258/P

9 780253 025883